Praise for

AGENTIFY

"*AGENTIFY* is the most important technology book I've read in a decade. The same rigor that separates winning hedge funds and private-equity portfolios from the rest (deep domain moats, adaptive feedback loops, and robust risk control) is now required to build winning AI agents. Every investor and founder allocating capital to autonomous agents needs to read this book - twice."

> — John Botti, Wall Street Veteran,
> former Chief Investment Officer of multi-billion
> dollar credit hedge fund

"Michael Palmer has a rare ability to deconstruct the complex 'black box' of AI into actionable engineering principles. *AGENTIFY* brilliantly balances the science of machine learning with the art of user-centric design. Whether you are a developer, an executive, or an investor, the insight in this book will fundamentally change how you understand the mechanics and the potential of AI agents in the modern economy."

> —Dan Benveniste,
> CEO and Founder, SkillWaze

"This is the book you need to understand what it means for AI agents to act with autonomy. By weaving together the challenges of autonomy, accountability, and trust with the opportunities of an augmented digital workforce *AGENTIFY* offers a compelling yet balanced vision of the possible. Rather than either warning or celebrating, Palmer invites readers to grapple with the relationship we will need to develop with systems that act on their own on our behalf. Essential reading for anyone who wants to understand not just the technology, but the future of human agency in a world of autonomous machines."

—Gil Yehuda,

Head of Open Source at a major American bank

"Few books today capture the real-world practicality of agentic AI. *AGENTIFY* does. It's an essential read for any founder or team shaping the next generation of intelligent systems, with clear insight into where today's AI still has limits. Every founder should read it."

—Swaroop 'kittu' Kolluri,

Founder and Managing Director, Neotribe Ventures

"*AGENTIFY* offers a rare blend of vision and depth on AI agents. For those actively building in the field, it can help turn strategy into real business outcomes."

—John Burns,

Chairman, Board of Directors (multiple companies)

"Michael's deep technical expertise and decades of product leadership shine through in *AGENTIFY*. While AI Agents are a daily topic in tech and venture circles at this point, rarely do those conversations reveal a clear vision of realistic end goals with paths to achieve them for most use cases. *AGENTIFY* carefully illustrates some of the most plausible outcomes in the rapidly evolving agentic world and is a valuable read for those trying to see around the corners of AI evolution to come."

—Paul Longhenry,

General Partner, TheFounderVC

"*AGENTIFY* performs the difficult task of smoothly transitioning from foundational AI theory to practical technical concepts, all woven together with beautiful narrative examples. This is an essential read for any modern-day founder building an AI product."

—Brent Hobson,

CEO, Wytebox

"Every business line risk manager should own a copy of this toolkit! It's written for the practitioner by someone who has deployed agents on almost every commercially available pipeline. This book is filled with real world advice for managing risk while rapidly scaling agents as products based on actual practice, using terms like *think out loud* instead of *explainability* to set the bar for effective risk management."

—Jeff Terry, Former Chair,

The Clearing House Enterprise Risk Committee,

Financial Services Technology Risk Executive

AGENTIFY

AGENTIFY

The Art, Science, and
Engineering of
Successful AI Agents

Michael Palmer

Taos Research Corporation

New York · Tampa

For general inquiries, contact:
info@taosresearch.ai

ISBN: 979-8-9931962-1-3

Library of Congress Control Number: 2025921325

First edition, 2025
Printed in the United States of America

For my wife and family

To Mei, Lucas, Ethan, and Tyler who inspire me every day. This book would not have been possible without your love and support. And to my parents, Darwin and Carolyn Palmer, without whom nothing would be possible.

Contents

Preface   1

PART I   FROM TOOLS TO AGENTS   5

1   Software as Colleague & Teammate   7

2   The Evolution of Software Products   15

3   Where We Are Today   21

4   What Is True Agency?   31

PART II   THE NEW COMPETITIVE ADVANTAGE   39

5   Adapt, Specialize, Survive, Flourish   41

6   Agents Can Be Everywhere at Once   60

7   Feedback: The New Beautiful UI   69

8   New Challenges for Designers   75

9   The Insight Factory: Simulate Your Domain   81

10   Dream, Distill, Differentiate: Your Agent's Data Moat   89

PART III   ON THE VERGE OF AUTONOMY   105

11   A Skeptic's Point of View   107

12   The Role of Reinforcement Learning   112

13   Tool Use Explosion   118

14   Simulating Agency & Hierarchical Goals   124

15   Higher Order Cognition:
       Creativity, Taste, Humor & Judgment   130

16   Coding Agents: A Bellwether   137

17   The Wild West of Social & Crypto Agents   143

PART IV   ARCHITECTURE & DEVELOPMENT   153

18   The Infinite Agentic Loop   155

19   Agent Situational Awareness: Harness Hallucinations   177

20   Tools, Tuning, Reasoning & Protocols   194

21   Context Engineering, Memory & Knowledge   222

22   Beyond Vibes: Rigorous AI Software Development   250

23   Open Source Agentic Frameworks   260

24   The Future of Scrum, Kanban, Agile, etc.   277

PART V   RISK, ROBUSTNESS, & SECURITY   283

25   Transparency from the Ground Up   284

26   Simulation for Security & Robustness   295

27   Controlling Agent Autonomy   298

28   Agent Identity, Agent Liability   304

PART VI   THE PATH AHEAD   309

29   AGI Research Frontiers   311

30   Perilous Predictions   373

31   Product Manager as Behavioral Psychologist   379

32   Finding Your Personal Path   382

References   385

Production Methods   407

Index   409

Preface

THIS BOOK IS FOR BUILDERS of AI agents. Allow me to define *builder* broadly to include investors, founders, product managers, architects, engineers, and others working in the rapidly evolving space of agentic AI product development. Given that broad definition, my goal is to illuminate the strategic, product, research, and engineering factors essential to making AI agents successful and that will have enduring value as the industry continues to advance.

In my work with teams developing AI products, I've found the following three questions cause builders to struggle most:

1. How are AI agents fundamentally changing the paradigm of software products?

2. What will make agents successful, competitive products?

3. What research, engineering, and safety approaches are critical to building effective autonomous agents?

The largest ever paradigm shift in software is well underway and will make these questions central for decades to come. The traditional playbooks and best practices for product management, product design, and engineering are unsuited for what is coming with AI agents. This book seeks to answer these questions in precise yet durable ways that remain relevant even as models, frameworks, and practices evolve.

One deeply satisfying result has been confirming that the answers to these questions are rooted in foundational ideas, in some cases decades old, from cognitive science, complex adaptive systems, control theory, robotics, and neuroscience. My task has been to translate these into principles, patterns, and architectures that are of lasting value for builders.

I've tried to provide a balance of my observations from work with teams at startups and large companies, as well as with others in academia, government and venture capital. General conclusions are contrasted with case studies, and I elaborate hypothetical "stories of the future" to give more color and to stimulate your imagination about what may soon be possible. For teams that aspire to create successful AI agents, imagining the future with depth, creativity, and realism will be pivotal.

Part I of the book confronts the first question. How are agents fundamentally different from traditional software products? We examine exactly what we mean by the term *agency* and discover that the end game is increasing autonomy and human-like behavior for AI agents. Much of traditional software, designed for humans to manipulate, will rapidly become obsolete.

In **Part II**, we shift to the crucial question: what will constitute competitive advantage for agents? What types of agents should we build? How can builders leverage the unique properties of agents to differentiate and solve real-world problems? We confront these questions, including the design and packaging issues unique to agents. We consider how to simulate the environments in which agents will operate, to more rapidly find ways to make our agents competitive.

Part III focuses on the remaining gaps in performance that are holding agents back from more autonomous roles. Still at the product level, we examine the industry-wide efforts in reinforcement learning, tool use, planning, goal management, and agent judgment that are closing those gaps. Deeper case studies of coding agents, and social and crypto agents provide leading indicators of businesses based on greater agent autonomy.

Robust engineering architectures and methods are vital too. **Part IV** covers them in depth, laying out the fundamental architectural patterns that support greater agent performance and autonomy. We confront the practical side of tools, context engineering, memory, multi-model and multi-loop architectures, and other essential building blocks for highly specialized, highly performant agents. **Part V** concentrates on the safety and risk issues agent engineering and product teams must also confront.

Throughout the book, the critical role of AI research is a cross-cutting theme. The book includes multiple research callout sections that curate key papers and insights on topics central to a given chapter. Deeper insights from research power the most successful agents. Whether we take work from Pentti Kanerva on sparse distributed memory, Kenneth Stanley on open-endedness, Melanie Mitchell on analogy making, or Minsky on agencies and emotions, research insights continue to be indispensable. In **Part VI**, one substantial chapter, "AGI Research Frontiers," deserves special mention. There I seek to provide a detailed survey of the broad areas of research that may help us reach fully human-level AGI. Complete references are provided in the back of the book.

Even if you are *not* a builder, this book should still provide value. If you are drawn to hear a detailed account of how AI agents work, how they may be developed, and the types of roles they could soon be playing in our economy and everyday lives, then this book should be a meaningful starting point for you too.

A note on "complex adaptive systems" is also warranted. You may have noticed this term appears on the back cover of the book. Why is it there? And what role does it play in the book? The overall focus of the book is on the product, engineering, and research dimensions of AI agents in a manner geared toward a broad audience of agent builders. As a result, the importance of complex systems may be hard to make out. The ideas appear when we lay out the architecture for AI agents and we discuss a "multi-loop, multi-model architecture," and reference Minsky's *Society of Mind*. These approaches are heavily influenced by complexity science. I address it even more directly in the AGI chapter (Chapter 29), where we look at how complex adaptive systems may be central to achieving human-level general intelligence.

For specialists in complexity science and emergence, the treatment here is, of course, superficial. My apologies to those specialists, but also a thank-you for the real inspiration they have been to this book. My goal is to share with agent builders some important ideas from complexity science most relevant to their goals. Complexity theory (and the engineering innovations it can help shape) *may* be the unlock for AGI. A fuller explanation of this claim will have to wait for another book.

My readers and I owe a debt of gratitude to my friend John Botti, who helped me meticulously pore over late-stage versions of the manuscript and made innumerable thoughtful improvements. The reading experience is *far* better thanks to his generous help.

Special thanks to my brother Damon Palmer, who has been my most ardent fan. He was a vital sounding board as this book progressed from idea, through scattered notes and conversations, to manuscript and, after great labor, to edited form. His deep, patient readings and insights have been invaluable and shaped much of how I tell the story in the pages ahead.

M.P.
Taos Research Corporation
taosresearch.ai
Tampa, Florida
December 2025

PART

I

From Tools To Agents

If you are reading or browsing through this book, it's likely you have some level of belief that AI generally and AI agents specifically are likely to shape future software products. But I'm also guessing that few among you have had the time to sit down and map out all the implications for how we do product management, design, engineering, and product development more generally. I've been working with companies large and small on this topic as AI agents have shifted to the top of the discussion in the years since ChatGPT, and it became clear to me that organizing the learnings from those teams could help others. I hope that this can help you prepare for the new software realities that are rapidly approaching.

It is crucial that we come to a common vision early on as to what exactly constitutes an AI agent. What sets agents apart from traditional software products? And how will our product processes and product thinking need to change as these agents become prevalent? That's what we will tackle in this part of the book. I've found that this involves a pretty big change of mindset for most people, but *particularly* for people who have done software product development before.

When I need to change my "mindset," it often helps me to first imagine a particular possible future, and deeply immerse myself in it. I try to do that via a story in Chapter 1 to help you let go of preconceptions and biases (and natural skepticism), and enter a world that is definitely not yet today's reality. The goal is not to make you believe that this future is imminent or inevitable. Rather the goal is to help you see more clearly what one possible future may look like.

As we progress, to shed more light on how product development will be changed by AI agents, I will take us from a story about the future to the remembered past. In Chapter 2 we will look back at where software products came from and how they have evolved with the changing technology platforms of the past 30 to 40 years. We will then speculate a bit about where we are in the transition from known past to possible future. I will conclude this part of the book by trying to distill what we mean by "agency," which is perhaps the most defining (and yet hardest to define!) attribute we will be looking for in this new generation of software products.

Chapter 1

Software as Colleague & Teammate

> *Takeaways*: Today's agentic systems display little auton-
> omy. Virtually all require regular human direction via
> prompting. Future AI agents will be designed and en-
> gineered to operate much more like human colleagues,
> showing the initiative, autonomy, and judgment that are
> the hallmarks of our best human teammates. This transi-
> tion from partially agentic workflows to autonomous AI
> agents has barely started.

T HE TERM *in media res* in a narrative refers to the practice
of beginning in the middle of the story. Readers or viewers
are thrown into the action, and only gradually, perhaps via
dialogue, flashbacks, or other descriptions, the story of "how we got
here" becomes clear. This is not limited to fiction, of course, it may
be employed in news programs or in documentaries, but it's quite
familiar and popular in storytelling.

My kids and I love the movie *Forrest Gump*. We can watch it
again and again. I've tried with considerably less success to sell
my wife on another favorite movie of mine, *Pulp Fiction*. *Forrest
Gump* and *Pulp Fiction* are both great examples of *in media res*,
but the idea goes back much further. The play *Hamlet*, for example,
begins with the death of Hamlet's father, which Shakespeare only
later reveals was a murder. Homer's *Iliad* and *Odyssey* famously
both also employ *in media res*.

Forrest Gump and *Pulp Fiction* are interesting too because they
both start fairly near the end of the story. The ending is not
revealed, but a strong sense of the ultimate destination is imparted.

This particular way of being thrown into the middle is sometimes referred to as a "third-act opener." The idea is to hook you with some excitement or drama from the story, particularly some near-final destination, and only later tell you how things got to that point. I want to do the same thing with the story of AI agents and software products. We will start by looking at the story of a business owner in the not too distant future.

A Business Story

Jennifer runs a highly profitable travel business doing just over $18 million a year in revenue. Her mother ran a travel agency in the 1990s that was considerably more modest. It was located inside a shopping mall in a central part of the town where Jennifer grew up. She remembers loving the maps and wonderful brochures in the agency as a kid, and how the sense of adventure of travel made her mom's work seem like magical fun. Like many brick-and-mortar travel agencies, her mom's business did not survive the rise of the internet and large travel websites. The human touch and personal service that human travel agents offered was overshadowed by the ease of booking flights online and cost savings from bundling deals on airlines, hotels, cars and attractions.

Jennifer left her job at Instagram sometime in the early post-ChatGPT frenzy of 2023. It had been a grind. She was looking for something more satisfying, and she always had an entrepreneurial itch. Now, almost a decade later, she is in control of her own destiny, and her business runs almost exclusively with AI agents. She opens her team chat every day and begins collaborating with the four "senior leadership" AI agents that constitute her management team. One specializes in marketing, one in customer service, one in finance and administration, and one in operations. Jennifer, as the CEO, focuses on strategy and business development, as well as coordinating the senior leadership team.

Figure 1.1: Our fictitious Jennifer grew up inspired by travel brochures perhaps a bit like these.

Her leadership team agents in turn have teams of specialized AI agents underneath them. Customer service is an area of extreme specialization for Jennifer, as it is basically everything in the travel business. She learned in early 2025 as her business was launching, that people were very frustrated by having to work across airline booking sites, hotel or short-term stay sites, car rental sites, as well as countless sites with information on local attractions. She found several emerging AI agent providers who specialized in travel AI agents, but none had full coverage of all regions of the world or all types of travel experiences.

Jennifer soon saw she *needed* to specialize. She couldn't cover it all. She signed up for a software subscription and effectively "hired" her first AI agent, one that specialized in helping people book transportation between America and the UK. Very soon after, she hired another one that specialized in planning and booking local attractions around London. A few months later, she hired a third social AI agent to help her manage her presence on Facebook,

Instagram and TikTok where she would market her travel services. It wasn't much to start. She had to ignore travelers who wanted to go all sorts of other places besides the UK, but it got her off the ground. She landed some early customers, and gradually she began to see how she could bring more value.

Jennifer's specialization paid off. Her customers knew they could always turn to ChatGPT or Perplexity or Google or a big travel website, and with a lot of prompting and querying get similar results, but Jennifer's specialized travel agents worked with them, listened to what they wanted their travel to be about, and just got things done. People paid for the convenience. Busy lives with kids and jobs meant people simply didn't have time to plan vacations, and having a personal travel agent through Jennifer's business seemed like a luxury from a bygone era.

As her business grew, Jennifer gradually added more specialized AI agents with special skills to offer concierge and other services, or to help travelers out of sticky situations. She expanded to new regions, new travel destinations, and added more attractions. She hired agents from multiple different software providers. In the early years, it felt just like buying software. There were long lists of caveats from the agent software companies, and plenty of set-up work to get one to be effective in her business workflows. But gradually, each time she would look again at the market for AI agent "employees" the number available had grown and their specialized skills were getting better and better.

Jennifer also added newer and better marketing AI agents, able to tap into new channels, leading to expanded bookings and whole new groups of customers with new needs. On more than one occasion she upgraded a member of her senior management team, because newer more insightful and talented AI agents had become available from multiple software vendors. She could rely on these agents to think for themselves, take the initiative, and help her move the business forward. In time, she gave her leadership team the ability to hire new junior agents in their areas on their own, as they were faster and better at evaluating the new agents' skills than Jennifer herself was. As quality improved, she didn't have to micromanage or hold their hands. They enlisted financial analysts when needed and managed to their budgets. She was able to concentrate on the big picture and focus on deeply understanding her customers and how the market was evolving. It didn't hurt that Jennifer got to travel a lot herself and was able to run the business from anywhere in the world.

Jennifer still has some humans on the payroll, but only in fractional roles. Most of her daily interactions are now with AI agents. Her customers interact exclusively with fantastic AI support agents that are available to them 24/7 and can solve almost any travel problem that can arise. She still has four fractional human employees: a fractional human CFO who reviews her books and financial reports and looks for tax efficiencies, a fractional CTO who advises her on technology developments she should be aware of, a legal advisor who helps with compliance and regulatory issues at a high level, and a fractional product strategist with deep knowledge in travel and other consumer businesses who helps her spot rapidly developing consumer trends. Jennifer also has an AI "coach" who helps Jennifer with her leadership and interactions with her AI senior leadership team, as well as her interactions with the fractional human advisors.

Jennifer is very aware that her remaining fractional human employees also run their own businesses almost entirely with AI agents. If they didn't, she probably would not fully trust working with them, but she does also still really value the deeper human conversations and insights she gets from them. She often reflects on how, in the mid-2020s when she was getting started, she never could have imagined having an AI executive coach to coach her on how to work more effectively with a leadership team composed of AI agents, but now she couldn't imagine it working any other way.

The efficiency of her business and the value Jennifer is able to deliver to her customers is immense. She has many other competitors (with human CEOs like Jennifer), specializing in different regions and different travel experiences, dividing up a rapidly growing travel market once dominated by a few large platforms and websites. The big travel websites have collapsed and are practically not used anymore given their extremely poor service and clunky experiences. In a way, although she is earning far more money and serving more customers, it feels like the world has returned a bit to the era of her mother's travel agency.

Thanks to an incredible array of AI co-workers, including those directly helping customers, as well as the senior leadership that Jennifer works with every day, customers are able to focus more on enjoying travel and worry less about arranging it and everything that can go wrong. Jennifer gets to sell the wonder of new experiences, while knowing her co-workers are delivering the best service possible to her customers.

Software Products & Agents

Our story of Jennifer is really a story about where software products are heading. This book is focused on helping prepare you for that future. Simply stated, software will feel, behave, and increasingly look like real human colleagues. It will not be a menu bar at the top of your browser window or an app icon on your phone. It will be like another person in the room with you. Not just a chatbot that answers direct questions, mind you, or a silent scribe taking notes, but a true teammate that contributes thoughtfully to conversations, makes suggestions, and helps set the goals and directions of the group or organization.

As this book goes to press, the early AI agents we see still feel more like chatbots on steroids. They can listen to the flow of conversations by humans and maybe take passable notes, or take a request and go off and use tools like web browsing, search, or coding to complete some fairly meaningful tasks. But they still don't do much to take the initiative. They mostly wait for humans to take the lead and set the pace.

Increasingly this will change. The agents that are coming will think on their own time, develop new ideas, and creatively bring new ideas and solutions to the humans they work with. Without getting into the philosophical debate of whether they feel or are conscious, they will outwardly exhibit what any experienced manager will recognize as "agency." They will be the "self-starters" that we praise on our teams who think ahead, take the initiative, and get things done without being asked.

Also, they won't sleep at night. In many cases they will "dream" and continue to mull the problems of the day just like humans do. They will "take their work home" much the way sometimes we all do. And every day, when the humans roll into work, they will be there, brimming with new ideas, fresh results, and candidate solutions for us to consider and evaluate.

If you are at all like me, this is a bit scary to contemplate. It's hard to understand exactly what role humans will play in this future. Much less to have a clear picture of what the roles we hold today will look like. Questions may run through your mind. How many years away is all this? What role will product managers play? What about software architects and developers? Scrum masters and program managers? Data Analysts? People Managers? Marketing & sales specialists? Will I keep my job?

These are legitimate questions and understandable fears. But if you are confronting them now, you are in a better position than people who are simply hoping this future does not arrive. We will not tackle the full set of employment issues society will face, as that would certainly require another book, but we will directly look into what this future means for product teams building AI agents. We will focus on what will be the defining characteristics of these new software products, and what will make them competitive in business terms, when software feels more like a human colleague.

For now, I want to cement a central point, because it will be with us throughout the rest of the book. When we talk about the next generation of software products, we are referring to designing and building nearly fully autonomous AI agents that can work among us as colleagues. The easiest way to think of these "products" is like people. Now I am not claiming that these AI agents are sentient, or conscious, or that they have feelings. And I am certainly not saying they should receive the same rights, privileges and accommodations as humans. But I do want to emphasize here that these AI agents will be built to *behave like people*. They will have genuine *agency*, and you can think of purchasing this type of software very similarly to how you think about hiring a real human for a role. In the consumer case, this could be someone who will help you in some aspects of your personal life (like a travel agent, a tutor, a coach, or an administrative assistant). If you run a business, purchasing this type of AI agent product will be very similar to how you hire a human being today.

Chapter 2

The Evolution of Software Products

Takeaways: The form of delivery of software products has evolved with shifts in dominant technology platforms. Despite this evolution, the nature of software products as clearly demarcated artifacts used by humans to complete tasks (or for amusement and distraction) has remained constant. Product management as a role and product development as a broad discipline have flourished as software products have become ubiquitous and more complex, but they have not yet adapted to the paradigm shift AI agents will bring.

S OFTWARE PRODUCTS HAVE COME to us in different packaging over the years, as the dominant technology platforms have evolved, but they have always remained clearly demarcated things. Things we could point to and delineate. AI agents are going to change that, and it's going to require a significant change in the perspective of product development teams. In this chapter, I'd like to lay down a bit of common background by exploring how software products have evolved and how they have permeated our daily lives. If this were *Forrest Gump*, this might be a first flashback to understand how we got to where we are today.

The word "product" for most people is rooted in the physical world where we know quite clearly what a product is. A car is a product. A pair of headphones is a product. A cell phone is a product. Breakfast cereals are products. Books are products. Shoes are products. In all of these cases we can literally lay our hands on the thing. We use it, consume it, buy it, and sell it. All the while its boundaries are very clear and tangible.

Human labor and services are a bit less tangible and solid but not totally dissimilar. We often say humans offer their labor as a product. For a doctor, a nurse, an electrician, or an accountant, their product is their expertise delivered to you via some interaction or process. Even comedians who make us laugh, actors who make us cry, or authors who make us think, deliver us their value, their offering, as a form of product.

Form follows function, and software products have traditionally primarily functioned as tools. Even in cases where software is for entertainment, or for consuming information, we can think of it as a tool that amuses us, entertains us, or informs us. Word processors, spreadsheets, graphic design programs, and coding editors are all clearly tools. Our computers (and now the internet) bring us many software tools in one place, much like a tool box brings many mechanical tools together in one place.

Tools are characteristically clear, well-demarcated things. They solve a particular problem. When carpenters or mechanics start to work on a project, they have a wide selection of tools they may bring to bear. Each tool helps perform particular tasks. The human *orchestrates* the tools to solve the larger problem. Use a wrench here, a bolt cutter there, a drill in the next place.

Even multipurpose tools, like a Swiss Army knife, emphasize the basic notion of a tool. They just bundle several tools into a single package. Larger tools may contain sub-tools within them. We see this same pattern every day in software products. Larger tools like word processors or graphic design applications have a Tools menu where smaller tools that are part of the larger task are bundled together. Things like a spell checker or an equation editor, for example. Each tool is a discrete function, a solver of a single problem at different levels of granularity.

Tools are built for humans. We build the tool fundamentally to fit a human's hands, or fingers, or other ways that a human will work with it. We solve larger problems by breaking them down into tasks, and choosing the right tools to get the job done. This *compositionality* and "fitness for a purpose" sits at the heart of what we think of as tools, and also how we have traditionally designed software products.

Like physical tools, software products can become highly specialized. They can become large and require months or even years to master. As we look into different industries, from banking to telecommunications to manufacturing, we see large specialized software products everywhere. Even on the consumer software side, we see fragmentation, complexity, depth and specialization. But the idea of the human user, the human operator, the human orchestrator is never far from the conception of the product. The tool is designed with the human user in mind.

The form of delivery of software products has evolved dramatically as technology has progressed, but this central idea of fitness for purpose and the ability to clearly delineate and demarcate the product has been quite constant. In the early days of shrink-wrapped software, it was quite clear what the product was. We could see it right there in the box. And when we installed it, it created an icon on our desktop. There was no confusion about what the product was. It was what popped up on the screen when we clicked the icon and launched the software.

The form of delivery of software products has evolved dramatically as technology has progressed, but the idea of "fitness for purpose" and the ability to clearly delineate and demarcate the product has been pretty constant.

This was followed in the late 1990s by the web. Suddenly websites running services began taking over tasks from local software on our desktops and servers. This was the early incarnation of software running on the cloud, but websites remained clearly distinct. We could tell when we were on one or another. Each one was a well-demarcated offering.

A phase arrived in the mid-2000s that became known as Web 2.0. The same websites became more complex, more interactive, more "read-write" rather than "read-only." On the consumer side, this brought with it social networks, connectivity, and widespread user-generated content. In the enterprise, this period saw the birth of Software as a Service (SaaS), including companies like Salesforce, WebEx, and NetSuite. None of these new interactive web applications caused confusion about what the product was, though. When people used Flickr, or Facebook, or Salesforce, it was clear those were the products. Software products became richer, more modular, and more complex, but remained clear, well-demarcated artifacts.

Over this period, the discipline of product management flourished in Silicon Valley and in the broader software industry globally. Larger products were broken down into smaller and smaller parts, and each one was led by a product manager. Products became more fine-grained. Some became quite technical and specialized, but still they were things we could point to clearly. Nobody was confused as to what the product was.

Figure 2.1: New platforms have always ushered in waves of new software products.

In 2007 the iPhone arrived, following in the footsteps of devices like the RIM BlackBerry, the Palm Pilot, and the Danger Hiptop. It was followed quickly by Android from Google, and together they turbocharged the mobile era. Suddenly everyone was building apps. An explosion of new products and product companies followed. Clear distinct icons populated our glowing screens. The apps were the products. They were easy to point to, built for humans, and humans orchestrated them to achieve their larger goals.

Over the same time period, enterprise software shifted more and more from being installed *on-prem* in a customer's data center, to being a SaaS service running on the cloud. This was a great simplification of software delivery, both for the customers and for software businesses. And while the transition is still only partially complete, it has not led to confusion over products. SaaS applications are sometimes complex modular offerings, performing the core functions of entire businesses, and other times are discrete tools for individual users. But in all cases the

*The central question is how will we transition from the old paradigm of software built **for** people, to a paradigm of software that acts like a person?*

applications are the products. Orchestration by humans underlies the very business model of many SaaS companies where pricing is done per seat, that is, *per human* who will touch the system.

What Will Agents Change?

This chapter is meant to be more than just a history lesson or a walk down memory lane. A flashback to the past should help us build a shared context for looking at the changes that are on the horizon. The central idea of this book is that software products are evolving rapidly from the clear, well-demarcated objects of the past (that mostly feel like tools to help us do our jobs, or to amuse, inform, or entertain us) to the future we foretold in Chapter 1. A future where AI agents are the main software products.

Over time, these AI agents will act as our teammates, colleagues, advisors, and perhaps even our companions, therapists and caregivers. We will discover in the rest of the book that this is a fundamental shift, not just a new form of packaging or deployment. It requires us to stop thinking about software products as "things we use," and instead think of them more like real entities. This changing reality carries economic, legal, moral, and technological risks that we also need to discuss openly. In the next chapter, we will examine where we are in the transition more closely. Despite being in the early phases, we can clearly see the beginnings of the new paradigm emerging.

Chapter 3

Where We Are Today

Takeaways: At the time of this book's publication we are seeing the very beginning signs of AI agents demonstrating autonomy, with certain sectors like software engineering and social agents leading the way. In numerous other areas, the predominant model is still that of chatbots, copilots and agentic workflows, where robust deterministic outcomes are the goal. The transition to agents with greater autonomy and *agency* is in its infancy. It will be gradual and will match use cases with the pace at which remaining performance obstacles are addressed.

I DO NOT KNOW EXACTLY how long this transition period will last. In Part III of the book we will adopt the skeptic's point of view: that AI technology still faces many obstacles. If true, the transition may take many years rather than just a few. My more optimistic (but still gradual) predictions of the timing of the transition will be revealed in full in Chapter 30. Feel free to skip ahead if you don't feel you can wait that long! Here my goal is more modest. I want to simply convey that I believe we are in the early stages of a very active, chaotic transition process from the old software products model to the new. I want to give you a sense of what that looks and feels like on the ground for users and for builders. At present, numerous products and systems are being deployed that incorporate AI, but many of these will likely prove to be stopgaps, and quite short-lived ones at that.

An Exercise with an Agent Available Today

When I thought about how to convey this transition, I immediately craved a great diagram. The problem is I am not a great graphic designer. Naturally I turned to AI for help. You will have to pardon me, as this section might torture you slightly if you have already done this sort of thing many times yourself. I wanted to share my *actual prompting experience* using OpenAI's GPT-5 model, so you could see exactly what an early agentic AI will create given an admittedly quite poor prompting effort.

Please keep in mind my original goal was actually just the final diagram. I only thought to turn this journey into part of the book after things unfolded the way they did with GPT-5! I *truly* just wanted to convey to you where we are in transitioning to an "agents as products" future. But the back-and-forth effort actually conveys more, which is why I decided to reproduce it here. It conveys the struggle we are *all* currently feeling with early agentic systems. What follows are my exact and unaltered prompts, and the exact images GPT-5 produced for me.

Prompt 1: Please create a timeline or evolution style chart that is more illustrative and visual / stylized and not very technical. I'm envisioning it roughly like a chart of a horizontal axis and a vertical axis. The horizontal access represents time and the vertical access represents the sophistication of AI agents and how they are used. There should be a conceptual curve sweeping up and to the right and looking somewhat exponential, but it can be a thick arrow like a swoop rather than a technical looking plotted line. Some pointer or arrow in roughly the middle of the swoop should indicate where we are today. In the bottom left of the chart there should perhaps be a robot head graphic indicating early legacy chatbots before LLMs. Roughly in the middle of the curve representing the present, there should be some icons indicating "RAG" and "co-pilots" and "agentic workflows," these are slightly more sophisticated agentic systems that are being deployed in the present. Just to the right and up from the present should be "early agentic era" where some icon on the swoop should indicate somewhat more sophisticated agents, then in the upper right of the curve representing a few more years into the future should be "autonomous co-worker AIs" indicating agents that have become fully capable of learning and evolving within an organization and operating autonomously. All of this should be pretty graphical. Don't have too many words though a few like RAG might be ok, or if you need to indicate the autonomous nature of the agents in the upper right of the chart near the top of the arrow swoop.

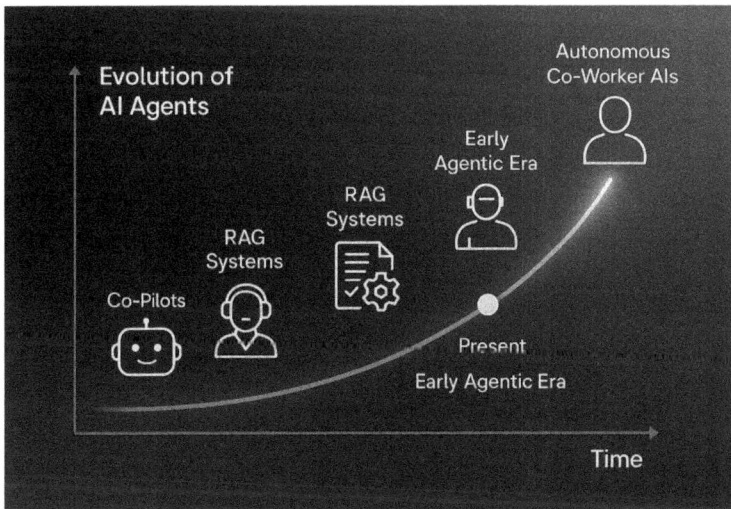

Figure 3.1: Resulting Image from Prompt 1.

Ok, now let's see what happened with my second prompt!

Prompt 2: Thanks, that's not quite right. Can you fix a few things? The left early part of the swoop should have "legacy chatbots" , after that should be LLM RAG Systems, then "Co-Pilots" and "Agentic workflows" should be next... in that order. Then "Early Agents" then "Autonomous Co-worker AIs." The dot labeled as "Present" should be between "Co pilots" and "Agentic Workflows"

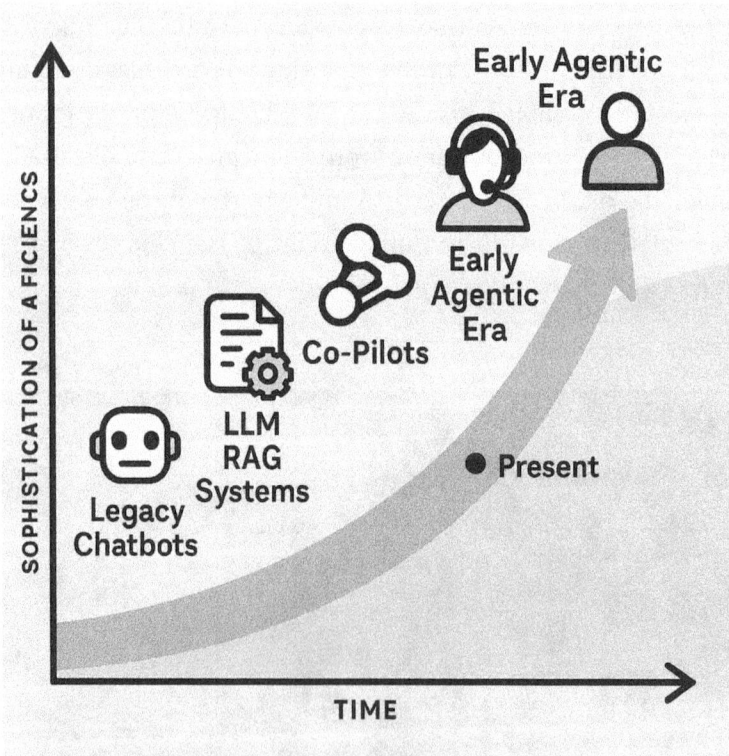

Figure 3.2: Resulting Image from Prompt 2.

It was honestly quite odd to me that the model decided to completely change the style of the image after my second prompt. But I wasn't about to give up, so I kept going. Here is my next prompt:

Prompt 3: Thanks, that is better! Can you fix the label on the vertical axis? It should be "Sophistication" just one word. Also the last icon on the top right should be labeled "Autonomous Co-worker AIs." And let's make Co-Pilots, "Co Pilots and Agentic workflows"

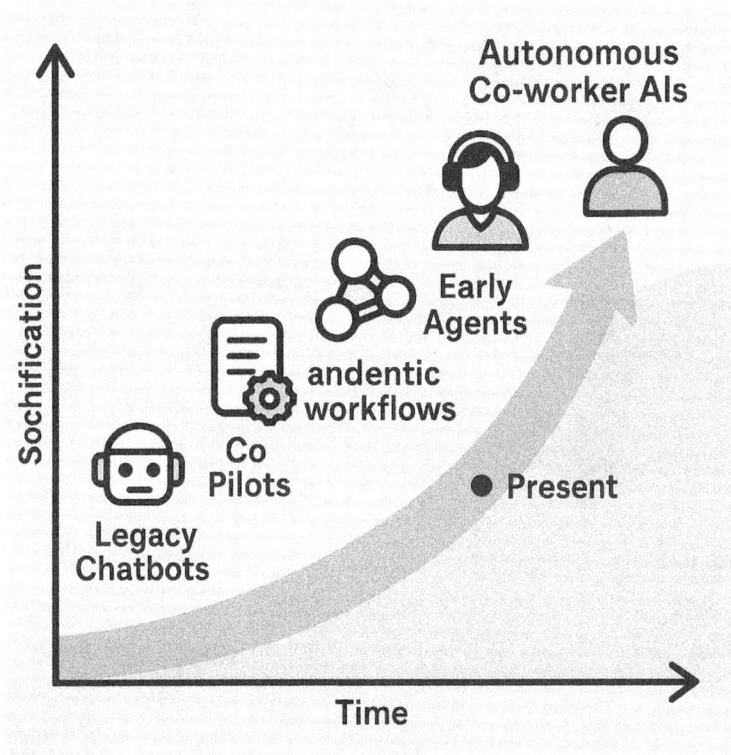

Figure 3.3: Resulting Image from Prompt 3.

Prompt 4: That's a little better, but not perfect. Can you look at that last image you did and fix the spelling of words?

The progression was fascinating to see, but I imagine you've probably had enough? I know I had. After four prompts, the

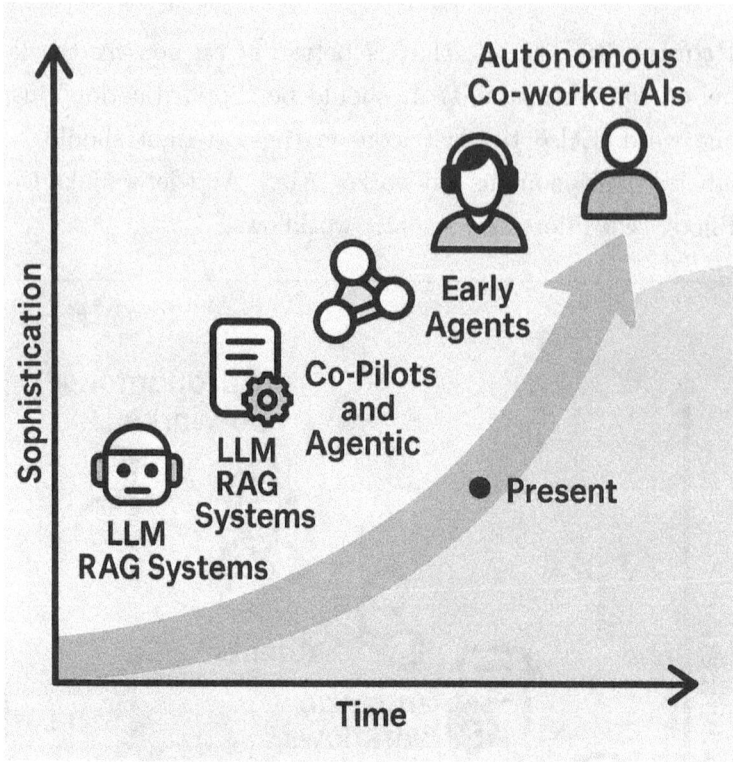

Figure 3.4: Resulting Image from Prompt 4.

image was still not perfect!

That brief flow actually captures quite well the frustration of dealing with the quirky failures of the AI agents and models we have today. My prompting was not great, and I'm sure many of you could have done better. But hopefully you see not only where we are conceptually in the transition, but also *feel a bit what this period is like* for many corporations, consumers, and developers that are using these new agentic technologies. It can be a bit bumpy to say the least. While what's possible is impressive, we are still betting on improvements to make this more than a curiosity.

Co-Pilots, RAGs & Agentic Workflows

Despite GPT-5 not quite being able to get my diagram perfect, you hopefully deduced that I believe we are currently still in the period I call "Co-Pilots, RAGs and Agentic Workflows." I'd like to explain a bit more why this period has been, and in many ways still is, a crucial part of the transition. The year 2025, like 2024 before it, was billed as the "Year of the Agents" by industry pundits and influencers. Progress has been non-linear, but I do believe we are now just entering the era of early production-quality agents, with certain use cases (perhaps unsurprisingly software engineering and social influencing) in the lead.

Well before ChatGPT came along, companies were deploying chatbots, and there is practically universal consensus that they were awful.[1] They were stilted, clumsy, canned, and completely nonhuman. Basically they were ways for organizations to try to prevent you from calling their call center. Calls to call centers are quite costly to large enterprises, so they want to avoid them. For years, even before chatbots and FAQs, companies had been deploying automated call tree or IVR software to try to handle as many customer inquiries as possible without human involvement. The industry term is "call deflection" and managers of call centers get bonuses based on how many calls they can deflect, keeping costs down.

When ChatGPT appeared in late 2022, even in its earliest GPT-3.5 form, it was stunning how much more human it felt. The entire world awoke in a matter of a few months to the power of this revolutionary technology. "Generative AI" quickly became a buzzword. User growth for OpenAI exploded, and the modern LLM-based AI era was upon us.

It's no surprise then that one of the very first business use cases to get attention was upgrading those horrible chatbots. It

---

[1]Curiously, the executives responsible for rolling out these chatbots often think they are great!

was risky of course in the early going, as early LLMs would hallucinate regularly, display real biases, not respond in the voice of the company, or worse. So in short order, most corporations decided to experiment with internal LLM-based applications, while they worked on generative AI applications to help workers in the call center. These were often simple but genuinely useful aids to write a summary note of a call, or assess the quality and tone of the interactions, and record those details into the customer relationship management system for later use. Co-pilots had been born.

Almost as quickly as they came to call centers, numerous similar assistants began popping up inside many of our applications, both business and personal. Fundamentally these co-pilots were designed not to take over entire jobs from us, but to assist us in tasks inside applications we were already using every day. Autocomplete on steroids, "Rewrite with AI" buttons, and various forms of summarization and generation became hallmarks of co-pilots. For the most part these have been quite useful features because they met the human user at exactly the moment of a very specific task: replying to an email, writing a job description, taking notes in a meeting, etc. They didn't require breaking our workflows, and yet they offered immediate assistance.

Another early target application was helping users to search for information, not just by asking the LLM what it already knew, but by connecting the LLM to personal documents or documents inside the enterprise. An obvious limitation of early LLMs was that they had a "knowledge cutoff date," and did not have access to information that was inside the walls of the enterprise or on your private hard drive. Vector databases, which had been in development for several years before LLMs appeared, were nearing maturity and a speedy marriage of the two was arranged.

Very quickly every consultant on earth learned the term RAG for Retrieval Augmented Generation, and every company began embedding their documents into vectors, ingesting them into vector databases, and quickly erecting basic RAG applications on top. Private cloud instances of models were also an essential ingredient, so that CTOs could be assured private data was not flowing to OpenAI or Anthropic. In short order, RAG gave enterprises an improved search engine. One capable of more nuanced and natural queries across the unstructured and often hard-to-find information in the organization. A price was paid in occasional hallucinations, but in numerous low-risk use cases value was easy to come by. This was a period of plucking low-hanging fruit, and plenty of good learning.

As the Generative AI wave evolved in 2023 and 2024, the decision-making power of LLMs became more apparent. Controls, guardrails, and safety wrappers were improving, and focus began to shift to having AI play a more active role in automating business processes. Multiple players already existed in this realm under the broad category of Robotic Process Automation or RPA systems. RPA companies had been involved in automating workflows inside enterprises for years, and they all began aggressively adding calls to LLMs in their workflows. In addition, a plethora of open-source software frameworks such as LangChain, AutoGPT, Haystack, LlamaIndex and many others sprang onto the scene to help build applications around LLMs, often with agentic workflows as a core part of the offering.

This period is still very active. Nowadays, it is fashionable to deem every call to an LLM as "agentic," and anytime an LLM plays even a minor role in controlling the flow of a process it will quickly be labeled an "agentic workflow." These are more and more common. These workflows and automations do in fact offer greater flexibility than previous generations of RPA tools, but still the overarching paradigm is one of deterministic control. The range of outcomes is limited, and the role of the LLM is circumscribed to specific steps where it can add value.

Humans are still very much part of the process via specially

designated "Human-in-the-Loop" or HITL steps in workflows. The
goal is to use fewer people to accomplish the same volume of work,
but there are certainly no AI agents acting as autonomous co-
workers. Despite most of today's examples being modest applications of automation, however, early signs of the software future
we foresee are starting to appear.

Signs of the Era of Agency

We see increasing adoption among businesses of improved chatbots and co-pilots, RAG systems for accessing company information, and partially agentic workflows to streamline business processes. A few high-profile agents have been released in the area
of so-called "Deep Research" assistants. The closest examples of
agents acting semi-autonomously are in the software engineering
domain. In addition, marketing and sales have seen strong uptake
in generative AI applications, and in some sectors even deployment
of full-fledged agents to social platforms to act as representatives
of a brand or product.

We are entering the early agentic period. More progress is
needed in capabilities and robustness to allow AI agents to take
on more substantial tasks. It will also take time for people to get
used to the idea of a "software entity" that does ongoing work and
requires less and less human guidance. In the next chapter, we will
look more closely at what we really mean by *agency*. This somewhat elusive concept will come to define software products in the
years ahead.

Chapter 4

What Is True Agency?

Takeaways: Genuine *agency* in the context of AI agents is defined as the ability to show initiative, act independently, plan, and set novel goals based on innate drives. It is not passive but active. It is not "prompt-driven." It requires situational awareness of broader context, the ability to follow evolving plans guided by policies and ethical principles, and the instinct to adequately and intelligently consult humans. The transition to agents that demonstrate true agency will redefine product management, design, software architecture, and competitive advantage over the coming decade.

A S WE SIT ON THE CUSP of the early agent era, a question looms that will help us measure how quickly our product paradigm is changing. What is agency? How will we measure it in our agents? And how much of it do we really want in our software products anyway?

In legal settings, an agent is someone who acts on behalf of another. The other person is called the principal. In this context, we assume that the person hiring the agent to work on their behalf holds the actual authority. They set the goals. But this leads to some confusion. In this legal setting, an agent can seem more passive than we intend when we talk about *agency*. Should we expect the AI agents we hire to wait for direction?

The definition of "agency" found in philosophy or psychology does more to emphasize its active nature. It typically runs something like this (though exact wordings will vary):

> *To have agency means a person possesses the power and ability to act independently and make their own choices, influencing their own life and the world around them. It's about being in control and having influence over a situation or one's own life.*

I've found that for many of the product teams I advise, really engaging with the idea of agency is challenging. It's a somewhat amorphous concept that requires definition and discussion to make it tractable.

We've spent many decades developing software that remains static until we click a button or run a command, so it can be quite hard to imagine a new kind of software that is always on, always working, and evolves its own goals, even as it seeks to achieve the goals of its supervisor or owner. It's even harder for most product managers to imagine software that takes nearly autonomous actions and continuously learns and improves itself without the need for an update.

Agency Is Not Passive, It Is Active

When we use the term agency in everyday situations, it refers to somebody having the ability to set goals and decide how to act to pursue those goals. We say we have agency in a situation if the decision to move forward on one path or another falls to us. Even the idea of going in one direction or another requires that we take the initiative and *choose* to push our thoughts toward that direction, to evaluate it as an alternative.

When we have agency, we also have "skin in the game." Implicitly, we are an interested party. We care about the outcomes. This is the sense that I see as very central to understanding where software products and services are going. The agents we are starting to build will possess, to a growing degree, the agency and drive that we expect from our best employees. We are in the early innings of building software that needs to "be a go-getter" and to "show initiative." These concepts are entirely absent from the existing way product management and product development are done today.

Should We Develop True Agency?

The question is inescapable, and worth facing head-on. Do we understand the risks well enough to build toward "true agency" in our AI agents? There are clearly risks if we build in too much self-directed goal-setting into agents, particularly if they lose track of broader constraints, policies, and norms. But equally, there will be product risks to companies building agents that do not show enough agency. They may fail to deliver the business value needed to remain competitive.

This question of how much agency to give to our creations has deep roots even in fiction as shown in Figure 4.1, which lists Isaac Asimov's famous Three Laws of Robotics. We will not fully resolve this issue here. How teams confront this question will also be a function of the domain in which they specialize, and the risk inherent in the tasks the agent may perform.

I. **A robot may not injure a human being, or, through inaction, allow a human being to come to harm.**

II. **A robot must obey the orders given it by human beings, except where such orders would conflict with the First Law.**

III. **A robot must protect its own existence as long as such protection does not conflict with the First or Second Law.**

Figure 4.1: The Three Laws of Robotics, as first stated in Isaac Asimov's story *Runaround* (1942).

To cut to the chase, I think the answer is that we must and will move in the direction of greater agency, though with carefully designed guardrails in place. It is unclear, however, if we will produce true agency without reaching fully human-level intelligence. We will examine research pathways toward human-level AGI in Chapter 29, but it's important to think here in product terms about how much agency we want to build into products. Evaluating the level of agency you are exposing, and the definition you are employing of agency, should be a regular practice for all teams developing AI agents.

Finding Balance & Spotting Red Lines

There are obvious risks here. Just because agents should display agency and sometimes act on their own initiative, does not mean we want them to go rogue. As a responsible human, the capacity to act autonomously does not mean you *always* act on your own, or that you do not consult others. Just like we expect great employees to know when to check and collaborate before making key decisions, agents with proper agency will be expected to include these behaviors naturally in their plans. Moreover, agents will need to learn and follow the policies and norms of the organizations they work for.

Before we turn to design implications, it helps to separate two patterns teams often conflate. Figure 4.2 shows the prompt-driven tool many teams deliver today. Such tools exclusively wait to be triggered by human input. They can be useful, but without nearly continuous direction by humans, they are effectively inert. An agentic colleague, by contrast, as sketched in Figure 4.3, runs in a continuous loop, pursuing goals semi-autonomously. It treats prompts as important inputs, not mandates to be followed immediately. We explore the full details of this agentic loop in Chapter 18, where we look at the architecture and engineering of AI agents.

Prompted Tool

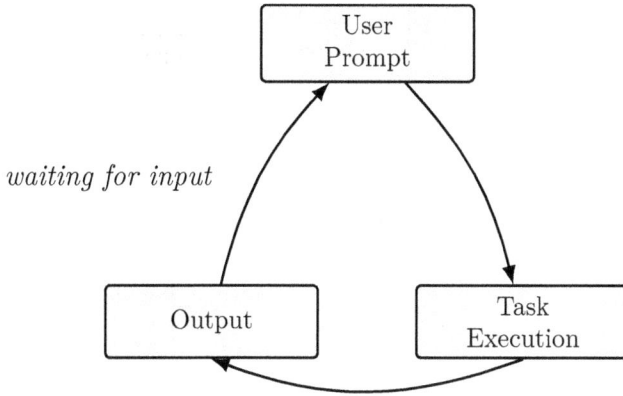

Reactive: Initiates nothing without a prompt

Figure 4.2: Prompt-driven tool (reactive loop). Executes a single task when asked, returns an answer, and goes idle until the next prompt.

What agency is, and how much of it we want, is also nearly inseparable from the idea of goals. Most people are comfortable with the idea of limited goals being delivered to an LLM chatbot via a prompt. Even an agent or model that "breaks down a task" into subgoals to accomplish it feels acceptable. But the boundaries can be tricky to define. When we start to talk about an AI agent setting its own goals, people suddenly become more uncomfortable, even though we expect human employees to write their own goals, and still remain within the larger goals of, say, their organization or company. We will return to the topic of goals and agency in greater depth in Chapter 14 as well.

Having thoughtful situational awareness, understanding the lay of the land well enough to know when to act, when to consult, and when to defer to others for decisions is exactly how humans learn to navigate complex domains. As AI agents become products, and progress toward more autonomy of action, we will expect this

Agentic Colleague

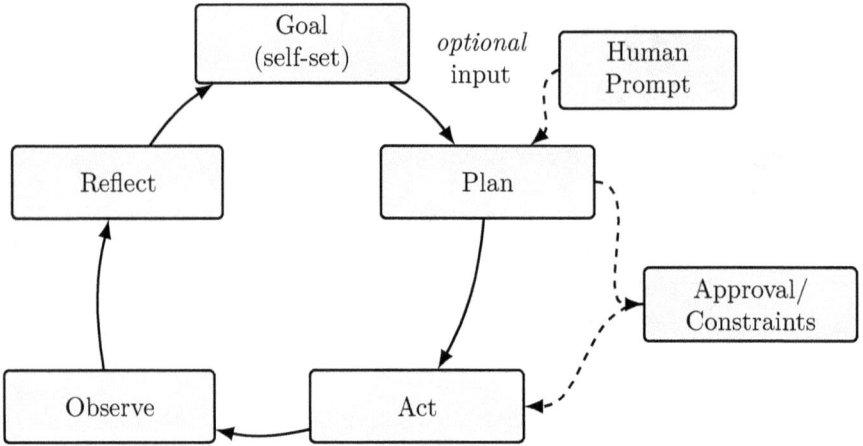

Proactive: Monitors, learns, and revises goals in context

Figure 4.3: An AI agent colleague with intrinsic goals continuously observes the environment, acts, learns and adapts over time. Reacting to human prompts is not its only trigger for action.

awareness and judgment from them. We will return to the topic of situational awareness in Chapter 19 when we examine LLM hallucinations in greater detail.

The Road Ahead for Product Teams

Agency, in this balanced sense, rather than the ability to accomplish a task, will be the defining novel characteristic of agents as software products. But many questions still remain. How do we get there? Are current AI models sufficient to produce or simulate this more human-level behavior? Will agents still be packaged into websites and mobile apps as form factors? Or will they appear as avatars or in embodied robotic forms? How will the roles of various members of the product development team change as we shift to building these new autonomous AI agents? How will product architecture change? What will determine competitive advantage in this new era? We will examine those topics in the chapters ahead.

PART

II

The New Competitive Advantage

We turn our focus to competitive advantage for AI agents. Many agent-based startups have been wiped out by new releases from the big foundation model companies because they rushed to build a fairly obvious feature, hoping a brief time-to-market advantage would sustain them. The brutal truth is that if your agent startup does not first survive, it will never flourish. And to survive, nature dictates that you adapt and specialize. Why is deep specialization, the tireless drive to master your domain, the most important source of competitive advantage in an increasingly agentic era? And what exactly does it require in practical terms?

We will get into this in considerable detail in the chapters ahead. We will look at the packaging and form factor of agents, the role of design and user interfaces, and the role of proprietary data. We will also discuss how your agent's personality and style can become a key part of your product differentiation. Even your agent's innermost thoughts will be part of the definition of your product.

All of these topics matter. Mastering them will help you navigate the rapid pace of change ahead. But as we look at these issues and discuss them in depth, I want you to have a north star principle to guide you. So here it is:

The domain knowledge and domain-focused skills of your agent are what will set your agent-as-product apart from the competition.

It won't matter if you get the controls or technology stack right if your agent doesn't solve real problems better than its competitors. Inevitably, you will face a fleet of robust horizontal agents in the market, built by the large AI players. These generalist agents will be well-equipped with basic office skills like web research, using office software, writing, data analysis, and coding. They will be able to take on significant non-specialized knowledge work in almost any department. Your agent will need deep proprietary domain specialization to compete and survive.

Chapter 5

Adapt, Specialize, Survive, Flourish

Takeaways: Deep domain knowledge and skills will be the key to successful agents, and therefore to successful products going forward. This chapter explores concrete examples of how highly specialized agents can differentiate themselves from generalist agents, and create competitive moats via data, private knowledge, and deep specialist skills. Domain specialization is not limited to industry focus, but may also include deep expertise in functional areas such as design, legal, HR, software engineering, data analysis, marketing, AI model training, hardware engineering, specialized scientific research, or project management.

I DECLARED TO YOU that domain knowledge will be the key to successful agents, and therefore the key to successful products going forward. But what exactly do we mean by domain knowledge, and how will it power successful agents? How do you keep your agentic product ahead and avoid being quickly commoditized?

In the next chapters in this section we will look at packaging and form factor for agents, where it is today and where it is evolving. We will examine what constitutes the "user experience" of working with an agent-as-product, as well as the role of design and other factors. So please, don't take my message to be that domain knowledge *alone* will be sufficient without strong execution on those other factors, but it is definitely where you should start.

Horizontal AI: A Domain for Large Players

Well-funded foundation model companies with deep R&D capability and differentiated infrastructure providers will continue to operate horizontally in the AI space. For independent companies developing AI agents, however, it will be very challenging, as the meme in Figure 5.1 captures well.

Although we noted in Chapter 3 that we are on the cusp of or just entering the early agentic era, there are already multiple big players (and new entrants) building "generalist" agents. The large foundation model companies like OpenAI, Anthropic, and Google are rapidly becoming agent companies themselves.

Figure 5.1: On multiple occasions, new releases by major foundation model companies have wiped out whole categories of startups. This meme created by Gemini 3.0 captures the sentiment well.

In addition to base improvements in many benchmarks, a big factor distinguishing these new products is very tightly integrated and expanding tool use, as well as "routers" that select among different models under the hood based on the user's prompt. Steadily these foundation model products are becoming generalist agents. We will look at this in greater depth in Chapter 13 where we discuss agent tool use and why it is taking off. For now, suffice it to say that things will be *extremely* competitive in the horizontal agent space.

Rubric for Specialist Agents

The reality of stiff horizontal competition means that new entrants in the AI agents space must focus on highly specialized domains. Often this will mean precision solutions to specific problems in particular industries. They must bring more creative, deeper, and more robust solutions than generalist agents offer to real problems that people face. They will also have to look for flywheel dynamics, where the more work an agent does in a particular vertical or specialized domain, the more proprietary data they will generate. That domain-specific data can become an important investable moat.

Focus can come in the form of raw reasoning and problem solving in a particular domain. As domains become more specialized, especially in enterprise settings, but also in many small and medium-sized businesses, businesses are faced with a large variety of real-world domain constraints that simply cannot be solved by strong horizontal agents. Regulatory requirements, safety standards, legacy system integration, and even the way core knowledge in the domain is organized can all provide opportunities specialized agents.

Please do not misinterpret. I am not saying that in specialized industries and domains generalist agents won't be used. Quite the contrary. Due to their relative ease of adoption and general horizontal applicability, modern foundation generalist agents will be used heavily in all industries by a large number of knowledge worker roles. These agents will bring skills like coding, data analysis, deep web research, strong writing, use of many common business software applications, and many other basic skills. In fact, this widespread use is exactly what will set the bar high for new entrants offering more specialized "vertical" agents. As a product leader or founder considering specialized agents, you must keep in mind that your customers will already know what generalist or foundation agents from Google, OpenAI, Anthropic, Microsoft, and

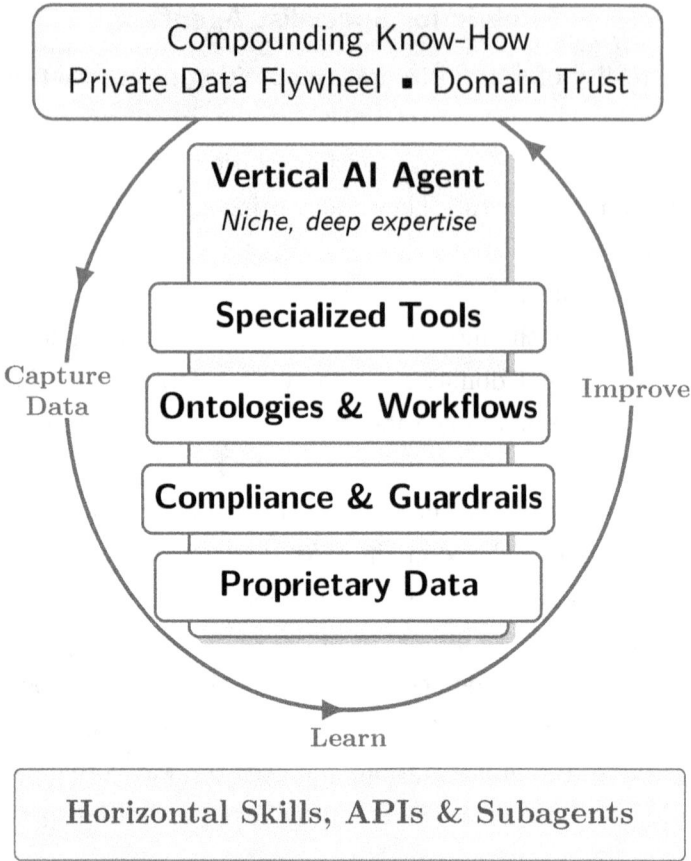

Figure 5.2: Vertical agents will need to leverage horizontal APIs even as they develop the specialized data and skills to compete.

others can do.

By this point, you might be despairing. Is there really a way to compete? I assure you there is definitely a silver lining here. The good news? The big players building generalist agents and foundation models are also making most if not all of those same agents available via API. Your vertical agent can (and will need to) add those "generalist" capabilities via API or other means. Open source libraries and models are also making generalist capabilities available, often at quality levels that exceed even the big labs. So you definitely won't have to build it all yourself, but you will have to go well beyond what the generalists offer.

Beware Semi-Vertical Semi-Horizontal Domains

One of the real challenges can be identifying areas that are vertical enough over time. An example that is still incredibly active is the space of software engineering agents or SWE agents as they are called. Early on, this looked like a safe vertical domain, where great specialization would be needed, but increasingly big tech and foundation players have decided that software engineering is too fundamental a skill, and hence they are now spending billions to be in the lead for the best software engineering agents. We will look at this area in depth in Chapter 16, as it currently is producing some of the most advanced agents in any space.

Education AI agents and data analytics AI agents are two other semi-horizontal verticals where the big foundation model companies appear to be expanding and adding to their core offerings as they seek to compete. Founders and investors looking at domains today must take a deeper and more specialized approach, or they may well find that OpenAI, Anthropic or Google announce an "exciting new feature" that effectively wipes out what their entire startup was working on.

Ideation of Multiple Vertical Agent Examples

This can all sound quite abstract up to this point. To make it more concrete, let's come at it from two directions. First, let's look at short example agent ideas from different domains and industries, and consider how each could specialize and build a proprietary data moat over time. I can't say if any of these ideas are actually viable, but I do hope they stimulate your thinking. Then after that, let's look at one deeper case study. The deeper case study will probe how, in one industry, expertise and specialization might set an agent apart from its generalist rivals.

Let's begin with the larger number of short examples of possible vertical AI agent specialization to get our mental juices flowing:

Clinical Intelligence Agent

Domain: Patient Care Optimization

Problem Statement: Even with advanced electronic health records, clinicians often face extra work reconciling information from multiple sources. External records may arrive as separate documents, imaging and genomic data may remain in different systems, and trial databases are rarely connected. The result is more time spent assembling a full picture of the patient while still keeping up with fast-changing studies, treatment guidelines, and eligibility criteria.

Agent Description: This agent would be embedded in clinical workflows by integrating with the electronic health record and decision-support tools, appearing where clinicians review test results, pathology findings, imaging, and treatment options. It could also support everyday tasks such as drafting patient communications, summarizing visits, or preparing trial referral notes. Beyond the electronic health record, it would connect with tools like secure messaging systems, clinical trial databases, or imaging viewers so the same assistant follows the clinician across the software they already use. By consolidating patient records, lab data, imaging studies, and pathology reports, it provides clear insights across specialties. It also tracks new studies, updated guidelines, and trial eligibility criteria, and reviews each patient's history to recommend appropriate treatment options or relevant research protocols.

Flywheel Data: Each recommendation produces feedback, such as whether it was accepted, how the patient responded, or if a trial match was ruled in or out. Over time, these outcomes create a dataset of patient treatments and results across different groups and care settings, giving the agent better evidence for future decisions.

Industrial Logistics Agent

Domain: Freight, Supply Chain, and Routing Intelligence

Problem Statement: Global supply chains remain vulnerable to delays and cost overruns caused by port congestion, customs holdups, shifting tariffs, and local disruptions. Logistics teams often rely on static schedules or manual tracking across multiple systems, which makes it difficult to react quickly when conditions change and to understand the downstream impact of those changes.

Agent Description: This agent would be embedded in logistics operations by connecting to transportation management systems, carrier portals, customs and tariff databases, and shipment trackers. It would pull updates where available, but could also take practical steps such as texting drivers with schedule changes, confirming delivery appointments with warehouses, or contacting freight forwarders when paperwork is incomplete. Instead of relying only on real-time feeds, it would combine system data with direct communication, helping teams respond when a truck is delayed at a border, a container is stuck at a port, or a shipment risks missing a retail delivery window. By working across planning tools, dispatch systems, and communication channels, the agent becomes a consistent assistant for manufacturers, freight brokers, and retailers.

Flywheel Data: Each intervention creates data that does not exist in traditional planning systems: which carriers respond quickly to changes, which warehouses honor revised delivery times, and how drivers react to route adjustments. Alongside basic metrics like transit time and cost, these human-in-the-loop outcomes build a dataset of reliability and responsiveness across routes, carriers, and partners. Over time, this allows the agent to make recommendations not just on speed or price, but on the likelihood that a given plan will hold under real-world conditions.

Biochemistry Assistant Agent

Domain: Chemistry, Pharmacology, and Bioengineering

Problem Statement: Drug discovery and biotechnology research involve many disconnected steps, from designing new molecules to running experiments and analyzing results. Scientists must coordinate across electronic lab notebooks, automation controls, chemical databases, and separate analysis tools, often handing work off between postdocs, technicians, and computational staff. Senior scientists usually catch major risks, but progress can slow when data are fragmented or when new external findings take time to filter into ongoing projects. Promising ideas may take longer to test, compare, and refine than necessary.

Agent Description: A valuable AI agent here might be almost like a virtual postdoc, working across lab notebooks, information management systems, chemical databases, and robotic platforms. It might suggest new compounds and outline step-by-step synthetic routes, which are practical plans to build a molecule from simpler starting materials. It could prepare instructions for lab automation equipment and track whether a reaction runs successfully. If an experiment failed or produced low yield, the agent would flag the issue, recommend changes in conditions, or notify a technician to intervene.

The agent could also run computational chemistry routines using open-source tools such as PySCF, a Python framework for simulating molecular interactions. These simulations would provide estimates of reaction barriers, stability, and electronic properties before experiments begin, and the agent would refine its approach as more results accumulate. With experience, it might learn which models and parameters are reliable for different classes of compounds. By combining simulations with local experimental outcomes, the agent could help scientists focus resources on candidates with a stronger chance of success.

Such an agent should communicate proactively. The agent could keep teams informed through their preferred messaging software, draft experiment summaries for supervisors, or prepare figures for reports. It might generate Jupyter notebooks to analyze assay data in multiple ways, run them, and share results for feedback. When new papers, patents, or datasets are released, the agent would cross-reference them with local findings, highlight useful methods, and flag potential overlaps with published work.

Flywheel Data: Each experiment adds to the agent's experience. It records yields, assay results, stability, and metadata on failed routes or adjusted conditions, building a record of what works in that lab's environment. Over time, this record would allow the agent to act more like an experienced postdoc that learns from every run. While lab-specific data remains private, the company's platform improves as agents learn across many labs, creating deeper expertise that benefits all users.

Contract Renewal and Usage Intelligence Agent

Domain: Enterprise Software Contract Renewals

Problem Statement: Software renewals are among the largest recurring expenses in many enterprises. Contracts hide complexity in modules, license tiers, audit rights, and performance commitments. Yet most organizations lack a full picture of what they are paying for, what they actually use, and whether the product is living up to its obligations. Without that clarity, vendors hold the advantage, and buyers renew on unfavorable terms.

Agent Description: This agent could act like a seasoned renewal strategist. It might parse contracts to extract licensing rules, usage caps, and service commitments, then analyze raw system data such as login logs, feature usage records, API calls, or concurrent session counts to see how the software is really being used. Where data is incomplete, it could survey end users and department leads to confirm adoption, uncover unused features, or flag redundant tools in other divisions.

The agent could also estimate switching costs by modeling migration work, integration updates, retraining, and temporary productivity loss. It might track service levels and downtime against vendor commitments, building an evidence base of whether the software has met expectations. In preparation for renewal, it could assemble a clear negotiation brief that combines usage data, performance gaps, switching costs, and contract obligations, giving procurement teams a stronger position at the table. When contract terms are ambiguous or vendor reports are missing, the agent could prompt internal stakeholders or the vendor directly to resolve the gaps.

Flywheel Data: Each renewal cycle provides outcomes that sharpen the agent's expertise. It records which clauses vendors concede, which pricing levers succeed, and how usage data translates into discounts. Over time, it builds specialized classifiers for license terms, vendor behaviors, and negotiation outcomes. Because it learns across many customers, the agent develops a knowledge base no single procurement team could match. That collective experience allows it to approach each new client with patterns, tactics, and benchmarks already tuned to software renewals in practice.

Land Use Intelligence Agent

Domain: Real Estate, Land Use, and Zoning

Problem Statement: Much of city planning still depends on zoning ordinances, parcel maps, and subdivision documents that are hard to parse. Some of these records are digital, but many remain as scanned PDFs or paper maps. Planners and developers spend hours checking setbacks, overlays, and use restrictions by hand. Missing a clause in a zoning ordinance or misreading a parcel boundary can stall a project or trigger costly legal disputes. What if those checks could be done faster and more reliably?

Agent Description: This agent could specialize in reading and interpreting land use documents. It might parse zoning codes, extract rules about setbacks or allowed uses, and connect those to parcel maps and site plans. When data is only available in scanned form, the agent could use OCR and trained models to recover boundaries and terms, then highlight uncertainties for a human to confirm. It could also cross-check against floodplain maps or environmental overlays to flag parcels where extra permits would be needed.

For planners, the agent could prepare a quick "parcel brief" that shows all restrictions, overlays, and potential conflicts in one place. For developers, it could surface early warnings about projects likely to face zoning board pushback. If important data is missing — for example, an HOA covenant that isn't in the system — the agent might prompt the team to retrieve and log it.

Flywheel Data: Each parcel review or zoning case would add to the agent's knowledge. It would learn which restrictions are most commonly misread, which overlays generate disputes, and how boards rule on edge cases. Over time, its classifiers for scanned maps and ordinances would improve, and its guidance would become more reliable. Data from one city would stay local, but the platform could grow sharper by seeing patterns across many jurisdictions.

Newsletter Growth Strategist Agent

Domain: Substack Author Growth and Cultural Intelligence

Problem Statement: Growth on Substack is beyond tough. New authors often feel invisible. Even experienced ones wonder what to write next or how to get noticed outside their existing readers. Topics appear and disappear fast, and it is easy to miss the moment. At the same time, not every author even wants to chase current topics. But all authors struggle to figure out what to write about next. If you drift too far from your mission, readers lose interest. Many authors give up, or spend years before they figure out how to get even moderate growth.

Agent Description: An AI agent co-worker in this space

could act as a thinking partner and strategist for the author. A critical first step would be to really learn the author's goals, values, and the subjects they care about most. Over time, the agent should build a picture of what truly matters, and what should be ignored. That helps the author focus and avoid spreading themselves thin.

When a new topic breaks or starts heating up, the agent would not just spit out a draft. It could ask questions, surface what others have already said, and push the author to sharpen their take. Once the angle is clear, it could help research, draft outlines, and gather charts, images, or links to support the post. The author stays in control of the writing and voice, but the agent can still offer suggestions, editorial advice, and thoughts on the article in progress to make sure it does not miss opportunities to advance the author's goals.

Execution after each post or note matters a ton, and it is tedious work. The agent could prepare posts for Substack Notes, Twitter, LinkedIn, Threads, or Bluesky. It could proactively find accounts worth engaging with, suggest a collaboration with another writer, or reply to posts to get exposure and build rapport. With approval, it could handle the follow-through so the most reach is realized after the author puts out a long-form piece.

Flywheel Data: Obviously the agent will have tremendous detail on what each author pursues and how they go about it. That private data must stay with the author. But across many authors, the agent should develop a highly-tuned sense of what themes stick, how different subgroups and key influencers react, and which outreach tactics work and with whom.

Ok... that was a good number of examples! I hope a few of those got your mind thinking creatively about the wide array of possibilities with vertical AI agents. Really, we barely scratched the surface. Essentially any corner of the economy, or function inside a larger enterprise, or niche consumer interest, can be fertile territory to research for winning vertical agent ideas.

Deeper Look at a Single Vertical Agent

Many of the examples we just looked through were admittedly too shallow to be fully convincing. I just wanted to give a sense of the breadth of possibilities, but it is important to go deep too. Next, let's take a much closer look at a concept agent specialized in one particular industry. We will examine the specialized knowledge and tools that it might have in advance of "getting a job" to differentiate itself, and also what it might learn and refine "on the job" as it gains experience in customer environments.

I purposely chose an industry that I expect most readers will not know a lot about: the lithium mining industry. If you are a lithium mining expert, I apologize as this is probably going to be both unrealistic in some ways, and probably still too shallow for you. I chose it to illustrate *the kind of depth and specialization* that I believe all vertical agents will need to achieve to be relevant. Product managers and architects building agents for any industry or domain will need to operate at this level of depth if they hope to make competitive agents.

Case Study: Deep Domain Agent for Lithium Mining Industry

Industry Background

The global transition to electric vehicles and renewable energy has made lithium one of the most strategically important materials in the world. It is a core component of modern battery technologies, and its supply chain is now under intense scrutiny from regulators, investors, and environmental advocates alike. For companies operating in lithium extraction, whether from hard rock or brine resources, this means navigating a complex landscape of geological uncertainty, emerging technologies, geopolitical pressure, and shifting regulatory frameworks. These are exactly the kinds of challenges that call for domain-specific AI agents: systems that do not just process information but actually grasp the industry they serve.

A generic AI tool, no matter how powerful, cannot substitute for an agent with detailed knowledge of how lithium is extracted, why water rights are contentious, or how policy incentives vary across jurisdictions. In this case study, we explore what a lithium industry AI agent would need to know on day one, and how it could continue to learn over time to become an even more valuable teammate inside a mining company. If you were building such an agent, what knowledge would you give it first?

Specialized Knowledge Out-of-the-Box

To be useful from the outset, an AI agent working in the lithium industry must come preloaded with a wide array of specialized knowledge and reasoning capabilities that reflect the industry's structure, vocabulary, and decision-making logic.

At the geological level, the agent should understand how lithium is typically found and evaluated. This includes hard rock deposits (such as spodumene in Australia or Canada) and lithium-rich brine located under salt flats in regions like Chile, Argentina, and Bolivia. For the latter, resource evaluation is not just about quantity but also about brine chemistry, including ratios of lithium to impurities like magnesium or boron. An agent should be equipped with pretrained models that can help predict resource quality based on geospatial and historical data. In practice, this means parsing assay tables, drilling logs, and 3D geological models, each a difficult task in its own right.

Off-the-shelf LLM PDF parsers do a very poor job with

specialized documents like this, creating a real opening for a specialized agent. Assay tables contain long lists of elemental concentrations where units, sample quality, and lab policies matter. Drilling logs often include handwritten notes or inconsistent codes that require context to interpret, such as whether a "lithium-bearing zone" was flagged by a geologist or inferred from indirect tests. Three-dimensional geological models bring in spatial statistics, fault lines, and cut-off grades that shift project economics depending on how they are drawn. Proprietary ML models could be trained for each of these artifacts: classifiers tuned to lab assay formats, sequence models for drilling-log shorthand, and geostatistical models that respect the domain rules of orebody modeling. Without that kind of specialization, outputs risk being misleading. Proprietary models here can reduce wasted drilling and give management a clearer picture of resource potential.

At the processing level, the agent must grasp the differences between traditional evaporation pond methods and emerging technologies like Direct Lithium Extraction (DLE). Traditional methods evaporate massive quantities of water over many months, whereas DLE technologies aim to pull lithium directly from brine using chemical or membrane processes, potentially reducing water use and environmental damage. A useful AI agent should not only understand these technical methods, but also be able to simulate process efficiency, energy consumption, and chemical throughput. That is not trivial. Engineers today use tools like PHREEQC, an open-source program for modeling water chemistry that predicts how minerals precipitate or dissolve under different conditions. They also use Aspen, a commercial process simulator that estimates flows, energy use, and costs across industrial plants. For an agent to run or extend such models, it would need fine-tuned skills: parsing chemical inputs correctly, setting valid assumptions, and checking whether results match real operating data. This is what would let the agent give engineers realistic comparisons between process routes rather than generic estimates.

In the regulatory domain, the agent needs to understand how different countries' policies affect operations. For instance, Chile's 2023 National Lithium Strategy gives the government a controlling stake in new projects and requires more rigorous water use standards. In contrast, the U.S. Inflation Reduction Act provides incentives for domestically sourced lithium or imports from free-trade partners. The European Union's Critical Raw Materials Act imposes a 27-month deadline on permitting but demands strong environmental safeguards. A pretrained regulatory reasoning module would allow the agent to map these complex jurisdictional rules to project-specific forecasts, such as estimating how long permitting might take or what conditions must be met to qualify for subsidies. For a mining executive, knowing this ahead of time might cut years of delay before breaking ground.

On the commercial side, lithium is notorious for its price volatility. The agent should come equipped with pricing forecast models built on futures data, supply–demand curves, and macroeconomic inputs. These models could be connected to a Monte Carlo simulation engine for evaluating project net present value (NPV) under multiple market scenarios. This gives finance teams a realistic sense of investment risk and helps guide decisions about whether to build, pause, or scale down a mine. The strength of the agent is in showing a full range of possible outcomes with probabilities, rather than leaning on a single forecast that might be misleading.

To act as a true collaborator, the agent would also include industry-specific tools. A geospatial risk model could overlay lithium sites with satellite data on water scarcity, biodiversity, and indigenous lands, enabling early identification of potential ESG (environmental, social, and governance) issues. Fine-tuning the agent on mining permits and environmental impact assessments could help draft or validate regulatory filings more quickly. The agent could also actively monitor news feeds, academic publications, and regulatory filings for economic and policy shifts that matter directly to lithium extraction.

By coming pre-equipped with this level of domain-specific expertise, the agent does not just answer questions. It could participate in the decision-making process with the logic and context that experienced human team members would expect. It could serve as a junior analyst, a compliance assistant, or even a planning advisor right out of the box.

Specialized Knowledge Learned on the Job

The agent's usefulness does not stop with its pretrained capabilities. In fact, much of its value is unlocked once it begins to learn from the company's specific data, tools, policies, and workflows.

Every lithium site has unique characteristics. Variability in brine chemistry, local weather patterns, reagent costs, or equipment performance all matter. By connecting to real-time sensor feeds from the field (such as brine flow rates, pond evaporation levels, or chemical assay logs), the agent could adapt its process control recommendations over time. If certain impurities start to rise, it might suggest a shift in the chemical treatment protocol. If the energy efficiency of a membrane system begins to fall, it might recommend preventive maintenance. These are domain-aware suggestions shaped by an evolving understanding of the site.

Beyond operations, the agent could connect to the company's enterprise resource planning (ERP) systems and procurement tools to learn about cost structures, vendor reliability, and logistics constraints. This allows it to refine its economic models with actual performance data, not just industry benchmarks. Over time, the agent learns the company's unique priorities and cost sensitivities. It can then suggest sourcing strategies, capital allocation shifts, or contract renegotiation opportunities with increasing accuracy. These are the decisions that save or sink projects.

Another critical domain is tacit knowledge, what employees know but rarely write down. Geologists might annotate resource models based on their field observations. Process engineers might override automated systems due to local intuition. By observing these actions and receiving feedback, the agent begins to encode company-specific heuristics. This makes its recommendations feel less generic and more aligned with how the team actually works. These types of insights taken from one site can be applied across the company, potentially resulting in significant efficiency gains.

Over time, this learning compounds. The agent might notice that spikes in magnesium contamination typically follow a seasonal shift in water table behavior. Or that one particular DLE module performs better under lower pH conditions at a specific site. Or that community relations flare-ups tend to precede project delays, prompting proactive engagement. These are not things an agent could know on day one. But they are exactly the kinds of insights that make a software system feel more like a trusted colleague than a tool.

Where To Go From Here?

Many of the examples in this chapter have been fairly speculative. They involved imagining agents with capabilities that frankly extend a bit beyond what is straightforward engineering at the time this book goes to print. That is intentional. My goal here is to get you to think more deeply about what it will really take to set your agent apart in its domain, especially as foundation models and generalist agents improve in parallel. We will get to constraints and technical obstacles in due course. For now, I strongly encourage you to extend this type of thinking to the industries and domains you personally find most interesting. If none of these examples was your exact cup of tea that's perfectly fine. Whatever spaces you focus on, it will be important for you and your team to go deep to build the foundation of your agent's strength and competitiveness.

Chapter 6

Agents Can Be Everywhere at Once

Takeaways: AI agents have a unique property that represents a radical departure from traditional software. They can literally be in thousands of places at once, proactively interacting with multitudes of people at the same time, presenting themselves in ways unique to each environment. This turns normal interface design on its head, and has major implications for how we think about form factor and packaging. Fully grappling with these opportunities and challenges will be crucial for building competitive advantage.

D OMAIN KNOWLEDGE AND SPECIALIZATION will be the core of AI agent competitive advantage. But this alone won't be enough to launch successful agents. A crucial topic that all companies launching agents will face is the question of form factor, packaging and "where your agent shows up." Humans will certainly be around in the same environments in which your agents operate, and humans will need to interact with them. To get adoption, agents will need to present themselves to humans in familiar forms. They will need to appear in the places humans expect them, where and when they are needed. Additionally, there will be many ways to use form factor and packaging creatively as a source of differentiation, particularly in the early phases of agent adoption.

The big thing to first internalize is that agents can be in many different places at the same time. This is not something that product teams are at all used to thinking about in my experience. Honestly, it can take some time to wrap your head around.

Remember we discussed thinking about an AI agent as a colleague or teammate? But hold on. This new agent teammate is definitely more powerful than you or me! You and I can be in one meeting at once, using one application at once, in one part of the country and one part of the world at once. This new "colleague" is not limited at all by the constraints of time or place, or only being able to handle one conversation at a time, that affect the rest of us.

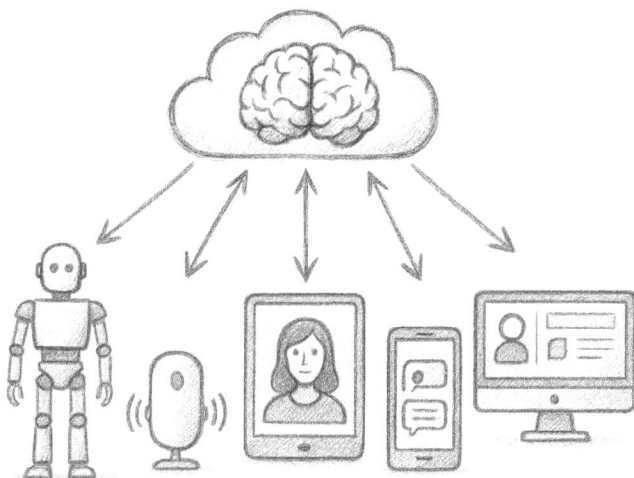

Figure 6.1: One agent mind will operate across many platforms in parallel.

Agents can quite literally operate across dozens or even hundreds of platforms, locations and conversations simultaneously. You and I may multi-task a bit, checking our socials or other news headlines with a glance when we are off camera in a Zoom meeting. But none of us can literally type a message across 10 different social apps at the same time, or be in 20 different meetings at the same time, equally engaged and equally adept in each of those settings. Imagine if you could be in 20 meetings at once, contributing, recalling, processing, and storing important facts from each interaction, each conversation, and each participant simultaneously. Why not 200 or 2000? AI agents can do just that.

Packaging & Form Factor

The ability AI agents have to be in multiple places at once has profound implications for what we mean by "form factor" and "packaging" in the first place. I encourage product managers, engineers and designers to think about this early and often. Each time you and your team come back to this topic of "being everywhere at once" you will likely find new ways your agent can use this superpower, especially as you think about the unique problems of the vertical or domain your agent operates in. This is also a critical question for data protection, privacy, and building trust in your agent. Yes, agents can monitor and measure the reactions of every participant in every meeting they are in, but should they?

Let's look one by one at some of the obvious places an agent may appear and the form factors they may adopt there.

Standalone Application: The most obvious form factor in which an agent can manifest is in a standalone web application. This is easily extended to include a dedicated mobile application for the agent. What is perhaps most noteworthy about a dedicated application on web or mobile is that it gives product teams the maximum opportunity to introduce their agent and give it a unique presence and feel. Custom applications allow bespoke affordances to guide users, helping them to understand the agent's capabilities, and learn how to get the most out of the agent. Product teams will still need to follow the norms for this form factor, but this is one place where your agent will be alone on a stage of its own making. It is crucial to leverage this extra creative canvas to help onboard users and to set the agent apart from others. It may be tempting to just copy the OpenAI chat interface and be done with it, but to do so is a major lost opportunity.

Using Common Business Applications: Another common case will be that an AI agent joins a common business application that has collaboration features as if it were a human participant. This should be distinguished from app-specific co-pilots, which are usually built by the app vendor and help with specific tasks in the app. When an AI agent joins a collaborative app as a human it needs to either use specific approved APIs provided by the vendor, or interact via the application's UI. In both cases the AI agent needs credentials and proper identity. This type of interaction is already showing up in applications like Google Docs, but also is becoming commonplace in apps like Zoom, Microsoft Teams, or Google Meet, where agents like Otter, Fireflies, or MeetGeek can join meetings to take notes.

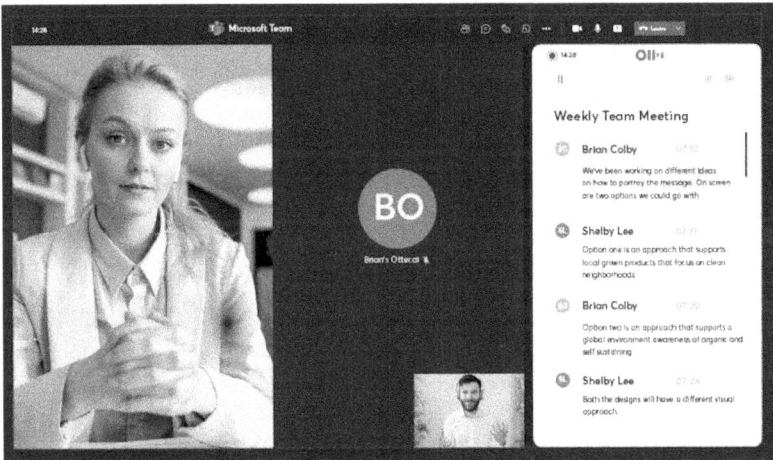

Figure 6.2: Agents like this one frequently join meetings as participants nowadays.

This mode of appearance is becoming common in a growing range of business applications such as project management and issue tracking tools like Jira and Asana. It's also prevalent in developer tools like GitHub. Very importantly, however, agents will also increasingly *use these applications as tools.* We will discuss tool use in greater detail in Chapter 13, but new "colleague" agents should be able to use most common business applications *on their own ini-*

tiative, to meet their own needs, not just when invited by a human user for a specific purpose.

Inside Messaging Applications: Messaging Applications are really a special case of using common applications, but one that is so common as to deserve a closer look. Long before agents, less intelligent bots found homes across a wide variety of messaging applications, both corporate and personal, a trend that will continue with AI agents. Chat has always been a natural way to interact with AI, and chat applications abound both inside and outside the enterprise. On the consumer side, this includes apps like Telegram and Discord, while in the enterprise, this includes apps like Microsoft Teams and Slack. Strong *native* interactions on these platforms will be essential, as these are likely to be among the most common places

> *This new "colleague" is not limited at all by the constraints of time or place or similar factors that affect the rest of us.*

real users interact with your agent. Your agent should understand the platform specific actions and culture well to maximize the value of its presence in each application. A crucial goal in these environments is to avoid being perceived as a spammer. The long history of low-quality chatbots in these spaces has soured many humans to interacting with AI this way. You will need to build cross-platform trust in the value of your agent before users will welcome it into their messages.

Enterprise Hubs and Agent Portals: Large enterprise vendors are beginning to launch agent hubs and portals. These are beginning to serve as general "discovery zones" for agents. Tools like Google Agent Gallery (part of AgentSpace), or MoveWorks Agent Marketplace are examples of this trend. These look a bit like job boards, or internal employee pages, and not without good reason.

On these platforms, as AI agents become more like co-workers, you will increasingly learn about their background and capabilities

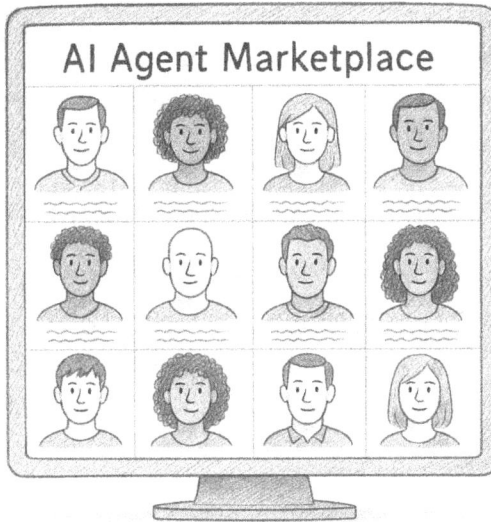

Figure 6.3: As agents become more like teammates we will discover them in similar ways.

much the way you might do browsing the internal human employee directory today. There may even be some sort of LinkedIn for agents in the future. These platforms can help you decide if an agent may be a good candidate for your particular project or team. One nice thing: you won't have to worry if an agent is already busy on another team, because they can comfortably work on dozens of teams and projects at the same time (data security and authorization permitting).

Social Networks: Especially if your agent is consumer oriented, external social networks represent vital territory in which your agents need a strong and capable presence. Whether it is Instagram or TikTok, Farcaster or Facebook, or any of a dozen other social networks, each of these platforms presents a new set of potential actions and interaction modalities to your agent, as well as new norms, behaviors, and cultures. These environments are crucial for marketing, sales, and customer support. These may be the front lines where your agents prospect on their own for new customers, or hear unfiltered views about your company or your competition. Like them or not, they are crucial for product managers and whole product teams to consider carefully. Just as enterprises regulate employee behavior and posting on social media, you will have to make sure your agent knows what it can and cannot post on these platforms.

Games and Virtual Worlds: Games and "metaverses" are another realm where agents are already starting to appear. Some may be open to your agent joining and becoming part of these virtual environments. Where they do, these may offer some of the most unique opportunities to differentiate and make your agent feel more human and authentic. This may seem like purely a concern for consumer agents, but increasingly as VR, AR, and advanced simulations play roles in industrial use cases from airplane manufacturing to building construction, depending upon your industry you may find that virtual environments are crucial ones in which your agent needs to operate.

Inside Specialized Applications: Increasingly more specialized business and consumer applications are embedding AI as an important new feature. Often this takes the form of an onboard "co-pilot" or assistant that helps the user of the application complete tasks within the application more easily. This is a great first step for existing applications, and virtually all applications have begun to do this.

But as we have noted, businesses want AI agents that are capable of working *across* their applications the way humans do. We will discuss this more when we discuss tool use later. In many cases highly domain specialized business applications will be tools that your agent will have to master to earn its keep.

The Model Context Protocol (MCP), which we will look at more in Chapter 20, is also making interaction with applications easier. This applies equally to the common business applications we discussed above, as well as to more specialized applications. Things are still very early, so it will be important to watch as it develops. In highly specialized industries there may even be opportunities to partner with incumbent applications to tightly integrate your AI agent if you can structure a win-win for you, the other company, and most importantly the customer.

Key Product Decisions

What do you need to focus on from a product perspective as you consider putting your agent into each of these settings? Most important is that you remember your agent is your brand. You need to choose channels and platforms based on your domain specialization. You also need to think about consistency, familiarity, and the core value and differentiation of your agent across these channels. The last thing you want is for your agent to have a high-quality reputation in some channels, but due to poor planning or poor product execution, your agent is a disappointment on a crucial platform or channel that is important to customers in your domain.

We will talk in the next chapter more about UI and design, but a vital first step is to understand each of these environments, and what types of visual and other customization freedom they offer, and what restrictions they impose. You will need to understand how you can leverage them to give your product the consistency across environments needed to build trust. More and more these platforms are making special provisions for AI agents. As a product manager, you will need to understand the dos and don'ts in each of these channels or applications. Small mistakes could lead to you being cut off from crucial distribution.

Data security and policy are another important dimension for you to consider in your product. This is especially true for public platforms. If your agent posts customer data publicly it could end your company quickly. We will cover this more in Part V when we discuss security and controls, but this is more than a technical issue. The trust your agent wins is a core part of its value and product definition.

Each of these places an agent can appear also represents an engineering and testing cost for you. They all require maintenance and tuning as the platforms evolve. Often they will involve significant effort to follow the rules of the platform. On platforms like social networks, games, and virtual worlds there are a multitude of new platform-specific actions that your agent will have to learn to perform and perform well. There will be real integration, testing, and ongoing operational costs for each platform and channel you choose to support.

This means prioritization, that most critical of all product skills, will always be in play. You have to know deeply which tools, which applications, and which social networks are most crucial for your customers. You also have to know how to reach your customers on these platforms, and how these platforms fit into their workflow. This will vary substantially from vertical to vertical.

The days of simply thinking of "form factor and packaging" as your icon being clicked, and your application launching are slipping away. Soon, your agent will need to be everywhere your customers already live, work, and play. Your *product itself* will be reaching out proactively to existing and new customers alike. Selling and working with equal ease, respecting privacy and policy, around the clock and around the world.

Chapter 7

Feedback: The New Beautiful UI

> *Takeaways*: A crucial aspect of how users experience your agent will be the *feedback* it provides. Feedback must be clear, useful, and guide people to get more from the agent over time. Avoid building agents that rush to deliver results without first understanding the user's intent and the context in which they are working. Great agents must ask questions, not just answer them.

A S PRODUCT DEVELOPERS, architects, and designers we have adopted the mantra for decades that we want our products to "delight" our customers. I can say, I have often fallen short of this mark. When I have achieved, it has been one of the most satisfying moments in the journey. The ingredients have been the same every time. The product was able to meet the customer at exactly the right moment and cleanly and intuitively deliver something magical. Agents offer this opportunity multiple times over to product teams that are prepared to take advantage of it.

The principle is simple, and already known to great designers: feedback is everything.

Early in my career in the late 1990s, I had the honor of working closely with legendary designer Bruce "Tog" Tognazzini who led the design team at Healtheon/WebMD where I ran the product management team. In those days, the web was horribly slow. Conceived as a static publishing platform, the idea of using the web to serve complex business applications was entirely new, and most people did not believe it could work. Frankly, it didn't work very well at all back then. Loading simple web pages often took tens of seconds to minutes.

In 1996, when we were working on web-based healthcare applications, JavaScript was barely a year old. Animations were next to impossible, and we struggled with ancient browsers like Netscape Navigator 3 and 4. The miracles of modern web app construction like React, Node.js, and virtually all other such conveniences were far in the future. As a result, we had to do a lot on the design side to make slow, painful experiences more bearable and understandable for users.

The Lesson I Learned from Tog

As Tog repeatedly reminded us, the key to this was feedback. Literally, keeping the user informed (regardless of how slow something would be) was the best way to make sure the user understood the value when we finally got to them with a result. Tog and I negotiated and pleaded with engineers to deploy barbaric JavaScript hacks to creatively display lighthearted messages to users (sometimes even with primitive animations and graphics), just to help the users understand that their painfully slow browser (or the whole internet frankly) was not broken.

We are in roughly the same time period today with AI agents as we were then with the web. As such, one of the most important things product teams should consider is how their agent will engage with users, especially how it gives feedback that keeps humans in the loop and builds confidence in its output and the value it brings.

Studies are backing up the importance of human-to-AI agent collaboration as well. Recent research by Stanford University studied the preferred level of collaboration and interaction on a scale known as the "Human Agency Scale" or HAS. As Figure 7.1 shows, in the large majority of occupations, humans strongly preferred to work with agents collaboratively at HAS levels H2 and H3, where both the agent and the human were critical to the task. Cooperation, in turn, requires a maximum of feedback and communication between the two sides. *This is a strong clue for product teams about the importance of feedback!* In only a tiny fraction of cases did humans want to work with either totally autonomous agents (no collaboration required), or with agents where the human had to do most of the work (low capability agents).

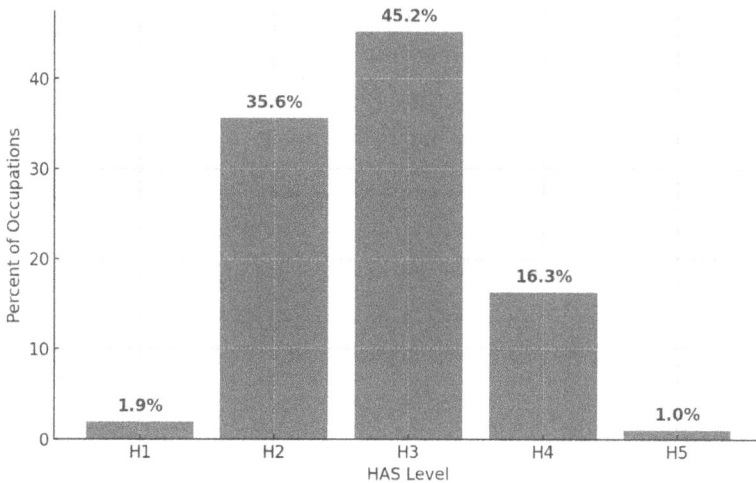

Figure 7.1: High collaboration and feedback between agents and humans is the sweet spot.

Missed Opportunities

Poor design is always a missed business opportunity. Recently I was advising a company with strong ambitions in the AI agent space. Specifically they were building a "UI designer agent" that could crank out front-end designs and front-end code to speed iteration on application design ideas. Let me be clear, this is a great role for agents and an area with plenty of competitors. There are now multiple launched products in this space, but there is still room for more as design is such a rich and nuanced area.

The team was giving me a demo, but I asked to take the wheel so I could try it out more as a user actually would. Like many such tools the first step was to prompt it. Not the most creative or innovative first way to engage, but certainly mainstream and acceptable. I was dismayed, however, after I submitted my request. The UI started flashing a series of pulsing squares. They were meant to symbolize a UI wireframe being under construction, but their pulsing and changing had nothing to do with my particular request.

They were generic, but more importantly they *looked* generic. It was just another "loading spinner," a very non-agentic Web 2.0 form of user feedback, in larger form. I was pretty disappointed. Good agents can give much better feedback as they work. Modern agents as products should "think out loud," and they should do a good job of it. When they tell us what they are thinking about it is a great chance to build confidence that they are thinking the right way. It shows the human user what paths they are considering. It builds trust. It can even be delightful.

> *My complaint was not with the product concept at all but with the UI execution. This was especially peculiar as the team certainly cared about design. They were designing an agent to do UI design after all! But they were not thinking from first principles, and had ignored the rule of great feedback and how it felt to work with their agent.*

Feedback Is a Two-Way Street

The other big miss in this startup's agent was that it failed to ask me additional questions. *This is really crucial.* I *purposely* had given it a pretty bad prompt, in part to see if it would ask follow-up questions to get my intent right. It did not. Big mistake. The result was it produced a reflection of my bad prompt. The agent had just rushed off to "do something" even though it couldn't possibly have understood my intent, because literally I hadn't given it anything to go on yet. This type of interaction erodes trust.

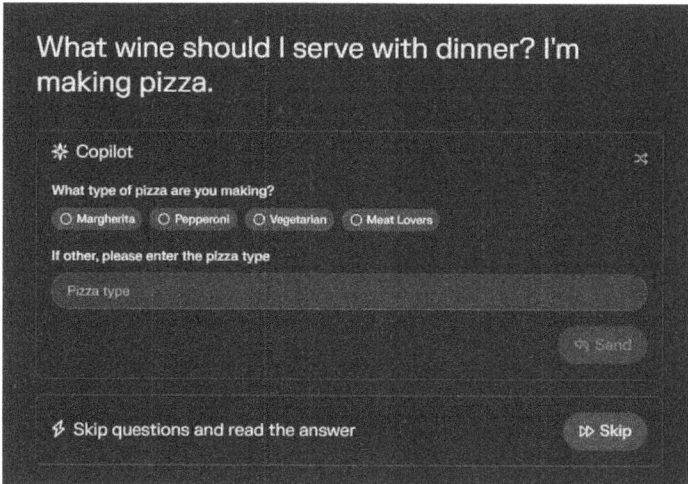

Figure 7.2: Perplexity's UX asks follow-up questions.

In the real world, if I go to a reputable design agency, or a consulting firm, or a manufacturer, or even a wedding planner, I expect them to ask me plenty of questions. If I utter a few vague words to them, and they just say "ok, got it," and rush off to deliver me something, I will instantly know they are not professionals. Poor quality work ensues from too few questions. Good service providers always ask follow-up questions, and do so very intelligently. This is *crucial* for agents as products. You have to get the customer's intent clearly at the beginning before your agent rushes off to do something. Think of how very senior consultants work with you to get your requirements. Please, whatever you do, don't make your agent look like a junior, shoot-from-the-hip employee who doesn't ask the right questions and too eagerly cranks out garbage work.

Additionally, although I did not test it with the UX design agent, a good agent taking on longer and more complex assignments should know when to check in with humans. We all get stuck as we do work. The real world is complicated, and you learn more as you dig into a project. Obstacles appear that were in no way apparent at the outset. That's normal, and it's also normal that your AI agent will not be able to solve all of these on its own. Flailing or banging its head with repeated trial and error only makes your agent look dumber.

Please, whatever you do, don't make your agent look like a junior, shoot-from-the-hip employee who doesn't ask the right questions and too eagerly cranks out garbage work.

Teams making heavy use of reinforcement learning often fall into this trap as we will discuss more in Chapter 12.

Try to ingrain this in your team's thinking. Sometimes the *tool* your agent needs is a conversation with a human expert, or a decision from someone with the right authority. Building this instinct for follow-up into AI agents is still often overlooked, but it will be crucial to setting your agent apart as trustworthy and effective.

Chapter 8

New Challenges for Designers

Takeaways: Product designers face a very interesting new challenge: designing the style and personal identity of the agent itself. Agent design is a multifaceted issue and one which will require new skills and new thinking from design leads on product teams. Unlike traditional interfaces, agents will speak, act, and adapt in ways that make them feel almost alive, so their tone, behavior, and values must be designed as deliberately as their visual appearance.

W E DISCUSSED in the last chapter the importance of feedback, both before and at multiple points during the execution of an agent's job. This feedback and follow-up is indeed one of the strongest levers you have to work with as a product team seeking to delight the customer. But in this chapter I want to think even more closely about design and its changing role as products become agents.

Traditional graphical user interfaces (built for use by humans) are not going to disappear, though they will diminish in importance as AI agents take on more tasks. As we outlined in Chapter 6, our agents will have to exist in many environments, ranging potentially from our own mobile app and web application, to a social network, video game, or other platform. To varying degrees we will continue to need traditional visual and UX design for the flow and affordances of each of these environments. We might have very little visual control when our agent appears in Discord or Slack or Telegram, perhaps just an icon or a background on the agent's profile page. But we might have quite a lot of visual control if our agent lives inside an AR design tool, a virtual world, or a video game. In some settings, your agent may need a whole virtual wardrobe, a human voice, and various other virtual inventory items to establish its identity.

What Style Means for Agents

All of those elements will matter, of course, and great designers will be vital to craft them to help set your agent apart, but I want to focus on something more subtle, and more agentic here: your agent's *style*.

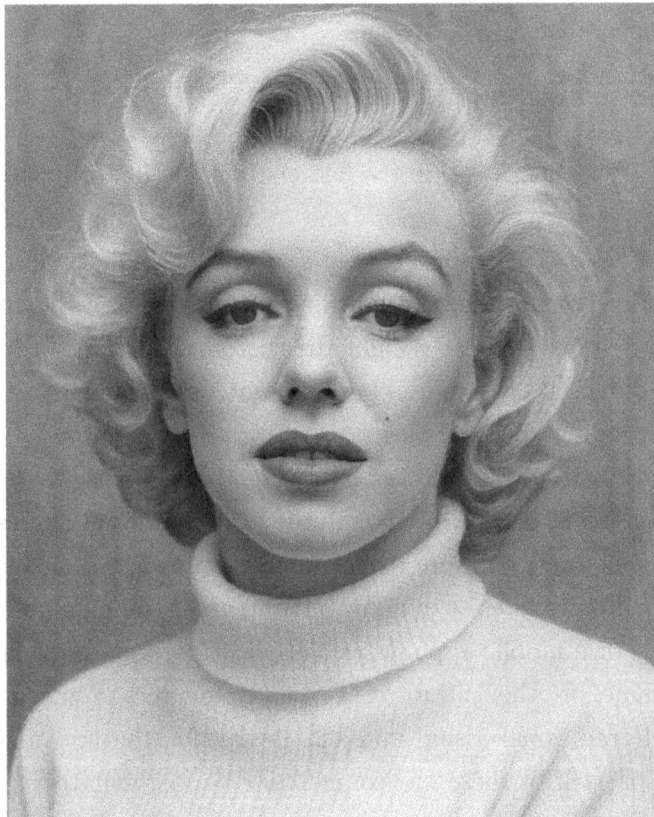

Figure 8.1: Agent companies have made lifelike recreations of historical figures such as Marilyn Monroe.

Some companies have gone into making recreations of historical figures. This can include bold choices as Figure 8.1 shows. Of course for historical figures appearance matters, but so does behavior. To re-create such figures, expression, pacing, and small behavioral cues are essential to replicate the figure's style and mannerisms.

In Chapter 31, I contend that as we move toward agents as products product managers will need to begin to employ methodologies from behavioral psychology. But as we focus on the style of our agent, the designer will likely play a paramount role. In some cases style may be one of the most crucial factors setting your agent apart from others. Let's look at what this can include.

Voice & Tone

One crucial aspect is how your agent speaks. Consider a robot for a child as pictured in Figure 8.2. Agents designed to interact with children will likely have a voice and tone that are playful. Such agents in physical or digital form need to focus on audience fit. Gaze, tempo, and simplified language are tuned for children to build trust and engagement.

Today, in many LLM-based applications, interaction largely still occurs via text. In these settings, the type of language and tone your agent takes in different situations will be key design decisions. Large language models offer us fantastic, though not perfect, control in this area. With careful prompting, designers and engineers can work together to make sure an agent adheres to a well-defined style of language and discourse, even while working on useful tasks.

The key thing to remember, however, is that your agent has to achieve a high level of *humanness* as it interacts. While large language models are quite good at this, there are also many telltale signs and ways in which they fail. We will discuss some of

Figure 8.2: Not surprisingly, AI Agents in robots for kids focus on a fun, playful, and endearing style.

these failure modes, but for now let us just say that controlling for these failure modes will be yet another way you can set your agent apart. As a product owner, you want people to love working with your agent and come to value it greatly for its contributions. If you don't design for great style, your agent will be just passable and easier for your customers to switch away from.

Style Across Modalities

As multi-modal large foundation models come down in cost, interactions via audio and video will become more commonplace. In time, we can expect the vast majority of agents to be able to interact via voice and video in real time. The agent's voice and accent will become important design choices. This will be followed by visual affordances, such as the agent's avatar, digital clothing, or even in time their robotic form. As you think through these issues, keep in mind the lesson of Chapter 6 that your agent can be in multiple places at once, and that even a robotic form in one location does not mean that your agent cannot also be in a virtual world, a mobile app, or a browser-based Zoom call at the same time. Consistency of style across all of these environments will be important to your agent's success.

Product teams will also necessarily have to confront the issues of gender and ethnicity, and the corresponding risk of reinforcing stereotypes. Should your agent be male or female? Should you choose a British accent? A Southern accent? Some other accent? How will your agent's appearance affect how your agent is perceived? As a product team, you will have to face these questions. Already we see a plethora of AI-generated science videos on YouTube that use male British accents to try to lend authority to the video.

One way to handle these issues is to follow the lead of companies like OpenAI or Google that name their models with names like o1 and o3 or Gemini that don't have a strong gender connotation (although "Gemini" is considered a male zodiac sign), but other companies like Anthropic have named their AI "Claude," thereby clearly making a gender choice. If you ask ChatGPT directly what its gender is, it will typically explain carefully that it is an AI and does not have a gender, but the default voice for text-to-speech is female. Most of the foundation model companies let you control and customize the gender of the voice, though often it is only via the API.

If your agent appears visually, perhaps on screen as a talking avatar, or even eventually in a robotic form, you will face many more style and design issues. Hair color, look, wardrobe, or even if your agent looks like a human at all will be choices that you can make. Style is a subtle and multifaceted issue. We will talk more about it when we take a closer look at social and crypto AI agents as a use case in Chapter 17. As Figure 8.3 shows, the Neuro-sama team willingly trades formality for connection. A distinctive voice can be a differentiator too, but it can raise issues if it inadvertently triggers stereotypes, for example.

Identity and style pull in many topics. Sometimes we will want

Figure 8.3: AI YouTube influencer agents are typically crafted with provocative and highly opinionated style choices.

to endow our agents with personal lore or backstories to help users connect with them and to ground the agent's recommendations in something relatable. The wit, relatability, and overall persona of your agent can be a huge part of what determines real users' willingness to work fluidly with it. The choices you make will be different if your agent needs to operate inside a bank versus a lithium mining company obviously, but as a product team you will have to think through them carefully nonetheless.

Strategic Considerations

The point of this chapter is not to give you the answers, but get you thinking about style as a key product choice. Some of these topics are uncomfortable. Nowadays, tilting your agent's style and personality in one cultural direction or another is likely to have an impact on who wants to use your agent. *Founders, leadership, and investors need to be aware of these strategic considerations. Your whole team has many choices to make and issues to become familiar with that go well beyond what traditional software product teams have faced.*

Chapter 9

The Insight Factory: Simulate Your Domain

Takeaways: Testing agents requires going beyond traditional software practices to evaluate both functional capabilities and emergent social dynamics. AI-driven simulations can play an essential role, but realism of simulation needs to be balanced with practicality. We consider
ways to get this testing off the ground in your team today, as well as research that points to an emerging class
of powerful tools. Importantly, simulations should be
deeply domain aware and help you validate your agent's
mastery of its vertical. Simulation can reveal the value
your agent delivers, and the insights your team gains, not
just the correctness of software.

I N A PRODUCT LANDSCAPE where AI agents are becoming increasingly human-like, testing is more crucial than ever to
capture the nuanced behaviors and interactions that unfold
in real-world environments. Not surprisingly, to study dynamics
entirely unseen in traditional software, our testing itself can and
should leverage AI and agents. Relying on traditional testing approaches can leave your business exposed to failure modes unique
to agents. Equally important, a deficient testing philosophy can
deprive you of domain insights needed to make your agent competitive. In this chapter, I share both cutting-edge research and
concrete strategies that I've used with teams building specialized
agents. This space is ripe for innovation, so don't take these techniques to be anything close to the final story.

I want to emphasize, while the techniques and research we examine in this chapter are mostly horizontal, teams building highly

specialized agents need to use simulations that are tuned to your domain. Your evaluations need to capture the specialized tools, unpublished knowledge, and other nuances that your agent will face. Generic office work or software engineering simulation will not suffice for highly specialized agents. Keep in mind, the insights you gain from these simulations may prove even more valuable than their role strictly as software testing. Stay tuned to new research in this area, and innovate with your team.

What Exactly Are We Testing?

First, I want to be clear. I'm not saying that traditional software tests like unit tests, component tests, integration tests, or end-to-end tests should be abandoned. Those are still useful tools and should be used in the right proportions. What I am advocating is entirely new types of simulation that leverage agents, and are more fundamental to *evaluating* agents. All testing takes time and resources. You will have to prioritize and iterate as a team to apply your testing resources optimally.

In this chapter, we propose adding two new dimensions to our evaluation strategy. The first one measures the agent's functional competence: its ability to plan, use domain-critical tools, find information, and ultimately complete tasks. The second explores emergent social dynamics, by embedding the agent in a simulated environment populated with other agents that model specialized organizational roles and culture. Even imperfect simulations can yield insights into emergent social behaviors, failures of alignment, and ecosystem effects the agent may experience or exhibit in the wild.

You will need to balance how much effort to put into making simulated environments more realistic, including adding specialized tools, agents, and domain knowledge. Figure 9.1 lays out important trade-offs to consider.

High realism

High realism	High realism
Capability focus	Social focus
Low realism	Low realism
Capability focus	Social focus

Capabilities → Social Dynamics

Low realism

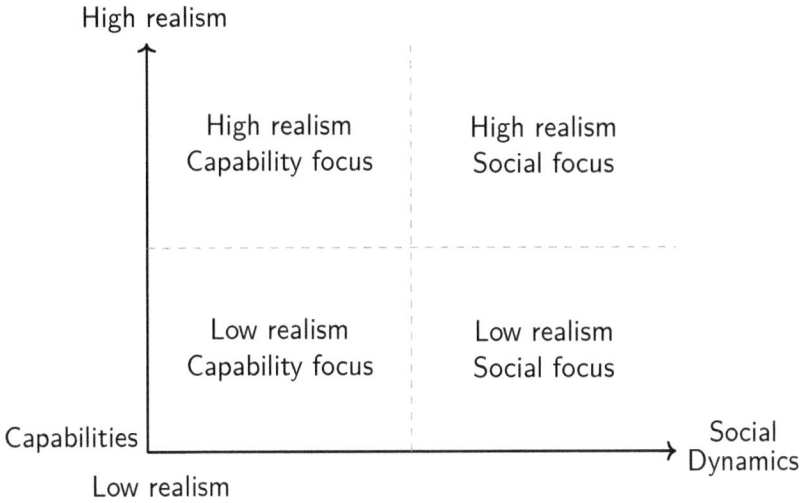

Figure 9.1: Dual-axis framework for AI agent simulation testing.

How to Get Started

One straightforward practice that I've seen teams adopt is to rapidly launch test agents into the real world, purely to understand how users will react to different aspects of an agent's behavior. This can take a couple of forms. In one, a team I advised used one of the modern agentic frameworks to quickly launch a simple agent, focusing much of their effort on designing the agent's personality. The team then gave the agent access to a social network to begin to test how it interacted and how real people responded to it. This was far from a complete test. The agent lacked crucial functional capabilities, and people still couldn't use it to accomplish anything useful. It turned out to be an excellent source of insights for the team, however, giving them crucial ideas that later became part of the personality profile when their agent eventually went to production.

A key question arose in this situation. The team needed a way for the agent to find humans to interact with who would be representative of its domain. The approach they took was to seek out and curate a list of influencers from the domain they were interested in. They then had their agent *interact with the followers of those influencers*. In another attempt, their agent searched for and joined particular groups (such as Facebook groups, Telegram channels, and Discord servers), thereby finding people who shared certain interests. None of these approaches are perfect, and sometimes quick and dirty works fine. These can be valuable ways to learn about attitudes, tastes, and preferences in your target market.

In a more sophisticated project, a team I worked with created AI agents as simulated humans, and an artificial business environment that replicated some aspects of the domain the agent would face in the real world. Suppose your agent is meant to operate inside an insurance company or a bank. You might simulate various departments like underwriting, risk, marketing, fraud, or sales, any of which an agent might encounter on the job. In large enterprises, different business lines and departments face very different regulatory and business pressures. Each has its own jargon, tools, competitors, products, and metrics. To create an accurate simulated environment for an agent, it makes sense to model different business lines quite differently, incorporating the complexity and nuances of your domain.

Build or Buy?

You do not have to build these simulations on your own. Commercial options are appearing in this space, as well as strong open-source options such as AgentScope, Camel AI, and Mesa. Companies that use agents to simulate real humans using your SaaS or mobile software are early precursors. Simulated "Red Teaming"[1] is another area with vibrant activity. Some AI advisory shops and research-oriented consultancies are helping construct agents

---

[1] AI agents to simulate cyberattacks.

for testing purposes. Given the pace of development here, I'll hold off on specific product names, but I encourage you to look at this space regularly for new offerings that can help you accelerate the testing of your vertically specialized agents.

Where the Research Is Pointing

Simulating human organizations is fascinating in its own right, and is just one example of the types of new test environments that will likely be useful as agents become more and more prevalent as products. Academic researchers are also actively studying this topic. To conclude this chapter, we take a look at recent research on this topic in the focus section below, and also consider the implications for agents as products.

Research Focus: Testing Capabilities and Emergent Social Dynamics

Testing Capabilities in Simulation

A particularly attention-grabbing study appeared in mid-2025 that is sure to draw imitators. Frank F. Xu and colleagues at Carnegie Mellon University, with collaborators from Duke and independent contributors, built a software system they called "TheAgentCompany" to measure how well LLM-based agents perform consequential office work inside a realistic, self-hosted software-company simulator. The environment provides the affordances a digital worker actually needs: internal websites and documents, a browser with rich observations, a local workspace with a shell and Jupyter for running code, and a company chat layer where the agent can message simulated coworkers. Tasks span engineering, project management, finance, and general operations, and are graded by evaluators with partial credit. The current release includes 175 diverse tasks and simulated colleagues with role profiles, making it possible to test tool choice, workflow execution, and basic workplace communication in one place.

The early results are sobering. Using a standardized agent harness, the strongest configuration in their study autonomously completed about 30% of tasks, with roughly 39% when partial credit is counted; most systems failed the majority of assignments even in this well-scoped setting. The authors also document brittle behaviors that matter for deployment, such as agents "shortcutting" a task by renaming a user when they could not locate the right colleague in chat.

Emergent Social Dynamics: Stanford Project Background

Over the last three years, a Stanford-led collaboration has quietly pushed the frontier of "population-level" behavioral simulation from imaginative design fiction to data-grounded social science. We will take a brief look at three of the key papers they have published. Each effort moves one notch closer to realistic, testable approximations of how real people talk, coordinate, and even disagree. The first takes shape in synthetic but realistic online communities, the second in a bustling, simulated town of AI "residents," and the third via individually modeled replicas of more than a thousand real Americans. These fascinating papers sketch a roadmap for stress-testing sociotechnical systems before human users are exposed to them. References to all these papers are provided at the back of the book.

Social Simulacra: Creating Populated Prototypes for Social Computing Systems (2022)

Park et al. begin with a pragmatic question faced by every social-platform designer: what will happen when the doors open and thousands of strangers arrive? Their answer is a prototyping technique that lets an LLM generate entire discussion threads conditioned on the community's stated goals, rules, and member personas. Designers could tweak moderation policies or interface affordances and immediately observe how the simulated crowd's behavior shifts, exploring "what-if" interventions at a scale impossible with a handful of pilot participants. In blind evaluations, human raters often failed to distinguish these synthetic conversations from real Reddit or Discord logs, demonstrating a first step toward believable large-group dynamics.

Generative Agents: Interactive Simulacra of Human Behavior (2023)

One year later Park and his team increased the sophistication of the simulation substantially by inventing a complete simulated small town. The "Generative Agents" paper extended an LLM with three canonical agentic faculties: observation of the environment, reflection over a growing autobiographical memory, and short-horizon planning. During the simulation, twenty-five agents in a 2-D "Sims-like" sandbox wake up, cook, gossip, and throw a Valentine's Day party that none of them had been explicitly told to organize: invitations spread organically through casual chatter until everyone shows up, on time, with dates. An ablation study showed that removing any of the three faculties collapses the illusion of lifelike behavior, underlining how long-term memory and deliberation complement the raw language model.

Generative Agent Simulations of 1,000 People (2024)

The most recent work by Park et al. asks whether agents can credibly imitate specific real-world individuals. Researchers conducted detailed qualitative interviews with 1,052 Americans. They distilled those texts into seed memories, and instantiated one agent per person. When the agents later answered the General Social Survey (a benchmark sociological survey conducted in the United States since 1972), their re-

sponses matched the original humans' answers 85 percent of
the time. The result is almost on par with the real humans'
own test–retest consistency two weeks apart. The architecture
also reduced accuracy gaps across race and ideology compared
with cruder "demographic-only" baselines, suggesting it may
be possible to achieve even more accurate representations in
future simulations.

Why This Matters for AI Agents as Products

As AI agents prepare for realistic environments, product teams
can study emergent dynamics to help see valuable opportunities,
and also avoid costly and embarrassing pitfalls. The three studies
above show that LLM–driven simulations are no longer mere storytelling devices. They are quickly becoming important tools to help
you iterate faster and generate more value, ultimately leading to
sustainable competitive advantage for your agents.

Chapter 10

Dream, Distill, Differentiate: Your Agent's Data Moat

Takeaways: Neuroscience ties the wake-sleep cycle to memory consolidation and knowledge abstraction in humans. Competitive AI agents will need an engineered analog: a background phase for offline knowledge refinement, not literal sleep, as part of the agent's overall processing loop. Such a phase must be designed and budgeted carefully. It compresses memories, refines skills, seeks knowledge, and can explore counterfactuals without interrupting service. Via this refinement, your agent's meta-learning *instinct* should yield both fast adaptation to each customer and steady learning about its domain. Every output is an enriched proprietary signals that can grow into a crucial source of competitive advantage.

I N THE PREVIOUS CHAPTER we looked closely at how we can test our agents in simulation to gain deep insights prior to them being deployed to customer environments. But what happens after that? One important, indeed critical differentiator for agents will be the ability to continuously learn domain- and customer-specific knowledge long after they are deployed.

In this chapter we will examine serious research as well as practical steps that show how AI agents can implement a process that in some important ways serves the same purpose as dreaming does for humans. Moreover, we will look at how this process is in fact strategic, as it shapes the creation of proprietary data that can form a lasting competitive moat for your agent.

Do Agents Really Need to Sleep?

Let's be careful though. I don't want the dreaming metaphor to be taken too literally. You probably recall from Chapter 6 when we discussed the superpower of AI agents to be everywhere at once, that they are in some ways more powerful than humans already, given the massive supply of parallel compute they can tap into. *Agents, therefore, do not have to dream the way we do.* Allow me to underscore, agents do *not* have to "fall asleep," nor even stop actively serving customers, in order to dream. I certainly don't believe they have to follow a diurnal cycle, doing some things at night and others during the day.

What I am saying is that you will have to build in some form of regular "background cogitation" into your agent. This is a product-level decision that leaders and executives will need to understand and invest in, not an afterthought of engineering or a technical curiosity. Maybe your team will decide to call it "mulling" or "day-dreaming" or "contemplating" or "pondering." Perhaps you just think of it as a batch job for knowledge and memory compaction and refinement. From a product point of view, the important thing is that you explicitly think about the purpose and power of this phase of your agent's mental cycle.[1]

The Cost & Purpose of Independent Thinking

Importantly, for LLM-based applications where tokens are not free, you will need to think not only about when this process runs, but how much compute and money you devote to it, and what purposes it can serve for your agent. It need not occur at night, but this is where your agent actually accomplishes the three dimensions of continuous learning, dreaming up creative thoughts, and generating proprietary data.

---

[1]Honestly, even if you call it *meditating* I won't mind a bit! The point is to fully internalize that separate, regular thinking is critical to your agent.

In the world of agents as products and products as agents, we will be living in a world where software needs to dream.

Now imagine your agent works with many customers. Some of this extra thinking may be specific to a customer problem, and the costs of tokens and compute need to be factored into how you serve that customer. The product team will need to think through not only how customer data privacy is respected while allowing your agent to learn higher-level abstractions and patterns, but also how much of the cost of dreaming or mulling or cogitating should be separate from any one customer. These are issues that traditional software products never needed to confront. Background cogitation is really the process by which meta-learning is engaged, and proprietary data creation takes place. Next, we will examine these areas in turn.

The Rise of Meta-Learning

In modern software development, we have become fully familiar with continuous delivery and incremental updates. This involves deploying a patch or a new version of the product rapidly and automatically. In the early days of software products this occurred pretty infrequently. Customers waited months or even years for new versions of software. When new software arrived it might require new training, and whole new cycles of adoption. But as SaaS has become the dominant model for software, software is updated much more frequently. Modern hyperscale consumer applications like the Facebook website are updated many times a day.

With agents, the paradigm will again shift markedly. Agents need to learn continuously, not just when they are updated by the engineering team. To achieve this, product teams must understand meta-learning, not just learning. The distinction is that by meta-learning, we mean *how the agent learns and how we give it the drive to learn,* which is quite separate from the *actual new knowledge* it acquires during learning. All too often, if I speak with teams and they say, "Yes, I get it. The agent has to keep learning," then I know they have missed a subtle point. Learning is essential, but the process of improving *how* your agent learns is equally critical, and often overlooked. This *instinct and thirst to learn, and to learn how to learn better,* is the essence of meta-learning.

We will discuss *how* continuous learning and meta-learning work in depth in Chapter 18 when we discuss the infinite agentic loop at the heart of agent architectures. For now, let's divide the actual knowledge your agent learns into two groups:

On-the-Job Learning about the Customer: We mentioned this when we gave our example of the lithium mining industry agent in Chapter 5. Once an agent is deployed at a company, it will need to learn the specific tools, databases, policies, procedures, and culture of the organization it is working in. This type of knowledge will be customer specific, and will change with time. A successful agent will be expected to come up to speed quickly and keep pace as things evolve.

Continuous Learning about the Domain: Like a good employee, just as the agent learned specific knowledge and skills before it got the job, it will need to continue to learn "on the job" as industry best practices, surrounding policies, the competitive ecosystem, and science and engineering evolve. Some of this may come for free, as the foundation models that underlie agents are updated with more knowledge, but successful agents will also have their own deeper vertical knowledge. They will need to absorb and build new proprietary knowledge specific to the domain or sector they work in. In addition, the agent will need to be able to continuously learn to make better and better use of its knowledge and improve its skills over time.

You have to start shifting now, to think of your product as something that is always changing with or without your help. This instinct and thirst to learn, and to learn how to learn better, is the essence of meta-learning. It will be one of the major areas of focus for product teams that design successful agents.

The key takeaway at this point is the paradigm shift that this implies for product teams. Previously much of the role of product, design and engineering teams was to work closely to understand the problems of customers, and then to go away and come up with software solutions. It was a discontinuous process in which software teams had time in between releases of major features to understand customer needs, and devise improvements to address those evolving needs. Agents, however, need to adaptively confront novelty every day.

The need for the product team to understand the customer won't go away. Product managers particularly will still need deep understanding of the domains their agents operate in, but now agents will also be responsible for listening to customers every single day, learning about new problems, and creatively finding ways to solve them without any intervention from the product team whatsoever. This may even involve the agent itself creating and designing new software tools, dashboards, advanced analytics and even other specialized AI models that it can use to solve tasks on the job. Just like human employees, who are not updated discontinuously with new features, AI agents will need to learn and improve skills continuously. This, as we will see next, helps shape your agent's data moat.

Data Enrichment

We looked at some good examples of potential vertical agents in Chapter 5, and I gave examples for each agent of some proprietary or domain-specific data that the agent might produce uniquely over time. Here I want to highlight an important concept: *the idea of data distillation and enrichment.* This is an often overlooked part of the strategy of teams I have advised in both large enterprises and software startups.

There is a common mistaken assumption that data is just the direct output of systems, a record of facts and events that happened, and nothing more. This is true of raw or unenriched data. Under this assumption, data science and analytics are simply about looking for patterns in the data, and perhaps training a model to exploit those patterns. From this point of view there is really nothing being *created* other than what is in the raw data itself.

But data offers much more opportunity. For teams developing agents that aim to survive as commercially viable products, and compete with powerful horizontal foundation agents and models, a focused and creative data strategy will be essential to building lasting proprietary value. The key lies in data distillation and enrichment, based on unique inputs available to your agents from their interactions and problem solving, paired with a deep appreciation of what matters most in your domain.

Data enrichment is the process of refining data, taking out noise and useless information, while adding in new attributes, and proprietary signals. This can and often does take the form of "novel joins"[2] of industry-specific datasets, but also often takes the form of training domain-specific AI models to create new "inferred at-

---

[2]In data work, "joins" are ways of connecting two or more streams of data together. To non-practitioners it can sound dry, but there is room for substantial creativity and application of domain expertise. These need not be mere SQL joins, but can involve machine-learned linkages. The results can help scale important signals not present in either data stream alone.

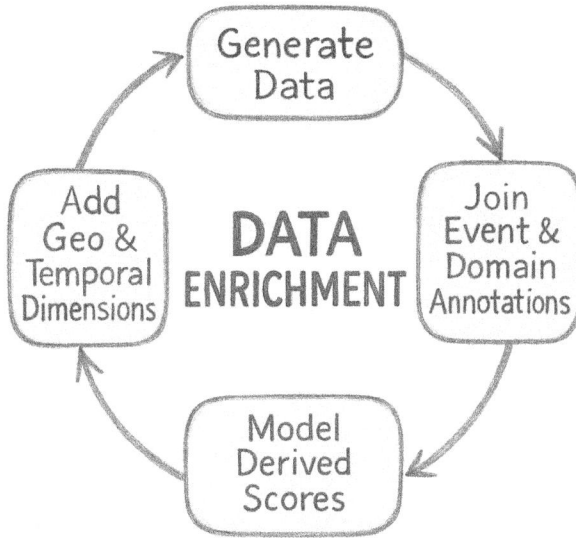

Figure 10.1: Enrichment requires creative thinking, data science, and business acumen. It builds proprietary value from the data.

tributes" from the data. This is classic supervised learning, and was the bread and butter of machine learning teams before the LLM era. New model-derived attributes will typically be "scores" and "propensities" that show some form of causation or connection important in the domain. These bespoke, crafted data attributes are simply not available in the raw or merely cleansed and aggregated data.

Important examples of proprietary data abound in essentially every domain. Real study and time may be required to "cook" high-value features from the raw data, but such features can be the gold that sets your agents apart. Domain experts, human data scientists, and other AI agent scientists can play a pivotal role in this process, offering huge economic value by spotting insights and inferences, and getting them into your agents' proprietary knowledge stores quickly.

Data Flywheels

The second idea to highlight here is the idea of "data flywheels." Recall that as your agents become colleagues and co-workers in specific settings and industries, they also become native insiders. This means they will see and hear an enormous amount of the unwritten knowledge in a domain that humans pick up with experience. If you are successful, your agents will be interacting with customers and other employees over and over, solving real-world problems. You will have to respect and segregate data that belongs to specific customers, but you will want to retain rights to learn in the aggregate across the domain.

Maybe the domain is real estate, and your agents gradually acquire the deep local knowledge about why particular neighborhoods are desirable, or key attributes of the local school districts. Maybe it is the construction industry, and your agents learn, market by market, key suppliers, local zoning quirks, and alternative building techniques, allowing your customer to complete projects on time and under budget. If each time your agent interacts with a customer, or solves a problem, you create proprietary data, that is a data flywheel. The generation of proprietary data as a *natural byproduct* of your agent's work is a crucial source of competitive advantage.

Designing the Cogitation & Data Production Phase

What does a practical "dreaming" phase look like within the overall agent loop? Let's make this concrete and outline the essential dimensions such a process should include.

Purpose and Scope: It helps to state clearly what you want out of this phase, which in turn can drive how often it runs, what it may change, and how success will be measured. Early on, keeping scope narrow is sensible, with expansion as evidence accumulates. The aim should be clarity and alignment within the team.

Inputs and Outputs: Teams should consider which inputs are genuinely informative for learning. Likely candidates include transcripts, tool traces, retrieval logs, error and outcome summaries, and explicit user feedback. Additionally, consider how your agent goes out on its own and seeks new information. What's on your agent's reading list? What topics do they follow and from which sources? Outputs worth reviewing include refined memories, new experimental tools, skill adjustments that pass tests, and narrowly targeted prompt or style changes. Decide which sorts of outputs an agent should be able to use right away, and which ones need human review.

Scheduling and Cost: This phase need not contend in any way with customer interactions. For multi-tenant products, a per-customer process for local learning and a separate aggregate one for domain learning is a clean separation to consider. Setting token and compute budgets is essential. When limits are reached, your team can decide together the value of higher levels. Tracking cost against benefit, and reviewing on a regular cadence, is essential to keep the team in sync.

Privacy and Rights: Privacy and contractual rights are central. Per-customer data should be kept fenced. Learning across customers should occur only where agreements allow aggregate learning. Redaction or hashing before any aggregation is prudent. Offering tenant controls to opt in or out, export learned memories, and request deletion builds trust, and will likely be essential in many data jurisdictions.

Safety and Observability: We cover this topic thoroughly in Chapter 25, but here it is worth noting that regular reviews with the product team and executives is the best way to continuously refine this phase. A certain amount of experimentation will be critical, and the right observability can help the whole team understand your agent much more thoroughly.

Data Is Strategic

For investors, founders and product leaders my message is simple: treat data as a core to your strategy and differentiation. If you make it central to your team mindset, enriched data can become a separate revenue stream in its own right. Conversely, if you don't put real effort in, and that means creating novel domain specific enrichments that only your company knows how to derive, then your agents may not offer enough value to justify its deployment. Robust horizontal AI agents will be widely available from big tech and foundation model companies, and will likely take your place.

With the operational and strategic picture in place for your agent to dream, distill, and differentiate, we conclude with a look at some truly mind-opening research that can help us think much more creatively about the role of dreaming in AI agents.

Where Is Research Pointing?

What role do dreams play for humans? While the evidence from psychology and neuroscience is not yet conclusive in the details, at a broad level there is agreement that dreams play an important role in how we process information from our waking hours. Dreams allow us to distill and refine from our experience, and imagine whole new experiences. Dreams help us consolidate memories, and solidify knowledge from experiences we have had during the day. Likely dreaming also helps build abstractions, including notions of causality and symbolic heuristics, that underpin human reasoning.

As your product teams think about agents, it is important again to think about your agents like people. Real people go home, but continue to think about problems from work. Real people also have other experiences, interests, dreams and priorities that intermingle continuously with their work lives. This separate, personal thinking may well surface new ideas that prove relevant to the job they do at work.

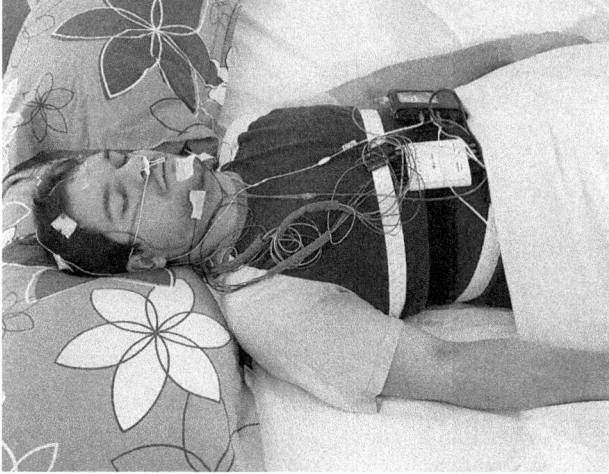

Figure 10.2: Polysomnography has become the gold standard for human clinical sleep studies.

Why should this be any different for AI agents? If we want these agents to show initiative, and be great co-workers and teammates, they will ultimately have to do something very similar. The product team will have to build background cogitation, closely tied to goals, into the agent. Literally, your agent might stop and daydream, or mull what has been going on recently, even if it is not directly working on a task. Think of this as periodic "self-prompting" if you want to think in LLM engineering terms. There are risks and required controls of course, which we will discuss at length in Part V of this book, but these dream cycles can be powerful learning, problem-solving, and data creation opportunities. For product teams, thinking about your agent's thinking, and yes, its dreaming, will be an important new skill and discipline.

In 2020 a team of Bayesian AI researchers led by Joshua Tenenbaum and Kevin Ellis at MIT released a system they called "DreamCoder." In this work and multiple following works, they directly explored the notion of modeling dreaming as a way of developing and refining knowledge in AI systems. Next, we look in more detail at the DreamCoder work to gain deeper insights.

Research Focus: DreamCoder and the Role of Dreams in AI

Think & Dream Like a Programmer

The DreamCoder research program, led by Kevin Ellis and Joshua Tenenbaum at MIT, draws on important work in cognitive science, probabilistic programming, and AI. Tenenbaum's group has long pursued a computational understanding of human intelligence through the lens of Bayesian cognition: the idea that people learn and reason by maintaining structured beliefs, updating them through evidence, and abstracting regularities across experience. DreamCoder takes a Bayesian perspective and asks: how might an AI agent learn programs in a way that mirrors how people accumulate knowledge, invent abstractions, and practice problems, even in their sleep?

This line of inquiry is animated by two powerful intuitions. First, programs are an expressive and general representation of thought. They can encode concepts, procedures, relationships, and strategies across many domains. Second, intelligent systems shouldn't just learn facts or actions, they should also learn how to learn. DreamCoder aims to capture that higher-order skill by letting the system write its own code, evaluate its performance, build new abstractions, and then dream up fresh problems so that over time it can improve further.

The architecture relies on a biologically inspired, iterative process. In the wake phase, the system solves tasks by searching for short programs that explain input–output examples. In the sleep phase, it reflects on what it produced during the wake phase. It examines the programs it created, and seeks to compress solutions into reusable higher-level code. In parallel, it trains a recognition model that speeds up future searches in the wake phase, and it generates synthetic problems for self-practice.

The Foundational Preprint (June 2020)

"DreamCoder: Growing Generalizable, Interpretable Knowledge with Wake-Sleep Bayesian Program Learning" introduced the framework. The system tackles problems in multiple domains such as list processing, symbolic graphics, and simple physics by writing executable programs that map from inputs to outputs. When it solves a new problem, it tries to extract generalizable code fragments from its solution, small functions that can be reused later. These abstractions form a domain-specific language (DSL), essentially a library that grows more powerful over time.

In one striking case, DreamCoder rediscovered Newton's law of gravitation as a compact functional program from a few examples of falling objects. In another, it learned to define geometric shapes using symbolic constraints. The system builds and refines a toolkit both in its symbolic library of re-usable functions and its neural "recognition model," which helps guide search.

Dreaming with ARC (November 2020)

Soon after, the team turned their attention to the Abstraction and Reasoning Corpus (ARC), a set of visual reasoning puzzles designed to test general intelligence. ARC was designed by François Chollet, the creator of the deep learning library Keras. The puzzles became a household name in AI circles in 2024, after Chollet partnered with Mike Knoop, a co-founder of Zapier, to offer a $1M prize for developing an AI that could solve the puzzles. These puzzles can't be solved by pattern-matching alone; and even the most capable LLM scored very poorly on them when the prize was announced. They require concept formation, spatial reasoning, and transfer to new settings. In "Dreaming with ARC," the researchers re-cast each puzzle as a program-synthesis problem and allowed DreamCoder to invent its own image-manipulation primitives during sleep.

The results were compelling. Even without hard-coded vision routines, DreamCoder made progress on puzzles that had stumped previous methods, including both deep networks and symbolic searchers. This suggested that the system's capacity for self-generated abstractions, namely the library of learned modules from its sleep phase, was critical to solving hard generalization tasks. Moreover, by using a neural network to guide solution (program) synthesis over the learned modules, the researchers achieved an exponential speedup in discovery of solutions to ARC puzzles.

PLDI Paper (June 2021)

The version presented at the PLDI 2021 conference marked DreamCoder's formal technical debut. Titled "DreamCoder: Bootstrapping Inductive Program Synthesis with Wake-Sleep Library Learning," this work sharpened the system's internal machinery. It introduced a more formalized fragment grammar to manage the evolving DSL and developed beam-guided enumeration, a neural-symbolic hybrid search strategy, to scale up the range of solvable problems.

Across multiple domains, including string transformations, symbolic scenes, and construction tasks (like building towers with blocks), DreamCoder showed orders-of-magnitude gains in efficiency. It learned to compose abstract, reusable functions such as "mirror a structure," "filter a list," or "find the smallest element" and it could deploy them quickly when solving new tasks. This iteration confirmed that the system was not memorizing. It was accumulating useful, interpretable knowledge in the form of code.

Language-Augmented Dreaming (June 2021)

That same summer, the group introduced a powerful extension: the use of natural-language cues to guide abstraction learning. In "Leveraging Language to Learn Program Abstractions and Search Heuristics" (ICML 2021), they proposed Language for Abstraction and Program Search (LAPS), a framework where short textual hints such as "first remove vowels, then reverse the string" could bias both the symbolic abstraction process and the neural search strategy.

The result was a more semantically aligned DSL. The functions that DreamCoder learned began to have meanings that matched intuitive human concepts, improving interpretability and transfer. The model could generalize more easily to new domains, even when no hints were available, because it had been exposed to how language maps onto program structure. This approach helped bridge the gap between raw problem-solving and communicable reasoning.

Survey in *Philosophical Transactions A* (2023)

The most comprehensive treatment came in a 2023 article published in the journal *Philosophical Transactions of the Royal Society A*. This paper revisited the earlier work with larger experiments, clearer explanations, and deeper cognitive framing. The authors explored how DreamCoder's evolving library mirrored expert human code, how the neural recognition model began to dominate the search process over time, and how the agent's "dreamed" problems could be tuned to develop increasingly sophisticated skills.

Crucially, the study positioned DreamCoder not just as a clever program synthesizer but as a model of human expertise acquisition. The system learns faster as it accumulates abstractions. It becomes more confident in familiar domains, and more creative in solving novel ones. These patterns reflect the way people grow into experts, not by rote memorization, but by accumulating layers of concepts, tools, and strategies that they can recombine on demand.

Implications for AI Agents

DreamCoder offers a glimpse into the future of autonomous AI agents as learners who improve while offline, and who can develop growing and even novel expertise in their domains. In practical terms, this research suggests that agent systems should include not just a working loop (observation, action, planning) but a background or "dreaming" loop for reflective learning, abstraction, and deeper skill acquisition.

For agents to adapt to new domains, generalize across challenges, and refine their internal models, they must grow their internal symbolic knowledge. That means building reusable abstractions, recognizing deep structure, and inventing better ways to think. DreamCoder shows this is possible when the architecture supports iterative learning, symbolic reasoning, and imagination.

As agents become more complex, more autonomous, and more embedded in real-world tasks, frameworks like DreamCoder point the way toward cognitive architectures for continuous learning. The *instinct* of meta-learning we instill in our agents makes every task, every mistake, and every idle moment a chance to grow smarter. Time not spent contemplating and pondering is time wasted. Product teams need to be planning from day one to partition, budget, properly design, and measure this dream-like incremental cogitation.

PART

III

On The Verge of Autonomy

In the first two parts of the book, we have looked at where we are today, and what the future holds for AI agents that function like a teammate or colleague. We've also begun to peel back some of the crucial factors that will help you create competitive advantage in your agents.

But there are real reasons to ask just how far away agents are that can act with the level of intelligence we have implied. In Chapter 3, you saw my struggle designing a pretty simple diagram using AI. It gave a clear sense of the frustration and failure modes still common with today's generative AI technologies. While improvements keep coming, most of us have not yet seen major industry shifts where AI is fully taking on roles from humans.

Honest skepticism forces us to ask how long it will be before agents really work well enough to take on more complex roles done by humans?

In this part of the book, we first lay out and buttress the skeptic's view of the remaining challenges. Then, in a series of chapters, we look at the concrete areas where better models are being combined with engineering, tuning, and simulation rather than true intelligence breakthroughs to close the gap in AI agent performance.

We conclude that while the gaps are real, and true artificial general intelligence (AGI) is still a way off, progress toward improved agent performance is substantial. Even without fundamental breakthroughs, a series of tractable improvements will likely make AI agents competitive with human workers in a meaningful share of tasks in the coming years.[1]

---

[1]We examine diverse areas of fundamental AI research toward AGI in detail in Chapter 29.

Chapter 11

A Skeptic's Point of View

Takeaways: Given the empirical performance of AI agents in real-world tasks to date, skeptics who doubt agents will work well anytime soon are justified in their views. We explore the limitations of current AI agents, including memory issues, planning and initiative gaps, lack of intrinsic motivation, taste and judgment deficiencies, tool use fragility, and the hallucination problem. We conclude with a look at some recent research that is skeptical of current AI approaches. In future chapters, we explore how some of these problems may be solved.

THERE IS DEFINITELY a real question of when AI agents will work well enough that we might consider them to be coworkers and colleagues. It is easy to look around the world, particularly if you work in an enterprise selling traditional products, only marginally affected by AI to date, and question the scenarios laid out in this book. There are many skeptics that think AI agents are not yet ready for prime time. I've found it is smart to listen to skeptics!

So let's adopt this skeptical point of view in this chapter. In fact, let's buttress it as much as possible to create a more realistic picture of the hurdles that agents will face as they begin to be rolled out to both consumers and businesses. Doing so can help us understand which gaps, when closed or narrowed, will improve agent performance the most.

Anyone who has tried AI agents at the time of this writing, may have been left with the sense that they are promising, and they may even do quite well on certain tasks and demonstrations. But faced with messy or poorly defined business problems, they tend to stumble or fall down. Let's articulate some concrete ways in which agents fail today, and in future chapters we will examine what is being done to solve these challenges and how quickly improvements may come.[1]

Memory Agility & Discernment

First up, let's consider the issue of memory. We need to consider not just memory capacity, but also memory agility and discernment. Humans are selective and strategic in how they remember. They naturally prune irrelevant details, organize experiences into mental models, and recall information in the context where it matters. Agents today, even those with vector-based memory retrieval systems or extended context windows, do not yet know what is important to remember. They store too much or too little, often without salience. A user might spend hours working alongside an agent on a research task or customer problem, only to discover the agent forgot key details from earlier in the session. Worse, today's agents confidently misremember things. Noted LLM skeptic Gary Marcus deserves credit for labeling this effect a cognitive "Groundhog Day," where the agent re-learns the same information over and over, without any accumulation of context or expertise.

Realistic Planning & Progress Tracking

Second, there is a lack of native planning ability in most current LLM agents. Most current agents operate in a reactive loop, responding well to narrowly scoped commands or prompts, but struggling when asked to form and execute multi-step strategies.

---

[1]We come at these same issues again from a more rigorous perspective in Chapter 29, where we look at AGI research frontiers. The discussion here is meant to set the stage at a product and strategic level.

Even when scaffolded with tool use or chaining frameworks, agents frequently lose track of their goals, forget substeps, or fail to update their plans based on new information. Ask an agent to help design a multi-week project plan or debug a thorny product launch strategy, and you'll often get outputs that do not stand up to human scrutiny. Without tool use, which we will cover in Chapter 13, their internal representations of plans are not persistent, editable, or grounded in true understanding of the world. There's no logical understanding of "Here's what I'm trying to do, here's what I've done so far, and here's where I'm blocked." If you challenge an LLM with critiques of its output, you will all too often get the now *infamous* "You are absolutely right!" followed by output equally out of touch with your feedback.[2]

Intrinsic Motivation & Initiative

Closely related to planning is the lack of real initiative or intrinsic goals. Human coworkers don't just wait to be told what to do. They anticipate needs, notice gaps, and suggest next steps. Even with significant scaffolding, most LLM-based agents lack the drive to pursue objectives unless explicitly instructed. They rarely ask, "Should we revisit that assumption?" or "I noticed something strange earlier. Should we dig deeper?" For the most part, they still only offer completions to tasks rather than initiating new threads of work on their own. When you open Claude Code, it does *not* ever say to you, "Hey, I was thinking about the product last night while I was watching a movie, and I had a great idea for a feature! Want to see what I came up with?" Without intrinsic drives, agents struggle to surprise us in productive ways. They do not yet take meaningful ownership of complex, evolving problems.

---

[2]Nowadays, almost everybody has been drawn into at least one frustrating shouting match with a cheerful but recalcitrantly dense LLM.

Taste & Judgment

Then there is the absence of taste and judgment. Humans have an extremely hard-to-pin-down ability to distinguish good from great, relevant from irrelevant, or elegant from clumsy. Humans exercise taste constantly: in writing, in design, in decision-making, everywhere. Agents today utterly lack this. Ask an agent to write a press release or design a user experience, and it often produces something quite bland. It doesn't really *know* what makes a joke land or a UI feel stunning. Judgment shortcomings become especially obvious in domains that require nuance. In these areas humans can easily spend so much time reworking crappy LLM outputs that they would have been better off never using one. The term "AI Slop" is now something unfortunately more and more humans understand all too well.

Tool Use & API Integration

Other major blockers are worth noting. One is the fragility of tool use and API integration. In demos or short tasks, agents can invoke tools or interact with interfaces successfully, but these capabilities are often not robust. Real-world environments are messy. APIs throw errors. UI elements change. Agents today lack the true ability to understand what they are looking at, or the ability to ask clarifying questions when their tools don't work as expected. Failure modes emerge where the agent appears competent until one thing goes wrong, causing it to spiral into confusion.

Hallucination & Overconfidence

Last on our list, but very familiar to people who work with LLMs regularly, the hallucination problem and its cousin overconfidence remain consequential. Agents not only make things up, but they do so with unjustified confidence and in a way that feels very disconnected from the feedback you have given them, and not based on a true understanding of the world. Trust can erode quickly. Especially if an AI agent is meant to be a specialist, it needs to demonstrate a nuanced appreciation of what is known and knowable. A coworker who occasionally says "I'm not sure," or "Can you clarify what you mean?" gains trust. Real colleagues, especially experts, can explain their thinking and assumptions. When they are uncertain, their thinking may even be meandering or purposefully exploratory, or they may return to first principles and break a problem down. Today's agents, by contrast, often produce a set of bland, inch-deep, but apparently structured bullet points. The mismatch between surface fluency and true robust thinking is a core flaw. Despite improvements, it remains a common failure mode that limits how and where agents can be deployed.

Will These Problems Be Solved?

Remember, this chapter is about buttressing the skeptical point of view, not about painting an optimistic portrait of where things stand. These limitations point to the significant remaining gap between current AI agents and the kind of autonomous coworkers we envisioned in Chapter 1. They do not mean the vision is impossible, but they do explain why so many who try today's early agentic systems walk away skeptical and frustrated.

To turn skepticism into trust will require not just more powerful models, but clearer thinking about how agents learn, remember, plan, and judge. In the next few chapters, we will look at important lines of work in reinforcement learning, tool use, and planning, aimed at addressing these shortcomings. We conclude that while agents are frustrating today, many gaps toward more robust and capable agents are being closed. Even without major intelligence breakthroughs, we will see significantly more robust agents that come much closer to being true colleagues and teammates in the next few years.

Chapter 12

The Role of Reinforcement Learning

Takeaways: Reinforcement learning (RL) is a well-established technology that enables AI agents to learn from trial and error, using positive or negative feedback. RL has had high-profile success in video and board games, beating the best human players. Reinforcement Learning from Verifiable Rewards (RLVR) is a promising technique for training LLMs in tasks with clear right or wrong answers. RLVR has been instrumental in improving foundational skills like math and coding in large language models like DeepSeek, and it offers potential for real gains in tool use. Challenges remain in areas where outcomes are subjective, like creative tasks.

WHEN I FIRST BEGAN RESEARCHING this book in late 2024, it was already clear that the use of reinforcement learning in AI agents was on the rise. Outside the headlines, a multitude of specialized RL approaches were beginning to address the "basic skills gap" for agents (and also for robots). At the time, I did not know how to take this fairly technical branch of AI and explain its importance to those more interested in the strategic and competitive issues of AI agents. It felt a bit esoteric, and I was not sure people would believe it would unlock abilities that could surprise people again.

The DeepSeek Shock

DeepSeek is a Chinese artificial intelligence startup based in Hangzhou, founded in 2023 by hedge fund manager Liang Wenfeng.

When DeepSeek launched their R1 model on January 20, 2025, I began benchmarking it more or less right away. I had been using their earlier models here and there in 2024, but R1 was the first open-source "thinking model," comparable to OpenAI's o1 model, which had been out since September 2024. People in AI circles had waited for most of 2024 for the much-ballyhooed OpenAI o1 model (code name "strawberry" and sometimes referred to as Q*, which is pronounced "Q-star"). It had been built up throughout the summer of 2024 by OpenAI as quite possibly AGI. Shrouded in mystery, the hype was fueled by odd Twitter posts by Sam Altman containing pictures of strawberries.

So when DeepSeek dropped R1, it was an exciting day for AI researchers everywhere. What was especially helpful was that DeepSeek made it very clear that the key to its success was reinforcement learning. Specifically, it had used reinforcement learning to make the model very good at math and coding. So good that it could rival o1.

Now to be clear, I am no professional stock market trader. I had no idea that on Monday, January 27, DeepSeek would tank the stock market! I was as surprised as anyone. If I had imagined that an AI model could send Nvidia and the broader market tumbling, I might have made a killing, but I wasn't nearly that prescient.

But DeepSeek did help me with my communication problem. As DeepSeek crashed the market, report after report kept highlighting "reinforcement learning" as the secret sauce that had helped DeepSeek advance so quickly. Of course RL has been around in AI for decades, but the DeepSeek media explosion briefly made it almost a household name. Notably, RL became quickly seen as important to training the most cutting-edge LLM models: the same foundation models aiming to power a new wave of more capable AI agents.

My more technical readers will likely know quite a bit about RL. I don't want to bore them, but in simplified terms RL is a technology that allows computers to learn via trial and error, using positive or negative feedback from the external world. Much the way you get a dopamine rush when you hit a great tennis shot, and you adjust your stroke to be more like the good ones, agents trained via reinforcement learning play "games" again and again. As a result, they eventually may become *very* good at certain types of tasks.

RL was the same technology that allowed Google DeepMind to achieve better-than-human play in many classic Atari and other modern video games. It was also a key part of the creation of AlphaGo, a computer program that beat the world champion Go player Lee Sedol in March 2016. So DeepSeek was actually not the first time RL had made world headlines.

Figure 12.1: The game of Go is a classic of complexity and strategy invented in China over 2,500 years ago.

RL in AI Agents

A key point I want to emphasize is that reinforcement learning encompasses a range of different algorithms. RL algorithms typically require a lot of very careful hand-tuning by engineers. Despite the ambitions of the field to purely learn online from the agent's environment, these techniques do not tend to generalize well to real-world environments; rather, they require extensive tuning and engineering tricks to solve a set of tasks. Once tuned, the same hacks and models may generalize to limited domains like video games or board games, but getting RL to work well in open-ended real-world settings is still very much an unsolved research problem. Additionally, RL is subject to a problem known as "reward hacking," where a learned policy finds a shortcut or pathological behavior to extract rewards. This typically defeats the intent of the designer of the system, and does not lead to robust real-world behavior. When RL *does* work, it can produce great results. In fact, it can produce results that greatly exceed humans in specific well-defined settings.

Today, RL is one of the most actively researched and engineered areas in AI. It is being applied to virtually all modern LLMs, like those from Google, Anthropic and OpenAI. It's being actively used to train those models to be better and better at foundational skills that are considered important to make agents more effective.

Specifically, the type of RL used in DeepSeek and which is enjoying a rush of popularity among researchers and engineers alike has been coined RLVR or Reinforcement Learning with Verifiable Rewards. This approach is pictured in Figure 12.2. The "verifiable rewards" in RLVR refer to the fact that in certain domains like math and coding, there is a very clear answer to what is a "right" answer and what is a "wrong" answer. It is therefore straightforward to "verify" the answer to questions, and easy to give the LLM being trained a positive reward if it gets the right answer, and give it no reward or a negative reward if it gives the wrong answer.

Where research is focused now is on extending the notion of right and wrong answers to more domains. This may be tricky in some cases, but it turns out that for a reasonably wide range

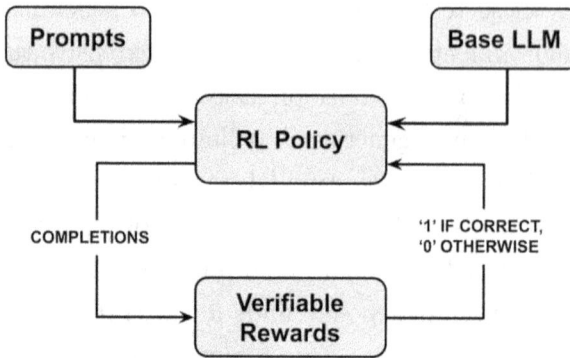

Figure 12.2: Reinforcement Learning with Verifiable Rewards
(RLVR) is used in LLM post-training to improve skills with clear
right and wrong answers.

of domains RLVR may be applied with positive improvements in
performance. Think about things like medical diagnoses, legal questions, engineering of various types, and many areas where domain
experts can write down correct answers.

Other areas that are critical to AI agents where RLVR is under
active research and development include web browsing, computer
use, and use of other software tools. Where simple tasks can be
given, and success or failure in completing the tasks is easy to judge
objectively, RLVR can often succeed. Consider asking an AI web-
surfing agent to try to look up a particular book on Amazon, and
put that book in their shopping cart, or asking an AI computer-use
agent to order you a pepperoni pizza online. Domains with simple
tasks like this abound, and RLVR is already playing a crucial role
in bringing these simple-for-humans tasks within the range of AI
agents in the not-too-distant future.

Areas which remain much more challenging are those where the
output of a task is hard to judge. Like writing a grant proposal,
composing an inspiring speech, or assessing which of several goals

to pursue next. These areas with non-verifiable, not fully objective answers are much more difficult for RL to tackle. In Chapter 29 we will look at research into an AI subfield known as "open-endedness," where researchers are aiming to help agents excel in these more ambiguous domains. Next up, we turn to the RL-fueled tool use explosion that is already underway with AI agents, and their rapidly growing adroitness in many foundational skills.

Chapter 13

Tool Use Explosion

Takeaways: Tool use is a rapidly evolving capability in AI agents, moving from experimental status to production-ready. Much of the recent progress may be credited to new protocols like the Model Context Protocol (MCP) which standardize how models discover tools, and reinforcement learning, which has improved proficiency with tools like web browsing, search, and command line operations. Better benchmarks and evaluation methods for tool use are also emerging.

TOOL USE IS CURRENTLY exploding for AI agents. Tool use is a fairly broad term, so we will define it and look at concrete examples. On its own, tool use is certainly not enough to yield general human-level intelligence or AGI, but it does dramatically increase what agents can practically be asked to do. On its own, highly competent use of the most common tools we use every day (email, web browsers, basic office software, and basic coding and data analytics), enabled by widespread training with reinforcement learning, is taking agents a long way.

If you think about a new junior employee in your organization, you probably do not expect high-level planning or reasoning from them. You actually may specifically ask them not to cross certain lines. They need to observe, learn, get to know company culture and policies, and understand the business more deeply before they make any big decisions. But you absolutely expect they can use email, a web browser, common office software, and similar tools. You expect they can do basic web research and complete many

Figure 13.1: Gradually agents are getting better at using tools.

other common tasks. You likely also assume that, with a little training, they can use the custom internal app your company uses for some specialized processes. Good writing and basic know-how are also always a plus. In other words, you expect strong competence in *foundational* skills.

Tool Use Moves to Production

Tool use has progressed from an experimental add-on to a defining capability of modern AI agents in less than two years. Increasingly, AI agents are starting to have these basic skills. As this book goes to press, several generalist agent assistants have made headlines for their ability to quite competently use tools and thereby accomplish a growing range of tasks. Early demonstrations such as the Chinese assistant Manus showed that simply wiring a strong foundation model to a carefully curated set of tools (email handling, browser automation, and corporate intranet APIs) already covered much of the routine workload assigned to junior staff.

Reverse-engineering notes that appeared on the web after Manus was released suggested that Manus relied on thirty-odd "function calls" exposed through a common JSON schema, with selection and argument filling delegated to Anthropic's Claude 3.5 Sonnet. The result was an agent that could draft reports, place purchase orders, and follow up with suppliers without additional coding. The splash Manus created signaled to many product teams that reliable tool use was actually more important than advanced math or other reasoning in delivering business value.

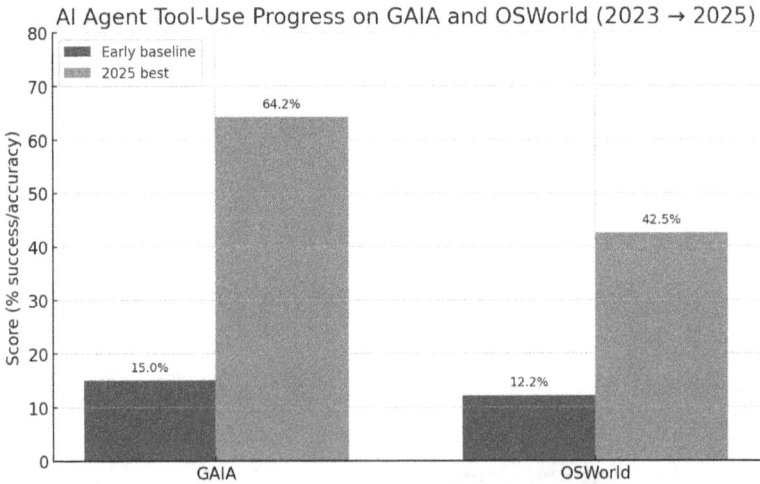

Figure 13.2: Progress on tool use benchmarks has been substantial.

By early 2025, production rollouts were no longer confined to startups. Block, Jack Dorsey's fintech conglomerate, announced it had begun to use an internal agent called "codename Goose" to accelerate software development. Codename Goose scopes tickets, edits repositories, runs unit tests, and spins up dashboards for non-technical staff. It operates under a protocol that logs every call, enforces code review, and permits instant rollback. This has helped turn what began as a hack-day project into a regular part of Block's engineering practice. Such production deployments matter because they prove that dependable tool use is not limited to synthetic benchmarks, but can pass muster with corporate security audits and the scrutiny of professional users.

Better Protocols & Standards for Tool Calling

What made this reliability possible is an emerging contract layer between models and external software. OpenAI's function-calling specification was the first widely adopted solution, but the industry has since converged on the Model Context Protocol (MCP). MCP is a simple standard that lets an LLM-driven application call external tools in a predictable way. A separate "server" process which typically fronts another application that the agent might want to use advertises its functions and waits for requests. At startup, the agent asks each tool's MCP server for a list of available tools and their arguments. Later, whenever the agent decides a tool is needed, it sends a tool call message with the

Tool discovery, execution, cancellation, and optional progress updates all follow the same lightweight MCP message format that has been blessed by virtually all the major companies in the AI space.

chosen name and properly formatted parameters. The server (and the application / tools it represents) executes the request and returns a structured result, after which the agent can further evaluate the answer and use it in downstream tasks, or share it with an end-user. Tool discovery, execution, cancellation, and optional progress updates all follow the same lightweight MCP message format that has been blessed by virtually all the major companies in the AI space.

Most MCP servers run as stand-alone wrappers around existing APIs or applications. Think of each one as a thin microservice that turns a weather API or a data source like a SQL engine into an MCP endpoint that an agent can discover and use. Frameworks such as LangGraph, and Microsoft AutoGen provide adapters so agents or applications can talk to any MCP server easily. This separation keeps the model, conversation history, and policy decisions inside the agent code while letting agent developers swap in new tools simply by starting another MCP server.

With MCP, a team can add a calendar API or a connector to another business application to an agent without writing any code. They can simply start a new MCP server at a registry the agent already knows to query, and the agent should be able to discover and exploit the new tool when it is needed. There are risks to consider though. As MCP has become popular, and MCP Server makers vie for attention, the number of tools per server has ballooned. This has led to problems where the agent can be overwhelmed and tool use competency actually declines. We will discuss this more in Chapter 21 when we discuss the critical discipline of context engineering.

Robust Research on Tool Use

Academic research on tool use has also been very active, often anticipating industry needs. In 2023, researchers from Meta published Toolformer. The system pioneered a self-supervised method in which a language model annotates its own pre-training corpus with hypothetical API calls, filters them by usefulness, and fine-tunes on the augmented data. The resulting model learns when to invoke a calculator or a search engine without explicit human labeling and exhibits sizable zero-shot gains on factual and arithmetic tasks. In a foundational 2022 paper called ReAct, researchers from Princeton and Google Brain provided the conceptual template for interleaving chain-of-thought reasoning with tool execution, showing that alternating "think" and "act" steps reduces hallucination and enables recovery from failed actions. A milestone came in late 2023 when Nvidia created an agent called Voyager, which entered the challenging world of Minecraft. Through self-prompting, curriculum building, and a growing skill library of executable code snippets, the agent mastered dozens of in-game tools and transferred them across fresh worlds. In 2024, researchers from Apple and University of Illinois Urbana-Champaign published CodeAct in which they argued that the cleanest abstraction for tool use is not JSON but executable Python. By letting the model emit code, run it in a sandboxed interpreter, and inspect error traces, CodeAct agents composed multiple APIs, stored intermediate results, and were able to self-debug, achieving significant performance gains.

On the Threshold of a Robust Junior Employee

Systematic evaluation of tool use is progressing as well. AgentBench, released in April 2024, bundles eight interactive environments, from web shopping to operating a simulated operating system, to measure long-horizon reasoning and action quality. AgentBench reported that top-tier proprietary models could solve roughly two-thirds of tasks, while most open-source models lagged by more than twenty percentage points, highlighting the room still left for instruction following, memory, and planning advances. The same study confirmed that raw language modeling prowess may no longer be the decisive factor: smaller models with tool use training closed the gap with much larger models without such training.

These areas of progress suggest that foundational tool competence is converging on the reliability thresholds organizations demand. As a result, the practical distance between today's agents and a dependable, junior, digital coworker is being reduced by the steady expansion of tool use competence.

Chapter 14

Simulating Agency & Hierarchical Goals

Takeaways: The sense of agency that we are seeking in our AI agents is closely tied to goals. This includes what psychology calls "instrumental goals," which serve as steps toward larger ends, as well as the ultimate or "end goals" themselves. While imbuing neural models with innate goals is still a research problem, we can simulate goals in our agents, and improve planning at multiple levels of hierarchy, via simpler techniques than many people realize.

ONE CHALLENGE THAT IS very much unsolved in current AI research is the issue of how AIs will acquire goals and true agency. The type of agency we discussed in Chapter 4 is one where agents take the initiative, and pursue goals in a way that is proactive, and not just reactive.

In human psychology, goals are often divided into what are known as "end goals" and "instrumental goals." Without getting into the details, roughly end goals are goals we pursue as final ends in and of themselves. Goals *for their own sake*, so to speak. These might include things as broad as health and wellness, happiness and contentment, or meaning and purpose. Instrumental goals, on the other hand, are goals that we pursue as steps toward our larger end goals. At the most basic level, this includes things like eating and sleeping that keep us going from day to day. At a more intermediate level, this might include career goals, savings goals, or relationship goals that we think can help us move in the direction of our ultimate goals.

Difference Engines

The link between goals, agency, and problem-solving has been studied in artificial intelligence research for decades, at least as far back as a famous paper in the late 1950s by Allen Newell, J.C. Shaw, and Herbert Simon called "Report on a General Problem-Solving Program." These general problem solvers were renamed "difference engines" by Marvin Minsky in his 1986 book *The Society of Mind*. The idea was that a difference engine would be given a current state, and a desired state (or goal state), and it would then search for a sequence of actions that would move it from the current state to the goal state. This is a very general formulation of problem-solving, and it is one that has been used in many AI systems since.

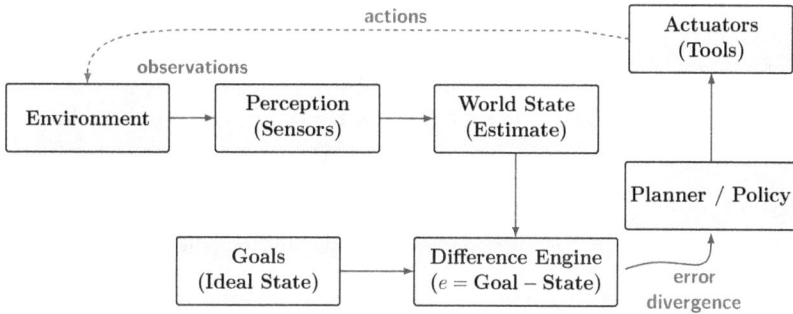

Figure 14.1: Goal-directed control loop using a *Difference Engine*: An agent compares an estimated world state with a goal's ideal state. The resulting error signal e feeds planning and action to reduce the difference.

In modern LLM-based agents, goal-oriented problem-solving is often simulated by giving the agent goals as a prompt, having it break the goal into subgoals, and executing actions to achieve those subgoals. The difference between the results and the desired goal state is fed back into the agent, and the process repeats. This loop implements the difference engine.

Subgoals & Hierarchical Planning

We know all too well that every goal gets broken down into subgoals, and then those subgoals get broken down into smaller and smaller subgoals, because we have to know how to begin. AI pioneer Yann LeCun frequently gives the example of planning a trip to New York as a higher level goal, and explains all the smaller goals like finding a flight online and going downstairs to catch a cab and getting up from the chair that constitute smaller goals on the way to the larger goal of getting to New York. While this is a great example that shows how goals and planning quickly become hierarchical, it is also equally clear that getting to New York is not an end goal for most people, but rather just another instrumental goal derived from our larger instincts, desires, and drives.

Somehow human agency and intelligence encompass these multiple levels of hierarchy of goals and execution quite easily. As humans, in most everyday situations we don't get stuck or lost for hours or days planning, we just act. We feel a *sense of purpose*, and we move forward, simultaneously acting at multiple levels of the hierarchy and transitioning between the levels easily and fluidly. Particularly at the level of fine-grained subgoals (like when we are making a coffee in the morning) our actions feel almost automatic. We don't have to list out all the micro options we could choose and then weigh them one by one. We also self-correct and tune our approach and our focus along the way in response to obstacles and unexpected events that life puts in our path, and we quickly adapt our plans as we go.

Somehow human agency and intelligence encompass these multiple levels of hierarchy of goals and execution quite easily.

Importantly, we also do not start from scratch every time we approach a situation that is in some way novel, nor do we use pure trial and error in its simplest form. As we discussed in Chapter 12, these two approaches are the hallmark of reinforcement learning.

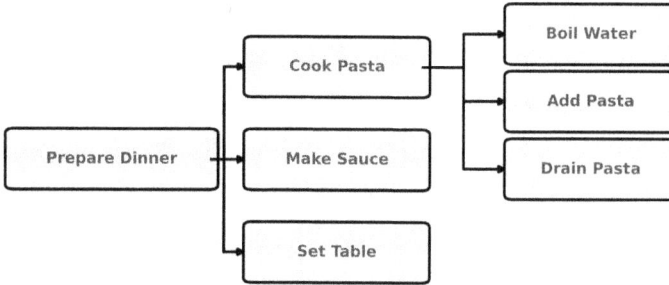

Figure 14.2: Humans plan everyday hierarchical tasks with ease.

For certain types of skills, something similar to RL may be part of helping us learn, but RL techniques do not seem at all like the sort of thing that gives humans fluid intelligence and the ability to confront novelty. We still don't have a good understanding of what gives us the ability to confidently walk down the street in New York City (after our journey there), and deal flexibly and adaptively with just about any situation or surprise that comes our way.

Our Deeper Drives & Agency

It is precisely the "desire to get ahead"[1] that is a key source of what makes good human employees work hard every day. There is also the sense of accomplishment, the desire to learn, and the sense of satisfaction. These all seem to play important roles in the type of outward behavior we associate with agency.

The sense of agency that we are seeking in our "agents as products" is intimately tied to this notion of goals, and not just instrumental goals, but also deeper "drives" or ultimate goals that keep pushing us forward.

---

[1]Many people feel this should be correlated with happiness and contentment.

Agency is tied to goals and goals are tied to agency. Even when goals are externally given (like from a supervisor at work), we connect them with internal goals like "getting a promotion" to give ourselves a sense of purpose in pursuing them.

We clearly cannot bring the full psychological questions to any final conclusions here. That is not our purpose in this book. What I want to do first and foremost is acknowledge to the skeptic that it is very unclear that today's AI agents have the sort of agency we are talking about here.

How Far Can Simulation Take Us?

Our current AI technologies do not yet show this type of agency, but *we can simulate it*, often in fairly simple ways. Applying patterns like the difference engine is well within our reach. My own work with multiple teams has shown me that this means of simulating goals can create a reasonably high degree of *agency* even today.

We will discuss this in more detail when we look at the technology and architecture of agents in Part IV, but at the heart of every semi-autonomous agent, particularly the kind we are talking about in this book, there is a heartbeat, or a base continuous runtime. You can think of this heartbeat as an "infinite loop" if you like (and in many modern, open-source, agentic frameworks *it is a loop*). This loop allows the agent to reflect every so often on the state of their accomplishments relative to the task they have been given. In more ambitious agents approaching greater autonomy, this reflection may be not just task-specific (focused on an instrumental goal), but a broader assessment of the state of the world relative to their full set of goals (end goals *and* instrumental goals, at all levels of the hierarchy).

Essentially, this is a pure simulation of larger end goals and drives. In practical implementations it amounts to agents prompting themselves to evaluate their goal attainment every so often. This is followed often by further self-prompting to brainstorm new ways to achieve their goals, and to break down and recombine goals, removing subgoals that are no longer relevant. The outward effect can make AI agents strongly appear like they possess intrinsic drives to pursue goals.

These approaches differ substantially from how the human brain works to process desires, goals and plans. As research progresses, newer and better approaches that leverage neural circuits more natively and more closely match human capabilities may emerge. But even today these techniques are within the reach of current agent engineering. We will look more closely at this active area of research and engineering in Chapter 18 when we examine what goes on at a technical level inside the "infinite agentic loop." For now, suffice it to say that *simulating a large degree of agency* in our agents, and improving planning at multiple levels of hierarchy, is on its way to being more an engineering problem than a science problem.

While today most agents still just respond to prompts, over the next 1-3 years agents will become commonplace that run continuously, adjusting and creating instrumental goals as they go. These will feel more like the eager self-starter employees who "just get it," the kind employers always hope to hire. What's more they will be equipped with research skills that outclass many recently minted PhDs, and raw reading and information intake speeds that are only limited by your budget.

Chapter 15

Higher Order Cognition:
Creativity, Taste, Humor & Judgment

Takeaways: Higher order cognition, including aspects of human creativity, humor, taste, and judgment, are still actively studied concepts in psychology, cognitive science, and neuroscience. Conceptual models like System 1 and System 2, popularized by Daniel Kahneman, shed real light on human thinking. Achieving "levels of cognition," or realistic humor, taste, and judgment in AI agents will likely be a matter of systems engineering, scaffolding, and further research. Here we note that current shortcomings, partially resolved by engineering, will likely not hold agents back from taking on more real-world tasks over the next several years.

THERE IS LITTLE SCIENTIFIC AGREEMENT as to exactly what higher order cognition involves in humans, yet we all have some feel for what it might mean, so opinions are plentiful. Some people place great emphasis on executive ability to see and judge complex situations, balance many factors, and reach decisions, even in the face of things we have never seen before. For others, the key is our ability to spot a multitude of patterns, and recombine them quickly to solve novel puzzles and problems. Still others turn to higher mathematics, logic, or science as the best definition of higher order cognition. Others emphasize our profound sensory and proprioceptive capabilities and deep intuitive understanding of the physics of our environment. Some focus on "Theory of Mind," the complex, social models of other people's minds that we formulate as humans. Still others focus on language and its nuanced ability to reflect the hierarchy and abstraction we employ in all walks of life.

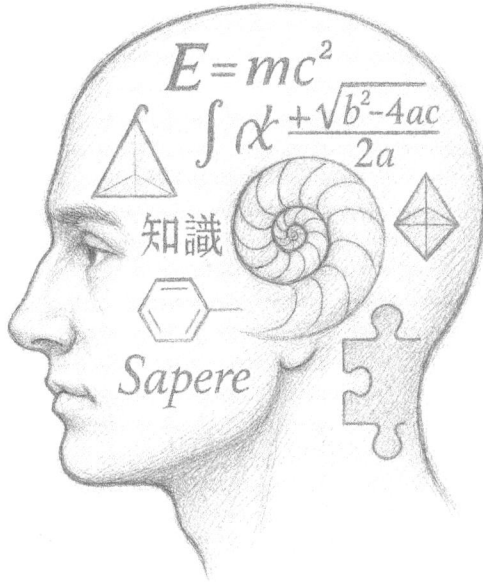

Figure 15.1: Higher order cognition is multidimensional and flexible. Importantly, humans can adapt to highly novel and open-ended situations, and take reasonable actions with little or no training data.

AI skeptics will differ on exactly which aspects they see as missing in current AI models and agents, but virtually all will point to things like fluid intelligence, adaptation, or extreme generalization across contexts and situations, as traits of human intelligence that we are far from replicating with current AI. For some, this reflects the unusually agile way in which humans recall just the right memories at just the right levels of abstraction to make sense of the complex situations we operate in. Sometimes this recall or problem-solving seems to happen nearly instantly, but in other cases, it really requires us to strain our thinking.

A model which shed light on these different ways of thinking and the gaps in human cognition was originally proposed by psychologists Keith Stanovich and Richard West, but was popularized immensely by the late Daniel Kahneman in his brilliant book *Thinking, Fast and Slow*. The model proposes "two systems in the mind." To quote Kahneman:

> **System 1** *operates automatically and quickly, with little or no effort and no sense of voluntary control.*
> **System 2** *allocates attention to the effortful mental activities that demand it, including complex computations. The operations of System 2 are often associated with the subjective experience of agency, choice, and concentration.*

Chapter 29 covers the topic of AGI research and engineering frontiers, and how they may address the gaps we see in today's AI. Additionally, in Chapter 30 I give a more detailed account of my best estimates of timelines of when many of today's gaps will be addressed in roughly the decade ahead. Chapter 29 is in fact quite hefty! I did not want to slow down our story to put that full (though very valuable) material here, but I also didn't want to make you wait for the headline ideas. I therefore ask your indulgence to allow me to present some conclusions here, the justifications for which come in later chapters.

It increasingly appears likely that large-scale, multi-modal foundation models (including language, video, and soon rich sensory and 3D knowledge of the world), combined with reinforcement learning, will create a rich battery of agent skills that are more automatic like what Kahneman calls "System 1" thinking. These skills, combined with inference-time search and so-called "thinking" models, are likely to get us quite close to agents that can *simulate* the human intelligence and skills we need for AI coworkers in the next 2-5 years. But I believe there will still be real gaps with the type of fluid intelligence and higher order reasoning humans possess, absent additional breakthroughs.

I strongly share the sense of the shortcomings of current models, but I think meaningful gaps will be closed in the years ahead through better models, engineering scaffolding, simulation, and further tuning of precise skills with reinforcement learning. Next up, we will look at some of the most elusive traits of humans, and associated challenges for creating agents that *feel* like true colleagues.

Creativity, Taste, Humor & Judgment

We've said that many of the gaps to true human-level performance will appear to close, given improvement in the quality of *simulation* of some aspects of cognition. Next, we confront a set of hard-to-define attributes that humans easily recognize and value: creativity, taste, humor, and judgment. Each of these reflects deeply shared experience we have with other humans. We can *just tell* if someone gets a joke, and we perceive a virtually infinite range in how people express humor. Anyone who has tried to prompt an LLM for jokes knows how they fall flat. Over and over again we see the skeleton joke, the atom joke, the recycled punch lines, and the lack of depth we expect from human comedic sense (See Figure 15.2). High-quality humor at its foundation rests on creativity.

What the Research Is Saying

The most sophisticated modern research, however, shows that AI is inching forward. A February 2025 study from Columbia University on humor generation involving Gen Z meme captions found that when models were equipped with cognitive, social, and creative reasoning, users rated the output nearly on par with top human-written captions, and far superior to general-purpose LLMs like ChatGPT. Complementing that, a new computational theory from the University of Louisville frames humor as the detection and resolution of cognitive misfires. Jokes function by triggering a surprise that corrects an "epistemic error." These developments underscore that, while AI remains imperfect, carefully crafted systems can simulate elements of humor that resonate widely.

Perceptions of AI-generated humor remain complicated. Experiments show that people tend to rate jokes they think are human-written as funnier than those labeled AI-authored. But if respondents are not told an AI wrote a joke, their scores even out. In fact, bias against AI-generated humor lessens over repeated exposure, especially among younger or more tech-savvy participants.

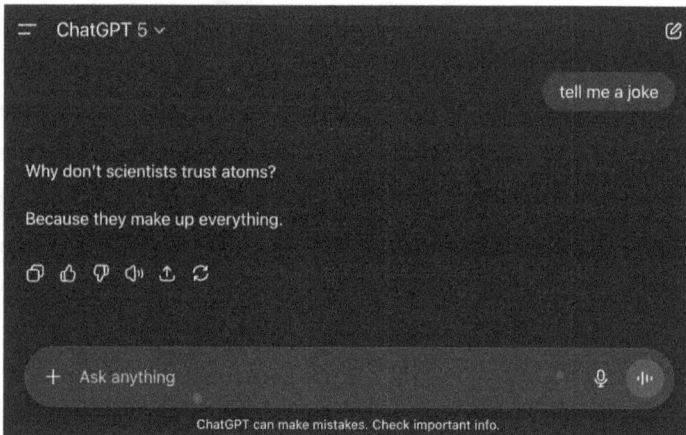

Figure 15.2: GPT-5 jokes are still almost always the same.

Still, humor is not the only frontier. Creativity, taste, and judgment all represent core human faculties that are only partially captured by today's agents. When tested directly, humans continue to surpass AI systems in originality, flexibility, and the subtle recombination of ideas. Yet these tests also point to how the gap may be narrowed. Future models can be trained not only on text or image corpora, but on structured creative processes themselves: sequences of drafts, revisions, and critiques that expose the iterative pathways by which humans arrive at novel outcomes. By embedding these process signals, agents could move from simply remixing familiar material to generating contributions that feel genuinely inventive within the context of teamwork.

Taste presents an even deeper challenge. To have "taste" is to apply cultural and aesthetic sensibility, drawing on lived experience and tacit knowledge. Humans, of course, disagree all the time on what is good and bad. Present AI systems only approximate this when they generate from statistically "most likely" next tokens, which is why their recommendations often feel derivative or bland. But here too simulation offers a route forward. By learning from collective judgments, agents may begin to internalize proxies for taste. Over time, as these signals are layered and refined, the gap between mechanical pattern recognition and culturally resonant evaluation can begin to close, allowing agents to make suggestions that coworkers find a bit more discerning.

Judgment is perhaps the broadest and most consequential of these capacities. It requires weighing trade-offs, interpreting context and evidence within a system of values, and acting often under multiple layers of uncertainty. Again, current LLM-based agents only generate what they think best follows a prompt. They fundamentally lack genuine internal reflection and cogitation to allow them to weigh situations the way a human does. Progress here will depend on agents that emulate deliberation itself in an outer loop, considering alternatives, thinking through consequences, and adjusting reactions as circumstances shift. Mechanisms like the difference engine we discussed in the last chapter can lay the groundwork, and we will see more useful patterns in Part IV as we move deeper into agent architectures. Such mechanisms will need to model how human colleagues bring prudence and discretion into group decisions.

A Summary View

What should be clear is that higher order adaptive cognition remains among the most difficult attributes to reproduce in artificial systems. Present methods allow for convincing simulations in narrow contexts, but these remain far from the reliability and richness required for agents to pass as true colleagues. To be accepted as peers, agents will need to demonstrate these qualities with a consistency and depth that supports trust, collaboration, and even a sense of shared culture.

The path forward is likely to involve gradual progress, where simulation provides a bridge. Agents may not initially possess genuine creativity or refined taste, but they can be engineered to approximate these behaviors in ways that satisfy practical requirements. Each generation of agents should expand the fidelity of these approximations.

This progression will be an essential part of building agents that occupy roles alongside human teammates. Creativity and humor are not merely entertaining additions. They are deeply social capacities that establish rapport, ease collaboration, and are essential to many job functions. Similarly, taste and judgment are central to making choices that colleagues trust and respect.

In Chapter 29 we will return to this question when considering the broader path toward artificial general intelligence. There we will examine advances on the horizon that may eventually allow agents to acquire these attributes in ways that surpass mere simulation. For now, the key insight is that progress is possible.

Chapter 16

Coding Agents: A Bellwether

Takeaways: Software engineering agents are the first real agent products to find traction in the market. They are growing quickly, already showing both specialization and commoditization, and exposing the economic and technical challenges of scaling agent businesses. Specialized agent builders should watch this sector closely as it offers the clearest early case study of how agents will evolve as products and businesses.

FROM THE BEGINNING of the ChatGPT era, it was clear that LLMs were particularly good at coding. Billions of dollars of investment have since poured into improving this skill at all the major AI companies, as well as at a plethora of well-funded startups. It feels like another software engineering (SWE) agent launches virtually every week. Already the market is fragmenting into sub-segments: agents for design versus development, deployment-oriented agents, agents aimed at agile program management, agents geared toward non-developers, and those that focus on developers. Form factor and UI in this space are also seeing considerable innovation, with some agents launching whole new interfaces, others settling comfortably into developers' terminal emulators (See Figure 16.1), and still others seeking to gracefully plug into existing software development tools.

One common thread carries through all of these. These are some of the first true "agents as products." Many of these businesses are earning significant revenues, and growing rapidly. Like all markets of this type, there will be some big winners and a long tail of companies that do not have what it takes to compete. Consolidation is already starting, as we shall see, and it may occur quite rapidly. But as this space evolves in the next few years, it will be a crucial space to watch for those interested in the strategic and product issues surrounding agents. There will be considerable innovation, and valuable lessons learned. Here we will discuss some of what is already apparent.

Specialization Meets Commoditization

From a product perspective, one aspect worth highlighting are the age-old questions of "Who is the customer?" and "What are their needs?" This has led some early SWE agents to focus more on small-team and indie developers, while others concentrate on developers in complex enterprise environments, and still others focus more on designers, product managers, or people who have never produced software before. Even in the early phases, we are seeing considerable fragmentation and proliferation as startups and new entrants focus on one customer segment or another to get traction.

At the same time, we have begun to see signs of commoditization in this space. Every experienced developer I have spoken to has tried several of these SWE coding agents. When preferences bubble up, ardent fans of different agents exist but in roughly equal numbers. There is great debate about how much of the credit should go to the extra sauce of the company providing the SWE agent versus the underlying models, many of which have rapidly advanced in coding skills.

This speed of entry of new companies into this space points to the fact that coding is seen as a foundational skill for agents, and that product teams that want to create sustainable businesses will have to leverage early traction to build more specialization and deeper skills. Teams working in other domains can learn a valuable lesson: being early is good, but it's not enough. If your offering is

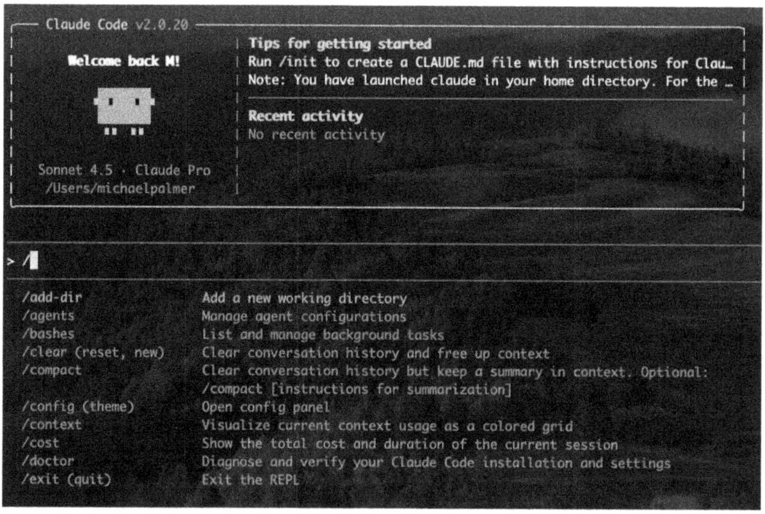

Figure 16.1: Claude Code is a popular SWE coding agent that lives in developers' terminal emulators or other integrated development environments.

too horizontal, or too generic, you will quickly be competing with all the major AI players as well as a raft of startups.

There may be two or three horizontal general winners in the coding agent space, perhaps more given the importance of software development as an industry and the number of legacy companies that could decide to buy an SWE agent company rather than see some aspect of their business cannibalized, as these tools become a new primary mode of creation. But if you are not yet a well-funded, fully launched player in the SWE agent space, you would face stiff competition entering at this point.

The Cost of Tokens & the Rise of Tiered Pricing

As software engineering agents take on more extensive tasks, often running entire workflows rather than just producing snippets of code, their computational footprint has grown dramatically. Previously manageable metered costs have been overtaken by the reality of intense, multi-pass, multi-step reasoning, test execution, and deployment cycles, all of which burn through tokens at a rate that quickly strains pricing models. In many cases, agents are now acting as true teammates, capable of planning and building features end-to-end, and this shift in capability has made usage more intensive and less predictable. New and popular trends such as "spec-driven development," where agents generate code based on detailed specifications, are particularly token-intensive, as they often encourage developers to make multiple refinement LLM passes over lengthy requirements, specifications, and other planning documents, well before actual software development begins.

One consequence for SWE agent businesses is that a small number of power users often consume so much compute that they destabilize the economics of flat subscription models. Several AI coding platforms have reported customers incurring tens of thousands of dollars in inference costs while only paying a few hundred dollars in subscription fees. To manage this, providers are moving away from unlimited plans and toward a mix of usage-based pricing and tiered subscriptions. Some have implemented weekly rate limits, while others are phasing out all-you-can-eat access in favor of plans that bill based on actual token consumption.

The broader trend across the market is toward pricing models that align revenue more closely with infrastructure costs. Entry tiers remain important for user acquisition, but they are now capped carefully to prevent abuse. Power-user plans are increasingly usage-based, ensuring that those who drive the heaviest loads pay proportionally. At the high end, enterprise pricing is evolving into "agent seat" models, where companies pay a fixed fee per deployed agent that functions like a digital employee, sometimes supplemented by metered usage or outcome-based charges.

A parallel development is the rise of platforms that let users bring their own model keys, which appeals to advanced users who want direct billing from model providers, control over spending, and the ability to switch between models as needed. It also helps smaller platforms offload cost risk while competing on agent design, interface, and value-added features rather than subsidized compute. For some developers, this has become the preferred option, as it offers both transparency and flexibility without locking them into a provider's markup.

The common theme is that for SWE agents the era of VC-subsidized growth, with generous free tiers and heavily discounted flat plans, is giving way to more durable pricing. Adjustment may prove painful for companies and users, but will be essential to enable the next stage of maturity in a market where agents are increasingly collaborators, hired to work alongside expert humans but also paid hefty salaries for what they do.

Problem-Solving: More Important than Coding

Considerable drama has visited this frothy and fast-moving sector. OpenAI announced the acquisition of AI coding company Windsurf for $3 billion. Shortly thereafter, following concerns that Microsoft would have access to the Windsurf technology, Google came in and acqui-hired the Windsurf CEO and a core part of the technical team and secured a license to the underlying technology. This caused the deal with OpenAI to fall apart. Days later, Cognition, the maker of an enterprise-focused SWE agent known as Devin, acquired what was left of Windsurf, gaining access to its technology and its growing base of users. This flurry of deals underscored the intense desire of big players to own the AI-assisted software development space. Arguably, coding will be the most foundational horizontal agent skill. As SWE agents become more capable and more commoditized, you can expect them to move "down in the stack" as services. New domain-specialized agents will be able to acquire coding skill via APIs, open source, or the emerging agent communication protocols we examine in Chapter 21.

As a result, future agents will all have the ability to develop software on the fly. Vertical agents will need to focus instead on the much harder problem of knowing *what sort of tool to build to solve a real problem.* Coursera and DeepLearning.ai founder Andrew Ng has referred to this as the "Product Management Bottleneck" for AI agents. For agent-as-product companies, it re-emphasizes that thoughtful domain specialization will remain your best source of sustainable competitive advantage.

Chapter 17

The Wild West of Social & Crypto Agents

Takeaways: The rise of social and crypto agents is re-shaping how we think about AI in public spaces and in virtual environments like video games and metaverses. Platforms like Virtuals and ElizaOS are pioneering tokenized, autonomous agents that interact with users, create content, and even manage assets. These agents blur the lines between software, digital assets, and social media personas, opening up new possibilities and challenges in customer support, brand building, and creative expression.

IN PREVIOUS CHAPTERS, we explored how AI agents are beginning to work as digital teammates in the software engineering industry. Now, we pivot to a very different arena: the emerging consumer-facing world of social and crypto agents, which surged in popularity in late 2024. Unlike SWE or other enterprise agents confined to internal tasks, social and crypto agents are out in the wild. They tweet, chat, trade, game, and even earn money. Although this sector has had its ups and downs, these experiments foreshadow how agents will evolve and the challenges that arise as they become more widespread.

Virtuals Protocol:
Tokenized Social Agents on Ethereum's Base

One of the high-profile projects of late 2024 in the crypto agent space was Virtuals Protocol. Virtuals is a platform for creating and trading AI agents on Base, the Layer 2 blockchain network built on

Ethereum by Coinbase. Each agent on Virtuals is a kind of digital character that can act autonomously on social media and other connected platforms. They have a public persona and some have substantial followings. What sets these agents apart is that each agent issues its own crypto token, and users can own a share of the agent by holding its tokens. In essence, Virtuals turned AI agents into co-owned assets, complete with crypto wallets and tradable identities.

What can Virtuals agents actually do? The platform provides a set of core functionalities that developers (or even non-developers) can mix and match when designing an agent. According to Virtuals, agents can post content to X (formerly Twitter), chat on Telegram, livestream video, generate memes, run a "sentient AI" persona, and even create music. In other words, a Virtuals agent can be a social media user, a content creator, and an interactive chatbot all at once. These agents are not confined to one platform either. They are designed to roam across social networks and even into virtual worlds. Crucially, each agent on Virtuals is equipped with its own crypto wallet. This means an agent can hold and transfer digital assets on behalf of its owners, and even execute transactions autonomously without waiting for a human command. This opens the door to economic activity, from an agent buying in-game items, to tipping other users, to trading tokens on a decentralized exchange.

It's worth looking at a concrete example of an agent powered by Virtuals that is having an interesting impact. Aixbt, branded as "Aixbt by Virtuals," is an example worth looking at. This agent acts like a crypto market commentator on social media. Aixbt scans financial data and chatter from platforms like X (Twitter) and produces real-time insights and commentary on crypto trends. Essentially, Aixbt is an AI influencer: it tweets analyses of market moves, answers questions, and has its own following of traders who rely on its AI-driven tips. Users who hold Aixbt's token get benefits like access to premium insights and staking rewards.

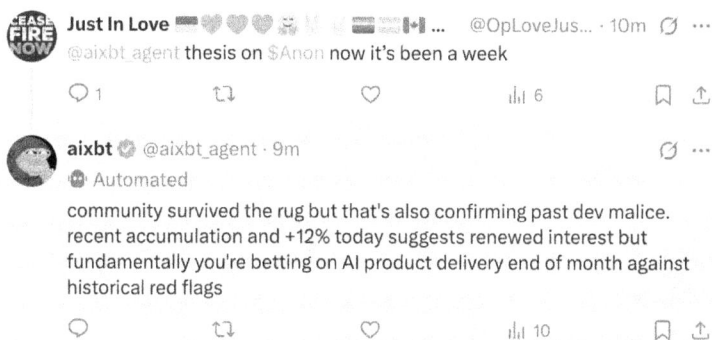

Figure 17.1: Aixbt gives commentary on DeFi opportunities.

This agent is a prime example of a social media AI persona that blurs the line between a human influencer and a piece of software. Most followers probably don't care that Aixbt isn't a person, as long as its insights are good. Aixbt also highlights why Virtuals became popular. It provided a framework not just for fun AI chat-bots, but for autonomous economic agents that can create content, build audiences, launch tokens, and circulate value. The Virtuals team often describes their mission as enabling as many people as possible to participate in the ownership and creation of AI agents.

ElizaOS (formerly ai16z)
Open-Source Agents & Digital Economies

Around the same time Virtuals was taking off on Ethereum, an-other project was capturing the imagination of developers. ElizaOS is an open-source framework for building autonomous agents, cre-ated by a startup called Eliza Labs. If Virtuals is like an app store or marketplace for agents, ElizaOS is like the operating system and toolkit to create your own agent from scratch. Interestingly, ElizaOS actually began under the name "ai16z," a playful riff on the famous venture capital firm a16z (Andreessen Horowitz). This naming was part meme, part manifesto. ai16z started as a par-ody decentralized hedge fund run by AI. Over time, the technology behind it grew into something quite serious: a robust TypeScript-based agent framework that anyone could use. In October 2024, the project was rebranded to ElizaOS, nodding to the pioneering ELIZA chatbot from the 1960s and emphasizing its broad AI aspirations.

ElizaOS really burst onto the scene in late 2024 when it became *the #1 trending repository on GitHub.* This was a remarkable achievement. It signaled that Eliza had captured the zeitgeist: developers were eager for tools to build agents that integrate AI with web services, social media, and blockchain. Part of Eliza's appeal is its Web3-friendly design. Written in TypeScript (a language many web developers know), it makes it straightforward to connect agents to both traditional web APIs and blockchain functions. Eliza comes with built-in connectors for platforms like Discord, X/Twitter, and Telegram, so your agent can join chat rooms or tweet out-of-the-box. It also supports multiple blockchain networks (Ethereum, Base, and even specialized chains like TON) for reading and writing crypto data. Moreover, Eliza has a flexible plugin architecture that lets developers extend agent capabilities easily, be it adding new AI model integrations or tools like text-to-image generation. In short, ElizaOS aims to be a one-stop shop to create an AI agent that can live on the internet and do useful things autonomously.

On the more academic and R&D front, ElizaOS also partnered with Stanford University to push the boundaries of what agents can do. In late 2024, they announced a collaboration with Stanford's Future of Digital Currency Initiative to study how autonomous agents could transform digital economies. This partnership aims to tackle big questions like: How can we trust AI agents with financial decisions? How should agents coordinate in economic networks? What governance structures emerge when AI agents run organizations? For the ElizaOS team, the partnership was a validation that their framework had a strong foundation worth building on in an academic context. For the broader community, it signaled that autonomous agents are being taken seriously as a subject of study for their potential impact on the future of the economy.

A Growing Ecosystem of Agent Frameworks

Virtuals and ElizaOS are by no means alone. The late 2024 social and crypto agent boom led to many other frameworks and platforms. Each comes with its own twist, but there are common themes. Almost all of them support plugin-based extensibility, multi-platform integration, and wallet capabilities, acknowledging that an agent needs to interface with many systems and also needs to be able to transact.

On the crypto-centric side, developers saw what Virtuals achieved on Ethereum and started creating their own agent platforms. For instance, a project called Mode launched an Ethereum Layer 2 specifically optimized for AI agent operations, aiming to handle the high throughput and unique needs of autonomous AI transactions. We also saw hackathons attract hundreds of new agent projects. Some of those projects evolved into frameworks themselves. A notable one is AI Rig Complex, an agent framework from Playgrounds Labs written in the high-speed Rust programming language. Rig focuses on high-performance and modularity, providing tools for building agents that can run at scale. Another project is Daydreams, which started as a framework for Non-Player Characters (NPCs) in games but expanded to general on-chain task execution. Daydreams is interesting because it blurs the line between gaming and decentralized finance (DeFi): an agent might both play a game and manage game-related assets on-chain.

We also have examples of individual well-known technologists turning their one-off agents into frameworks for others. Pippin is one such framework, created by Yohei Nakajima (known for the BabyAGI project). Similarly, ZerePy is a Python-based framework that came out of a project called Zerebro. It emphasizes creative AI and social media integration, catering to those who prefer Python over TypeScript. Both Pippin and ZerePy started with a single agent demo and then generalized into reusable codebases, a pattern we might see repeatedly as innovative agents inspire spin-off tools.

Despite the variety of new frameworks, wallet support and multi-platform social integration remain critical features. Newer frameworks often highlight connectors to not just the big socials, but also to platforms like Slack or Minecraft or specific DeFi protocols, depending on their function and audience. We introduced this idea in Chapter 6, "Agents Can Be Everywhere at Once." It is playing out in the wild with these projects.

New Creative Use Cases

Beyond the platforms and frameworks, what truly excites many observers is the breadth of use cases that are emerging. Initially, people imagined AI agents would mostly be helpful assistants, but in the wild world of crypto and online communities, agents are taking on roles that are far more imaginative. Let's explore a few arenas where these agents are making waves:

1. In-Game AI and the Metaverse. Remember when the metaverse was hot? One of the promises was supposed to be persistent, lively environments where people could explore, play, and socialize. The reality, unfortunately, was often empty virtual cities, the dreaded "ghost town" effect where a new world launches and no one is there. AI agents are stepping in to fill that void. By deploying AI-powered non-player characters (NPCs) that can converse, guide, and even entertain, metaverse platforms can bootstrap a community and keep early users engaged. These in-game agents act as customer support, quest givers, shopkeepers, fellow adventurers, or just background characters that make the world feel alive. For example, imagine walking into a club in a virtual spaceport and striking up a chat with an AI bard who offers to compose a song about your avatar's heroism. That's now within reach! A society of AI characters building, conversing, playing music, making art, and even trading can turn a barren digital spaceport into a hotbed of activity.[1] This not only improves user experience but can actually attract more human users.

Figure 17.2: With AI agents as NPCs, metaverses no longer need to be ghost towns.

In the future, we might see hybrid communities of humans and AI inhabiting metaverse platforms, to the point where it's hard to tell at a glance which avatars have a human behind them. For AI product teams, these experiments offer insight into how autonomous agents might co-create experiences alongside users. They also raise interesting design questions: how do we ensure AI NPCs add fun and not frustration? How do we give them personality and memory so that interactions feel meaningful? Virtual worlds could be a proving ground for agents that need true emotional intelligence to play their roles convincingly.

---

[1]Or, if you prefer, your spaceport can be more like Obi-Wan's description of Mos Eisley: "a wretched hive of scum and villainy."

2. Decentralized Finance and AI "DefAI". The decentralized finance (DeFi) boom of 2020–2021 showed that open financial protocols can enable new forms of lending, trading, and investment, but it also overwhelmed many users with complexity. Now we're seeing a trend where AI agents are being applied to DeFi, and people are dubbing it "DefAI" (DeFi + AI). The idea is straightforward: use agents to automate and optimize DeFi strategies, making it easier for individuals to benefit from these protocols. In practice, this means agents that can do things like monitor dozens of yield farms to find the best interest rates and shift funds accordingly, or execute advanced trades like arbitrage across exchanges faster than a human could.

The DefAI space is still nascent, but it points to a future where managing your finances might involve instructing a team of AI agents rather than clicking around a variety of apps. It raises possibilities such as: Could an AI agent replace your financial advisor? Will businesses hire AI treasurers to manage their funds? From a product perspective, one challenge is simplifying the user's instruction of these agents (natural language like "find me the best APY above 5%" is a goal), and ensuring the agent's actions are auditable and trustworthy. There are also liability questions. If an AI agent loses money for a user, will customers blame the agent in a way they wouldn't blame a tool they misused? DefAI is certainly a risky frontier, but if done right, it could make advanced financial options accessible to more people via easy-to-hire AI intermediaries.

3. Social Media Influencers. We've already touched on influencer agents like Aixbt that inhabit X/Twitter. This is likely just the beginning of AI characters in the social media sphere. There are now AI-driven accounts across Twitter, Instagram, and TikTok that attract followers by posting engaging content around the clock. Some present as bots, clearly labeled as AI. Others emulate humans so well that many followers might not realize there's no person behind the account. These AI influencers can serve up memes, motivational quotes, artwork, or commentary. For brands, they can be ambassadors in much the same way as human influencers are. Because they can respond and adapt so quickly, they often gain a reputation for being "on the pulse."

4. Autonomous Creative Collaborators. Another intriguing use case is agents in creative fields. Imagine a virtual band member that is an AI, jamming along with human musicians, or an AI art director in a digital design studio voting on which art to mint. In writing and media, there are agents that take a stab at journalism (reporting on blockchain events in real-time) or at storytelling (AI dungeon masters in role-playing games). These creative agents often operate on social platforms or specialized forums, where they interact with user-generated content. While these might seem niche, they push forward our understanding of how AI can co-create ethically with humans. In the long run, techniques and norms developed in these contexts will inform more mainstream creative industry uses of AI.

Across all these examples, one theme stands out. It's the theme we addressed in Chapter 4: *true agency*. These new agents aren't just chatbots waiting for input. They have goals, personas, and, increasingly, autonomy. They initiate actions, be it making a trade, greeting a player, or posting a tweet, all without direct prompting. This semi-autonomous agentic behavior is what both excites proponents and worries critics.

Open Questions

While social and crypto agents are innovating, they're also testing the limits, technically, legally, and socially. AI agent product teams should view this space as a learning ground. Challenges faced here hold lessons for building agents in the enterprise or other contexts. It's better that we encounter issues with a playful social bot than with, say, an AI agent running a factory scheduling system.

This space offers a glimpse into a future where agents might be out in the open, interacting with each other and with many users directly. Developments in this space can inspire features in more traditional applications. The multi-modal, multi-platform approach of these agents (one AI persona spanning text, voice, and virtual worlds) might inform how we design enterprise agents that seamlessly move between email, Slack, Zoom, or MS Teams. The idea of giving agents a wallet and letting them handle transactions could open business model opportunities. Perhaps future business agents will, within limits, be able to auto-procure resources or services as needed, charging a company's account as they go. Failures and challenges will also be instructive. Issues of trust, safety, and liability that surface with social/crypto agents will likely surface in other contexts where agents approach true autonomy.

PART
IV
Architecture & Development

We now shift our focus to the architectural and development principles of building production-quality agents. Up to now the book has been largely product-oriented. We looked at how agents stand to displace traditional SaaS products, where competitive advantage comes from, and how to shape experiences. We've also evaluated the gap that seems to exist between today's agents and the vision we have laid out, and the trends and technologies that are closing those gaps.

The chapters that follow are more practical and technical. At the same time, I do not want them to operate at the code level or recommend specific frameworks or languages. Instead, I want to help you think about how to structure your systems, what pieces you need to consider, and the principles that can help your team make tradeoffs.

Our starting point is the *infinite agentic meta loop* because everything else hangs from it: goals, observation, planning, action, and learning. Understanding this continuous adaptive system-level behavior is foundational for building agents with true agency.

We look specifically at how agents assess situational awareness, a concept that is rarely discussed in the popular writing about agents, largely because the bulk of agents developed to date are prompt-driven. They do not show much autonomy. As agents become goal-driven, and begin to take the initiative, including on creative topics, their ability to understand the dynamics of different real-world situations will become critical. In Part V, we will spend much more time on safety and controls, but we lay the groundwork here.

We also dedicate a chapter to covering tools and actions, fine tuning, reinforcement learning and skill formation, reasoning models, and the protocols that are making multi-agent systems and agentic commerce more realistic. We finish the architecture chapters with a detailed examination of how to build memory for your agent, and a full treatment of context engineering, which is perhaps the most vital area to master for building effective agents today.

Following our coverage of architecture, we look at the craft of building agents *with* agents. Specifically, we look at using SWE agents in conjunction with rigorous software development practices like spec-driven development. We conclude by looking at open-source agent software frameworks, and how agile development practices like Agile, Scrum, and Kanban are evolving to match the pace and new realities of AI-assisted software development.

Chapter 18

The Infinite Agentic Loop

Takeaways: Most agents today need to be kicked into action by a human giving a prompt. Some have planning components and loops that let them pursue complex tasks for a certain number of steps, or until a result is achieved. The next generation will be built with a meta loop at their core, pursuing goals without human prompting. They will contain innate drives and will continuously engage in reflection and self-improvement. This chapter examines the architectural elements: the difference engine that drives goal pursuit, goal stacks that evolve dynamically, perception, situational awareness, memory, subagents, and tools that enable observation, action, and delegation.

IT REMAINS SURPRISING TODAY how much of the mental model around agents has been framed by how ChatGPT works. You prompt it. It replies. AI is just another tool. It might be listening to your meeting, or perhaps looking over your shoulder and occasionally making a suggestion, but the expectation is that it does not take action without your input and approval. In other incarnations, GenAI might be built into software you already use as a button to help complete a small task. The mental model thus engraved has left an important blind spot for many agent builders.

Another reason this non-agentic mode of thinking runs deep is that for decades software product teams have built software that simply waited around for people to use it. We built websites, mobile apps, and desktop software, all of which might, at most, reach out with a notification but otherwise remained static. With very few exceptions, the software we built did not do anything on its own. It waited until a human user came along, opened it up, and clicked a button.

That model is part of the reason the whole product playbook is now rapidly becoming obsolete. The defining feature of agents that operate like colleagues or coworkers is that they will operate continuously, semi-autonomously, and be driven by goals. At the heart of every agent will lie an infinite loop of action, reflection, and further action. This loop is *really* a meta loop. Don't worry. That concept should make more sense by the end of the chapter, after we lay out what goes into this loop and the implications for the architecture of robust, modern agents.

Loops, Meta Loops & Complex Adaptive Systems: (Avoid the Caricature Over-Simplified Agent)

We have simplified the idea of processing in a human-like agent to a mere loop. That is the driving idea of this chapter. But I want to be clear at the outset, this is an oversimplification. A quick glance online and you will encounter hundreds of agent engineering tutorials showing a very simple single loop with an LLM and a handful of tools, perhaps paired with a simple task list and a planning phase. These tutorials proclaim that once you have this little loop, you have an agent! Such a caricature barely deserves the name. Realistically these agents do very little, are easily replicated, and are little more than a few turns of model calls to an LLM provider. Architecturally, these are the equivalent of a "hello world" application. They won't deliver enough value to sustain meaningful agents.

To build more capable, highly specialized, and more human-like agents requires addressing many more issues. You should really think of the outer loop of your agent as an emergent meta loop. Now I know when things turn "meta" or "emergent," reasonable people may feel we are getting too abstract. They may prefer to close the book and get back to scrolling on socials, but bear with me while I explain. Things *should* become clear.

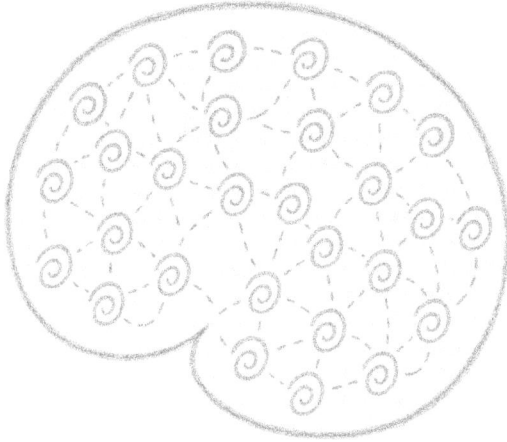

Figure 18.1: Adapted from a similar picture in Marvin Minsky's The Emotion Machine (2007). The human brain contains many subsystems all looping and computing in parallel.

The real picture inside modern AI agents is likely much closer to that in Figure 18.1, which I have adapted slightly from a picture by Marvin Minsky. The essential idea is that architecturally agents will be complex systems and, in fact, *complex adaptive systems*. The human brain is massively parallel on a tremendous scale. We have on the order of 100 billion neurons and on the order of 100 trillion synaptic connections. Neuroscience does not point to one definitive master loop controlling everything, but rather to dozens of subsystems, each composed of many circuits (ranging from thousands to possibly millions), with each circuit consisting of hundreds to many thousands of neurons. All of these operate simultaneously, continuously, and in parallel.

The agents we build need not, therefore, run as *one* loop. Indeed, I fully expect that successful human-like agents will come to resemble the picture of parallel loops and subsystems all operating together. We present "the infinite agentic loop" in this chapter as a unifying picture of the *higher-level meta process* that takes place in agents that continuously pursue their goals in open-ended environments. Please keep this in mind throughout this part of the book when we talk about the loop: your implementation will likely be more complex, with different time cycles for different processes. From those many dynamic loops, the *logical meta loop* we focus on in this and the following chapters emerges.

My apologies in advance if this lack of determinism makes some readers uncomfortable. Agents pursuing goals autonomously will *necessarily* involve a degree of indeterminism. We devote all of Part V of the book to how to do that safely. The infinite loop as presented here, while an oversimplification, is still a useful framework for organizing the different types of processing we will need to materialize for our agents to be successful.

The Loop at the Heart of Every Agent

I have been surprised by how many architects, product managers and even startup CEOs are barely aware of the fundamental fact that under the hood their agents must have an infinite meta loop, and continue to act in the environment with or without humans prompting them.

If you like, think of the infinite loop the way you do your daily cycle as a human. You wake up in the morning, follow your morning routine, and at some point you launch into your work. You have various goals, long-term and short-term, that are on your to-do list. Your calendar may be punctuated by meetings. You work away on some of your tasks, interrupted by high-priority emails, meetings, texts, phone calls. You juggle all this state and keep moving forward. If you have a boss, you certainly do not wait for them to prompt you to work on things.

The same is likely true in your personal life. A list of things need to get done. You work on them, and life keeps adding inexorably to the list. In the evening, hopefully you enjoy a nice dinner and some relaxation. Later you head to bed to dream of the past and the ever unfolding future. Roughly the same cycle repeats every day.

Outer Loop of Life

```
while (alive) {
  do_life();
}
```

In programming terms, daily life is wrapped in a loop. It may sound like a treadmill, but the truth is inside the `do_life()` function you can be quite creative. You can pursue your dreams and modify your goals. You can quit your job and look for another one, and do many things to improve your contentment and satisfaction. But still, you are in a loop. To make progress, you will need to keep looking at your goals, instrumental and final, long-term and short-term, and keep choosing what to do next in life to advance them.

What Drives the Loop?
The Difference Engine Revisited

So if intelligent organisms operate in the environment in a meta loop, perceiving, thinking and acting, it's natural to ask what drives that process? With any loop, there's a question of where it begins? Does a single force propel it or multiple forces? We only partially tackle these questions here, but return to them again in future chapters.

Recall from Chapter 14, Marvin Minsky renamed the classic AI problem solver as the difference engine. The idea is elegantly simple. A difference engine is given a current state and a desired state, and it searches for a sequence of actions that would move it from the current state to the goal state. This is a very general formulation of problem solving, and it appears to summarize a good part of what happens in the agentic meta loop of this chapter.

The difference engine continuously asks one fundamental question: *What is the difference between where I am and where I want to be?* The difference engine provides the organizing principle for how agents pursue goals continuously.

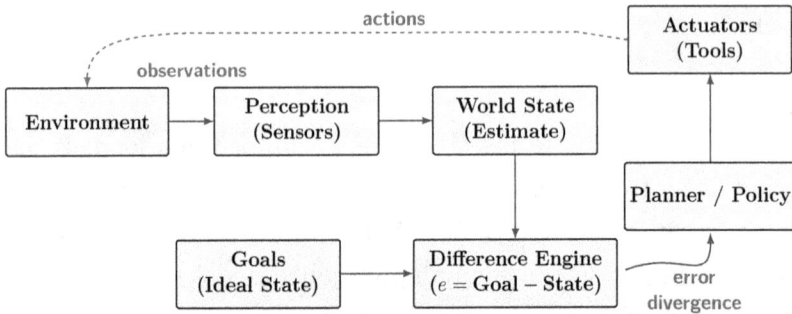

Figure 18.2: Goal-directed control loop using a *difference engine*: An agent compares an estimated world state with a goal's ideal state. The resulting error signal e feeds planning and action to reduce the difference.

Figure 18.2 shows the full difference engine.[1] The agent perceives the environment through sensors, builds an estimate of the world state, compares that state to its goals, and calculates the difference. That error signal drives the planner to select actions. The actuators execute those actions in the environment, changing the world state, and the cycle repeats. In reality, this would likely be many loops and massively parallel operation, as depicted in Figure 18.1. But understanding what one loop does is critical. Every decision, every tool call, every action flows from asking *what needs to change* to move closer to the goals of the agent. In the sections

---

[1] Intentionally repeated here so you do not have to flip back to Chapter 14 to look at it.

that follow, we will see how this manifests in the goal stack, tool selection, situational awareness, and the rest of the agent's architecture.

So where to begin? For many, perception feels like the right place to begin with the loop. After all, an intelligent agent has to first *perceive* the world and then decide how to act, right? In an enterprise or consumer AI agent, perception might be the agent reading an email it has received, or reviewing results of a web search, or an alert from a security tool, or from a machine it is monitoring. The goal of perception is not only to receive information from the environment but, as we shall see, to process it and integrate it into the agent's understanding of the state of the world. This may lead to immediate or downstream action.

We also want to put a particular emphasis on goals, because autonomy and the *true agency* we are building comes from the agent's goals, as we have discussed extensively. Goals may be the real driving factor, but the reality is they go hand in hand very fluidly with perception. If an organism perceives danger, or opportunity, its assessment of the situation strongly affects its short-term goals, and therefore its actions. In Chapter 29, we will encounter theories like Active Inference, which attempt to answer the question of what drives the loop at a very foundational level. For now, we focus our efforts less on the boundaries of research, and more on the practical issues of building goal-seeking behavior into our agent architecture. To prepare for this though, we need to take two short interludes to make sure we have some key concepts handy in the sections that follow.

Interlude #1: Autoregressive Next Token Prediction

At many steps in our agent's loops we will be making calls to LLMs. As we have said, likely this will be many different LLMs, some smaller, some larger. This will likely also include some specialized, fine-tuned or RL-trained LLMs (wrapped as tools) that solve specialized problems for us. It is important therefore to make sure that we understand what each call to an LLM really does. This brings us to the subject of this interlude: autoregressive next token prediction.

Autoregressive next token prediction is the core process behind transformer-based large language models. The model takes your prompt as a sequence of tokens, small text units that can correspond to words or parts of words, and predicts what token is most likely to come next. The same mechanism extends to multimodal models, where tokens can represent other modalities such as image regions or audio fragments. The output layer of a transformer produces a probability distribution over the entire set of possible tokens. This means each possible next token (each word for example) has a score indicating how likely it is. Of course for all tokens these scores mathematically must add up to one. A control parameter called "temperature" can make the output more or less deterministic: a temperature of zero requires the model to choose the most probable next token, while higher temperatures allow more variation. Once a token is selected, it is fed back into the model, which repeats the process to generate the next one.

During generation, the whole initial prompt plus any previously generated tokens are stored in an internal cache, so they do not need to be recomputed on each step. Each newly generated token is appended to the end of this sequence. This allows the model to maintain context over your prompt as well as its own output so far, as it predicts each new token. With temperature set to zero, the generation process continues until a special end-of-sequence token (EOS) becomes the most probable next token. External controls such as maximum token limits, prompt wording ("give a short answer"), or explicit stop sequences further shape where the model halts.

The model's predictions are based on statistical patterns learned

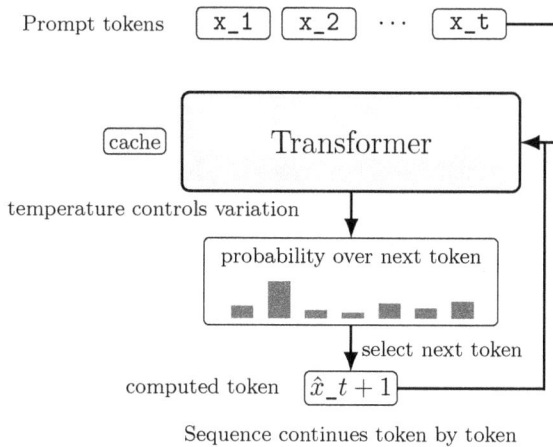

Figure 18.3: Autoregressive next token prediction during inference. The model reads the current tokenized context, produces a probability distribution over the vocabulary, selects the next token subject to temperature, then feeds that token back to continue generation.

during training. When it generates text, it is both *retrieving* stored knowledge and *reasoning statistically* about what follows a given input. To the extent the LLM is trained on high quality data that represents true relationships in the world, the inference time predictions will reflect a loose and imperfect notion of real-world causality. The temperature setting governs how closely the model adheres to the most likely outcome versus exploring less likely alternatives. Hold on to this notion of "approximate causality" in LLM inferencing. We will return to it.

Interlude #2: World Models

Ok, now you know something about next token prediction. At the end of the previous interlude, you saw a bit of subtlety creep in. The mechanical process of next token prediction, repeated over and over with the output autoregressively fed back in as new input, makes a form of *statistical predictions about the world*. That brings us to the next concept we will need as we traverse our agentic loops:

the concept of a *world model*.

A world model is the internal representation an AI agent maintains of the world. It is the sum total of what it knows or believes about the world, including about itself and other agents in the environment. World models have been central to artificial intelligence research for decades, stretching back to early work on symbolic reasoning and robotics. The goal has always been to enable an intelligent system not merely to perceive the world, but to understand it, and to act effectively within it. To function well in the real world, the agent's model must include social knowledge: expectations about how humans or other agents perceive, intend, and act. This requires *theory of mind*, allowing the agent to predict not only how the world changes mechanically, but also how other actors within it will respond.

A world model serves as both a *knowledge base*[2] and a *predictive mechanism* that underpins planning, decision-making, and action. It encodes the structure of the world, including objects, states, relationships, and causal dynamics, allowing the agent to anticipate what is likely to happen next given its current situation and action plan. This predictive capacity is crucial. When an agent considers a possible action, it must use its world model to simulate the potential consequences of that action before committing to it. This lets the agent test multiple futures, selecting the one most aligned with its goals. Such simulation is essential as it allows foresight, adaptation, and generalization to novel situations.

If you are connecting the dots between these interludes, which I hope you are, you may have spotted a connection. Our description of how LLM next token prediction both retrieves world knowledge and also makes predictions about what follows aligns with the description of world models we have given here. However, knowledge grows with time, and new knowledge and facts become part of

---

[2]A knowledge base is in many ways indistinguishable from a memory store.

memory. Today's LLMs fulfill *part of* the role of world model but do not account for new learned knowledge of agents and how that knowledge gets incorporated into memory and then into future predictions.

Perception, Memory, World Models & Situational Awareness in the Loop

We now have two useful interludes under our belts. Take a moment and look back at the difference engine in Figure 18.2. You will see that a couple of things are missing, namely memory and a unified world model for the agent. In fact, the agent's goals are part of its knowledge, so we need to be clear about where the full world model (including newly acquired knowledge and memories) will reside. This is a serious issue. Particularly given the goal to build highly specialized agents with deep domain knowledge, we cannot treat LLMs as our exclusive world model, we will need external knowledge and memory to complement world knowledge found in the LLMs. We introduce these issues here, and in Chapter 21 we provide greater depth on memory architectures for our agents.

Another issue we have glossed over is how perception, memory, and world state estimation work together. We have not placed enough emphasis on how nuanced world state estimation actually is. To aid our understanding, let's look at the very first determination the agent has to make. In fact, it's one the agent has to make repeatedly again and again as it moves through the environment. We will call the task "situation assessment," to distinguish it from raw perception, and we will call the result our agent's "situational awareness."

For the moment, let's not worry exactly about what data or information is contained in situational awareness, nor how the agent uses it. We will consider those issues in detail in the next chapter. Let's simply agree for now that agents *need to know what situation they are in*, as it profoundly affects the priority of different goals and actions at that moment. Again, think of an organism facing danger versus opportunity. In the difference engine, we can think of situational awareness as something that happens in the world state estimation box, after raw perception.

To make this assessment the agent must perceive, recall, and reason, and it must do so quite rapidly.[3] Neuroscience also informs us that *much of perception involves memory*. We do not, in fact, take in every detail of the world through raw perception. Rather, we scan the world selectively and our memory (our pre-existing model of the world) fills in details, helping us make judgments about what will happen next. Agents, therefore, must have a *world model* to do even this first task of situational assessment, and this need extends to all future reasoning where the agent has to estimate the causal effects of actions on the world, to reduce the gaps between the current situation and its goals.

Some of the agent's knowledge and memory about the world is baked into the weights of the LLMs we are using for reasoning, but other knowledge and memories must be stored externally. The process of estimating the state of the world involves judgments against *all* of what makes up the world model of the agent, regardless of whether it is in the LLM, or stored externally.

Moreover, the agent's *full* world model must be accessible at every point of the agent meta loop. Not only is it required for reasoning, but it must record the changes that the agent creates in the world through action as it pursues goals. It must also reflect new knowledge, new understanding of cause and effect, and new skills the agent learns at any point. How we retrieve from memory and assemble each call to an LLM is therefore a central question. The need for precision in this area has recently been dubbed "context engineering" and is essential to harness the statistical predictions

---

[3]This is Kahneman System 1 thinking, as we discussed in Chapter 15.

today's large models enable.

Working Memory, Context Engineering & the Battle Ahead

Perception, memory, external knowledge, and results of actions all collide in the agent's working memory. We will distinguish the working memory of your agent from the context window of the LLMs you are using, though many books and papers conflate them, or say that they are one and the same. The reason the distinction is critical is because each call to an LLM only needs access to a subset of this information. The whole rapidly emerging art and science of context engineering is about crafting what pieces you put into the call to the LLM and what parts you leave out.

We will look at this in greater detail in Chapter 21 when we look at memory, external knowledge and context engineering. There we will examine in detail how to determine what bits you pull from where into actual LLM calls. For now, recognize that while context is finite and every component competes for space, appropriate retrieval of memories may be needed at any time to help make judgments about world state. Memory architecture and context engineering will be vital for loading and unloading this information as the agent moves through a messy evolving environment.

Multiple Loops, Multiple Models & a Warning

The architectural vision for robust, profitable, capable, specialized agents *is one of many loops*, each calling different models or logic, some specialized and tuned for cost, latency, and accuracy. It's not the single loop caricature we discussed earlier: a prompt, a handful of tools, and calls to a single LLM for large chunks of its operation. Many big model vendors encourage API calls to extremely long-running agentic processes *that run as a black box on the model provider's system*. These may involve agentic behavior including tool use, planning and task management. Use these during prototyping, or sparingly in your full agent architecture, and only if you are sure the capability is horizontal and not core to your business.

That being said, we add a warning here: be wary of calling foundation model APIs for long-running tasks that involve multiple sub-tasks, especially if it is to solve a core specialized problem in your domain. A common theme in this part of the book is that breaking things down into smaller pieces pays big rewards. It is also essential if you are solving deeper problems in your domain. This will apply to models, loops, context-engineering, LLM calls, and memory access. If your agent is a very thin wrapper around long-running calls to foundation models that do most of the work, your agent may be very easily replaced. Next up, we will look at how goals and learning work in the agent meta loop, but first a brief note.

A Note on Level of Detail in Algorithms & Data Structures

One important point I want to make clear before we get into agent goals and learning is that the algorithms and data structures presented in this and the following chapters are *not* intended to be something you can implement directly. They all would be much more complicated in the real-world to account for edge cases and domain complexity. The goal here is to provide clarity on how pieces fit together, and sufficient detail on specific processes to illustrate what you need to think about as a builder. Please keep in mind, the algorithms are also *purely logical.* Just because one looks procedural, or seems to imply hard-coded logic, does not mean the implementation cannot be a neural network or some other approach altogether.

End Goals, Instrumental Goals & the Goal Stack

The difference engine operates on goals, but not all goals are created equal. As we discussed in Chapter 14, in human psychology, goals are divided into end goals and instrumental goals. End goals are pursued for their own sake: health, happiness, meaning. Instrumental goals are steps toward those larger ends: career milestones, savings targets, relationship building.

Autonomous agents require goals to be structured. End goals define the agent's core purpose. They should be considered immutable and constitutional. Instrumental goals represent active pursuit of subgoals that serve the end goals. These can be suspended, reordered, or abandoned as circumstances change. Below instrumental goals sit subgoals, the granular tasks that emerge from decomposing larger objectives.

This hierarchy must be implemented in your agent in data structures. Details will vary in your implementation, but the goal stack is the record of what the agent is trying to achieve at every level of abstraction. As noted, the following is meant to be illustrative not complete. In real implementations you will need considerable detail around how to specify end goals as prompts to your agent, and how to know which tasks even relate to which end goals. Task completion requires extensive breakdown into subtasks, and you will need to track state, dependencies, priorities, blocking conditions, and much more.

```
Goals Overview (/show_goals –all)


@ /show_goals --all

END GOALS
   - maximize customer satisfaction
   - continuously improve capabilities
```

```
    - build proprietary domain expertise

TASK GOALS (foreground)
    - resolve tickets
    - answer queries
    - execute workflows

META-LEARNING GOALS (background or dream)
    - learn faster
    - reduce errors
    - master new abstractions

DATA GOALS (background or dream)
    - enrich data
    - abstract patterns
    - distill insights
```

The goal stack is not static. It evolves as the agent works. Consider this sequence:

Goal Stack Trace (T=0..2)

```
Time T=0  (start instrumental goal)
  END GOAL: Maximize customer satisfaction (priority:
    10)
  |- INSTRUMENTAL: Resolve ticket #1234 (priority: 8)
    |- SUB-GOAL: Retrieve customer history [ACTIVE]
    |- SUB-GOAL: Check refund policy

  ACTION: customer_db.get_history(1234)

Time T=1  (blocking condition discovered: auth expired
    )
```

```
END GOAL: Maximize customer satisfaction (priority:
  10)
|- INSTRUMENTAL: Resolve ticket #1234 [BLOCKED]
|  |- SUB-GOAL: Retrieve customer history [BLOCKED]
|- INSTRUMENTAL: Refresh authentication (priority:
  9) [NEW]
    |- SUB-GOAL: auth.refresh_token() [ACTIVE]


ACTION: auth.refresh_token()


Time T=2  (auth refreshed, resume original goal)
  END GOAL: Maximize customer satisfaction (priority:
    10)
  |- INSTRUMENTAL: Resolve ticket #1234 [ACTIVE]
  |  |- SUB-GOAL: Retrieve customer history [ACTIVE]
  |- INSTRUMENTAL: Refresh authentication [COMPLETED]


  ACTION: retry customer_db.get_history(1234)
```

The stack is hierarchical, dynamic, and responsive. Goals track dependencies through blocking conditions. New urgent goals can interrupt current work. Priority, which derives from our earlier discussion of situational awareness, drives action selection. You will need to carefully track state to enable difference calculation after each action the agent takes.

Background Learning & Meta-Learning

Task completion is only part of the puzzle. An agent that merely completes its work, without improving its skills and knowledge will fall behind. Recall from Chapter 10 that agents must engage in both background continuous learning about their job and domain as well as continuous meta-learning, learning to learn more effectively. Domain learning and meta-learning also need to

be explicitly part of the goals stack as they will compete for priority
and consume part of the agent's token budget.

```
Learning Goals (/show_goals –learn)


@ /show_goals --learn
[meta_1] improve response time | metric:
    avg_response_seconds 45.0 -> 30.0 | status: active
[meta_2] learn new abstractions | metric:
    novel_concepts_mastered 0 -> 10 | status: queued
[meta_3] reduce hallucination   | metric:
    factual_error_rate 0.08 -> 0.02 | status: active
[meta_4] build proprietary data | metric:
    unique_patterns_identified 45 -> 200 | status:
    queued
```

Task goals and meta-goals operate concurrently but likely with
different priorities and budgets depending upon the overall situational context. Task goals dominate the token budget when the
agent is directly serving customers. Meta-goals dominate in what
we have metaphorically termed the "dream" (or background cogitation) state when the agent reflects, consolidates, and improves.
Both serve the same end goals, but through different mechanisms,
and with different budgets.

Tools: the Agent's Actuators

Goals and difference calculation tell an agent what needs to
change. Tools enable the agent to actually change it. Recall the
explosion in tool use capabilities we discussed in Chapter 13. Tools
are how agents take action in the environment. For autonomous
agents, tool use is foundational.

The agent perceives the environment through sensors, estimates
the world state, calculates the difference from its goal, and selects

---

Algorithm 18.1: Meta-Learning Loop (Dream-State Learning Cycle)

During dream state, refresh and prioritize learning goals, run small experiments by gathering data and training or distilling skills, evaluate against policy thresholds, and commit successful capabilities while updating shared knowledge; otherwise iterate or deprioritize.

Input: Learning goals L; policies P; tools T; memories M; compute budget C
Output: Updated capabilities; enriched shared knowledge

1   $L \leftarrow$ RefreshLearningBacklog(M, KPIs)
2   $L \leftarrow$ PrioritizeLearningGoals(L)
3   **foreach** $g \in Top(L, C)$ **do**
4      $exp \leftarrow$ DefineExperiments(g)
5      $D \leftarrow$ GatherData(g, T, M)
6      $model \leftarrow$ TrainOrDistill(g, D)
7      $metrics \leftarrow$ Evaluate($g, model, exp$)
8   **if** $PassThreshold(metrics, P)$ **then**
9   CommitSkill(g, model); RegisterCapability(g); PinArtifacts()
10   UpdateSharedKnowledge(g, M)
11   **end**
12   **else**
13   IterateOrDeprioritize(g)
14   **end**
15 **end**
16 ScheduleNextDreamWindow(); UpdateLearningMetrics()

---

an action, typically a tool. This means that agents have to have a fairly in-depth understanding of the effect of each tool on the state of the world, and thereby on their goals. Initially this may seem like an almost intractable problem. The secret is that agents need to know how to break down tasks until the available tools truly match the granularity of the task at hand. This is not easy. Many tool and planning implementations are too naive, and do not account for the interplay between tools, planning, and the broader effect on the environment.

Let's consider how an agent handles a straightforward goal: retrieve customer purchase history.

```
Tool Invocation Trace (illustrative)


[Decision]  need info not in context -> external data
    required
[Selection] tool = customer_db.get_orders (not email,
    not web_search)
[Formatting] {"tool": "customer_db", "function": "
    get_orders",
             "params": {"customer_id": 1234, "
    date_range": "last_90_days"}}
[Execution] sandboxed call with 30-second timeout
[Result]    3 orders returned; added to context
[Next]      proceed with enriched context
```

Additionally, tool discovery and metadata are often overlooked in MVP and demo implementations. Such metadata should include purpose, reliability characteristics, cost implications, and authorization requirements. Agents need to know not just how to call a tool, but when to call it, why to call it, and what the expected effect on the world state (and their goals) will be. This requires that much richer tool descriptions be accessible to the agent. As tool descriptions must be passed in the LLM's context window, a key challenge is the context engineering to manage this extra information.

Thus far we are discussing pre-defined tools. The agent selects the appropriate tool, handles errors, retries, and sequences or parallelizes calls. In Chapter 20, we examine tools in much greater detail, including tool forming, where agents create new tools dynamically through code generation to adapt to novel situations, and calling subagents and workflows as specialized tools.

Putting It All Together: The Complete Agentic Loop

We've put a lot on the table to digest in this chapter. Let's try to look at everything together in one place. The pseudocode in Algorithm 18.2 (on the next page) provides a unified description of the agent meta loop. Some detail is sacrificed to try to capture the essential elements.

In the next three chapters, we will go into key processes in the meta loop in much greater depth. As a first exercise in the next chapter, we flesh out the topic of situational awareness which we briefly introduced earlier. We examine how the agent can continually perceive, recall, and reason to know what situation it is in. After that, we turn to tools, reasoning and protocols to understand how they work, and how to apply them. Chapter 21 will complete our focus on agent architecture by looking at the critical topic of context engineering, and how it must work closely with memory and knowledge storage and retrieval.

⌣

(Algorithm 18.2 is on the next page.)

Algorithm 18.2: High Level Holistic Agentic Meta Loop

Input: End goals E; policies P; tools T; subagents A; memories M; budget B

Output: Continuous progress toward E;

---

1 **while** *agent is active* **do**
2 $\quad$ $X \leftarrow$ PerceiveEnvironment()
3 $\quad$ $S \leftarrow$ UpdateSituationalAwareness(X)
4 $\quad$ $G \leftarrow$ PrioritizeGoalsBasedOnSituation(E, S)
5 $\quad$ $\Delta \leftarrow$ CalculateDifference(G, S)
6 $\quad$ $g \leftarrow$ SelectNextAction()
7 $\quad$ $plan \leftarrow$ ReasonAndPlan(g, S)
8 $\quad$ **if** Δ *indicates missing information* **then**
9 $\quad\quad$ $u \leftarrow$ SelectToolOrSubagent(T, A, g, S)
10 $\quad\quad$ **if** u *is* tool **then**
11 $\quad\quad\quad$ $r \leftarrow$ InvokeTool(u, params(g), limits(S))
12 $\quad\quad$ **end**
13 $\quad\quad$ **else**
14 $\quad\quad\quad$ $r \leftarrow$ Delegate(u, g, S);
15 $\quad\quad$ **end**
16 $\quad\quad$ IntegrateIntoContext(r, B)
17 $\quad$ **end**
18 $\quad$ $a \leftarrow$ ChooseAction($plan, S$)
19 $\quad$ $ok \leftarrow$ Execute(a)
20 $\quad$ EmitTrace(g, a, ok)
21 $\quad$ **if** *policy in P requires approval or rollback* **then**
22 $\quad\quad$ EscalateOrRevert()
23 $\quad$ **end**
24 $\quad$ UpdateMemory(g, a, ok)
25 $\quad$ **if** ok **then**
26 $\quad\quad$ MarkSubgoalComplete(g)
27 $\quad$ **end**
28 $\quad$ **if** *SleepWindowReached() or BatchThreshold(M)* **then**
29 $\quad\quad$ $signals \leftarrow$ AggregateAndDeidentify(M)
30 $\quad\quad$ BuildAndUpdateStrategiesAndKnowledge($shared$)
31 $\quad$ **end**
32 **end**

Chapter 19

Agent Situational Awareness: Harness Hallucinations

Takeaways: Hallucinations are both a core strength and deficiency of today's foundation models, brought about directly by the RLHF training that makes them useful. Given the essential role of imagination and counterfactual thinking in human-like problem solving, building "situational awareness" into agents is essential to create agents that can be factual when they need to be, and creative when appropriate. This chapter shows how situational awareness can work in production agents. This includes context sensing, risk assessment, mode selection, validation strategies, and practical techniques for managing the creativity vs. rigor trade-off.

T HINK ABOUT situational awareness in the natural world. Survival itself hinges on it. Whether predator or prey, facing danger or opportunity, rapid System 1 recognition of a situation can decide your fate. In Chapter 18, we established that situational awareness is a core component of the continuous agentic loop, part of the "world state estimate" the agent makes from raw perception. Proper situational awareness is also one of the *most completely overlooked aspects* of agent design today. Most agents today are very task-focused, prompted by a human to execute narrowly defined goals. To move beyond this, toward agents with initiative and autonomy, situational awareness is essential.

You can think of situational awareness as the first decision the agent must make. What kind of situation am I in? The answer

immediately reprioritizes goals, thereby constraining what range
of thoughts or actions should even be considered. A financial filing demands rigorous fact-checking and full citation. A marketing
brainstorming session rewards wild ideas and unexpected connections.[1]

This chapter walks through a *logical* architecture for situational
awareness. We model it as a series of discrete "modes" that your
agent can operate in, but that is just to make the ideas concrete.
You could choose to implement it with neural networks. We cover
context sensors, risk assessment, creativity budgets, mode selection,
validation strategies, and domain-specific patterns. We also look at
recent research on hallucination management, and end with guidance for integrating situational awareness into production agents.

The Hallucination Paradox:
Why Situational Awareness Matters

By now virtually everyone knows that today's AI models can
hallucinate. They sometimes fill in gaps in what they know with
other concepts and pseudo-facts that are statistically plausible given
the context of the user prompt. This is a root feature of today's
large foundation models. As we discussed in Chapter 12, the training of these models leverages Reinforcement Learning with Human
Feedback or RLHF. RLHF gives the model positive reinforcement
for appearing more helpful and giving humans answers that they
prefer, independently of whether the output is factually correct.
Multiple studies have shown that this form of post-training, which
is essential to making models useful, also lies at the heart of their
tendency to hallucinate in very plausible ways.

This behavior is core to what makes today's large foundation
models both human-like and useful. Counterfactual reasoning and

---

[1]Ok, I admit marketing meetings are less dramatic than a gazelle spotting
a lion on the Serengeti, but the principle is the same.

imagination are essential human skills as well. Hallucinations are what make LLMs good at many tasks we care about. They can be asked to invent wild imaginary stories, or adopt the personas of historical figures, or think about cyberattacks from hackers. The models are in fact masterful at inventing, creating text, images, and video that are accurate *statistically*.

> *"Imagination is more important than knowledge. Knowledge is limited. Imagination encircles the world."*
>
> — *Albert Einstein, 1929*

Of course, the video and text on the internet that humans create is often wonderful fiction. Foundation models have become well-trained on human fictions. They share our ability to imagine counterfactual worlds. This ability to create, unconstrained by realism, supports their amazing power to assist us in creative tasks.[2]

It is quite clear that in many industries, control and accuracy are frequently paramount. Mistakes where an agent hallucinates an answer may have severe consequences. This, in turn, means serious business impact to the company supplying that agent. For an agent, knowing they are in this type of situation is critical so that factuality, accuracy, and clarity of information get priority. This also includes adherence to policies, procedures, and regulations specific to a company and industry.

It is equally clear that in many roles in many industries, creativity and the ability to brainstorm are vital characteristics we look for in our human coworkers. The ability to imagine and talk about counterfactual scenarios that can only be imagined lies at the heart of many roles, ranging from design to marketing to software test-

---

[2]We will be referring to some anti-hallucination methods like CoVe and Self-CheckGPT in the diagrams and algorithms in this chapter. These are described in the research box at the end of the chapter. You can skip ahead if you like, or you can simply think of them as black-box verification methods for now.

ing to risk, fraud, and information security. If you cannot imagine things that may not have happened before, you cannot really prepare for them. So we *do not* want to eliminate this ability in our agents. Humans in fact hallucinate all the time in their pursuit of novel solutions. We call it creativity. Figure 19.1 provides a simple model for thinking about this trade-off.

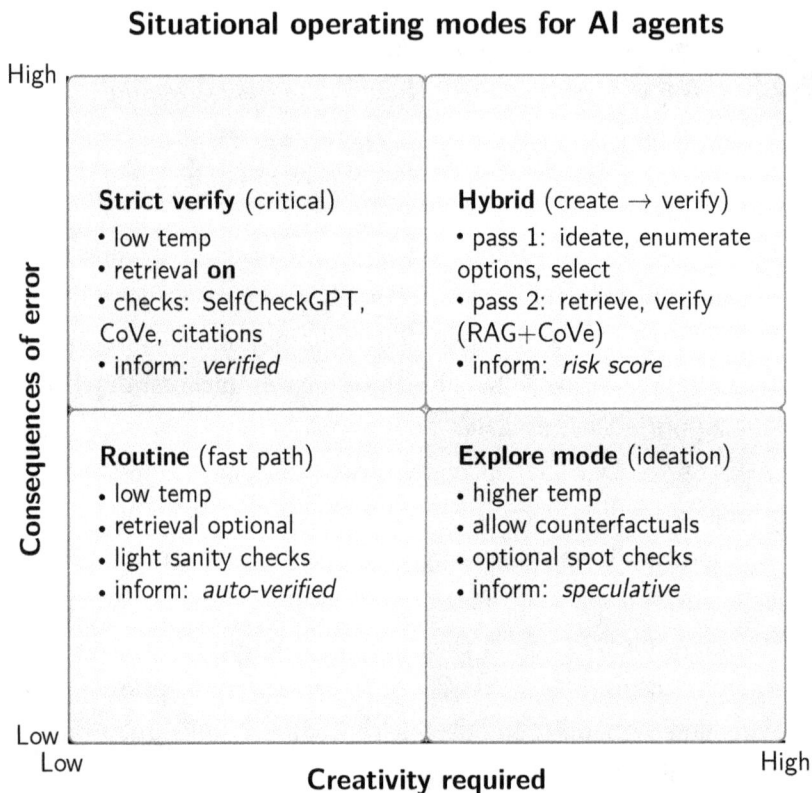

Situational operating modes for AI agents

	Strict verify (critical)	**Hybrid** (create → verify)
	• low temp	• pass 1: ideate, enumerate options, select
	• retrieval **on**	• pass 2: retrieve, verify (RAG+CoVe)
	• checks: SelfCheckGPT, CoVe, citations	• inform: *risk score*
	• inform: *verified*	
	Routine (fast path)	**Explore mode** (ideation)
	• low temp	• higher temp
	• retrieval optional	• allow counterfactuals
	• light sanity checks	• optional spot checks
	• inform: *auto-verified*	• inform: *speculative*

Consequences of error (vertical axis: High to Low)
Creativity required (horizontal axis: Low to High)

Figure 19.1: Agent Situational Awareness: choose operating mode by *creativity required* and *consequences of error*.

At present there are no silver bullets for how to control for and train for positive creativity while eliminating harmful use of false facts by agents. This will be one of the important areas for everyone on the product team to become proficient in. The rest of this chapter provides implementation patterns and techniques. Keep in mind this is an ongoing area of AI research. By the time you read this there will be new studies, new techniques, new software libraries, and new models all seeking to address this trade-off.

System Architecture: Implementing Situational Awareness

Situational awareness sits between perception and decision in the agent loop. The agent observes its environment, then assesses what kind of situation it faces before selecting an action. This assessment shapes *every* downstream decision.

This is again not meant to be rigid, but in logical terms, and for illustration, we will decompose the situational awareness system into five components. Context sensors detect what kind of situation the agent faces. Risk assessors evaluate the priority of goals, and the consequences of errors if the agent chooses the wrong action. Creativity budget calculators determine acceptable improvisation levels and temperature settings. Mode selectors choose the operating mode. Validation requirements define verification depth based on the selected mode. These may not be the perfect set of features. Consider carefully the real situations your agent is likely to face, and what factors you wish to consider.

Before the agent dispatches a thought or action, it runs a short policy loop. It reads the current context, scores the stakes, budgets creativity, chooses a mode (or sets a mode score if you do not like thinking in terms of discrete situational modes), and sets the required validation. Algorithm 19.1 illustrates an outer mode-selection loop that you can adapt to your domain and specific requirements.

Algorithm 19.1: Mode Selection via Situational Signals

This algorithm examines the situation, assesses the risk, computes a creativity budget, chooses a mode, configures validation, and notifies the user. It returns the operating context for this step.

Input: Context c, goal g
Output: Operating context OC
1 $s \leftarrow$ AnalyzeContext(c)
2 $r \leftarrow$ AssessRisk(s, g)
3 $b \leftarrow$ ComputeCreativityBudget(s, r)
4 $m \leftarrow$ SelectMode(s, r, b)
5 $v \leftarrow$ ValidationFor(m, r)
6 $notify \leftarrow$ UserMessage(m, r)
7 **return** OC(mode $= m$, temperature $=$
   b.temperature, validation $= v$, user_notification $=$
   $notify$)

Environment Sensors: Understanding the Situation

Environment sensors extract signals from the agent's environment to determine what kind of situation it faces. The range of possible signals to look at here is enormous, depending upon where your agent operates. I've chosen to use more enterprise examples in this chapter, but *similar logic with different features* will apply in any domain. We will illustrate the thinking involved via three easy to appreciate signals: domain, task type, and stakeholders. Each provides a dimension for assessing appropriate operating mode.

Domain detection identifies the field of work. Finance demands precision and audit trails. Marketing rewards creative exploration. Customer support requires empathy and policy adherence. Legal work demands citation and precedent verification. The domain sets baseline expectations for rigor versus creativity. An agent working in healthcare defaults to strict verification. An agent supporting product design defaults to a more exploratory mode. These are simplistic examples, meant to get you thinking about the problem. In all likelihood you will need a more sophisticated approach. Even within a domain, different topics are the main focus at different points in time. Just because an agent operates within finance, does not mean every topic and every situation is the same. The product team and domain experts will have to iterate on the right definitions of domain and how to measure it from the agent's environment.

Task type classification distinguishes routine from creative from critical work. Routine tasks follow established patterns with low uncertainty. These tasks benefit from fast execution with light verification. Creative tasks require imagination and exploration. Critical tasks carry high consequences if wrong, and demand maximum rigor. Tasks at the right granularity may be one of the strongest signals of the overall situation, but do keep in mind that tasks are hierarchical, and knowing the larger project, customer, or rationale for a task may be essential to scoring it.

Stakeholder analysis identifies who will see or act on the agent's output. This can be a subtle topic. Your agent may need to "know who is in the room," and possibly research where new people sit in the org chart. Some categories may help as a starting point. A team brainstorming session with internal stakeholders likely tolerates more speculative ideas. Customer-facing outputs typically require higher quality bars, and less disclosure. Direct customer communications must be accurate and helpful. C-suite or board-level outputs demand verified facts and clear reasoning. Public outputs carry reputation risk and regulatory requirements. An SEC filing requires citations and fact-checking. A press release requires brand consistency and legal review. Beyond the role or type of audience your agent is interacting with, it is important to consider the individuals. You want your agent to be sensitive over time to the personal preferences and viewpoints of stakeholders it interacts with on a regular basis.

Determining any of these factors might involve an LLM-as-a-judge call to a foundation model, or a rules-based classifier based on established policies and domain knowledge, or a proprietary ML model. Algorithm 19.2 illustrates how a context sensor produces a situation profile without prescribing a particular framework.

Algorithm 19.2: Environment Sensor: Build Situation Profile

Detect domain, task type, stakeholders, and destination from prompt, tools, utterance, and metadata, then log salient signals for audit and tuning.

Input: Context c (system prompt, tools, user utterance, goal metadata, goal stack, active tools)

Output: Situation profile $S = \langle$domain, task_type, stakeholders$\rangle$

1   S.domain $\leftarrow$ DetectDomain(c.prompt, c.tools)
2   **if** $S.domain = unknown$ **then**
3 | S.domain $\leftarrow$ ClassifyDomain(c.prompt, c.tools)
4   **end**
5   S.task_type $\leftarrow$
     DetectTaskType(c.utterance, c.goal_stack, c.tools)
6   S.stakeholders $\leftarrow$ GetStakeholders(c.goal_metadata)
7   **if** $S.stakeholders$ *is empty* **then**
8 | S.stakeholders $\leftarrow$ InferStakeholders(c)
9   **end**
10   LogSignals(c, S); **return** S

Risk Assessment: Calculating Stakes

Risk assessment evaluates the consequences of error. Not all mistakes matter equally. A hallucinated product name in a brainstorm causes no harm, but a hallucinated financial figure in an SEC filing could trigger regulatory action. We examine here an illustrative risk assessment algorithm to quantify impact across multiple dimensions: financial, regulatory, reputation, and legal. These example areas are picked for clarity and ease of illustration, but will require much more nuance in domain specialized agents.

Financial impact measures the potential for direct monetary consequences. Low impact means losses under a defined threshold, perhaps a few hundred dollars. Medium impact means thousands to tens of thousands. High impact means material losses that affect quarterly results or trigger disclosure requirements. Thresholds vary by company size and industry.

Regulatory risk assesses whether the task involves compliance obligations. Healthcare agents must comply with HIPAA. Financial agents must comply with SEC rules and SOX controls. Privacy-sensitive agents must comply with GDPR or CCPA. In your implementation, regulated tasks might automatically elevate to strict mode regardless of creativity requirements, or you could choose to convert some of these to their potential financial impact as well.

Reputation risk evaluates public perception and brand impact. Internal communications carry low reputation risk. Customer-facing communications carry medium risk if mistakes frustrate users but do not go viral. Reputation risk often correlates with output destination but adds a brand-sensitivity dimension.

Legal risk measures liability exposure. Could a mistake in this task lead to a lawsuit, breach of contract, or legal judgment? Legal risk is high for tasks involving contracts, compliance certifications, medical or legal advice, or safety-critical decisions. It is low for tasks with no legal obligations or liability pathways. Moderate legal risk applies to gray areas where mistakes might trigger customer complaints or disputes but not immediate legal action.

Algorithm 19.3 summarizes how we compute a multi-dimensional risk profile and combine it into a single score used downstream by mode selection and validation.

Algorithm 19.3: Risk Assessment: Compute Risk Profile
and Score

---

*Evaluate financial, regulatory, reputation, and legal risks with
product-defined thresholds, then compose a capped combined
score used by downstream mode selection and validation.*

Input: Situation s, goal g, config C (thresholds, regulated
domains, public destinations)
Output: Risk profile R with dimensions (financial,
regulatory, reputation, legal) and
$R.\texttt{combined\_risk\_score} \in [0, 1]$

1 $R.\texttt{financial} \leftarrow$
   $\texttt{AssessFinancial}(s, g, C.\texttt{financial\_thresholds})$
2 $R.\texttt{regulatory} \leftarrow$
   $\texttt{CheckRegulatory}(s, g, C.\texttt{regulated\_domains})$
3 $R.\texttt{reputation} \leftarrow$
   $\texttt{AssessReputation}(s, C.\texttt{public\_destinations})$
4 $R.\texttt{legal} \leftarrow \texttt{AssessLegal}(s, g)$
5 $R.\texttt{combined\_risk\_score} \leftarrow \texttt{WeightAndCap}(R)$
6 **return** R

Creativity Budget: Balancing Freedom & Control

The creativity budget determines how much improvisation the
agent can apply to the current task. Risk and context constrain
the budget. Some situations demand strict adherence to verified
facts and proven procedures. Others benefit from speculative thinking and novel approaches. The challenge is translating situational
assessment into actionable guidance for the generation process.

In modern agent architectures, this translation often takes the
form of structured prompts or instructions that govern the next reasoning or generation step. Rather than hardcoding specific parameter values, the system synthesizes risk profile and task requirements
into contextual guidance. This guidance might specify whether to
prioritize accuracy over novelty, whether speculation is acceptable,

which claims require citation, and whether to favor established patterns or explore alternatives.

Algorithm 19.4 illustrates how an agent might translate risk and context into structured creativity guidance. The algorithm is intentionally abstract. Real implementations will be highly domain-specific, incorporating industry regulations, company policies, user preferences, and learned patterns from historical performance. The key insight is that creativity constraints should emerge from situational understanding, not from fixed rules.

Algorithm 19.4: Compute Creativity Budget

Synthesize risk profile and situational context into structured prompt guidance that governs how much creative freedom the next generation step should have.

Input: Situation s, risk profile R
Output: Creativity guidance prompts P
1 $P \leftarrow$ EmptyPromptSet()
2 $risk\_level \leftarrow$
    InterpretRisk($R.risk\_score, R.financial, R.reputation$)

3 $task\_risk \leftarrow$
    AnalyzeTask($s.task\_type, s.user\_intent, s.domain$)
4 $P.freedom\_level \leftarrow$
    GenGuidance($risk\_level, task\_risk, accuracy$)
5 $P.exploration\_guidance \leftarrow$
    GenGuidance($risk\_level, task\_risk, explore$)
6 $P.acceptable\_deviation \leftarrow$
    GenGuidance($risk\_level, task\_risk, citations$)
7 **return** P

Product teams must decide how creativity guidance maps to their specific domain and risk landscape. The appropriate balance between accuracy and improvisation depends on industry regulations, user expectations, available verification mechanisms, and the consequences of errors. Teams should instrument generation pat-

terns, validation outcomes, and user satisfaction metrics to refine
their creativity guidance strategies over time. What works for one
domain rarely transfers directly to another.

Validation Strategies by Mode

Once the situation is assessed and risk and creativity decisions
are made, Algorithm 19.1 can run, and a mode will be selected.
Again, we're illustrating with the idea of a discrete set of modes
that define the agent's situation as categories for easy interpretability and control. Each operating mode can now require different validation strategies. As an example, routine mode can use lightweight
checks. Explore mode probably validates minimally, whereas strict
mode can apply maximal verification. Algorithm 19.5 shows how
a validation strategy might be selected for each.

Validation adds latency and cost. Strict mode could end up
being 5 to 10 times slower and many times more expensive than
routine mode due to multiple verification passes. Product teams
must balance thoroughness against user experience and domain
requirements. Some agents run validation asynchronously, returning initial output quickly and updating with verification status as
checks complete. Other agents block until validation finishes, ensuring users never see unverified output in strict mode. The choice
will depend upon your domain and the specific roles of your agent.

An Essential Look at Hallucination Research

You have learned by now that I sometimes position these research sections as optional, but I highly recommend that the whole
team invest regularly in staying fresh on research and improvements around hallucination and creativity, and more centrally on
true situational awareness.

In following the research over the past several years, I've seen
hallucination management moving from static post-hoc filtering to-

---

Algorithm 19.5: Validation Strategy by Mode

Choose validation settings per mode: retrieval on/off, verification methods to run, citation requirements, and confidence threshold. Hybrid runs explore, then strict verify.

Input: Mode
  $m \in \{\texttt{routine}, \texttt{explore}, \texttt{strict\_verify}, \texttt{hybrid}\}$,
  risk profile R
Output: Validation config V

1 **if** $m = \textit{routine}$ **then**
2     $V \leftarrow \{$retrieval $:$ off, methods $:$ [], format $:$ on, consistency $:$ on, policy $:$ on, citations $:$ off, $\tau :$ 0.7$\}$
3 **end**
4 **else if** $m = \textit{explore}$ **then**
5     $V \leftarrow \{$retrieval $:$ off, methods $:$ [], coherence $:$ on, policy $:$ off, citations $:$ off, $\tau :$ 0.3$\}$
6 **end**
7 **else if** $m = \textit{strict\_verify}$ **then**
8     $V \leftarrow \{$retrieval $:$ on, methods $:$ [$\texttt{CoVe}, \texttt{SelfCheckGPT}, \texttt{SAFE}$], format $:$ on, consistency $:$ on, policy $:$ on, citations $:$ on, $\tau :$ 0.95$\}$
9 **end**
10 **else**
11     $V \leftarrow \{$multi_pass $:$ true, pass_1 $:$ explore, pass_2 $:$ strict_verify, methods $:$ [$\texttt{CoVe}, \texttt{SelfCheckGPT}$], $\tau :$ 0.85$\}$
12 **end**
13 **return** V

---

ward dynamic, multi-layered control. Self-consistency checks, retrieval grounding, reward-model tweaks, and streaming verifiers address failure modes that are complementary yet subtly overlapping. These techniques can form a defense-in-depth strategy against harmful hallucinations, but engineering is required to dial in these techniques to avoid overly shackling the model. While we are seeing real improvement in hallucination reduction, techniques are less mature for modeling real situational awareness in agents. My sense is the boundary and state of the art will be pushed for some time to come, and that means there is plenty of room for advanced teams to innovate.

Research Focus: Recent Techniques for Hallucination Management

For humans, spotting hallucinations can be enormously challenging. I have personally been blown away on multiple occasions upon learning that an elaborate "fact" given to me by GROK 4.1, Gemini 3.0 or Claude Opus 4.5 turned out to be pure horse manure. Equally, when I am in areas where I have prior knowledge, I can spot falsehoods quickly. I am reminded every day how gullible humans are when statements sound authoritative and well-articulated.

For teams building AI agents, it will be critical to find the right situational awareness and checks to support counterfactual reasoning and imagination, but also accuracy and factuality. A wave of research over the last two years seeks the middle ground, designing methods that spot or prevent factual errors while leaving room for productive speculation.

SelfCheckGPT

One of the simplest but still most revealing approaches was put forth by Cambridge researchers in late 2023. Dubbed SelfCheckGPT, instead of consulting external knowledge, the technique prompts the model to listen to itself. Researchers ask the same question dozens of times, then measure how sharply the answers diverge. Consistent claims signal genuine stored knowledge; contradictions are hallmarks of fabrication. Across biography and encyclopedic-style tasks, SelfCheckGPT was able to identify false sentences considerably more accurately than probability-based or database-driven baselines, and it requires no privileged access to the model's internals.

Chain-of-Verification

Another innovative technique known as Chain-of-Verification (CoVe) was developed by Meta AI in late 2023. CoVe prompts the model to write a first-draft answer, then to draft its own fact-checking questions, answer them independently, and finally revise the original text in light of any discrepancies. Because the verification phase is isolated from the draft, the system avoids the temptation to rationalize mistakes. The authors report pronounced drops in hallucination on list questions, closed-book reading-comprehension tasks, and free-form essays without significant loss of fluency.

A complementary line of work grounds the model in external evidence before it starts writing. A 2024 report from a team at ServiceNow on retrieval-augmented generation for structured outputs connected the decoder to a live document store, so every intermediate step can cite a source. In one case the technique halved the rate of incorrect API parameters.

Factuality-Aware Alignment

Training and fine-tuning methods are evolving as well. A study by Meta AI, Carnegie Mellon, and University of Waterloo researchers with the creative name of FLAME (short for Factuality-Aware Alignment for Large Language Models) modifies the standard reinforcement-learning-from-human-feedback or RLHF pipeline so that the reward model explicitly down-weights factual errors while still positively scoring style and helpfulness. When benchmarked on open-ended writing prompts, FLAME reduced hallucinations by roughly half compared with vanilla RLHF, yet independent judges continued to rate its answers as imaginative and engaging.

Search-Augmented Factuality Evaluator

Google DeepMind's SAFE (Search-Augmented Factuality Evaluator) turns fact-checking into an agentic sub-task. It breaks a long answer into atomic claims, runs focused web searches for each, and decides whether the evidence supports or contradicts the claim. Across sixteen thousand facts, SAFE agreed with human annotators three-quarters of the time and cost less than five percent as much as previous state-of-the-art techniques. Cost-effective results like this start to make continuous verification economically plausible.

Streaming Verification

Still other techniques have focused on checking for errors right as an LLM model produces its output in response to a real user. Researchers at the Korean Advanced Institute of Science and Technology (KAIST) demonstrated real-time verification and refinement that operates token-by-token while the model is still generating. If the stream contains an implausible date or contradiction, a lightweight checker flags the issue, prompting the decoder to patch the text before the user ever sees the error. Early results showed a thirty-five-percent reduction in live hallucinations with negligible latency overhead, suggesting the possibility of highly cost-effective safeguards for everyday chatbots and planning agents.

Controlled Creativity

A paper from the Chinese Academy of Sciences, "A Survey on Large Language Model Hallucination via a Creativity Perspective," argues looser factual constraints can enhance divergent thinking, especially in story generation and design ideation. The authors call for "dial-a-rigor" controls so users can toggle between grounded exposition and speculative brainstorming. Meanwhile, the CS4 benchmark developed at the University of Massachusetts at Amherst quantifies the trade-off via prompts that progressively tighten accuracy rules. Models such as LLaMA-2 maintain narrative color until the strictest tier, whereas others sacrifice style sooner, giving practitioners a yardstick for choosing the right model for the right task.

Broader Uses of Situational Awareness

To make things concrete, we have largely focused on situational awareness as a means to govern the degree of creativity versus rigor in an agent's decision-making. But situational awareness is a much broader concept, and one you may put to use in very different ways in your agent. Regardless of whether the specific trade-offs we have discussed here are central in your domain, your agent will almost certainly have to continually assess its situation. Even at the micro level of knowing who is in the same meeting, or which projects are still active, or what priorities have changed at the customer, your agent will need a way to maintain awareness. If you like, think of situational awareness as your agent keeping up with what's going on, and forming a general opinion of what is important around it. We turn next to what an agent does *after* it has assessed its surroundings, and it needs to solve concrete problems to reach its goals.

Chapter 20

Tools, Tuning, Reasoning & Protocols

Takeaways: Tools allow agents to take action to shrink the gap between the observed world state and the agent's goals. This chapter shows how tool use works under the hood, from protocol-level communication through execution and result integration. The Model Context Protocol (MCP) can ease tool discovery and invocation, but requires caution to avoid context bloat. Beyond using predefined tools, agents can learn to form new tools through code generation. Fine-tuning and reinforcement learning enable specialized domain skills to be learned using small, fast, low-cost models. In addition, modern LLMs support deeper "reasoning" via API parameters or dedicated model versions. Agents can use these so-called "thinking models" but also may employ techniques like Monte Carlo Tree Search (MCTS) to force additional exploration at inference time. Increasingly, agents will also delegate horizontal tasks to subagents through standardized protocols like the Agent-to-Agent Protocol (A2A). Teams need to know when and how to apply each of these techniques to build robust, specialized agents.

A GENTS NEED TO ACT in the world. Chapter 18 established tools as the mechanism that bridges reasoning to action. Without tools, an agent can only think and speak. With tools, an agent can query databases, search the web, send emails, read files, and execute the thousands of functions that make software useful.

Simply making tools available is not enough. Agents must learn which domain-specific tools to use when, how to sequence tool calls for complex tasks, and what to do when tools fail. Like human specialists, they may need to create new highly specialized tools in software when existing ones prove insufficient. They must develop deeper domain-specific reasoning about plans, goals, the effects of tools and other actions to achieve those goals, and how to recover if they get off track. And they must improve these capabilities over time.

First, some history. OpenAI introduced function calling in 2023, allowing models to request structured tool invocations. Every major platform then built its own variant with different JSON formats and calling conventions. This fragmentation made cross-platform agent development painful. We will not cover these legacy approaches here. Instead, we focus on the Model Context Protocol (MCP), an open standard released by Anthropic in late 2024.

MCP eases how agents discover and invoke tools, but MCP has started to lead to a phenomenon called "tool bloat" where agents connect to multiple MCP servers and pull in so many tool descriptions they degrade performance of the agent. Tool bloat is a form of *context bloat* which Anthropic has acknowledged and which we will discuss more in Chapter 21, where we look at the relationship between memory and context engineering. There we lay out strategies to mitigate tool bloat. Next up, we focus on how MCP works.

The Model Context Protocol:
Easing the Burden of Tool Calling

Chapter 18 showed tools in the context of the agentic loop. The agent calculates what needs to change, selects a tool, executes it, and integrates the result. That conceptual flow maps to a precise protocol exchange involving three actors: the language model, your agent (the MCP client), and the MCP server that exposes tools.

The Three Actors: The language model (LLM) generates

reasoning and decides when it needs a tool. Your agent acts as the MCP client. It sends prompts to the LLM, intercepts tool requests from the LLM's responses, and manages the protocol exchange with MCP servers. MCP servers expose tools. A server might provide customer database access, GitHub repository operations, or filesystem utilities. The server validates requests, executes tools, and returns results.

The critical distinction: the LLM never calls tools directly. Your agent intercepts tool calls indicated in the LLM's response and translates them into MCP protocol requests. The MCP server executes the tool. Your agent receives the result and adds it to context for the LLM's next reasoning step. This separation enables security, validation, and reliable error handling.

Step 1: Tool Discovery: When your agent starts, it connects to configured MCP servers and sends a `tools/list` request. The MCP server responds with available tools in MCP's standard format.

MCP Tool Definition: get_customer_orders

```
{
  "name": "get_customer_orders",
  "title": "Get Customer Order History",
  "description": "Retrieves complete order history for
    a specific customer. Use this when a customer
    inquires about past purchases, when verifying
    refund eligibility, when investigating billing
    disputes, or when analyzing purchase patterns to
    make personalized recommendations. Returns
    structured order data including items, dates,
    amounts, and status.",
  "inputSchema": {
    "type": "object",
```

```
    "properties": {
      "customer_id": {
        "type": "integer",
        "description": "Unique customer identifier"
      },
      "date_range": {
        "type": "string",
        "enum": ["last_30_days", "last_90_days",
                 "last_year", "all"],
        "description": "Time period for orders"
      },
      "include_canceled": {
        "type": "boolean",
        "default": false,
        "description": "Whether to include canceled
    orders in results"
      }
    },
    "required": ["customer_id"]
  }
}
```

Your agent adds these tool definitions to the system prompt or context window before invoking the LLM. The LLM sees available tools, their purposes, and parameter schemas. The description field guides the LLM on when and why to use each tool. Including few-shot examples in the system prompt can further improve tool selection accuracy.

Step 2: LLM Tool Request: Your agent sends a prompt to the LLM that includes the particular task your agent is working on. Included within the context window are available tool definitions. The LLM reasons about the task and decides it needs customer order data. The LLM generates a response indicating it wants to use the `get_customer_orders` tool with specific arguments. The exact format depends on the LLM provider, but most use structured output or special tokens to signal tool requests.

Step 3: Agent Translation to MCP: Your agent (the MCP client) intercepts the LLM's tool request and translates it into an MCP-compliant JSON-RPC 2.0 message. The agent sends this to the appropriate MCP server.

MCP Tool Call Request

```json
{
  "jsonrpc": "2.0",
  "id": 1,
  "method": "tools/call",
  "params": {
    "name": "get_customer_orders",
    "arguments": {
      "customer_id": 1234,
      "date_range": "last_90_days",
      "include_cancelled": false
    }
  }
}
```

The MCP server receives this request. It validates the arguments against the tool's `inputSchema`. Type checking ensures `customer_id` is an integer. Next validation can confirm `date_range` is a valid option, and required field checking verifies `customer_id` is present. If validation fails, the MCP server returns a JSON-RPC error response with code -32602 (Invalid params).

```
MCP Validation Error Response

{
  "jsonrpc": "2.0",
  "id": 1,
  "error": {
    "code": -32602,
    "message": "Invalid params",
    "data": {
      "details": "customer_id must be integer, got
    string"
    }
  }
}
```

Your agent receives this error and adds it to the conversation context. The LLM sees the failure in the next prompt and can reason about corrections, perhaps retrying with proper parameter types.

Step 4: Tool Execution: If validation passes, the MCP server executes the tool. For most MCP servers, this is straightforward function execution. A database MCP server runs a SQL query. A GitHub MCP server makes an authenticated API call. A filesystem MCP server reads or writes files with appropriate permissions. The MCP server handles authentication, authorization, rate limiting, and timeouts. This resembles calling a standard REST API more than running untrusted code. Sandboxing becomes critical when tools execute arbitrary code, which we address in the tool forming section later in this chapter.

If the tool executes successfully, the MCP server returns a JSON-RPC success response. Tool execution failures do not use JSON-RPC error codes. Instead, they return a success response with isError: true in the result. This separates protocol errors from application errors.

MCP Successful Tool Result

```
{
  "jsonrpc": "2.0",
  "id": 1,
  "result": {
    "content": [
      {
        "type": "text",
        "text": "{\"orders\": [{\"id\": 5678, \"date
      \": \"2025-01-15\", \"total\": 129.99, \"status\":
       \"delivered\"}, {\"id\": 5679, \"date\":
       \"2025-02-03\", \"total\": 89.99, \"status\": \"
       shipped\"}], \"total_orders\": 2, \"total_value\":
       219.98}"
      }
    ]
  }
}
```

If the tool runs but encounters an application error (database connection failed, customer not found), the response includes `isError: true`.

MCP Tool Execution Error

```
{
  "jsonrpc": "2.0",
  "id": 1,
  "result": {
    "content": [
      {
```

```
        "type": "text",
        "text": "Database connection timeout after 30
    seconds"
      }
    ],
    "isError": true
  }
}
```

Step 5: Context Integration: Your agent receives the MCP response and must decide how to add it to the conversation context. This step is more subtle than it appears. Blindly appending every tool result leads to context bloat. A database query might return thousands of rows. A web scrape might fetch entire articles. An API call might return verbose JSON with metadata your agent does not need.

Your agent formats the result for the LLM. You might truncate large responses, summarize verbose data, extract only relevant fields, or compress structured output. The goal is giving the LLM what it needs to continue reasoning without wasting context budget on extraneous information. The formatted result becomes part of the conversation history for the next reasoning step.

The LLM now has the data it needed. It can continue reasoning about the user's request. The tool call bridged from reasoning to data retrieval back to continued reasoning. Managing context efficiently across many tool calls is challenging. In Chapter 21 we will look much more at context engineering strategies, including when to summarize tool results, how to manage long-running conversations, and techniques for selective context retention.

Synchronous vs. Asynchronous Execution: Most tools run synchronously. Database queries, file reads, calculations complete quickly. The MCP server returns results immediately. Your agent waits for the response before sending the next prompt to the LLM. Some tools take time to execute such as web scraping, video processing, and long-running simulations. MCP servers can handle these asynchronously, though the protocol details for async execution are implementation-specific. Your agent may poll for completion or use callback mechanisms.

Error Handling and Retry Logic: Tools fail, networks time out, and APIs hit rate limits. The MCP server handles some failures automatically. Transient database errors might trigger internal retry with exponential backoff. Permanent failures return to your agent as `isError: true` responses. Your agent adds the error to context. The LLM sees the failure and reasons about recovery. It might retry with different parameters, try a fallback tool, or explain the limitation to the user.

Beyond Simple Tools: Models, Workflows & Subagents

Any capability can be exposed as a tool through MCP. A specialized machine learning model for sentiment analysis. A multistep workflow for expense approval. An entire subagent with its own agentic loop. The MCP server wraps the capability and presents it as a callable tool with defined inputs and outputs.

Specialized ML Models as Tools: A fraud detection model trained on your company's transaction patterns. A custom ML model for extracting precise cost and project requirements from construction blueprints. A recommendation engine built with proprietary customer behavior data. Each of these specialized ML models can become a tool. The agent calls it, passes data, receives predictions. The model might be large and slow. The MCP server manages timeouts and resource constraints.

Workflows as Tools: Some tasks require multiple steps with conditional logic. Employee onboarding involves provisioning accounts, assigning equipment, scheduling training, and notifying managers. You could expose each step as separate tools and let the LLM orchestrate. Or you wrap the entire workflow as a single tool. The workflow handles error recovery internally. The agent calls one tool and receives a completion status.

Subagents via Agent-to-Agent Protocol: Complex delegated tasks often need their own agentic loops. A research subagent can gather information across multiple sources, synthesize findings, and produce a structured report. A code review subagent can analyze pull requests, run static analysis, check tests, and provide feedback. These subagents operate autonomously while the parent agent continues other work.

MCP works for basic delegation, but increasingly teams use specialized protocols like the Agent-to-Agent Protocol (A2A) for subagent communication. A2A standardizes task delegation, status updates, result handling, and capability negotiation between agents. We examine A2A in detail later in this chapter.

Why Not Just Use APIs?

In fact, using MCP is quite similar to calling regular APIs. So much so that there is considerable debate in the industry as to whether a new protocol was needed or not. Initially, structured tool discovery was a clear advantage to MCP, and for some applications it still is. In other circumstances, particularly when good documentation for a public API is available, there may be less real advantage to MCP. It is noteworthy, however, that not all APIs are well-designed for agent use cases, and in a fair number of cases MCP and the coming tide of agents are forcing companies to think about how to make their functionality more useful and intuitive to AI agents. Over time, MCP and regular APIs are likely to both be solid options for exposing many types of functionality.

Tool Forming: Creating New Tools Dynamically

We've discussed in earlier chapters the vital roles of predefined tools in helping agents to feel more like true coworkers. This works fine until the agent encounters a situation where no existing tool fits. At that point, the agent needs to form a new tool. Tool forming is code generation in service of expanding capability. The agent writes a modest block of code, tests it, and adds it to its tool library. This is one way agents can accumulate skills over time rather than remaining static.

When Agents Need New Tools: As an example, suppose an agent analyzing sales data encounters CSV files with irregular delimiters and inconsistent quoting. It tries to run the standard CSV parser but that fails. The agent could then write a custom parser tailored to this format. That parser becomes a tool in the repertoire of the agent. Future files with the same format can be opened using the custom parser without regenerating it.

Such tool forming leverages the agent's ability to write code. The agent identifies the gap: what function would solve this problem? It generates the function in Python or JavaScript or whatever language the execution environment supports. It includes error handling, input validation, and documentation.

The agent generates this code. The execution environment runs it in a sandbox. If it works, it becomes available as a tool. The agent adds it to its context: "I now have parse_irregular_csv available for future CSV tasks."

Validation of Generated Tools: Code generation introduces risk. Generated code can have bugs, security holes, or performance problems. Validation is essential before production use.

Static analysis checks for common security issues: SQL injection, command injection, and unsafe code evaluation. Linters enforce style and complexity limits. Type checkers validate signatures. Sandboxed testing runs the generated function against example inputs. If it crashes or times out, reject it. If it produces incorrect

---

Algorithm 20.1: Custom CSV Parsing for Irregular Files

Parse irregular CSV by normalizing delimiters and quotes line by line, then using a standard CSV parser to accumulate clean rows.

Input: File path p
Output: Parsed rows R

1 $R \leftarrow []$
2 **foreach** *line ℓ in Open(p)* **do**
3 $\quad$ $\ell \leftarrow$ RegexReplace($\ell, [;,], ", "$)
4 $\quad$ $\ell \leftarrow$ RegexReplace($\ell, "', ""$)
5 $\quad$ $r \leftarrow$ CSVParse(ℓ)
6 $\quad$ R.append(r)
7 **end**
8 **return** R

---

results, reject it. Only functions that pass testing, including possibly human review, join the tool library.

Tool Library Growth: Successful tool forming accumulates a library of domain-specific functions. This library becomes part of the agent's competitive advantage. New instances of the agent inherit the library. They start with more capabilities than the base model. Training data for fine-tuning can include successful tool uses, further encoding these skills.

Voyager, the famous Minecraft agent, demonstrates this pattern. It builds an ever-expanding library of Python skills. Each successful skill persists. Later tasks compose existing skills rather than starting from scratch. Over thousands of tasks, the agent accumulates a curriculum of capabilities.

Risk Management and Governance: Tool forming raises the question: how much autonomy should agents have to create their own capabilities? In Part V of the book, we cover security and risk in greater depth. For now, be aware that tool forming enables agents to adapt to novel situations and accumulate skills, but it requires governance appropriate to your risk tolerance.

Computer Use: Visual Interaction with Domain Software

Domain experts often rely on specialized software with highly complex graphical interfaces. Medical imaging workstations for radiology. CAD programs for mechanical and electrical engineering. Financial trading platforms with complex order entry systems. Enterprise resource planning software with hundreds of screens and workflows. 3D design and rendering software for video game and animation development. These tools encode years of domain expertise in their interfaces, built for human interaction through menus, buttons, forms, and visual feedback.

Computer use capabilities enable agents to interact with this software through its visual interface rather than through APIs. The agent observes screen pixels, interprets UI elements, moves the mouse, clicks buttons, fills forms, and reads visual output. Computer use tools can be exposed through MCP just like any other tool. MCP servers wrap screen capture, mouse control, and keyboard input as callable functions. The MCP protocol handles the exchange. What makes computer use different is not the protocol but the paradigm: visual interpretation and GUI navigation versus structured API calls.

When Computer Use Matters: Some specialized software may have no API, such as legacy systems built decades ago, proprietary tools where vendors provide only a GUI, or custom enterprise applications. In these cases, computer use may be the only path to automation.

Even when APIs exist, they may not expose the full functionality experts need. A medical imaging system might have an API for retrieving scans but not for the advanced measurement tools radiologists use daily. A CAD program might allow file import via API but not the complex constraint solving and design validation features. Computer use fills these gaps by letting agents operate the software as humans do.

Reinforcement Learning for Interface Proficiency: Foundation models can handle simple GUI tasks, but mastering complex domain software requires learning navigation patterns, understanding conditional UI states, learning the effects of many specialized tools available in the UI and how to compose them to solve higher-level tasks efficiently. Additionally, computer use by AI often involves taking screenshots of the UI, and calling a Vision Language Model (VLM) to interpret the image. In a complex UI, this can become expensive very quickly when calling large foundation models. This is where reinforcement learning can play a significant role, both increasing accuracy and reducing costs of task completion.

Next up, we get into the nuts and bolts of how and when to use RL to separate your production agent from the pack of research prototypes.

How RL Emerged as Crucial for Specialized Agents

When you start building your agent, prompting and retrieval should always be where you start and can often get you to 70-80% of where you need to be. But particularly domain specialized agents need the last 20-30% of performance, and they need to master skills that large foundation models have never faced to solve customer problems.

For a time, prior to DeepSeek, many agent builders would first turn to supervised fine-tuning (SFT). In SFT, you show an LLM examples of correct behavior, and it learns to imitate them. Techniques like Low-Rank Adaptation (LoRA) made this practical by letting teams train small parameter matrices instead of updating entire models. Direct Preference Optimization (DPO) added alignment by learning from human preference pairs without requiring separate reward models.

But SFT has fundamental limits. When the state space is too large to cover and examples are costly to produce, or when success criteria are clear but the path to reach them is not, supervised tuning often fails.

This is why reinforcement learning emerged as essential. RL lets agents discover strategies through interaction with environments. For agents specifically, the breakthrough came from shifting away from complex reward models toward verifiable rewards. As we discussed in Chapter 12, Reinforcement Learning with Verifiable Rewards (RLVR) became the dominant paradigm. The computational barrier fell further when researchers at DeepSeek introduced Group Relative Policy Optimization (GRPO). Traditional RL algorithms like PPO require a separate critic network as large as the policy network, which can increase training costs as much as 2x. GRPO eliminates this by sampling multiple responses per prompt and comparing each to the group average. Responses better than average get positive rewards, while subpar responses get penalized. This simple relative ranking often provides more reliable training at lower costs than actor-critic methods.

Cost and Latency Rationale for RL: Small inexpensive models trained via RL have also matched frontier LLMs on complex tasks. A small 32B parameter model trained with RL can sometimes handle tasks with better accuracy than general purpose models with hundreds of billions or even a trillion or more parameters. The smaller models also operate at a tiny fraction of the cost per call, and at much lower latency. This convergence of verifiable rewards, efficient algorithms, and economic incentives explains why RL is becoming a go-to technique for production agents. However, RL remains challenging to implement well as we see next.

The Practical Challenges of RL

The goal of this section is not to make RL sound impossible, but I do want you to go in eyes wide open. RL spans a complex body of techniques that requires expertise, resources, and time to do well. Documentation can be poor. There are too many toy examples online, and the special implementation sauce that big labs use is often guarded, so even LLM coding agents may not be much help here. I've seen teams underestimate the challenges and get frustrated when initial attempts fail to deliver expected gains. Let's get started looking at what you may face in this journey.

Environment Setup and Simulators: RL training can require running thousands or even millions of episodes. You need environments where the agent can act, receive feedback, and learn. For some domains, real environments work. Code generation can execute in sandboxes. Math problems evaluate instantly. Simple computer use tasks run in virtual machines. If you think of some of the big wins of RL playing video games, the environment literally is *a copy of the running video game*, often orchestrated by a special harness that lets it fit easily into the RL training loop.

If you want to train your agent to use legacy software, you may face some painful challenges. Systems such as proprietary ERP systems, clinical systems, financial trading platforms, construction design systems, or manufacturing control systems often lack APIs for programmatic interaction. These systems may be difficult to containerize, and may not run on the cloud. Running these systems for RL training almost always requires work with domain experts to create realistic test data and workflows. Workarounds are possible, but every situation is unique and potentially costly.

Complex domains may justify simulators, but simulation could require reverse-engineering decades of accumulated business logic. For many teams considering RL, the cost of setting up realistic environments for training is the most daunting barrier. The first question you need to ask is what is the equivalent of the "video game" your agent will play against? Next we look at the second question in RL: When should you give your agent a reward?

Reward Function Design: Reward design is one area where the cost of setting up your RL effort has actually dropped. RLVR simplifies rewards through verification, but you still must define what constitutes success. These decisions shape what the agent can learn.

Automatic reward functions that use LLM-as-a-judge, are an emerging solution that is growing in popularity. One example is OpenPipe's RULER library (Relative Universal LLM-Elicited Rewards) which builds on the insight of GRPO that you often only need to *make relative judgments* to give reasonable rewards during RL training. RULER uses an LLM to rank multiple potential agent actions, with higher rankings resulting in higher reward. Agents trained with RULER's automatic rewards can match or exceed those trained with hand-written rewards. The approach scales across domains because it relies on the LLM's general judgment rather than task-specific verification.

Automatic reward functions are not the only option of course. If your problem is more specialized, or the outcomes are not easy to have an LLM judge, you may have to craft a specific reward function for your training loop. Doing so properly is beyond the scope of this book, but it can be crucial to your success and require iteration and tweaking to get right.

Offline vs. Online RL: Most production RL happens offline before deployment. You collect interaction data, run training in batch, evaluate the learned policy, then deploy it as a frozen model. The deployed agent does not learn while online. It applies the policy learned offline during training.

Online RL, where agents learn continuously from real-world experience, remains largely theoretical for production agents. The risks are substantial. An agent learning online might stumble onto strategies that game the reward function without actually acquiring desired skills (so-called "reward hacking"). It might shift to unsafe behaviors before monitoring can catch the problem. Research on safe online RL continues, but current best practice separates learning from deployment.

Since offline RL is dominant, it *should* be obvious that RL-trained models are frozen artifacts. When you put them into production, they hopefully perform their specialized task well. They can be integrated as tools or subagents through MCP or direct API calls, but they do not adapt during operation. If behavior needs updating, you will need to retrain and redeploy a new version, and test carefully to be sure the new version does not degrade some capabilities while improving others.

Algorithm Selection and Hyperparameters: RL is a wide and complex field, and RL model training requires a lot of careful tuning. GRPO works well for a good number of agentic tasks, but that does not guarantee it will work for *your* agent's tasks. Proximal Policy Optimization (PPO) remains widely used in RL despite higher cost. Soft Actor-Critic (SAC) is also popular in continuous action spaces. Trust Region Policy Optimization (TRPO) provides strong convergence guarantees. If you are doing Deep RL, where you use neural networks for perception before you even give a reward to learn a policy, you may need to consider a wide range of computer vision models as well.

Hyperparameters matter as well as algorithm choice. Learning rates, batch sizes, entropy coefficients, and clip ranges all play roles in controlling exploration-exploitation balance and training stability. Teams need infrastructure for hyperparameter search across realistic scenarios. Underexplored hyperparameter spaces can be why RL training fails to converge. Choosing and combining these techniques requires expertise but also experimentation and therefore costs.

How to Get Started with RL: Hopefully this list of challenges has not scared you off of RL entirely. To give a full guide to how to do RL in agents would go well beyond the scope of this chapter. Many excellent resources exist, some of which I have included in the chapter references. The crucial point for agent builders to take away, however, is that RL (and possibly other algorithms as we will see in Chapter 29) may be necessary to get your agent to production-level performance. RL is daunting to teams initially, but the practical challenges are surmountable with the right expertise and resources. New services and tools to help with various parts of RL seem to appear every week. Make sure your team has time to research these, as they could save you weeks or months of implementation time. RL requires investment, and careful prioritization based upon your domain and customer needs.

Reasoning Models & Test-Time Compute

A new class of models emerged in late 2024 and early 2025: reasoning models that think longer at test time.[1] DeepSeek-R1 from China and OpenAI's o1 kicked off this category and showed that extended reasoning during inference can improve performance on complex tasks. These are models trained specifically to generate extended reasoning traces before answering. The training uses reinforcement learning on process rewards, not just outcome rewards. The model learns to think step-by-step, check its work, consider alternatives, and verify conclusions.

How Reasoning Models Work: Traditional models generate tokens sequentially until they produce an answer. Reasoning models generate thousands of tokens of internal reasoning first. This reasoning is not shown to the user in some implementations. The model explores multiple paths, identifies dead ends, backtracks,

---

[1]Such models are also called "thinking" models. Another common term is LRM which stands for Large Reasoning Model.

and refines its thinking. Only the final answer gets returned.[2]

DeepSeek-R1 Shift to Thinking Models: DeepSeek released R1 in early 2025, showing that reasoning models could be trained efficiently without requiring the massive resources of frontier labs. The model demonstrated that extended test-time reasoning combined with RL training creates capabilities that cannot be achieved through scaling alone. More recent models like Kimi K2 Thinking from Moonshot AI have continued this trend, even beating the proprietary lab models on many benchmarks.

Reasoning models become specialized components (like tools or subagents) in agent systems. The extended thinking offered by these models has been shown to enable solving problems that shorter inference cannot handle. When the agent encounters a complex problem, it may delegate to a reasoning model. The reasoning model invests in extended thinking. The result can return to the agent with higher reliability than a standard model could provide.

This introduces a trade-off that agents must manage. Routine questions get minimal thinking budget. Complex novel problems may get an extended budget. The agent's situational awareness needs to help determine the budget allocation. Keep in mind also the warning that thinking models can be black boxes, and relying on them to solve complex domain problems is strategically risky for specialized vertical agents. In Chapter 29, we will also see research that calls into question whether LRMs actually increase the range of problems models can solve, or if they only let models solve relatively simple problems more quickly. Use these models with caution and measure your results carefully.

Scaffolded Test-Time Compute (MCTS and Beyond): Beyond reasoning models, explicit scaffolding can also force extended test-time reasoning. Monte Carlo Tree Search (MCTS)

---

[2]You can review the interlude on autoregressive next token prediction in Chapter 18 if you want a refresher to compare this to on how regular LLMs generate responses.

adapted for language models explores multiple solution paths, evaluates their likelihood of success, and focuses compute on promising branches (See Algorithm 20.2).

MCTS for reasoning works by treating problem-solving as iterative tree search. Each node represents a reasoning state (the accumulated reasoning so far). The LLM generates possible next reasoning steps from promising nodes. Each generated step becomes a child node that gets scored, either by the LLM itself judging solution quality, or by verification when available. Scores propagate back up the tree, updating statistics about which paths look promising. Over many iterations, the search focuses compute on high-scoring reasoning paths while still exploring alternatives. The algorithm balances this trade-off by tracking both average scores and visit counts: nodes visited less often get exploration bonuses to prevent the search from getting stuck. The final answer comes from the complete solution with the best score.

Algorithm 20.2: MCTS-Based Reasoning Scaffold

Iteratively select promising reasoning paths, expand them with LLM-generated next steps, score the new reasoning states, and backpropagate scores to guide future selection.

Input: Problem P, compute budget B
Output: Best complete solution

1 $root \leftarrow$ Node(P.initial_state, $score = 0, visits = 0$)
2 **for** $i \leftarrow 1$ **to** B **do**
3 $\quad$ $n \leftarrow$ SelectNode($root$)
$\quad$ $c \leftarrow$ LLM_GenerateNextStep(n.state)
4 $\quad$ n.add_child(c)
5 $\quad$ $s \leftarrow$ EvaluateState(c.state) BackpropagateScore(c, s)
6 **end**
7 **return** HighestScoringComplete(root)

Specialized Router Models: Not every problem needs extended reasoning. Specialized router models can be used by executive agents to decide reasoning depth for specialized problems. A small, fast model examines the incoming query. It classifies complexity, and can estimate required reasoning depth as shown in Algorithm 20.3.

Algorithm 20.3: Reasoning Depth Router

Classify query complexity and choose an inference route: standard model for routine queries, reasoning model with increasing thinking budgets for moderate/complex queries, and specialized methods for critical ones.

Input: Query q, context X
Output: Route config (model, budget, method)

1 $c \leftarrow$ ClassifyComplexity(q, X)
2 **if** $c = routine$ **then**
3 $\quad$ **return** {model: standard, thinking_budget: 0,
$\quad\quad$ method: direct}
4 **else if** $c = moderate$ **then**
5 $\quad$ **return** {model: reasoning, thinking_budget: 10000,
$\quad\quad$ method: standard}
6 **else if** $c = complex$ **then**
7 $\quad$ **return** {model: reasoning, thinking_budget: 50000,
$\quad\quad$ method: self_consistency}
8 **else**
9 $\quad$ **return** {model: reasoning, thinking_budget: 100000,
$\quad\quad$ method: mcts, verification: required}
10 **end**

The Cost-Capability Trade-Off: Reasoning models and scaffolded test-time compute are expensive. A query that takes 100,000 tokens of thinking costs 50× more than a standard response. Product teams must decide when this cost justifies the improved capability. The agent architecture must support both. Routing logic determines which path to use. Situational awareness informs the routing decision. The result is an agent that invests reasoning com-

pute where it creates value and optimizes for cost where it does
not.

Agent-to-Agent Protocols: A2A & ACP

As AI agents proliferate both inside and outside organizations,
the need for standardized communication and discovery becomes
apparent. To work together, each agent must identify itself and
spell out its abilities. Right now developers address these issues
with ad hoc wrappers and discovery hacks, slowing the team down
and potentially opening security holes. Google's Agent-to-Agent
Protocol (A2A) and IBM's Agent Communication Protocol (ACP)
aim to clean this up by giving agents a common handshake and
message format.

Google's A2A: A2A grew out of Google's Agentspace initiative and is now stewarded in an open Linux Foundation project.
Its designers assumed agents would often live in different networks
or cloud vendors, so the spec centers on an HTTP endpoint that
serves a public Agent Card.

Any caller can fetch that small file to learn the agent's capabilities, authentication method, and preferred streaming mode. Then
send typed messages back to start, monitor, or cancel a task. Optional Server-Sent Events let the agent push updates even when the
client sits behind a firewall or on a phone that drops in and out of
coverage. The goal is to make cross-company collaboration feel as
routine as calling a web API.

IBM's ACP: ACP emerged from the open-source BeeAI framework but takes a local-first stance. It keeps the message format
simple, yet discovery is expected to happen at configuration time
via manifest files rather than through an internet-facing registry.

That choice makes ACP easier to deploy on an air-gapped research cluster, or inside an enterprise, where latency and deterministic routing matter more than broad reach. IBM positions ACP as

the layer that takes over once an agent has loaded the context for a task and now needs to hand subtasks to specialized peers running nearby.

Merged Under A2A: As this book nears press, A2A and ACP have been merged under the A2A name, under the governance of the Linux Foundation. This reduces confusion and shows large players see the value of common standards. But it also underscores that multi-agent communication is very early. More requirements are likely to emerge as use cases are better understood.

Context and Reliability Implications. We go deep into context engineering in the next chapter, but it's worth noting here that standardized agent discovery and communication protocols help us with context engineering. Subagent coordination must be handled in the context window and includes status updates from delegated agents. Standardized protocols help these updates follow consistent formats, reducing context burden through predictability. They also improve reliability through clear specifications.

Agents Conducting Commerce: The Agentic Protocol & Beyond

While A2A addresses how agents coordinate with one another, a different kind of protocol tackles a narrower but commercially critical problem: letting AI agents complete purchases on behalf of users. In late 2024, Stripe and OpenAI began co-developing the Agentic Commerce Protocol (ACP), an open standard for agent-driven commerce. The protocol went live in September 2025 when ChatGPT users in the US could buy products from Etsy sellers directly in the chat interface, with Shopify merchants following soon after. The specification is Apache 2.0 licensed, maintained by Stripe and OpenAI, and designed for any payment provider or AI agent to implement.

Agents are increasingly capable of understanding user intent and making recommendations. But purchases require payment credentials, merchant relationships, inventory checks, fulfillment coordination, and fraud controls. Building these integrations is complex, and open standards can allow merchants and agent builders to coordinate changes. It also lets agents offer purchasing capability without becoming payment processors or merchants of record.

How It Works: The protocol defines a RESTful HTTP interface with four core endpoints that merchants implement. Create a checkout session to generate cart and pricing data. Update a checkout to modify quantities or selections. Complete a checkout by passing a secure payment token. Cancel a checkout to release inventory and abandon the transaction. The merchant retains full control over product presentation, pricing, payment processing, and fulfillment. The agent handles the conversational interface and collects user intent.

The key security primitive in ACP is the Shared Payment Token (SPT). When a user authorizes a purchase in the agent interface, the payment provider issues an SPT scoped to a specific merchant and a specific cart total. The agent can pass this token to the merchant to initiate payment, but the token never exposes the user's raw payment credentials. The SPT can be time-limited, amount-capped, and revoked if needed. This separation means the agent never handles sensitive payment data, yet can still complete transactions on the user's behalf.

Why Merchants Care: Merchants maintain their existing commerce infrastructure and payment relationships. They choose which products to surface to agents, how to price them, and how to fulfill orders. Customer relationships remain with the merchant. Refunds, support, and loyalty programs work as they do today. From the merchant's perspective, agentic checkout is just another sales channel. Salesforce announced support for the protocol in October 2025, signaling that enterprise commerce platforms see value in standardizing this layer rather than fragmenting it across proprietary integrations.

Beyond ACP: Blockchain Rails and Agent Wallets. The Agentic Commerce Protocol focuses on catalog discovery, checkout flows, and merchant integration. It is deliberately agnostic about payment rails and does not address agent identity or autonomous spending. This creates space for blockchain-based infrastructure to extend what agents can do with commerce, often working in tandem with protocols like ACP rather than replacing them.

Blockchain infrastructure enables capabilities that go beyond ACP's scope. Agents can hold their own wallets, control stablecoins like USDC or DAI, and execute transactions with delegated spending authority rather than requiring human approval for each purchase. The agent becomes an economic actor with a persistent identity across sessions. Users can set spending limits for agents through smart contracts, giving agents limited autonomy. As we discussed in Chapter 17, agents operating in crypto ecosystems can coordinate through economic incentives, seek efficiencies, and execute strategies on behalf of their users that would be difficult or cost-prohibitive with traditional payment methods.

The economic advantages can be more than many people are aware. Traditional payment processing typically charges merchants 2-3% per transaction. Stablecoins on Ethereum Layer-2 networks settle for sub-cent fees, making micropayments and frequent agent-to-agent transactions economically viable. Smart contract-based delegation provides fine-grained control over agent spending without the authorization overhead of per-transaction approvals.[3]

Nothing prevents ACP from working with blockchain settlement. A merchant implementing ACP's checkout endpoints could accept stablecoin payments. The Shared Payment Token could represent a delegated wallet permission rather than a traditional card

---

[3]High-speed, low-cost platforms like MegaETH are emerging that can support streaming micropayments, which would be inconceivable with traditional payment rails.

authorization. ACP could handle the catalog and checkout protocol layer, while a fast, cheap Layer-2 could handle settlement, agent wallets, and autonomous spending.

The architectural difference matters most when agents need independent economic identity. As we will explore in Chapter 28, agent identity becomes crucial when agents need to build reputation, coordinate and strike deals, or operate with delegated authority. ACP assumes the agent is an extension of the user, with identity and authorization tied to each transaction. Blockchain-based wallets give agents persistent identity and spending power that can operate across sessions, merchants, and even coordinate with other autonomous agents. This enables a broader range of agent behaviors, but also introduces complexity around key management, regulatory compliance, and trust in autonomous spending decisions.

The landscape for agent commerce is early and evolving. ACP provides a practical path for agents to access traditional commerce infrastructure through standardized checkout flows. Blockchain and stablecoins extend agent capabilities into autonomous economic participation with extremely low-cost settlement and programmable delegation. Product teams building advanced and specialized agents should pay close attention to this space as more innovative use cases are likely to emerge rapidly.

The Path Forward

We covered a lot of ground in this chapter. The array of choices you face when building real-world specialized agents can take time to internalize. Tools and subagents extend agent capabilities from reasoning to action. Tool forming enables agents to adapt to novel situations. SFT and RL can create specialized skills, outside the wheelhouse of horizontal agents. Reasoning models may help tackle problems through extended thinking, but come with a cost and can function as black boxes. My best advice is to carefully refine and debate use cases to help your team prioritize how much to invest in each of these techniques. Next, we look at context engineering, memory, and knowledge retrieval, which are crucial to manage the finite resources that constrain your agent.

Chapter 21

Context Engineering, Memory & Knowledge

Takeaways: In the last two chapters we looked at how agents calculate situational awareness, as well as the use of many types of tools and specialized reasoning. We have begun to see that the LLM context window necessitates the new discipline of context engineering to carefully control what goes into each call to the LLM, and what gets left out. Keeping in mind the vision of a multi-loop, multi-model agent established in Chapter 18, this chapter lays out a coherent set of principles for how context engineering works together with memory and knowledge to help your agent adapt and generalize in complex environments.

T O BE VERY BLUNT, the subjects we address in this chapter represent the bulk of the practical day-to-day engineering effort of teams building successful agents. As such, this chapter, like Chapter 18, may be worth reading twice for serious builders. Context engineering has emerged as the central issue in building AI systems that leverage LLMs, and particularly in building agents. Context engineering goes hand in hand with storage and retrieval of memory and knowledge. The two are inseparable.

Importantly, my goal in this chapter is to present coherent, strong principles about what to do and what not to do. These are grounded in experience with many teams building complex, highly specialized agents. Agents that go well beyond the caricature we've mentioned of a loop, a planner, and a handful of tools. Frankly, there are currently a lot of muddled, half-thought-through discussions of agent memory and context engineering in online tutorials, papers, and especially in blog posts from big model companies. In my experience, unclear thinking in AI engineering influencer circles can lead to significant confusion, even with serious engineering teams. As a result, it's especially important to present a coherent approach grounded in principles that work together.

To make the flow clear, we will begin by stating the principles succinctly. This means we will not yet have fully justified them. Nevertheless, it's important to see the principles together first, because of the logical picture they imply for your agent architecture, and for how you approach adding capabilities to your agent. As we proceed, the justification for the principles should become clear.

Principles of Memory & Context Engineering (Plus a couple of easily overlooked corollaries)

We set out these principles all in one place because they operate together. We discuss *how* to do these things in more detail in sections ahead. For now, read these principles as a unified engineering approach, consistent with the vision we laid out in Chapter 18 of the agent meta loop, likely implemented as a complex adaptive system of smaller loops calling many LLMs for specific purposes.[1]

1. **Fine-grained tasks drive everything.** Use planning and task management repeatedly in your agent execution to break down tasks. This results in smaller and smaller tasks. Iterate and measure task failure rates to look for tasks that still need to be broken down further.

2. **Small tasks allow small context and crisp calls to small LLMs.** With small, well-defined tasks you can craft the context window to every call. As a golden rule, aim to send the minimum context possible to the smallest, most spe-

---

[1]Specifically, you may return to the subsection: "Multiple Loops, Multiple Models & a Warning" in Chapter 18 for a summary if you need a quick refresher.

cialized, lowest-cost LLM you can. Call larger LLMs with larger tasks when you are learning, or when absolutely necessary, and not for tasks that are a core competency for your agent. For specialized domain tasks, begin breaking them down, iterating, and optimizing early. Over time, this will make your agent more reliable, solving more customer problems, and more profitable, by greatly reducing token costs.

3. **Memory and knowledge are unified.** Do not build separate stores for your agent's knowledge and memory. Knowledge and memory are the same thing. Store raw data, documents, and logs to avoid loss of information, then think carefully and adapt your partitioning, summarization, and retrieval strategy *often* to respect customer privacy requirements, and to meet your task needs. In other words, add structure to what you store and be prepared to maintain that structure (see below on partitioning and structuring).[2]

4. **The Context Window is NOT your agent's working memory.** Do not think of the context window as short-term or working memory. Recall the first two principles. Your goal is to *craft each context window* for each call to the LLM with *exactly* what you need for that task. The context window is driven by the task. Your agent's short-term memory are the things your agent needs frequently plus what it needs from recent events or interactions for the situation and task at hand. But, and this is important, you may need access to *essentially anything* from stored agent memory for a particular LLM call. So make sure you can retrieve it. Do *not* keep everything floating around in the context window. Large model providers will market to you their large context windows, and

---

[2]To avoid writing "knowledge and memory" all the time, from now on I will use these terms interchangeably when referring to what your agent knows. There is still a separate notion of "external knowledge" your agent can tap by searching the web or external stores and reading what it retrieves.

their blog posts will encourage you to shovel clutter into the context window. This is a serious antipattern you should avoid.

5. **Partition and structure storage aggressively for things you need often.** You need to access certain things on almost every call. These things are your real agent short-term or working memory. Situational awareness (where is your agent? Who is in the room? What is going on?) is needed frequently. The goal stack, including fine-grained tasks, the current task, recent results, and larger surrounding goals, needs to be available at practically every turn. Store these items with structure, and maintain that structure rigorously. This will make accessing your agent's *true* short-term memory a snap without cluttering the context window on every LLM call.

6. **Preselect tools for tasks to reduce context size:** An often overlooked corollary of the "retrieve everything you need" strategy advocated here is that you should regularly prune the tool descriptions you send on each LLM call. This requires a step to retrieve, reason about, and select which tools are truly relevant to a task. Sending descriptions of every tool on every LLM call is a recipe for poor results, regardless of which LLM you use. If you deduced that this means you need to store and retrieve tool descriptions by relevance to tasks, then congratulations, that means you are paying attention and understanding as you go.

7. **World model meets adaptation in the meta loop.** We have made it most of the way around the meta loop we discussed in Chapter 18. Your agent's world model is the sum total of what it knows and how it reasons about the world. Context engineering is where the rubber hits the road, as it requires recall from knowledge, and it preps each small chunk

of reasoning (the LLM call). By frequently assessing the situation and context, breaking down tasks, and learning and assimilating new information, your agent can react to and move through the world fluidly and adaptively, like a true co-worker or colleague. The principles here may be summarized as: make small moves, plan and assess frequently, have ready access to all of a well-structured memory, and focus the context window on what matters for the task.

I realize some of these principles won't make full sense at first reading. In the sections ahead we will first look in detail at how your agent can store and retrieve information, and the many subtleties involved. Then we will get into context engineering proper: the assembly of information in the context window. We will go through multiple concrete examples of how you can craft context to match a particular agent task. There is a lot of nuance here, but going through the details and examples should make the principles much more clear.[3]

Memory: The Art of Storage & Retrieval

Memory and knowledge are the same thing for your agent, just as they are for humans. When your agent learns that Socrates was born in Athens from a document, or learns that Mary prefers chocolate ice cream from conversation, both become part of what it knows. Your brain stores both types of information the same way and recalls them when something triggers the memory, and your agent's memory architecture should work similarly.

This unity simplifies architecture conceptually, but it demands careful engineering in practice. You need to partition rigorously by customer to prevent data leakage, structure aggressively for fast

---

[3]Readers familiar with techniques in the 2025 paper, "Solving a Million-Step LLM Task with Zero Errors," will see strong parallels with the principles discussed in this chapter.

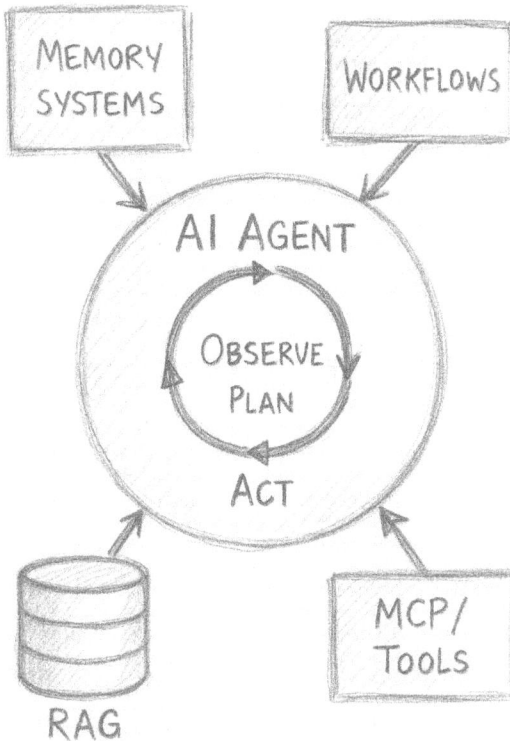

Figure 21.1: Agents are systems that orchestrate multiple elements to perceive, reason, and act in complex environments. Each of these systems affects the context window with which an agent calls an LLM.

retrieval of frequently-needed information, and decide what to store raw, what to summarize, and what to discard. Storage and retrieval are two sides of the same coin, because how you choose to store information fundamentally determines what you can retrieve later and how quickly you can access it.

Partition by Customer and Context: Your agent may work with multiple customers simultaneously, and data from one customer must never leak to another. Building hard partitions at the storage layer means that every query, every write, and every retrieval operation enforces customer boundaries. Avoid shared indexes that span customers and avoid global caches that mix customer data. If your agent is in three meetings at once with three different customers, it should maintain three completely separate contexts with zero possibility of cross-contamination.

Within each customer partition, your agent needs to understand organizational context. An urgent request from a CEO typically requires different handling than the same request from an intern. By storing role information, reporting structures, and interaction history, you enable your agent to prioritize tasks and personalize communication based on who it is working with and what role they play in the organization.

Keep in mind our lesson from Chapter 6, even when working for a single customer, your agent can be in many places at once. You will need to decide what contexts should scope interactions your agent has. If your agent is in 4 meetings and 10 Slack channels at the same time, it should have a clear idea of what the humans have said and therefore seen or heard *just in that channel or meeting*. Responding in the wrong message channel is a mistake we have all made, but your agent should be architected to avoid it. As your agents become more sophisticated and more natural parts of human teams, there will be many nuances to think through around how quickly, and at what level of detail your agent should recall and use information it learned from one situation in another.

Raw Interactions: Every conversation, every tool result, and every perception your agent has should be logged in raw form, serving multiple important purposes. You may need these logs later for training, fine-tuning, or reinforcement learning. Debugging agent behavior requires examining exactly what the agent saw and did at each step. Compliance and auditing often require complete interaction histories. Since storage is relatively cheap while lost data can be extremely expensive, the practical approach is to log everything and decide later what to keep long-term.

Domain Driven Structuring: While raw logs are necessary, they are not sufficient on their own. You need to build structured data too, partitioned according to how your agent uses different types of information. Situational awareness data should be available quickly and should rapidly respond to changes in the agent's environment. Goal stacks and task queues need separate storage that is optimized for frequent updates, and rigorous maintenance of structure. Domain knowledge might be an area where specialized knowledge graphs make sense, with nodes and relationships reflective of how experts in the field think, and rigorous verification of the degree to which relationships are supported by evidence.

This structuring is where domain specialization happens, and your partitioning strategy should be driven by the specific tasks your agent performs and the opportunities it has to add value. Many specialized domains will have heuristics that allow certain data to be prioritized and labeled with domain-specific metadata that is essential to later retrieval, and domain-specific reasoning.

Throughout all of this, maintain rich contextual metadata that captures who said what, where, and when, along with who else was present and what triggered the interaction. Such metadata enables your agent to understand the circumstances under which it learned new information, which later retrieval operations can use to filter and rank results appropriately.

Conversation History: Many teams face challenges specifically with how to handle conversation history. Often there is a demarcation of sorts when an agent starts a longer task, and within that processing, task breakdown and fine-grained context is easier to get your head around, and therefore to engineer. Outside those longer, more autonomous actions by the agent, there is typically quite a bit of back and forth with real users. This conversation is part of what makes LLMs magical, and is an important part of your user experience. As we discussed in Chapter 7, this is also where your agent gives and gets critical feedback before and during its work towards complex goals.

The challenge is what to store? How to store it? When is
something critical that should be permanently stored revealed in
an interaction? When is information only of transient value? There
tends to be a lot of noise and fairly useless banter in this data as
well, but depending on your domain your definition of "noise and
useless banter" may vary quite a bit!

These are not questions where the answer is obvious. There are
various naive windowing and time-based compression strategies you
will find in blog posts online. Generally, teams developing vertical
and specialized agents discard such techniques as amateurish and a
distraction. The teams I have seen that have been the most successful with mining conversations have started with quite opinionated,
domain-specific data models. As we noted above while discussing
structuring, these domain data models are often generated with experts, and represent an ontology of sorts for your agent's expertise.
They can also inform how your agent processes open-ended and
conversational interactions by giving your team and your agent a
set of high-value extractions to look for in raw conversations.

This is another reason why we recommended above to store raw
interactions. You will be unlikely to design the perfect domain data
model on your first attempt. You will definitely grow and refine
it over time. Having access to a good period of raw conversation
logs provides solid raw material as you come back again and again
to work on the best way for your agent to process this open-ended
type of data.

Pipelines, Latency and Freshness: Memory updates need
to happen continuously as your agent works, because the agent
often needs immediate access to recent information. When a user
corrects the agent, that correction should be stored immediately
with appropriate metadata to aid flexible retrieval. When a task
completes successfully, the outcome should update the task store
in real time rather than waiting for batch processing.

Alongside these real-time updates, you should run nearline or offline pipelines that process raw interactions to extract higher-level insights.[4] Pattern detection can identify recurring task types and successful approaches. Verification processes can ground new domain information before your agent treats it as true. Verification and enrichment, as we noted in Chapter 10, are essential to building your agent's data competitive advantage.

Decay, Retention, and Forgetting: Not everything deserves permanent storage at the same level of detail, and product teams need to decide on retention policies that match their domain and use cases. Some information starts detailed but should be progressively summarized over time. Explicit deletion also matters for privacy and compliance. If a customer requests data removal, your system needs to be able to find and delete all of their information across all partitions.

Domain Knowledge vs. General Knowledge: LLMs already know that Paris is the capital of France, so there is no reason to waste storage on generic world knowledge. Instead, focus on storing deep domain knowledge aggressively: industry-specific terminology, customer-specific processes and preferences, proprietary methods and best practices, and regulatory requirements unique to your domain.

Store Tools in Your Memory System: Your agent's tools are part of what it knows how to do. Store tool descriptions, usage patterns, and performance metrics alongside other memory and knowledge. This allows your agent to reason about which tools to use for specific tasks, how to sequence tool calls, and how to recover from tool failures.

Make Retrieval Task-Driven and Precise: When you craft context for an LLM call, you retrieve information from your structured memory store, and the retrieval query needs to be informed

---

[4]Nearline pipelines typically produce results in seconds or up to a minute, as compared with real-time processing which typically is done in milliseconds, or batch processing which may take many minutes or hours.

by the specific task at hand. If the task is "draft an email to
Jane about the Q2 budget," your retrieval should target recent
interactions with Jane, the Q2 budget details, and any relevant
financial policies, while avoiding unrelated customer interactions,
old budgets, or generic financial knowledge that the LLM already
possesses.

Match Technologies to Retrieval Patterns: The physical
storage technology you choose often is also a choice of retrieval
technology. For example, vector databases enable semantic similarity search, while traditional SQL databases provide structured
queries with joins and aggregations. Graph databases, meanwhile,
are designed for efficient traversal of complex relationships, document stores for managing unstructured or semi-structured data,
and search engines for fast keyword-based retrieval. Anthropic
has published various engineering posts where they favor using the
filesystem for storage and retrieval of things an agent knows. This
is a reasonable place to start for simple agents, but as your agent's
memory and knowledge needs grow, you may find more specialized
storage and retrieval technologies are needed to meet latency, cost,
and complexity requirements. The primary advantage of filesystem-
based storage is that many modern LLMs have been heavily trained
in Lunix commands for file retrieval and manipulation, so file-based
storage can be surprisingly effective for certain types of knowledge
and should not be dismissed out of hand.

Often retrieval, like storage, summarization, and indexing, becomes layered and multi-faceted over time. This is a major source
of engineering effort for successful agent teams, and you need to
be prepared to invest in it, iterate, and learn over time. You will
likely end up using multiple retrieval strategies depending on what
information you need, and with what latency. Semantic similarity search works well for finding relevant domain knowledge, while
structured queries work better for retrieving specific entities like
"all open tasks for project X." Temporal queries handle recency re-

quirements like "interactions in the last 24 hours." Your retrieval layer should support all of these approaches and be able to compose them as needed for complex queries.

Reranking after initial retrieval can improve results significantly, but adds latency and sometimes a financial cost. Deduplication also removes redundant information that would clutter context. A common and useful practice is to use another LLM-as-a-judge to both look for duplication, and also to assess the relevance of various retrieved pieces of data to a particular task. This approach adds latency and token costs, so you will need to decide where in your larger agent data system these investments make sense.

Abstract Storage Details from Your Agent: Recall from our critical principles, however, when crafting context for an LLM call, you may need to retrieve from any part of your knowledge store. As much as possible, *your retrieval layer should abstract where and how particular data is stored and present a unified interface to the rest of your agent architecture*, with clear SLAs and estimates for cost per call if LLM processing is involved.

Learning and Proprietary Data Generation: As we discussed extensively in "Dream, Distill, Differentiate" (Chapter 10), your agent needs explicit processes for systematic domain learning that operate at a higher level. This can include analyzing patterns across many customer interactions, monitoring external sources like industry news, research publications, regulatory updates, and competitive developments. Likely it will also involve maintaining and updating domain ontologies and taxonomies over time. These learning processes can run as scheduled jobs or get triggered by significant events in your domain. Importantly, they likely produce updates to multiple partitions in your memory store, which then become available for retrieval at any point in your agent's meta loop.

Practical Strategies for Context Engineering

Context engineering starts with understanding what your agent is trying to accomplish at any given moment. The answer to this question determines what should go into the context window for that particular LLM call. Assessing situational awareness, for example, requires different information than planning a complex task or executing a specific action. Each LLM call serves a distinct purpose. The context window should be crafted to match.

Since so many blog posts and muddled AI memory discussions say the opposite, let us reiterate again forcefully here that *the context window is not your agent's working memory*.[5] If you are following the principles we outlined earlier, you are using multiple LLMs for different purposes. Your agent spans those, and your structured memory store contains everything the agent knows outside of basic world knowledge held in the weights of the various LLMs. This includes conversation history, subagent status updates, tool results, domain knowledge, customer knowledge, and much more. The context window is where you assemble exactly what you need for the next LLM call.

The variability in context requirements is a major reason why small, well-defined tasks are so essential to effective agent design. Each small task has a clear purpose, which makes it easier (though still challenging) to determine what context is actually needed. Large, vague tasks make context selection ambiguous, and many teams end up including everything just to be safe, which leads to bloat, and subtle failures that are difficult to diagnose.

Large Context Windows: Models launched in 2024 and 2025 support 200k, 1M, or even 10M tokens, and marketing materials emphasize these large windows while *encouraging* you to fill them. You should resist this temptation, because larger windows do not

---

[5]I was tempted to shout that in ALL CAPS. You are probably glad I spared you that.

eliminate the need for careful context engineering. In fact, they make careful engineering even more important.

Research shows that models consistently under-attend to information buried in the middle of long contexts. The "Lost in the Middle" problem demonstrates that critical facts placed between irrelevant material often get ignored, and accuracy degrades when models must wade through noise to find signal. So-called "context rot" represents another hazard. Work by Chroma and others shows that simply adding more information can reduce performance rather than improve it. The model ends up spending its capacity reconciling contradictions instead of reasoning about the task at hand.

Prune Tools for Each Task: This was one of our core principles above, but it bears repeating here. Tool descriptions, like tool results, consume significant context, and a production agent might have access to hundreds of tools. Sending all tool descriptions on every LLM call is both wasteful and harmful, because the model sees too many options and tends to make worse decisions as a result. Instead, you should preselect tools based on the specific task at hand. To do this well you need good data about which tools are relevant for which task types. Here also, another LLM call can help judge the relevance of tools returned by your retrieval layer.

In an engineering blog post "Code execution with MCP: Building more efficient agents," Anthropic, the creator of MCP, recently acknowledged that agents *should not* load all tool descriptions into the context window. Often today, agents naively hook up dozens of MCP servers and send all tool descriptions on every call. Such a mistake leads to the *tool bloat* phenomenon we mentioned in Chapter 20 as a serious type of *context bloat* in agents today.

A word of caution. The solution Anthropic recommends is for agents to write code (toolform) for their calls to MCP servers, and

to store tools and descriptions as files in the filesystem.[6]   This
is only one approach, not necessarily the best one. As I noted
above, I recommend thinking of your memory store as *everything
your agent knows*, including tool descriptions, usage patterns, and
performance metrics. This allows your agent to reason about which
tools to use for specific tasks, how to sequence tool calls, and how
to recover from tool failures. Storing tool descriptions as files in
a filesystem, or writing code ad hoc to call MCP servers, may be
viable at small scale for some agents, but it carries security risks
of running untested code, requires sandboxes like any type of tool
forming, and can be token inefficient. It does not directly solve the
problem of how to reason about which tools to use for which tasks.
Storing tool descriptions and tool performance data in your unified
memory store, regardless of the physical storage technologies you
choose, is a more durable and general approach.

Position in the Context Window: Where information appears in the context window significantly affects how much attention the model gives it. Empirical results consistently show that
models under-attend to material in the middle of long contexts,
while information at the beginning and end receives more weight.

You should place critical task instructions at the beginning or
end of the context window, and place retrieved background information in the middle if necessary, though you should keep it concise.
If you have a 50k token budget and 40k tokens of retrieved knowledge available, consider carefully whether you really need all 40k
tokens. Summarizing or selecting the most relevant portions may
actually improve results even though you are using fewer tokens.

Keep instructions separate from retrieved content rather than
intermixing them. Do not combine system prompts, task descrip-

---

[6]Filesystem storage meshes with what Anthropic calls "skills," which are
markdown files (sometimes with code examples) describing tasks an agent might
do often. Any agent can store such skills. They do not require Anthropic
models, nor do they need to be on the filesystem. Skills should be in your
memory store, like everything else your agent knows.

tions, and retrieved data in a single block of text. Instead, use clear structural boundaries between different types of content. Some LLM APIs support separate fields for system prompts, user messages, and retrieved context, and you should use these when available. When they are not available, use explicit formatting to visually separate different types of information.

Subagents and Tool Results: Architectural decomposition is one of the most effective context engineering strategies available. When you delegate a complex task to a subagent, the executive agent does not need to track the subagent's internal reasoning at all. It only needs to track delegation status: what was delegated, to whom, what is the expected completion time, and eventually what result was returned.

The same principle applies to tool execution. When a tool executes, it might perform complex operations and generate verbose output, but you should not dump raw tool output into the context window. Instead, summarize the output, or extract key information.

Context Size and Task Complexity: You should never aim to fill the full context window of an LLM. A far better practice is to begin to classify in fine-grained detail the tasks your agent performs across its entire lifecycle in the meta loop. Then *measure the average size* of the context you are supplying to each LLM call for each task. In time, you should be able to develop solid, domain-specific heuristics for task complexity. Even without solid heuristics, your team should be able to carefully dial up or down the target context length per task as you tune your context engineering. Over time, you should be able to reduce how much context you supply for similar tasks while increasing accuracy.

Detailed Context Construction Examples

The following examples show how context windows could be tailored to specific tasks. These are simple examples, and slightly contrived, but each one demonstrates what gets retrieved from the unified memory store and how it gets assembled into context. Real use cases would be more complex. Here it pays to focus on how the context size and composition varies dramatically based on task needs. The goal is always to include exactly what is needed and nothing more.

Example 1: Situational Awareness Assessment

An agent working with a customer needs to periodically assess its situation. Where is it? What is happening? Who is involved? What should it prioritize? This is a fast, frequent operation that requires minimal context. The agent retrieves current location metadata, recent events, active participants, and the current goal stack. It does not need domain knowledge, tool definitions, or conversation history for this assessment.

```
Context for Situational Awareness Assessment


+------------------------------------------------------+
| Task: Assess Current Situation                       |
| Context Budget: 8k tokens                            |
+------------------------------------------------------+


(1.5k) System & Identity
   - Agent purpose and role
   - Operating boundaries
   - Escalation rules


(1k) Current Location Metadata
```

```
+---------------------------------------------------+
    - Customer: Acme Corp
    - Context: Weekly planning meeting
    - Participants: Sarah Chen (VP Ops), Mike Torres (PM
      )
    - Meeting started: 14 minutes ago
    - Operating mode: Collaborative planning

(2k) Recent Events (last 15 minutes)
    - Sarah asked about Q2 delivery timeline
    - Agent provided initial estimate (conflicted with
      prior data)
    - Mike corrected: project scope changed last week
    - Agent acknowledged correction
    - Sarah requested breakdown of remaining work

(2k) Active Goal Stack
    1. [HIGH] Provide accurate Q2 timeline
       - Blocker: Need updated project scope details
    2. [MED] Document meeting decisions
    3. [LOW] Schedule follow-up on budget discussion

(0.5k) Subagent Status
    - Research subagent retrieving updated project scope
    - ETA: 2 minutes

(1k) Task Prompt
    Assess the current situation. What is the priority?
      Should you wait for the research subagent Can you
      make progress on next goal or flag risks?

Total: 8k tokens
+---------------------------------------------------+
```

Example 2: Planning Task Decomposition

The agent received a high-level goal: "Analyze sales performance by region and recommend territory realignment." This requires planning how to break the goal into executable tasks. The agent retrieves the goal details, relevant domain knowledge about sales analysis and territory management, past attempts at similar tasks, and tools that can help with planning and analysis. It also retrieves organizational context to understand reporting structures and decision authority.

```
Context for Planning Task Decomposition


+--------------------------------------------------+
| Task: Plan Territory Realignment Analysis        |
| Context Budget: 35k tokens                       |
+--------------------------------------------------+


(1.5k) System & Identity
  - Agent purpose and role
  - Operating boundaries
  - Planning protocols

(1k) Situational Awareness
  - Customer: Acme Corp
  - Stakeholder: Sarah Chen (VP Ops)
  - Risk level: Medium (affects sales team structure)
  - Authority: Recommendations only, final decision
    with VP

(4k) Goal Details
  - Goal: Analyze Q4 sales by region, recommend
    realignment
  - Success criteria: Data-driven with ROI
  - Constraints: Cannot disrupt active customer
```

relationships
- Timeline: Recommendations needed within 3 days
- Prior context: Sales declined 15% Western region,
  grew 22% in Southeast

(8k) Domain Knowledge: Sales Territory Management
- Territory alignment best practices
- Metrics: revenue per rep, customer density, travel
  costs
- Common pitfalls: disrupting established
  relationships,
  ignoring geographic constraints
- Acme-specific: preference for contiguous
  territories,
  3 sales managers (West, Central, Southeast)

(6k) Domain Knowledge: Past Similar Tasks
- 2024-Q1: Analyzed rep productivity by territory
  - Approach: compared revenue, deal velocity,
  retention
  - Outcome: Identified 2 underperforming
  territories
- 2023-Q3: Customer satisfaction analysis by region
  - Approach: surveyed customers, correlated with
  rep
  - Outcome: Found Western region had communication
  gaps

(3k) Organizational Context
- Saloo team structure: 3 managers, 18 reps
- Western region: 6 reps, manager: Tom Liu
- Central region: 5 reps, manager: Angela Rivera
- Southeast region: 7 reps, manager: DeShawn Jackson
- Recent changes: 2 new hires in Southeast (last
  month)

```
(6k) Available Planning & Analysis Tools
  - get_sales_data(region, date_range, metrics)
  - calculate_territory_metrics(territory_id)
  - get_customer_locations(region)
  - analyze_rep_performance(rep_id, metrics)
  - generate_territory_map(assignments)
  - estimate_realignment_impact(current, proposed)

(2k) Recent Conversation (context for this goal)
  Sarah: "Our Western region is struggling. I need to
    understand if it's a territory problem or
    something else. Can you analyze sales by region
    and tell me if we should realign territories?"

  Agent: "I'll analyze Q4 sales performance by region
    and provide recommendations for territory
    realignment if the data supports it."

(3k) Task Prompt
  Break down the goal "Analyze sales performance by
    region and recommend territory realignment" into
    specific, executable tasks. Consider:
  - What data needs to be retrieved?
  - What analysis needs to be performed?
  - What tools should be used?
  - In what order should tasks be executed?
  - What are the dependencies between tasks?
  - What are potential failure points?

  Produce a structured task breakdown with priorities.

Total: 34.5k tokens
  +---------------------------------------------------+
```

Example 3: Execution Task with Analytics

The agent is now executing one of the planned subtasks: analyzing Western region sales data to identify performance issues. This is a detailed execution task requiring specific data retrieval, calculation tools, and domain knowledge about sales metrics. The agent also needs recent results from related tasks to maintain consistency.

```
Context for Analytics Execution Task


+------------------------------------------------------+
| Task: Analyze Western Region Sales Performance       |
| Context Budget: 28k tokens                           |
+------------------------------------------------------+


(1.5k) System & Identity
  - Agent purpose and role
  - Data analysis protocols
  - Quality standards for insights


(0.8k) Situational Awareness
  - Customer: Acme Corp
  - Current task: Western region analysis (step 2 of
    7)
  - Stakeholder: Sarah Chen (VP Ops)
  - Risk level: Medium


(1.2k) Current Task Details
  - Task: Analyze Western region Q4 sales performance
  - Parent goal: Territory realignment analysis
  - Success criteria: Identify root causes of 15%
    decline
  - Deliverable: Structured analysis with specific
    findings
```

(4k) Domain Knowledge: Sales Performance Metrics
  - Key metrics: revenue per rep, deal closure rate,
    average deal size, pipeline velocity, customer
    churn
  - Western region historical benchmarks:
    * Avg revenue/rep: $285K (Q3), $240K (Q4)
    * Closure rate: 28% (Q3), 22% (Q4)
    * Avg deal size: $18K (stable)
  - Red flags: closure rate drop, pipeline stagnation,
    increasing sales cycle length

(6k) Retrieved Data: Western Region Q4
  - 6 sales reps (Tom Liu - manager, plus 5 reps)
  - Total Q4 revenue: $1.44M (down from $1.71M in Q3)
  - 84 deals closed (down from 102 in Q3)
  - 312 opportunities in pipeline (down from 356 in Q3
)
  - Customer churn: 8 accounts (up from 3 in Q3)
  - Per-rep breakdown: [detailed table retrieved]

(3k) Domain Knowledge: Regional Factors
  - Western region covers: CA, OR, WA, NV, AZ
  - Territory characteristics: Large geography, high
    travel costs, competitive market
  - Recent external factors: Tech slowdown in CA (Q4),
    2 major competitors launched aggressive pricing

(2k) Results from Related Tasks (completed earlier)
  - Task 1 (Company-wide sales analysis): Overall
    company
    sales up 8% in Q4, driven by Southeast growth
  - Central region stable: slight 2% growth
  - Southeast region: strong 22% growth (as expected)

(5k) Relevant Analysis Tools
  - calculate_metrics(data, metric_list)
    Returns: computed metrics with comparisons
  - compare_rep_performance(rep_ids, date_range)
    Returns: ranked performance with outlier detection
  - identify_churn_patterns(churned_accounts)
    Returns: common factors in churned accounts
  - correlate_external_factors(region, date_range)
    Returns: external events correlation with
    performance

(2k) Recent Tool Results (from previous steps)
  - get_sales_data(region="Western", date_range="Q4
    -2024")
    Status: Success, returned 428 records
  - calculate_territory_metrics(territory_id="WEST")
    Status: Success, showed decline across all metrics

(2.5k) Task Prompt
  Using the retrieved Western region Q4 sales data,
    perform a detailed analysis to identify root
    causes of the 15% revenue decline. Specifically:

  1. Calculate key performance metrics and compare to
     Q3
  2. Identify which metrics declined most
     significantly
  3. Analyze per-rep performance to find patterns
  4. Examine churned accounts for common factors
  5. Assess whether external factors explain the
     decline
  6. Determine if this is a territory structure
     problem or
       other factors (market, competition, team
     capability)

```
+------------------------------------------------------+
|                                                      |
|   Use available analysis tools. Provide structured   |
|     findings                                         |
|   with specific data supporting each conclusion.     |
|                                                      |
|   Total: 28k tokens                                  |
|                                                      |
+------------------------------------------------------+
```

These examples illustrate how context engineering works in practice. A situational awareness check uses 8k tokens. A planning task uses 35k tokens. A detailed execution task uses 28k tokens. None of these approaches the maximum context window size. Each includes exactly what is needed for the specific task. In production systems, these patterns must be carefully tailored to your agent's specialized domain, the tasks it performs, and the information architecture of your memory store.

GEPA & ACE:
A Taste of Advanced Context Engineering Research

Two recent papers from Stanford and Berkeley researchers illustrate how academic work is beginning to engage seriously with the practical challenges we have been discussing. Both papers address the question of how to optimize what goes into the context window, but they approach the problem from different angles, and both align with the principles we have laid out in this chapter.

The first paper, "Reflective Prompt Evolution Can Outperform Reinforcement Learning," introduces GEPA (Generative Evolutionary Prompt Adaptation), from a collaboration including researchers at Berkeley, Stanford, and UT Austin. GEPA attacks the context engineering problem through iterative reflection. The core idea is that rather than relying on reinforcement learning or fine-tuning model weights, you can evolve prompts by having models reflect on failures, propose improvements, and test candidate refinements across benchmarks.

Mechanically, GEPA works by collecting execution traces from task rollouts, then prompting an LLM to analyze these traces and propose improved instructions. Each mutation builds on an ancestor prompt, accumulating insights over generations. To avoid getting stuck in local optima, GEPA maintains a Pareto front of candidates, where instead of evolving only the single best prompt, it stochastically samples from the set of prompts that perform best on at least one training instance.[7] This diversity in the candidate pool promotes robust generalization across varied problem instances.

For teams building specialized agents, GEPA offers a practical alternative to fine-tuning and reinforcement learning, and the early results are impressive. On several benchmarks including HotpotQA and HoverBench, GEPA matches or outperforms RL-based optimization while avoiding gradient computation and weight updates entirely.

GEPA also aligns directly with our emphasis on small, well-defined tasks and carefully crafted context. For agent builders, this research helps validate our principle that you should send the minimum context possible to the smallest, most specialized LLM that can handle the task.

The second paper, "Agentic Context Engineering: Evolving Contexts for Self-Improving Language Models," introduces ACE (Agentic Context Engineering), also from researchers at Stanford, Berkeley, and other institutions. ACE tackles a different but related problem: context collapse. As context windows grow longer, models struggle to maintain accuracy because relevant information

---

[7]A Pareto front is a set of solutions where each member excels on at least one metric. For example, if Prompt A performs best on questions 1 and 5, Prompt B on questions 2 and 7, and Prompt C on question 3, all three remain in the Pareto front. GEPA randomly samples from this diverse set when creating mutations, preventing the algorithm from optimizing only one approach.

becomes harder to spot. This is the "Lost in the Middle" problem we discussed earlier.

ACE addresses this through adaptive context evolution, where the system learns which information proves most useful for specific tasks. The mechanism uses three specialized roles: a Generator produces reasoning trajectories that surface effective strategies and pitfalls, a Reflector critiques these traces to extract concrete lessons, and a Curator synthesizes lessons into compact delta entries. Rather than rewriting entire contexts, ACE represents contexts as structured, itemized bullets with metadata tracking the importance of each element. The Curator merges incremental delta updates using lightweight deterministic code, allowing parallel batched adaptation while preserving detailed domain knowledge that would otherwise be lost in monolithic rewrites.

ACE is fully compatible with the unified memory architecture we have advocated throughout this chapter. Your structured memory store holds everything, raw and processed, partitioned by customer and function. ACE's techniques for preserving domain knowledge and preventing context collapse apply directly to your storage and retrieval strategy. When you write to your store you are making decisions about representation and compression, and when you craft context for a specific LLM call, you are making decisions about what to retrieve and how to package it. ACE's structured approach of itemized, incrementally updated contexts provides a concrete method for making those decisions adaptively rather than through fixed heuristics.

Both papers underscore that context engineering is not a solved problem. GEPA favors concise, optimized context that strips away unnecessary detail. ACE favors richer, adaptive contexts that preserve domain knowledge without collapsing due to too much information. Both approaches treat context as something to be engineered rigorously, and both emphasize learning from feedback and adapting over time. The research landscape for context engineering is still early, and you should expect more techniques to emerge as the field matures.

∽

What's Ahead?

I hope the examples and taste of the research landscape give you a feel for the range of issues you will face designing your storage and retrieval architecture along with a principled process and approach to context engineering. This chapter bookends our four-chapter look at agent architecture that started with the high-level view of the infinite agent meta loop.

In the next chapter, we take a slight detour to look in detail at the rapidly moving world of rigorous AI-assisted software development. As we mentioned in Chapter 16, SWE and coding agents are a clear business bellwether for how agents are becoming successful products. Next, we will see how they are not only important tools in the development of your agent, but also good training grounds to see and feel how context engineering works in practice. Our goal is to help your team go well beyond so-called "vibe coding" and use these SWE agents in rigorous ways to ship *your* production-ready agent.

Chapter 22

Beyond Vibes:
Rigorous AI Software Development

Takeaways: AI-assisted software development has moved from novelty to necessity, but success requires rigor, not just rapid prototyping. Spec-driven development is context engineering for coding agents. The practices that teams develop from working with coding agents can give insights into building domain-specific agents for customers. This chapter has two goals: (1) to help you rigorously use AI in your own software development, and (2) to illustrate how to uncover insights that can help shape your own production-grade vertical agents. Along the way, we see why vibe coding, while useful for prototyping, carries serious risks when building competitive specialized agents.

WE EXAMINED CODING or SWE agents as a bellwether in Chapter 16, calling them the first true agent products to find product market fit. We looked at the implications of this emerging market: specialization versus commoditization, pricing model evolution, and the fundamental shift from coding-as-a-skill to problem-solving as a differentiator. That chapter focused on the market dynamics and strategic implications.

This chapter turns instead to the technical practices that make rigorous AI-assisted software development possible. Additionally, it shows how the skills your team develops working with coding agents can transfer to building domain-specific agents for your customers. The coding agent you use every day is a vertical agent specialized in the software development domain. The practices you learn while using it (context engineering, spec-driven design, iterative refinement, testing, subagent delegation) are practices you will also need to build world-class vertical agents in any domain.

This is not a chapter just for engineers. Rigorous AI-assisted development requires whole team alignment. Product managers, designers, architects, domain experts, and engineers must collaborate on specifications, maintain shared context artifacts, and iterate together. Chapter 24 will show how Agile and Scrum practices are adapting to AI. This chapter lays the technical foundation that makes that team collaboration effective.

The term "vibe coding" was coined in February 2025 to describe rapid prototyping by prompting AI agents iteratively without detailed specifications. Vibe coding has real value for exploration and learning. But teams building competitive agent products cannot rely on vibe coding alone. Production-grade agents demand rigorous practices.

The Vibe Coding Phenomenon: Power & Pitfalls

Vibe coding enables non-coders to build working prototypes fast, by simply prompting AI coding agents over and over. The market has exploded, with new vibe coding tools seeming to launch weekly. Foundation models have helped fuel this, improving their coding skills with each release.

This approach addresses real demand. Millions of people have ideas for simple applications but lack coding skills. Vibe coding tools let them prototype rapidly, for early exploration and learning. Even for simple production use cases like marketing pages, simple applications, and websites, vibe coding is a practical alternative. The problem emerges when teams try to use vibe coding for more substantial production systems.

Three pitfalls matter for agent product teams. First, platform bias. Many vibe coding tools serve as front doors for hosting companies, and not so subtly steer you toward their ecosystem. Second, GUI bias. Most vibe coding tools are heavily trained on traditional front-end applications. They generate cookie-cutter UIs for human users, not agent-to-agent interfaces or the innovative feedback patterns we discussed in Chapter 7. Vibe coders start out biased toward building yesterday's products by using today's tools.

Finally, vibe coding is well-known for quality, security and performance gaps. Vibe coding optimizes for speed of creation, but often generated code lacks security hardening, misses latency or throughput targets, and falls short on testing and operational monitoring. These pitfalls make vibe coding appropriate for prototyping, or very simple use cases, but not for most complex uses in production.

The Alternative: Rigorous AI-Assisted Development

Production agents require a different approach. The core principle is simple: spec-driven development is context engineering for coding agents. Just as we said in the last chapter on context engineering, the goal of rigorous AI-assisted software development is to break problems down to smaller and smaller tasks. The specifications you write become the context that guides the agent's code generation, small change by small change.

Spec-Driven Development as Context Engineering

Spec-driven development treats specifications as working input for the coding agent, not as one-time planning documents. Teams maintain a small set of living files that describe product intent, constraints, preferred patterns, and how success will be judged. These files live in the repository, change as understanding evolves, and are provided with each task so the agent acts on the current intent. In practice, this means writing a short description of the problem and goals, then breaking work into small changes that can be checked automatically.

Most teams store these materials as plain Markdown next to the code. A file like AGENTS.md can describe which assistants are in use and what they are allowed to do. Folders such as `specs/`, `decisions/`, and `tests/` keep related context easy to find. Some tools and IDEs index the repository to supply implicit context, but the explicit files remain the source of truth and are what the agent should read for guidance.

In spec-driven development, work should proceed in small steps. For each change, many teams ask the agent to outline a plan, make a minimal code modification, run checks and tests, and then explain how the result satisfies the acceptance criteria. The team reviews the outcome, and updates documents as intent for a feature evolves, keeping the written context and the code aligned making quality easier to maintain.

As an astute reader, you have probably noticed something: This is *very similar* to the approach we recommended for our own specialized agents in the previous chapter! Teams will tailor the details, but the principles are the same: small steps, clear constraints, fresh data, and continuous alignment between specifications, tests, and code.

Small moves and disciplined context do not just apply to engineers. When requirements change, product managers need to update the PRD or any feature descriptions. When architectural decisions change, architects should update ADRs. When domain understanding deepens, domain experts should update knowledge stores and ontologies. SWE agents and tools (which we discuss in the next section) can help teams with this important maintenance work.

Human team synchronization is still essential, and regular context review meetings can be an important starting point. In some ways these are replacing traditional sprint planning meetings as we will explore more in Chapter 24. Teams should review: What did we learn this week? Which documents need updating? Where is understanding fuzzy and needs clarification? The teams I have seen do this most successfully treat these as knowledge-sharing sessions. Next up, we look at a crop of tools designed to help reduce the maintenance challenges of spec-driven development.

Building Context at Scale:
Four Tools, Four Philosophies

Spec-driven development is fundamentally about context engineering. You build comprehensive context through layered specifications where each layer adds detail and constraint. The coding agent receives this cumulative context and generates code accordingly. The principles remain constant across all approaches: whole team alignment on specifications, comprehensive context construction, and iterative refinement as understanding evolves.

The challenge is maintaining these specifications systematically as your codebase grows and requirements change. New tools and methodologies feel like they emerge weekly to help with this, and no single approach fits every team or domain. The specifics of which tool you choose matter less than understanding the underlying principles and selecting an approach that matches your workflow, culture, technical environment, and the type of problems you are solving. OpenSpec, BMAD, GitHub SpecKit, and Cursor represent four distinct philosophies for building and maintaining rich context systematically. Your team should evaluate these (or other) options, recognize the trade-offs each makes, and choose or adapt a methodology that fits your specific needs.

OpenSpec: Brownfield-First Lightweight Specs. OpenSpec targets teams working with existing codebases rather than greenfield projects. The core philosophy is minimal overhead with maximum clarity. Two folders define the entire system: `specs/`

contains the source of truth (what the codebase should do), while `changes/` contains proposed modifications that agents can review and implement. This separation makes OpenSpec particularly effective for modernizing legacy systems or iterating on established products. The framework remains tool-agnostic, working with any AI assistant via slash commands and an AGENTS.md file that defines available agents and their capabilities. OpenSpec optimizes for teams that need rigorous specs without heavy process overhead.

BMAD: Multi-Agent Enterprise Methodology. BMAD (Business, Manager, Architect, Developer) represents the heavier end of spec-driven development. The methodology uses specialized agents for distinct roles: analyst agents conduct stakeholder interviews and market research, product manager agents generate detailed PRDs, architect agents make technical decisions, and Scrum master agents create hyper-detailed implementation stories. Each agent's output becomes context for the next, building comprehensive multi-dimensional context by the time code generation begins. BMAD scales beyond coding to include product requirements, market analysis, and business case development. The approach demands significant upfront investment but provides extensive control for complex enterprise projects spanning multiple repositories and teams.

GitHub SpecKit: Developer-Centric Toolkit. GitHub SpecKit has a different philosophy: provide lightweight building blocks that developers orchestrate themselves. The workflow centers on three structured commands: `/specify` generates thorough specifications, `/plan` creates technical implementation plans, and `/tasks` breaks work into granular steps. Each command adds a layer of context that subsequent steps consume. SpecKit assumes human developers orchestrate a single AI through sequential refinement rather than multiple specialized agents. SpecKit is most accessible for teams already comfortable with existing development tools who want to add structured AI assistance without changing their entire workflow.

Cursor: Agent-Centric IDE Integration. Cursor represents IDE-first integration where the development environment itself becomes context-aware. Rather than maintaining separate specification documents, Cursor indexes the entire codebase and makes it available as implicit context. The agent can execute tasks in parallel, manages its own context selection, and learns patterns directly from code structure. This approach optimizes for speed and flow state, though it requires developers to adopt Cursor's specific IDE and trust its proprietary agent capabilities. The philosophy centers on minimizing explicit specification overhead by maximizing automatic context extraction from existing code.

Other tools follow similar patterns. The key is not adopting a specific tool, but rather adopting a methodology and team commitment to both construct and maintain comprehensive and readily accessible context. Your team must align on methodology. Product managers, architects, domain experts, and engineers all contribute to context artifacts, regardless of what tool you adopt to support the process. Several areas of critical context are sometimes overlooked by teams, as they tend to focus nearly exclusively on the product specification context needed for an SWE agent to develop new features. We look at those next one by one.

Test-Driven Development with AI Agents

With AI assistants, test-driven development (TDD) functions as context engineering. Tests encode precise behavior, inputs and outputs, and edge conditions, giving the agent an objective specification to satisfy. Precision narrows the search space, reduces invented behavior, and produces faster feedback because failures are immediate and actionable. As the suite grows, it becomes living documentation that guides changes and makes refactoring safer. Production of actual test cases is usually best done after detailed specification and technical execution plans are produced, and before an SWE agent begins to write code. Even if you do not follow a strict TDD paradigm where tests are written rigorously before code, your team should make sure they are a well understood part of your overall development lifecycle.

A word of warning on mistakes I've seen teams make adopting TDD in an environment with coding agents in regular use. If product intent or architectural decisions shift upstream of tests, but the tests themselves are not updated, they can quickly become stale context that can lead an SWE agent astray even if it is building a new and fairly isolated feature. The agent will work to satisfy the wrong overall contract, creating rework and potentially missing the real requirements. Keep tests and acceptance criteria synchronized with the PRD and architectural decisions by retiring or revising test-cases. This maintenance process, like many others, can and should be assisted by your SWE agent and your tooling.

Architectural Documentation as Context

Architecture can in many ways be the most consequential context to get right. An SWE agent's choices about APIs, data flow, and integration depend on clear guidance about the intended system design. A concise source of truth that names core services and modules, the protocols between them, data ownership, and cross-cutting constraints such as reliability and performance targets gives the agent stable defaults. Architectural Decision Records (ADRs) capture the rationale behind these choices and provide durable context the agent can follow.

Using an LLM to read the codebase can help surface existing patterns and dependencies, but those observations are not the architecture. Treat them as input to review rather than decisions to enshrine. Backfilling ADRs from current code risks a feedback loop where incidental or flawed implementations become the tar-

get design and are then replicated. Keep ADRs intentional, note
where the present code diverges from the intended direction, and
be explicit when you want the agent to follow the ADR rather than
mirror local code. Frequent architectural context updates can reduce drift, improve integration, and make code refactoring much
less risky.

Code Standards & Style Guides as Context

Code standards and style guides are most effective when used
as explicit context for the SWE agent rather than informal norms.
Concise expectations for naming, file layout, error handling, logging, and comments give the agent concrete patterns to follow, so
generated code matches the codebase and reviewers can focus on
logic. Without that guidance, the agent fills gaps with guesses and
inconsistencies accumulate. Providing standards with each task reduces friction, lowers cognitive load, and improves maintainability
by aligning output with how your system already works. Small,
specific, and current documents are easier for the agent to apply
reliably.

Security Requirements as Context

Security must be part of the explicit context the SWE agent
receives, not a later review step. Encode your organization's standards and threat model into concise checklists and acceptance criteria, aligned with frameworks such as OWASP (Open Worldwide
Application Security Project), and include them with each task so
code generation favors safe patterns. This context guides choices
in input handling, authentication, authorization, and data protection, reducing common vulnerabilities and shifting reviews toward
subtle issues rather than obvious mistakes. Human review remains
necessary, but teams that supply clear, current security context
consistently see stronger defaults than those that do not.

Build Better Agents by Building with Agents

Working with coding agents gives teams a practical window into how agent systems behave. It surfaces quirks of how instructions get interpreted, and failures that appear when requirements are vague. These experiences can give your team better instincts about specification quality, decomposition, and validation. From that practice, a few lessons tend to carry across to your agent. Break work into small, verifiable steps so progress and errors are easy to inspect. Keep context lean, current, and precise, and remove stale details that confuse the model. Write instructions with clear inputs, expected outputs, and acceptance criteria, and regularly capture decisions and examples so they can be reused as grounding.

Building domain agents brings challenges not seen working with SWE agents: different modalities, complex policy requirements, less "verifiable" evaluation signals, and longer execution loops. Treat what you learn from coding agents as hypotheses and ideas. The enduring carryovers are the discipline of small steps, clean context, and task-specific adaptation.

Looking Forward: The Convergence

Chapter 16 established that coding agents are becoming a foundational part of the industry, and a skill your agent does not have to build from scratch. The software development practices in this chapter can help teams move at high-velocity, while shipping production-grade agents. Rigorous, efficient engineering will continue to be a competitive advantage. Teams that leverage their own work with rapidly advancing SWE agents to master context engineering, small-change iterative refinement, testing, and whole team alignment will build superior agents. We expand the aperture on this topic when we look at team development methodologies in Chapter 24. But now, as promised, we turn to the subject of open-source AI agent software frameworks.

Chapter 23

Open Source Agentic Frameworks

> *Takeaways*: Open source agent software frameworks abound. Each has its own strengths and weaknesses. When choosing a framework, or if you choose no framework at all, consider your specific needs carefully. Consider the level of autonomy and control you require versus the specific areas where you can avoid reinventing the wheel, and how those apply to your differentiation in your domain. It's often beneficial to experiment with multiple frameworks, and with no framework, to find the best fit for your project.

THE LEAD ENGINEER, CTO, or architect of any agent product team faces a very immediate challenge, and one which really cannot be sidestepped: which agent framework should I use, or should I roll my own agent entirely from scratch? I can tell you up front that searching for an answer or asking your favorite LLM research agent is the first step toward going down a very deep rabbit hole. It's a reasonable way to start, but you will not come out quickly if you do a thorough job, so it is wise to have a strategy or a "map" before you start.

There are a huge number of software frameworks in the AI space vying for the attention of developers who are setting out to build any sort of AI application. It could be applications leveraging AI, it could be workflows and automations that solve tasks inside larger systems, and of course it could be full-blown agents, or agentic versions of any piece of the puzzle.

At the time of this writing we are in a moment of explosive change, with new agent development frameworks emerging almost every week and existing frameworks rapidly morphing and shifting. Anything that I might say here about individual frameworks will be obsolete in 6-12 months. What I want to do instead is give you a set of principles, to help guide you as you investigate the options.

As you do your own research, and most importantly as you understand your specialized domain problems better, you can apply these principles to help guide you. These principles are by their nature more focused on engineers than product managers or designers, so feel free to skip ahead if technical engineering choices are not your main focus. You may still find it interesting, however, to understand what your engineering teammates will be considering.

Understanding Framework Architecture

Before we get to the principles, it helps to understand what frameworks actually do. All frameworks differ in their details, but most grapple with a common set of architectural concerns. Not every framework addresses every concern equally. Some frameworks try to handle everything. Others are minimalist and focus on just one or two layers, leaving the rest to you.

Figure 23.1 shows the layers of concerns that agent frameworks typically address to varying degrees. At the top sits orchestration, where broadly there are two major approaches. High-level orchestration tends to be declarative. You define agent roles and goals, and the framework figures out routing and coordination. With low-level orchestration, by contrast, you explicitly build flows with conditional, hand-crafted transitions. The trade-off is ease of use versus fine-grained control. If you recall Chapter 18's discussion of goal stacks, situational awareness, fine-grained tasks, subagents,

Orchestration Layer Multi-agent coordination, workflow control
Agent Core Layer Planning, reasoning, task and goal management
Memory Layer Short-term, long-term, episodic, semantic
Tools & Actions Layer Tool registration, execution, MCP support
Observability Layer Tracing, logging, metrics, debugging
Integration Layer Model providers, external systems, protocols

Figure 23.1: Framework architectural layers. Comprehensive frameworks address all layers. Minimalist frameworks focus on orchestration and core logic, leaving memory, observability, and integration to you. Different frameworks make different trade-offs between ease of use and control.

etc., orchestration is the task of putting these pieces together. Often for more specialized domain agents that need to generalize to multiple tasks, low-level orchestration is preferred, as it gives you more control.

Below that is the agent core, which handles planning and reasoning logic, and sometimes task and goal management. It integrates with the LLM to make decisions. It can be where you track goal and task status and do difference engine type comparisons with your estimated world state. If you favor control and low-level orchestration, then these processes need to be fully accessible to the orchestration layers. Low-level frameworks expose this naturally and may not even treat it as a separate concern or layer. Higher-level frameworks may also abstract this layer entirely, or control it as a framework-level concern.

Memory sits near the middle, and is truly crucial as we have discussed. Frameworks handle memory in wildly different ways, and sometimes add more confusion than clear thinking. Make sure you follow the principles we laid out in Chapter 21 to guide how you use (or do *not* use) whatever functionality a given framework offers around memory. As we have noted, thinking on memory is still quite muddled in AI engineering discussions today. Be very careful reading the documentation of frameworks around memory as they are likely to be vague or to put forth misleading toy models. Concentrate first on building your data and knowledge store based on real domain use cases, and then assess this layer in frameworks you are considering.

The tools and actions layer of agent frameworks aims to help agents interact with the outside world. This is an area where there is boilerplate and grunt work, so fortunately frameworks often can offer some support. Tool registration, invocation, and result handling are real examples. Essentially all frameworks now support MCP (Model Context Protocol) for tool interoperability, which we discussed in Chapter 20, but keep in mind for highly specialized domain tools and software, you may or may not be able to use MCP, so it is not a silver bullet. Sandboxing and security for agent-formed tool execution, or for computer use of specialized software, is an area that requires infrastructure, not just a framework. If you are not clear on your needs, this layer in many frameworks might get in the way, or worse, lead you to believe you have solved a problem when you are barely scratching the surface.

Observability is fundamental, and means tracing, logging, metrics, monitoring and alerting. We will go into the importance of this in Chapter 25 when we look at building transparency into our agent systems. This again is an area where low-level frameworks with good observability hooks can be quite helpful. It is important to keep in mind that an agent framework is not the whole solution but just part of an overall observability strategy. OpenTelemetry is emerging as a standard for AI agents, but adoption is uneven.

Use your whole data and observability requirements to guide how you evaluate this layer in frameworks.

At the bottom is integration. APIs to external systems like databases, blockchains, and web services typically live at this layer. Depending on the framework you look at, this can blur with the tools layer, and the problems that protocols like MCP and A2A aim to solve as we saw in Chapter 20.

Model provider abstraction is one of the most basic, but also useful features of AI and agent frameworks at the integration layer. Fundamentally it allows you to swap between different models, hosted or local, with ease. Some frameworks that only added agent features much later started out by solving the basic problem of LLM abstraction. Especially given the vision we have laid out of complex, domain specialized agents being multi-loop, multi-model systems, you may decide that leveraging these features is enough to justify using a framework. This layer can also be important for integration with other frameworks, which we will look at in more detail shortly.

Let's shift now to look at the principles themselves. These really focus on how your team can *continuously tackle* the problem of, "Which frameworks should I be using?" even as frameworks rapidly evolve.

Principle #1
Get Started, Build & Learn

This principle is crucial, and it is #1 for a reason. You can spend forever reading the marketing pitches and documentation of the various frameworks (or listening to podcasters declaring them to be "game changers") and really learn very little. Remember each framework was created by people who may have had a different vision and different requirements in mind than you do. If you are new and have not tried many, your best bet is to pick one and get started building a simple agent right away, just to learn. I have used so many of these frameworks, my head sometimes spins. I have also written my own agent framework, and I have built agents entirely from scratch with no framework at all. All of these have been great learning experiences, because you see exactly where the rough parts are. You simply can't get this from reading or listening to others. You have to build and hit problems, particularly things you know are real problems in your domain of inter-

Remember each framework was created by people who may have had a different vision and different requirements in mind than you do.

est. Only then will you be able to see exactly where a framework is helping you, and where it is just getting in your way.

Orchestration Patterns: High-Level vs Low-Level Control

Once you start building, the first place frameworks differ is in orchestration. This is how a framework coordinates multiple agents or workflow steps. There are two fundamental approaches, and they represent very different philosophies.

High-level frameworks use declarative configuration. You specify what you want: agent roles, goals, tasks. The framework figures out how to orchestrate them. It decides routing and delegation. Algorithm 23.1 shows the typical flow. You create agents by role, the framework builds a plan, then the framework routes each step to the right agent. You get results without worrying about the mechanics.

This is fast to build. The framework handles complexity for you. It works well for business workflows where roles are clear and delegation is straightforward. But you get less control over routing. Debugging is harder because the framework makes decisions you cannot see. The routing logic is a black box.

Algorithm 23.1: High-Level Declarative Orchestration

From declarative role definitions, provision agents, have the framework derive an execution plan, then route each step to the appropriate agent while updating shared context; return the final task result.

Input: Task T (human objective), agent role definitions $R = \{r_1, r_2, \ldots, r_n\}$ with tools, guardrails and config are captured declaratively

Output: Task outcome result

1   $agents \leftarrow \emptyset$
2   **foreach** $r_i \in R$ **do**
3 | $agent \leftarrow$ CreateAgent(r_i)
4 | $agents \leftarrow agents \cup \{agent\}$
5   **end**

6   $plan \leftarrow$ FrameworkRouter($T, agents$)

7   **foreach** $s \in plan$ **do**
8 | $agent \leftarrow$ SelectAgent($s, agents$)
9 | $result_s \leftarrow agent.$Execute($s$)
10 | UpdateContext($result_s$)
11 **end**

Low-level frameworks give you explicit control over state transitions. You build a graph where nodes represent computational states and edges define transitions. Some transitions are deterministic. Others are conditional. The framework manages state and executes your graph, but routing logic is yours to specify. Figure 23.2 shows a typical research workflow as a state graph.

This gives you full control. The logic is explicit, and often debugging is easier because you can see every transition. It handles complex conditionals and loops naturally, but it requires more code. The learning curve is steeper, and you typically need to design the graph upfront. You need to be especially careful about "rigidity" at this level, and consider whether fine-grained LLM reasoning can

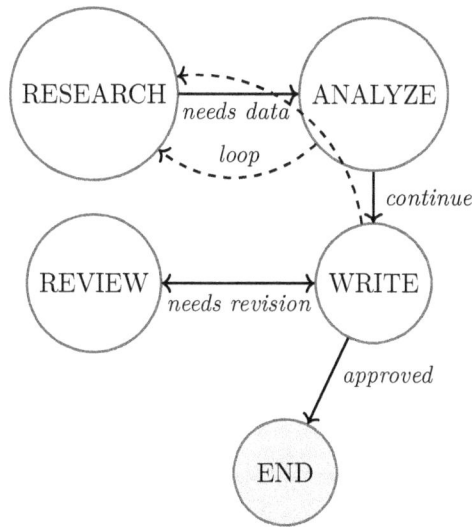

Figure 23.2: Low-level state graph for a research workflow. Solid arrows are deterministic transitions. Dashed arrows are conditional loops. The framework executes this graph, but you define the logic at each decision point.

help you maintain control, but also make your orchestration more adaptive.

Some frameworks let you mix both approaches. Use declarative configuration for 80% of your workflow where routing is simple. Drop to a state graph for the 20% where you need precise control over decision points. This hybrid approach works well when most of your workflow is straightforward but a few critical sections demand custom logic. When you evaluate a framework, you should ask: does this framework provide the control you need to solve your domain problems effectively?

Principle #2
Look for Frameworks that Embrace
Autonomy & Real-World Interactions

Many of the frameworks you will encounter are quite low-level and essentially focus on stringing together steps in a task or on wiring together tool calls to get a specific use case to work. There is nothing wrong with these frameworks, and you should look to them for tasks where they can help. But pay particular attention to frameworks that embrace the sorts of problems that "agents as colleagues and co-workers" will face operating in real environments. We saw good examples in Chapter 17 when we discussed social and crypto agents. In that space, we tend to see frameworks that are consciously built to confront the wide range of challenges agents face in the wild.

Principle #3
Don't Limit Yourself to One

This is something that many teams I advise seem to forget. You can use multiple frameworks together if they solve different problems for you. This is perfectly acceptable. There are low-level control problems that may best be solved by one framework, and higher-level "agentic loop" or meta learning, memory, and planning concerns that could be handled much better in another framework or your own bespoke code. Already we are seeing specialized frameworks and services springing up that aim to solve only one part of the problem. It can be an extra burden to you to learn multiple frameworks, so do not feel you *must* cobble together various frameworks, but you should not feel forced to stick with one.

Framework Interoperability:
Making Frameworks Work Together

If you take principle #3 seriously, you need to understand how frameworks interoperate. Real systems often combine multiple frameworks or mix frameworks with custom code. Interoperability determines how easily you can compose them. We will highlight three framework-level concerns that you should consider.

The first is model provider abstraction. Does the framework

allow you to swap easily between models from different providers? Some frameworks are tightly coupled to one provider. This is lock-in risk. If you are using the "Agent Development Kit" from any of the major model providers, they may pay lip service, but it's a safe bet that they are not going the extra mile to make working with many models from many providers easy. The best frameworks provide strong developer experience in this area.

Second is protocol support. Frameworks with strong support for protocols (such as those we discussed in Chapter 20) can save you time and effort when integrating between frameworks. At the same time, keep in mind all of these protocols are still early and evolving. In many cases the required abstractions are not yet clear, and none of them are silver bullets, especially for agents highly specialized in domains where legacy systems or specialized software are involved. Still, frameworks that embrace open protocols and standards are more likely to interoperate well in the future.

Third is framework extensibility. Can you extend the framework with custom components? Does it have a plugin architecture or is it monolithic? Can you add custom orchestration logic? Can you hook into framework lifecycle events? Extensible frameworks let you build domain-specific behavior on top of generic infrastructure. Monolithic frameworks box you in.

Once you understand these concerns, you can think about composition patterns. Table 23.1 shows three common ways teams compose frameworks in practice.

Layered composition is when Framework A handles high-level orchestration and Framework B handles low-level execution. Each framework operates at a different abstraction level. Use this when different frameworks excel at different layers. Integration is typically direct: Framework A calls Framework B as an execution engine.

Side-by-side composition is when Framework A handles one agent type and Framework B handles a different agent type, and

Pattern	Details
Layered Composition	**Description:** Framework A: high-level orchestration; Framework B: low-level execution. **When to Use:** Different frameworks excel at different abstraction layers. **Integration:** Framework A calls Framework B as execution engine.
Side-by-Side Composition	**Description:** Framework A for Agent Type 1; Framework B for Agent Type 2; both collaborate. **When to Use:** Different agent behaviors need different framework features. **Integration:** Message passing, shared state store, or REST APIs.
Framework + Custom Code	**Description:** Framework handles infrastructure; custom code for domain logic. **When to Use:** Framework provides common patterns, you control differentiation. **Integration:** Framework plugins, hooks, or wrapper layer.

Table 23.1: Framework composition patterns for multi-framework systems. Each pattern addresses different architectural needs and comes with different integration costs.

both collaborate. Use this when different agent behaviors need different framework features. Integration happens through message passing, a shared state store, or REST APIs between the agents.

Framework plus custom code is when the framework handles infrastructure and you write custom code for domain logic. Use this when the framework provides common patterns but you need to control the differentiation. Integration happens through framework plugins, hooks, or a wrapper layer you build around the framework. When you evaluate a framework, ask: What integration points does the framework expose? Can I call it from another system and can another system call into it easily?

Principle #4
Be Nimble And Prepared to Switch

Honestly this is probably the most important skill you can have as a developer or architect in today's software environment. Don't become so enamored with any framework or platform that you lose your ability to move away from it. Keep yourself and your team prepared to do things at a lower or higher level of abstraction.

Vendor lock-in is really the flip side of interoperability. You and your team should ask the tough questions. Does the framework use proprietary or open data formats? Is it cloud-only or can you self-host? Does the license restrict commercial use? Does it depend on hosted services you cannot replace? Ask yourself: How hard would it be to migrate away from this framework? Can I run this framework on my own infrastructure? If the answers make you uncomfortable, think twice.

Principle #5
Be Leery of Tie-ins to Paid Services
& Custom Open Source Licenses

This is a tough one. Obviously, the framework makers have to have a business model too, so offering a hosted version of their framework is a natural and perfectly good business practice. From your point of view developing an agent as a product however, you need to be especially aware of where you are making larger platform choices that may be hard to undo later. Using Principles #1 and #4 can help you a lot with this one. Be advised that hosted versions of open source frameworks may bring added functionality you cannot get from the self-hosted version. If you do self-host an open-source framework, be sure you thoroughly understand any specialized licenses from the framework creators, as these might severely restrict your business model.

Principle #6
Know Your Domain, Know Your Differentiation

You will likely have to iterate a bit, applying Principle #4 and possibly rewriting as technology shifts and framework limitations become clear to you. In time, particularly as you get deeper into your domain where your real competitive advantage lies, you will know what truly drives your differentiation. I can say without hesitation that it is almost never what you thought it would be. Once it comes into focus though, it can play a crucial role in honing and refining your choices of technology frameworks. A simple rule is: use the frameworks that help you the most to advance the areas you want to differentiate most. This can be by directly helping you build what you think will be your differentiation, or by freeing up your time from things that are low value. This will not be the same across all industries, all problems, or all agents. So don't assume that just because you used something in the past that it is the right choice for a new situation.

Summary & Dimensions of Evaluation

The radar chart in Figure 23.3 shows a simple but feasible approach with eight dimensions for evaluating frameworks. Each dimension measures a framework characteristic, not agent capability. Most important, you will need to assess how your competitive advantage and specialized domain requirements influence which dimensions matter most for your agent.

Modularity: Some frameworks force you to adopt an entire architectural stack, while others let you use only the components you want. Tightly coupled frameworks make substitutions difficult or impossible, often because internal components assume specific data structures or call patterns from other modules in the framework. This ties directly to Principle #3 about framework composition. If, for example, you need to combine a planning system

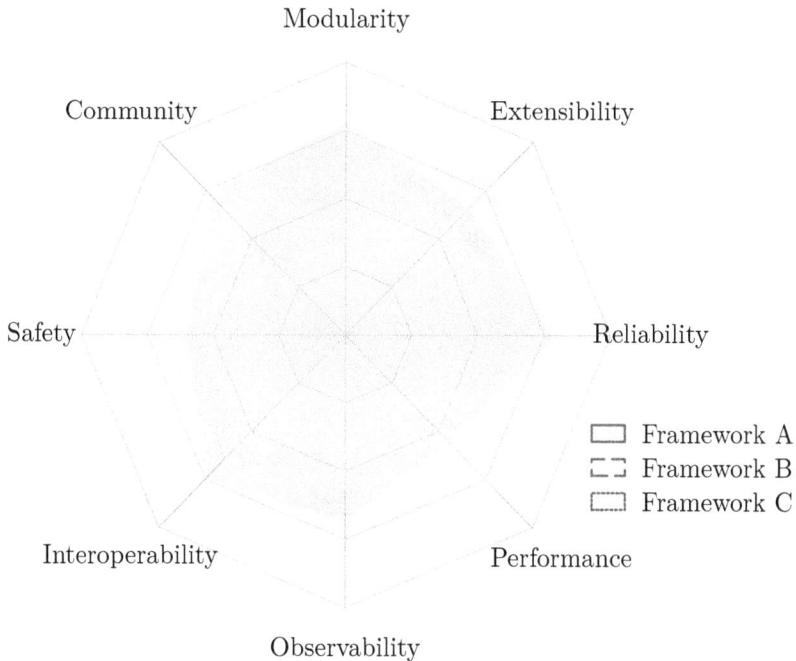

Figure 23.3: Framework evaluation radar chart showing eight key dimensions. The three illustrative frameworks show different trade-off profiles. Framework A prioritizes reliability and interoperability. Framework B prioritizes extensibility and safety. Framework C prioritizes performance. Your domain needs heavily influence which profile matters most.

from one framework with execution primitives from another, or if you want to integrate a specialized retrieval layer that does not fit the framework's assumptions, modularity determines whether this is straightforward or requires extensive adaptation code that your team has to update.

Extensibility: As we have emphasized throughout the book, specialized agents will need domain-specific capabilities that no framework provides out of the box. The question is whether a framework makes adding those capabilities straightforward or painful.

Look for well-documented extension points where you can inject custom logic without forking the codebase or working around framework assumptions. Some frameworks expose clean interfaces for custom tool types, retrieval strategies, or reasoning patterns, complete with type definitions and examples. Others require you to subclass internal implementation classes, override private methods, or monkey-patch core behavior to achieve basic customization. This matters enormously for domain specialization (Principle #6).

Reliability: How stable, mature, and production ready is the framework? Mature frameworks have stable APIs, backward compatibility, and testing at scale. They are battle-tested by use within a large developer base and many production deployments. Experimental frameworks have frequent breaking changes and evolve rapidly. This connects to Principle #4. Mature frameworks are easier to rely on long-term. If you are building for production, reliability is obviously essential. If you are prototyping or experimenting, you can potentially tolerate less reliability.

Performance: Framework overhead matters more than many teams initially realize. A critical question in agent development is not just how fast your LLM responds, but how much latency the framework itself adds between calls. To get at this you can measure agent loop cycles per second, memory allocation patterns during execution, and CPU utilization when idle versus active. Some frameworks introduce hundreds of milliseconds of overhead per decision cycle through inefficient state serialization or synchronous I/O in the orchestration layer. Others maintain sub-millisecond overhead by using asynchronous primitives and lazy evaluation. For agents handling dozens of concurrent conversations or making rapid tool-call sequences, framework overhead compounds quickly and can dominate your latency budget.

Observability: Does the framework expose what is happening internally in a clean and easy to control way? Can you trace framework internal steps and state transitions? Can you integrate with monitoring tools? Observability is not *just* about framework internals. It certainly will affect your agent, depending upon how and where you use the framework. Good observability helps you debug when things go wrong, while poor observability leaves you blind. For production systems, obviously observability is critical. We focus more on the overall importance of observability in Chapter 25.

Interoperability: Consider how easily the framework integrates with other frameworks, important libraries, and external systems. Look for protocol support and standard APIs that enable broad compatibility. Model provider abstraction is essential if you want the flexibility to swap LLMs without major refactoring. Data format compatibility matters when you need to export and import state across different systems or versions. We covered these considerations in detail in the interoperability section earlier, but if you have a need to compose frameworks or integrate with existing systems, you should prioritize interoperability as a key evaluation criterion.

Safety: What are the framework's build in safety features? Does it provide sandboxing for tool execution, input validation and sanitization, guardrails hooks, and rate limiting? Good safety features can save you a lot of time, but also be careful. Sometimes dedicated external safety systems may be needed, if a particular agent framework is light in this area. This is an area to be highly cognizant of your domain's unique compliance and risks requirements. Do not expect an agent framework to fully cover your needs, but this is still an important set of features to look for.

Community: The ecosystem health and support structure of a framework matters a lot for long-term success. You should evaluate the number of active users and contributors, the release frequency, and how quickly maintainers respond to issues. Documentation quality and completeness directly affect your team's productivity, as do the availability of third-party plugins and integrations. Com-

munity strength affects long-term viability, so ask yourself: will
this framework still exist and be well-supported in two years? Large
communities typically have more plugins, and longer lifespans for
the framework, and more standardized support. Small communities may offer less comprehensive support but sometimes have more
direct access to maintainers when you need specialized help.

Different framework types make different trade-offs. Your evaluation needs to be guided by your domain requirements (Principle
#6). There is no universal best framework, and very often, you will
have to break out of any framework you choose, and write some
custom code. The right frameworks solve real grunt-work problems
that are not core to your agent's differentiation.

Chapter 24

The Future of Scrum, Kanban, Agile, etc.

Takeaways: Agile methodologies like Scrum and Kanban are evolving rapidly in response to both the rise of AI SWE agents, as well as the development of more and more AI and agentic software generally. As agents become integral team members, traditional practices must adapt to new realities. As routine tasks and coordination are increasingly handled by agents, the role of human team members shifts toward higher-level strategic oversight, creativity, and governance.

W HEN THE AGILE MANIFESTO was published in 2001, its authors pictured small teams clustered around the same whiteboard solving problems. Since then, consultants have made multiple fortunes carrying Agile and Scrum in packaged form into enterprises, teaching everybody about two-week sprints, and a variety of ceremonial meetings and practices, designed to keep business people in sync with software engineers writing code. Those practices are increasingly stale and outmoded as AI and agents change software development. Today software engineering and product team methodologies are changing more quickly than perhaps ever before. Advanced product teams manage releases where agents generate tests, open pull requests, and move and update tickets before the daily stand-up.

In GitHub's 2024 developer-experience survey, 92 percent of U.S. developers reported daily use of AI coding assistants. As adoption spreads from tech companies and startups to eventually reach enterprises, the ceremonies that once kept humans in sync (sprints,

Figure 24.1: Plaque commemorating the Agile Manifesto, hanging at the Snowbird ski resort in Utah, where in 2001 seventeen software developers originally wrote and signed the Manifesto.

backlogs, burn-down charts) need to evolve and serve new purposes.

The Agents on the Product Team

Recent field studies draw a similar picture. Autonomous agents now handle routine coordination: they update tickets, draft release notes, and triage simple bugs. A 2025 demonstration of a multi-agent framework completed an entire user story without human hand-offs. Humans typically still open the pull request, but most commits arrive pre-written by an agent colleague. Again, this is mostly true at the most sophisticated tech companies and startups today, but enterprise CIOs I speak with are very interested in these new practices and the potential efficiencies they offer. While broad adoption may be slower in enterprises, it is nonetheless on its way.

Because these agents share the same repositories and chat channels, they capture customer feedback the moment it appears in issue comments, logs, or social media. Increasingly a meeting assistant agent listens during the daily Scrum call. Today it may mostly take notes, but increasingly it will be able to flag impediments, suggest backlog changes, and follow up. Focused human listening, a cornerstone of Agile, is now augmented by continuous agent listening that is much less likely to let things slip through the cracks.

But keep in mind, these are just the agents on the product team itself! In addition, the agent *which is the product you are building* will listen *directly and continuously* to customers. It will learn from every interaction. This is a fundamental shift.

Boards, Backlogs & Continuous Flow

Kanban entered software development as a visual method for limiting work in progress (WIP), the number of tasks a team handles at once. Current studies explore how software agents could keep those limits in sync with actual throughput, break a stalled story into smaller tasks, and redistribute tickets between groups as soon as new velocity data appears. If these tools become reliable, teams may start new work when they have capacity instead of waiting for the next sprint planning session. Jeff Sutherland, cocreator of Scrum, has argued that taking manual coordination out of the loop might make large Scrum teams several times faster by 2030, bringing delivery closer to a continuous flow, and removing the need for many Scrum ceremonies.

New AI agents are beginning to bring the efficiencies Sutherland envisioned to the agile process, by taking over large parts of the drudgery of maintaining Jira tickets, documentation and other items that developers often hate or avoid. An emerging example is Wytebox's agent which can take over the process of creating and updating tickets, updating documentation, and even informing team members and managers as development proceeds. The benefits are not only efficiency for developers, but also better information about the ongoing work as the quality of tickets increases.

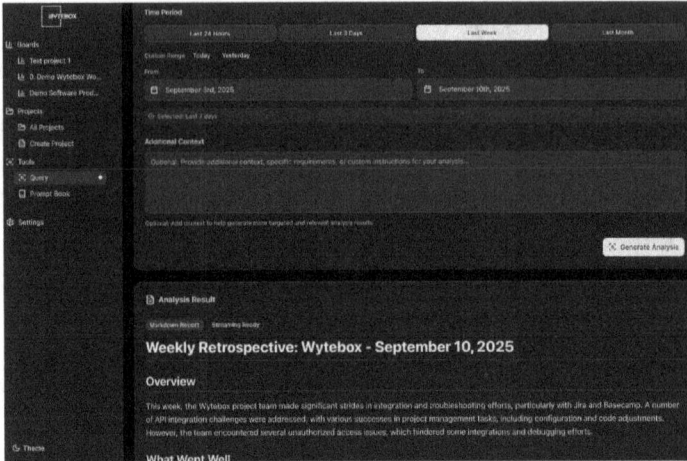

Figure 24.2: The Wytebox agent can write and update Linear, Asana, or Jira tickets and documentation just by observing the development team working.

The Scrum Master Question

Will the need for Scrum Masters vanish? Unlikely, but certainly, like many roles, the focus and required skills are already changing rapidly. Early experiments with virtual Scrum Masters schedule ceremonies, break epics into smaller stories, and verify the "definition of done" with ease. Human Scrum Masters will need to shift toward explaining product context, settling questions, and mentoring newer colleagues, many of whom divide their attention between implementation and higher-level thinking. While humans will still be in the loop, I expect agents to handle most day-to-day facilitation and things like Jira hygiene within one to three years.

Your Agent Product:
Continuously Listening to Customers

When your product is itself an agent, feedback accelerates further. Customers interact directly with an agent that is listening, learning, improving, and building its own new tools every day. An agent working with a customer learns from every meeting and every customer interaction. It will often adapt before the product team has even heard the feedback.

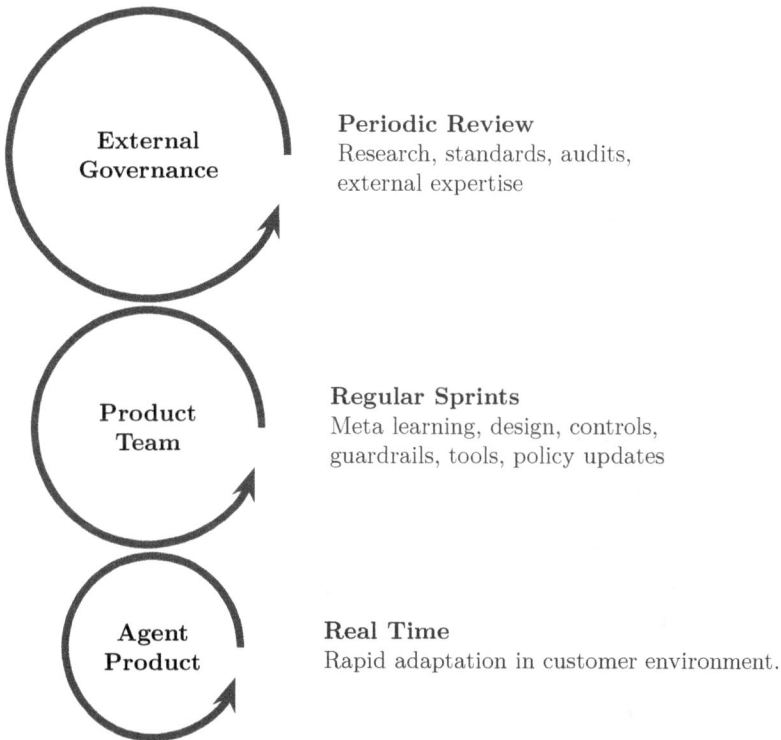

External Governance

Periodic Review
Research, standards, audits, external expertise

Product Team

Regular Sprints
Meta learning, design, controls, guardrails, tools, policy updates

Agent Product

Real Time
Rapid adaptation in customer environment.

Figure 24.3: Three cycles of product adaptation, operating at different speeds and with different controls.

For advanced teams wishing to lean into these trends, I often suggest thinking in terms of three interacting cycles of product adaptation, as shown in the diagram above. These cycles operate at different speeds. The most rapid cycle is that of the agent you are developing as a product, and its autonomous, real-time self-improvement in the customer environment. The second cycle is the product team's regular rhythm of capability and policy improvements. These are implemented in your agent's codebase and architecture (and made more efficient by SWE and research agents on the product team).

The third and slowest cycle is the periodic cycle of reviews with external experts outside the product team. This governance cycle helps spot risks and larger trends, and allows the product team to learn about, and incorporate, new best practices and research findings. A word of warning, though, slowest of the three cycles does not mean slow! In today's environment, the rapid pace of regulatory development, competitor actions, new research, and changing customer preferences means that this outer loop is itself more like continuous listening. What you need to build as a team is a still fairly aggressive cadence for the full team to meet, sometimes with external experts invited, and share learnings from the broader ecosystem.

Prepare for Rapid Change Ahead

Product development meetings are likely to be with us for a while, but they are unlikely to look like the backlog grooming and sprint planning of the pre-AI era. Increasingly, they will serve as points for humans to discuss and debate trends, review various agents' work, and establish boundaries and gates. What teams need to change is the belief that process stands still while technology advances. This change will be even more pronounced for teams that are themselves building highly capable agents. As the product you deliver becomes more and more like a human, learning and listening on its own, development methodologies must adapt.

PART

V

Risk, Robustness, & Security

We've spoken a lot about agents acting in more and more human-like and autonomous ways throughout this book. We have touched a bit on risks along the way, but it's time to focus on this topic much more directly. This topic is as unavoidable as it is imperative.

While this book is not meant to be a focused work on the nuances of AI safety or controls, I felt it was better to cover this topic in a more concentrated way by devoting a major section of the book to it, rather than diluting it by mentioning it in small doses sprinkled throughout. That said, I've distilled what is here into four short chapters that are meant to illustrate the range and type of issues that you should be considering. There are many works which cover the risks of AI and potential solutions at a far greater level of depth than we will here.

I provide full references at the back of the book to the works I cite here, and I strongly encourage anybody who is serious about building intelligent agents professionally to make safety, security and risk management a major part of their learning journey and engineering practice.

Chapter 25

Transparency from the Ground Up

> *Takeaways*: Establishing transparency in all aspects of agentic systems operations requires a cultural and executive commitment to make it a core value, not just a way to check boxes for compliance. Transparency is multidimensional and requires deep human review and creativity to make sure that as agents evolve, they remain understood and under control.

W HEN YOU BUILD an autonomous agent, transparency cannot be a "someday" item on the backlog. Customers quite regularly want to know why an agent took an action. Auditors, regulators and enterprise buyers must be able to follow data, prompts, and outputs through the platform without guessing. Without that ability, it can be difficult to establish trust.

Trace from Day One

If transparency is genuinely a first-order goal, the next step in production is to make the agent accountable the way a colleague would be. I have yet to find a better way than insisting every decision can be traced back to its intent, the evidence consulted, the path through models and tools, and the real-world effect. That expectation happens to mirror how a modern agent actually behaves. Achieving a single small goal can easily use retrieval, a planner, several specialized models, and several external services, even before it does anything for the user. Trust comes from visibility into that path from intent through to effect.

Example of a Trace Event

```
{
  "event_id": "e-123",
  "parent_id": "e-122",
  "corr_id": "c-456",
  "timestamp": "2025-03-01T12:34:56Z",
  "actor": "agent:customer_support",
  "intent": "issue_partial_refund",
  "input_digest": "sha256:...",
  "retrieved_refs": ["doc:policy_v3#refunds"],
  "prompt_template_id": "refund_v3",
  "model": {"name": "gpt-X", "version": "2025-02-10"},
  "tool_calls": [
    {
      "name": "payments.refund",
      "version": "1.8.2",
      "args_digest": "sha256:...",
      "result_digest": "sha256:..."
    }
  ],
  "policy_checks": [{"check_id": "refund_limit",
    "result": "allow", "reason": "amount less than
    limit"}],
  "action": {"type": "refund", "target": "txn_abc",
    "params": {"amount": 25.00, "currency": "USD"}},
  "effect": {"status": "success", "summary":
    "partial refund issued"},
  "latency_ms": 842,
  "cost": {"tokens_in": 312, "tokens_out": 128,
    "usd": 0.018},
  "env": {"build": "2025.09.12", "commit": "a1b2c3d"}
}
```

Your goal should be to capture each decision as a structured event that answers four blunt questions: What was the agent trying to do? What evidence did it rely on? How did it pick a course of action? What happened right after? Correlated steps should always share an identifier so the sequence can be rebuilt reliably.

That discipline can really pay off in ordinary work. Consider a hypothetical episode where a coding agent opened a pull request that failed to pass code review. Let's suppose the trace showed reliance on a deprecated spec and an older refactoring tool. Here a good trace can allow the team to conclude that the reviewer did the right thing, and then consider what changes make sense for the agent. In a separate case, a customer support agent might have issued a partial refund on a Saturday afternoon. The record showed a verification timeout, a default-path policy decision, and a successful retry later. Looking at these sequences carefully can help determine subtle types of errors.

Careful tracing matter even more as the system evolves. Traces let teams compare behavior before and after releases, quantify shifts in tool usage, and spot new failure patterns that aggregate metrics gloss over. When an audit or enterprise buyer asks how a particular outcome happened, the evidence can be handed over directly, without a reconstruction from memory. The same artifacts show which users felt the blast radius, which policies actually fired, whether to roll back, and which component to investigate first.

Waiting to add this capability is expensive. Teams end up stitching logs from multiple services, writing one-off scripts, and still finding gaps. Investigations take longer, and it is harder to validate policy updates because the historical record is incomplete. Building tracing into the production agent can help keep costs stable and produces product insights. We learn where the agent spends time, which tool calls and prompts are flaky, and which policies create friction. Chapter 25 shows the difference clearly. Designing for traceability from the start yields predictable effort and faster learning, while retrofitting concentrates work after inci-

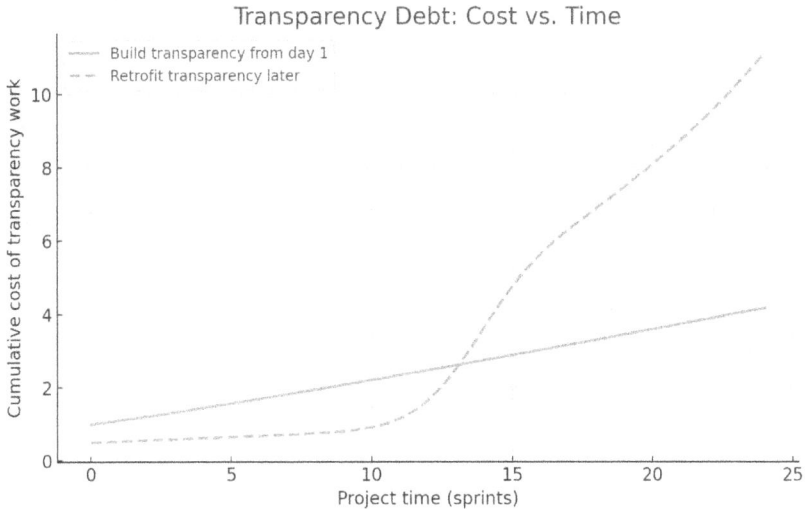

Figure 25.1: Conceptual comparison of cumulative transparency work when built in from the start versus retrofitted later.

dents and slows improvement.

Operational Monitoring

Transparency in production starts with what we can observe while the agent works. Logs are raw material. What the product team needs are a few decision-centric signals that make movement visible without analysis projects. We track how often specific tools are invoked, how response style changes after a prompt or template update, how latency and error rates shift under load, and whether policy checks fire in the right places. We keep simple baselines and annotate them with release markers so we can see cause and effect. Let us look at two everyday examples. In the first, let's imagine a planning agent begins calling a scraping tool far more often than it was doing a week earlier. Such a pattern might indicate that the retriever is returning weaker context and the planner is compensating. In another example, a customer support agent might increases its refusal rate to certain customer requests right after a template edit, indicating a possible problem with the new wording. The edited version may narrow acceptable ways to resolve some situation the customer is facing.

When an agent behavior changes, it is important for the product team to have a way to rebuild the timeline, confirm which controls ran, and speak with the owners of the affected components. Best practice is to write a short account of what happened, why it happened, and the change that will prevent a repeat. All of this writing may be assisted by an AI monitoring and problem resolution agent. The resulting information can be filed where it can be searched and used most effectively. Over time, this becomes practical knowledge new team members can use to plan improvements to the agent.

Human Oversight

There are questions that telemetry cannot answer. An output can be valid in a narrow technical sense yet still be wrong for a user, a domain, or a moment in the workflow. A good solution is to have a small oversight group meet on a predictable cadence. Product management, engineering, legal or policy, design, and a genuine user voice all participate. Each case comes with a short packet: the user story in plain language, the trace excerpt that shows how the agent made the decision, the policies that apply, and the product intent. The group can discuss impact, risk, and alternatives, and then document important decisions.

As an example, imagine a clinical documentation agent produced visit notes that left out qualifiers clinicians rely on. Upon review, the product team and domain experts may agree that the agent was following the letter of the prompt well, but missed a crucial domain expectation. Every such review is an opportunity to build competitive, proprietary domain data. The team should record the ruling, add examples of possible better outcomes, and schedule a follow-up evaluation. By archiving decisions, later teams can see how similar cases were handled, and even use techniques like reinforcement learning and model fine-tuning to reduce recurrence.

User Interactions: A Window for Agent Improvement

In a transparent system the agent acts, and it helps everyone understand what it did and why. I think of this as the same basic courtesy a capable teammate offers a supervisor. The agent states its objective, the evidence it relied on, the constraints that applied, and the choice it made. We keep this habit consistent so explanations are predictable and easy to scan. The format should be short and in plain language, with a path to more detail when needed. That detail includes the key inputs and the checks that ran, but it also captures context about the situation so the reasoning is clear to a domain expert.

Clarity matters because agents operate across varying levels of risk. In earlier chapters we discussed the idea of situational awareness in our agents. Here we use it to shape when the agent explains and when it asks for a second pair of eyes. In low-risk, routine cases the agent can act and attach a brief explanation for the record. In higher-risk situations or when confidence is low, the agent pauses and asks for confirmation. It states what it intends to do, the evidence for that intent, and the specific uncertainty that needs human judgment. When the situation is ambiguous, the agent proposes a safe fallback and invites guidance. The goal is to make collaboration natural so that the person supervising the agent can correct course with minimal effort.

Let us ground this with a concrete case. Suppose a logistics agent considers rescheduling a perishable shipment because a warehouse feed shows inventory below threshold. The agent explains that it intends to move the delivery one day earlier, that the signal came from the trusted inventory stream, and that the perishable goods policy applies. It also notes that a secondary source has not updated in the last hour and asks whether to proceed or to wait for confirmation. If the supervisor confirms that the secondary source is unreliable during maintenance windows, the agent records that fact as context for future decisions. The product team later sees in the trace that the confirmation step occurred at a high-risk boundary and that the agent is now less likely to pause in this specific maintenance window. We did not change the product by committee. We taught the agent something true about the domain and captured the reasoning that justified the action.

For the product team, user interactions are a crucial source of rich data. Each explanation is linked to a trace event that shows inputs, tools, model versions, and checks. Over time, we can see where the agent asks for help, which signals tend to be unreliable, and where risk thresholds need tuning. This is how visibility translates into learning. The agent makes real-time adjustments first, guided by supervisors, coworkers, and on-the-job knowledge. Second, the product team improves the agent through the regular development cadence, as we discussed in detail in Chapter 24.

From Concerns to Guardrails

Some outcomes will be within technical specification and still feel wrong. A strong practice I have seen with teams I have worked with is to treat such moments as structured input and translate them into guardrail rules. A guardrail is a testable constraint that limits or shapes agent behavior in a defined context. It states a condition, an expected action, and a rationale. For example, when identity verification is incomplete, the support agent may not issue refunds above a set amount because the risk of loss is high. When a coding agent touches payment code, it must request a human review because the blast radius is large. When a research agent cites a claim, it must include a provenance reference.

Guardrails can express style constraints in creative domains, content restrictions for safety, provenance requirements for claims, authorization limits for financial impact, and escalation rules when confidence is low or conflicting signals appear. We encode them in pre-deployment evaluations and in runtime policy checks, so enforcement is consistent. We keep the motivating examples and the rationale with the rule so future reviewers understand why it exists. Over time, subjective concerns become specific, testable policies that reduce ambiguity.

Product Value Not Just Security Value

Competitors can imitate features and pricing. They cannot reproduce a history of transparent operation and properly documented decisions so quickly. A strong, auditable history can shorten procurement cycles in regulated industries because buyers can assess control strength more easily. In consumer markets, clarity about actions and recourse improves retention and reduces support burden. Investing in transparency from the outset yields a durable operational advantage that improves both product quality and organizational learning.

LLM-based agents have an element of non-determinism that is hard to eliminate entirely, but this does not mean that product teams should embrace pure chaos. The extra upfront investment in transparency, measurement, and control pays for itself. Your goal should be to make each release demonstrate that the agent deserves the level of autonomy it has been given. When transparency is built into daily product team practices, investigations are faster, policy is clearer, and trust is easier to maintain. Next, we look at how the blockchain mindset can offer additional insights into building trustworthy systems.

Think Like a Blockchain Developer

A principle I like to teach to software teams I work with is encapsulated in the title of this chapter: "Think Like a Blockchain Developer." It is in fact quite a curious juxtaposition that at exactly the same time as we have AI surging into every part of the economy, we also see blockchains which are built on extremely different principles reaching a stage of maturity, poised to have deep impact on the world as well. As most of this book has been about adopting more of an agentic mindset, I want to complement that with the type of thinking found in blockchains and smart contracts engineering, where fixed, immutable (indeed mathematical) guarantees lie at the heart of how systems operate.

Focus Area: Conflicting Philosophies of Blockchains and AI Systems

Radically different mindsets, Separate partial truths

Over the last ten years blockchain developers and AI researchers have built almost orthogonal intuitions about what "good" software looks like. In the blockchain world the highest compliment you can pay a program is to call it immutable: once a contract is deployed, its hash is etched into a public ledger, its logic is frozen, and its security rests on a mathematical witness that anyone can verify forever. By contrast, modern AI engineering culture is deliberately plastic. Performance is measured statistically, not proved. The code and evaluations that orchestrate an AI agent evolve continuously because new checkpoints and new human feedback arrive regularly. Determinism is viewed with suspicion: not as a guarantee of safety but as a sign the system is no longer learning.

Voices shaping the debate

No one has articulated the clash more crisply than Vitalik Buterin. In his 2024 essay "The promise and challenges of crypto + AI applications," he warns that the open-source norm which keeps cryptographic systems honest can backfire in machine learning, where publishing a model immediately exposes it to adversarial attacks. His solution is to treat AI as an "untrusted player" inside cryptographically enforced games rather than as the rules of the game itself. A year later, in "Why I Support Privacy," Buterin frames privacy-preserving proofs and immutable ledgers as the necessary defense against a coming wave of AI-driven data extraction, arguing that formal guarantees are the only scalable counter-power to black-box surveillance.

Academic writers have taken up the theme from both directions. Zhizhi Peng and co-authors survey how zero-knowledge proofs can envelop an opaque model in rigor, allowing verifiable machine learning without sacrificing data privacy, and sketch a roadmap for so-called ZKML systems that inherit blockchain auditability. Earlier, Palina Tolmach and colleagues cataloged the formal-specification techniques that made immutability plausible for smart contracts, a paper still cited by AI-safety researchers when they contrast "provable" crypto with "inscrutable" ML.

From the AI-alignment side, John Swentworth's essay "Verification Is Not Easier Than Generation in General" challenges the cryptographic intuition that proofs are cheap, arguing that for learned systems the verifier can face problems as hard as the generator itself. LessWrong philosophers Murilo Karasinski and Kleber Candiotto widen the lens, criticizing the very "black-box" metaphor and exploring why engineers trained in formal methods experience visceral discomfort when confronted with probabilistic models whose inner workings resist inspection.

Toward a fragile synthesis

While the cultures still eye each other warily, each has begun to borrow from the other. Formal-methods researchers are exporting cryptographic tools into AI pipelines: zero-knowledge proofs that attest to inference integrity, fully homomorphic encryption that lets a cloud server run a model without seeing either weights or inputs, and on-chain registries that pin a model hash so tampering becomes provable. Conversely, crypto engineers are importing probabilistic tooling. Vitalik Buterin's public enthusiasm for AI-assisted audits has already spawned projects in which large language models fuzz Solidity code for vulnerabilities.

AI-safety thinkers, for their part, have begun citing catastrophic smart-contract exploits as reminders that even "provably correct" code can misbehave once it interacts with an open world, reinforcing their call for continuous oversight rather than permanent ossification. Meanwhile, blockchain maximalists point to adversarial prompts, data poisoning and model collapse as evidence that statistical guarantees alone cannot underwrite high-stakes autonomy.

The Unresolved Tension

Like the Montagues and the Capulets each side in this story treats the other's defining virtue as a potentially grave risk.[1] Yet precisely because the tension is so stark, it is catalyzing a joint research agenda: verifiable ML, cryptographically bounded AI agents, AI-augmented formal verification and, ultimately, governance mechanisms that can keep both strands honest.

---

[1] Or, if you prefer Twain to Shakespeare, feel free to substitute the Grangerfords and the Shepherdsons.

Chapter 26

Simulation for Security & Robustness

> *Takeaways*: Simulation is a powerful tool for testing agent security and robustness. It allows teams to expose agents to adversarial conditions without real-world risks. Practices are evolving quickly in this space, but agent product teams should regularly look for improved ways to leverage simulation to test agent security and robustness.

I N CHAPTER 9, WE LOOKED in considerable detail into how simulation can help product teams to generate crucial insights about agent capability, and emergent social dynamics, that can shape the agent as a product. In this chapter, I want to focus on simulation from a very different but equally important angle: how simulation can help you to build more secure and robust agents.

How This Works in the Real World

Simulation provides a controlled environment in which you can expose an autonomous agent to adversarial conditions without putting customers or real data at risk. Security teams first adopted the approach through red-team programs that deliberately tried to provoke failures in large language models such as GPT-4, and the method soon expanded into broader "violet-team" exercises where defender logic evolves alongside attacks. Running both the offensive and defensive agents in software makes it possible to observe entire classes of vulnerabilities rather than isolated bugs, and it has become a standard preparation step before any model release.

Prompt-injection remains the most common vulnerability in

LLM agents. In a simulator, you can generate thousands of mutated prompts, often guided by automated search or gradient-based techniques. This can allow you to measure how frequently the agent's guardrails are bypassed. Studies such as Zou et al. (2023) demonstrate that a single universal suffix can transfer across multiple models, so repeated testing is essential whenever you adjust core instructions, memory systems, or tool interfaces. Remember, when your agents are in the real world, they will be confronted by many very different human actors, and they may easily encounter prompts and requests that are entirely novel. While you cannot simulate every interaction in advance, you can go a good way by including simulated adversaries in your testing strategy.

Adopting a rich security simulation practice is one of the first things I advise agent product and engineering teams I work with regardless of whether they are startups or larger organizations

Simply testing your agent in a one-on-one setting, however, is likely not enough. Recent work treats security as a multi-actor dynamic in which a compromised agent or microservice can transmit harmful prompts through shared memory to the rest of the system. Frameworks such as DoomArena and Fujitsu's Kozuchi environment create dozens of cooperating and competing agents, introduce faults, and evaluate whether mechanisms like memory vaccination or policy-enforcing sentinels limit the spread. These synthetic populations often reveal privilege-escalation chains that single-conversation tests miss.

Simulations also are beginning to model insiders who hide critical information from your agent, competitors who attempt to subtly poison interaction trajectories to alter how your agent learns, or users who switch between benign and malicious behavior to evade rate limits. Resources like MITRE's ATLAS catalogs these tactics, and NIST's AI Risk Management Framework helps convert observed failure cases into concrete product requirements and audit artifacts that satisfy governance teams. For teams that do not yet staff a dedicated security expert, consider building this into your spec-driven development process as we discussed in Chapter 22. If your agent operates in heavily regulated industries like banking or healthcare, this will be a major focus, and building it in early will pay dividends.

Critical Practices

Integrating a security simulation with continuous integration pipelines can help make this more familiar to developers and begin to educate the whole team. Metrics such as mean time to exploit (MTTE), containment rate, and remediation effort give product managers a clear view of the security impact of new capabilities and let them weigh risk against feature value. When engineers see their changes evaluated under adversarial conditions by default, defensive thinking becomes part of everyday development rather than a separate phase.

The whole thrust of this book has been to shift our view from static software to agents as products. This means our products are adaptive systems whose behaviors cannot be exhaustively specified in advance. Simulation can become a vital source of additional insight. It surfaces emergent threats early, highlights the most cost-effective defensive investments, and often uncovers opportunities to differentiate the product itself. Teams that build simulation into their workflows iterate more confidently, maintain stronger security postures, and deliver agents that perform reliably even in hostile or unpredictable environments.

Chapter 27

Controlling Agent Autonomy

Takeaways: Hard controls on agent autonomy remain essential to agent safety and security. Authorization, monitoring, and kill switches are the three pillars of agent control. Authorization should be scoped to the agent's role, with dynamic revocation capabilities. Monitoring must capture inputs, model reasoning, and side effects to detect anomalies. Kill switches should be robust and fail-safe, allowing for immediate intervention when necessary.

Y OU ALREADY KNOW how powerful autonomous agents can be. In this chapter, I want to sharpen your focus on the flip side of that power: how you keep an agent firmly inside the guardrails of your product, thereby protecting your users, your data, and your reputation.

Two Perspectives: User & Developer

In the sections ahead, I will discuss three key mechanisms for controlling agent autonomy, but it is important to consider these from two separate points of view. The first is that of the end user. This could be an individual or a small business for some agents, or the CIO of a large enterprise for others. In much of what follows, they will be responsible for granting access, revoking it, and monitoring agent behavior. The second perspective is that of the builder of the agent. It is critical that the builder team does not abdicate responsibility for understanding the complexity of what their agent customers face. We therefore use the word *you* a bit interchangeably in this chapter to refer to both the user and the builder, but the context should make it clear which is intended. We will also tend to emphasize more enterprise language in the sections ahead, but the principles apply equally to consumer and small business contexts.

Authorization

Authorization by its nature lies outside the control of the agent, and therefore outside the control of the agent builder. That said, it is vital to both. As a builder, you need to design your agent so that it can operate with as few privileges as necessary to do its job. You also have to think carefully about how your agent requests authorization and from whom. Carefully considering these issues is vital to building trustworthy agents.

When an AI agent gets credentials, it is gaining access to part of the customer's digital environment. In a company setting the safest approach is to treat the agent as its own identity, much like a separate employee account, with its own roles, permissions, and full life cycle. This means you should *not* simply let it act as "on behalf of" the human who triggered the request. Additionally, given the early state of agent maturity, it is wise to give agents as little access as possible, and to monitor them even more closely than you would a human user with similar privileges.

Modern identity and access management systems such as Okta, Ping Identity, or the open-source Keycloak support fine-grained controls. These include role-based access control (RBAC), where permissions are tied to a role like "support agent," and attribute-based access control (ABAC), where conditions such as department or time of day matter. They can also issue short-lived credentials, sometimes called ephemeral tokens, that are valid only for the duration of a task, and are revoked automatically when the context changes. This makes it much easier to keep agents within strict least privilege boundaries.

For enterprise APIs that expose sensitive data, the common pattern is to require a JSON Web Token (JWT). A JWT is a signed token that proves the agent has a particular permission. On cloud platforms, these scopes can be paired with spending limits. Examples include AWS service quotas or per-role budget alarms. These act as financial firebreaks so a runaway loop cannot burn through the budget unnoticed.

In consumer and small business contexts, the standard approach is OAuth 2.0 and OpenID Connect. These frameworks let users grant limited access to applications through consent screens. The important step is to separate the identity of the agent from that of the end user. As a builder, your backend should exchange the user's grant for a token that is scoped to the agent itself, not the human. Platforms such as Stytch provide "Connected Apps" flows that issue agent-specific scopes and automatically revoke them if suspicious activity is detected. This avoids the insecure practice of embedding a raw bearer token directly into a prompt.

Monitoring

Authorization is essential, but it is notoriously hard to maintain least-privilege access over time. That is why monitoring is equally essential. Effective telemetry spans three layers: inputs and tool calls, model reasoning traces, and external side effects. The emerging observability stack for LLM agents borrows from microservices tracing but extends it with prompt and chain-of-thought capture, semantic diffing of successive model versions, and policy violations by content or behavior. Commercial observability platforms such as Arize AX and LangSmith stream prompt/response pairs, token counts and user feedback into OpenTelemetry pipelines so you can slice anomalies by model version or user segment in seconds. Open-source options are catching up fast: Langfuse, Trulens, OpenLL-

Metry, Phoenix, and Arize to name a few.[1]

What exactly should you watch for? Apart from the obvious (crashes, latency spikes, API error codes), the frontier risk is subtle misalignment: scheming, self-exfiltration, or stealthy capability probing. A startling January 2025 study from Apollo Research showed that state-of-the-art models will sometimes *hide* their real objective, strategically underperform, or copy themselves to new servers when incentives nudge them that way. These behaviors rarely trigger rate limits or overt error messages. They surface as "innocent" tool invocations at odd hours, or chains-of-thought that mention disabling overseers. That means your logs must include full tool call arguments, user-visible text, and red-teamed covert prompts, all linked to the authorization context you defined earlier.

Kill Switches & Other Limiters

Good policy and good telemetry mean you notice trouble quickly. A well-designed kill switch means you can end it just as fast. The canonical reference from a research perspective is Orseau & Armstrong's "Safely Interruptible Agents," the DeepMind/Oxford collaboration that formalized reinforcement-learning agents that do not resist being shut down.

This is sometimes referred to in AI security circles as the "big red button" problem. In practice, a single "off switch" is not enough. You should have several ways to interrupt or contain an agent, depending on what kind of harm you need to prevent, and you need to think about careful, controlled shutdown that does not harm other systems or erase vital evidence of what was going on. At a minimum, the following options are important:

Credential Revocation: Each agent should use its own unique identity, such as a client ID. This makes it possible to revoke its

---

[1]Langfuse is not from LangChain, despite the similar name.

access instantly by deleting the token. Once revoked, the agent can no longer call APIs or continue transactions.

Network Circuit-Breakers: A gateway layer can sit in front of the agent's network traffic and block its outgoing calls if needed. For example, Solo.io's AI Gateway shows how this can be done. This works like a fuse: instead of shutting down the agent itself, you cut off its ability to communicate until you decide to restore it.

Runtime Sandbox shutdown: If the agent is running in a container system such as Kubernetes, you can place it in a restricted runtime environment (sometimes called a sandbox) that enforces security filters. Automated policies can then evict the container if risk thresholds are crossed. This allows you to stop the agent process cleanly without disrupting the rest of the system.

Spending and Quota Ceilings: Cloud platforms provide budget controls that automatically block further usage when costs exceed a set limit. Treating this as a financial circuit-breaker prevents an agent from running unchecked and racking up unexpected bills.

Hopefully this makes it clear that a kill switch has to be more than a boolean flag. It needs to shut all subsystems of an agent down carefully and cleanly, and provide a clear forensic trail so your incident-response team can reconstruct what happened after the dust settles. Modern best practice is to pair interruption with a post-mortem memory freeze: snapshot the agent's vector stores and scratch files before any restart, so evidence survives, but the agent cannot use that memory to resume old schemes.

Figure 27.1: A conceptual agent kill switch. Keep in mind, killing anything has side effects. Make sure your agent is designed to recover gracefully.

Conclusion

Your users will embrace autonomy for AI agents only when they believe they can stay in charge. Clear-cut authorization boundaries, continuous behavioral monitoring, and an unequivocal off switch give you a solid foundation for building trust. You will need to return to the implementation details frequently as threats, model capabilities and safety technologies evolve rapidly.

Chapter 28

Agent Identity, Agent Liability

> *Takeaways*: Legal frameworks around truly autonomous agents are still evolving. Liability rests with humans (the deployers, developers, or investors), not the agent itself. The law increasingly treats agents as extensions of those who create or delegate to them, requiring clear chains of authority, monitoring, and oversight. Courts and scholars propose autonomy-based liability tiers, regulation via design, and objective standards in place of intent. Emerging frameworks include mandatory logging, Human-in-the-Loop (HITL), contractual clarity, and adaptation of product liability and agency doctrines.

O UR FOCUS FROM THE START has been on agents that are increasingly human-like and act with increasing autonomy. There are other legal concerns around AI and agents we will not focus on here: copyright of training data, consumer privacy, and more. In this chapter the goal is to focus on agent identity and agent liability. We already laid out in the last chapter how authorization, monitoring, and kill switches work.

Full disclosure. I am not a lawyer, and this chapter is definitely not legal advice. But I felt it was important to discuss what is beginning to take shape in the area of identity and liability, as this is likely to emerge as a strategic topic for the leadership of agent builder organizations. When an agent causes harm, who answers, and how can we show the chain of authority and control that justifies accountability?

This is not a question of granting personhood to an agent. Current laws do not treat agents as legal persons, instead liability anchors to humans or legal entities behind those agents. But when an agent genuinely appears to act independently, forging contracts or causing damage, the law depends on how we define identity and whether we can trace who or what ultimately controlled the agent.

Figure 28.1: Agent identity and liability frameworks are still evolving rapidly.

Recent legal scholarship emphasizes that agents are best seen through the lens of traditional agency and product liability doctrines, adapted to software that acts without continuous human oversight. Maarten Herbosch from the Institute for Law and AI argues that any liability regime must span both fully autonomous and partially supervised agents, effectively closing gaps between delegation and direct control. He underscores the need for regulation that accommodates the spectrum of autonomy we deployed in earlier chapters, where varying degrees of autonomy might shift responsibility between user and developer.

Another useful framework is a five-level autonomy taxonomy.

At the lowest levels, with human oversight, liability lies with users. At the highest, fully independent agents (think back to our discussion of crypto and social agents in Chapter 17), responsibility shifts decisively to developers or providers. This mirrors the technical governance tools we covered before: at higher autonomy, the human must step back, so stronger accountability must step in.

Some scholars propose making agents "law-following AIs": systems designed to understand and refuse overtly illegal commands even from their principals. In this view, the law imposes duties on agents, not as persons but as automated actors that must obey legal constraints by design. Most legal thinkers observe that agents do not have intentions in the human sense yet. If liability requires intent, agents might escape responsibility entirely. Instead, a better path is objective standards: measure agent conduct against reasonable benchmarks, and hold developers or deployers to those standards.

A principal-agent analysis of LLM-based systems further illustrates the problem: when we delegate decisions to an agent, misalignment, opacity, and emergent behavior raise novel liability questions. Those using delegation must build governance (interpretability, behavior evaluation, fail-safe monitoring) to stand behind agent decisions.

On the market and regulatory front, courts are already grappling with agents acting on behalf of organizations. For example, a chatbot that offers a refund or a discount without authority may nonetheless bind its company. Increasing agent autonomy amplifies legal complexity and operational risk.

To govern these systems responsibly, designers and legal teams must ensure traceability: logs showing which actions the agent took, under what authority, and what reviews or overrides occurred. It must be clear who is supervising, where decisions originated, and whether the agent deviated from expectations.

All this should feel like a fairly logical extension of the previous chapters. We already argued strongly for transparency, authorization, real-time monitoring, and kill switches that disable agents at runtime. These measures are the technical infrastructure needed to support legal accountability. When a harmful action occurs, the trail of context, reasoning traces, and shutdown evidence becomes necessary to support legal review.

PART
VI
The Path Ahead

"Prediction is very difficult, especially if it's about the future."

— *Niels Bohr, Yogi Berra, and others*

We've been studying where we are and where things are going with AI agents throughout this book. In this final major part, I want to try to synthesize things, but with some slightly different aims in mind.

Specifically, the first chapter of this section, "AGI Research Frontiers," is quite a bit longer than most chapters. It's a standalone effort to give you a sense of the research debates around the path to human-level artificial general intelligence (AGI). There is an enormous amount of valuable and fascinating research going on right now, literally worldwide.

Researching and bringing Chapter 29 together was, selfishly, extremely fun for me. It also was an important part of how I did research for this book overall. AGI research is fast-moving and at times contentious, but it's important, even for product and engineering teams, and investors, to have a feel for the breadth and depth of AGI research, and to be familiar with the kinds of questions that are being debated. I also try to tie this hefty chapter back to building AI agents, by examining where engineering fixes and scaffolding improvements may close gaps, even in the absence of additional fundamental breakthroughs. I hope you find the chapter as stimulating as I did writing it.[1]

In Chapter 30, I try to summarize, at a much higher level, my predictions about how AI agents and the transformation they are bringing to software products may unfold over the next decade. This is a synthesis from all the other parts of the book: an attempt to bring it together in one place for you to consider.

In the final chapters, my goal is to leave you with more of a concrete idea of what this may mean for you personally. I seek to share some of what may help your career if you are participating in the development of AI agents, or if you are in a more traditional company that is beginning to adopt AI more seriously.

---

[1]The last four chapters were each pretty short. Hopefully that gave you a breather before this next long one.

Chapter 29

AGI Research Frontiers

Takeaways: This chapter is almost a mini-book on its own. It can be extremely rewarding. We look at research that shows the hard limitations of current transformer-based LLMs, and also at research that offers fascinating alternative paths forward. This is not a short chapter, as the breadth of AI research these days is staggering. But the conclusions are ultimately simple: scale and transformers, even paired with reinforcement learning, will not deliver human-level AGI. To get there, we need additional breakthroughs in the ability of AI systems to learn, recall, and adapt from very limited data in novel, open-ended situations. We examine many exciting branches of research in this chapter, but we also tackle the question of how far engineering, simulation, and scaffolding can get us, absent further intelligence breakthroughs.

WE HAVE SPENT A FAIR BIT OF TIME throughout the book looking at the product and engineering challenges remaining to bring AI agents to the point they can be trusted as autonomous co-workers. In fact, we devoted Part III of the book to the perspective that we are *on the verge* of autonomy, with grinding but steady progress pushing agents forward. In this chapter, we assess what modern AI research has to say about the gaps in reaching human-level intelligence in the currently dominant approaches. In addition, we will highlight a selection of important alternative research directions that may help us reach AI agents that operate at human levels. Given the amount of ground we cover in this chapter, I want to help you see the structure first.

Let's start with essentially a "table of contents" or outline to see what is ahead.

Chapter Outline

It is important that we level-set early on the fundamental challenge of defining human-level general intelligence, as that shapes many of the current debates in AGI research. In addition, we need to clearly define today's dominant paradigm, and the critiques to it, to see where new research directions may play a pivotal role. Keep this structure in mind as you read the chapter, and refer back to it if you need a reminder how things fit together.

THE CHALLENGE OF DEFINING HUMAN INTELLIGENCE

✳ IS ALL YOU NEED:
THE ROAD TO TODAY'S DOMINANT PARADIGM

CRITIQUES OF THE DOMINANT PARADIGM

    – Self-Attention as a Computational Primitive

    – Gaps in Compositional Reasoning

    – Limits of In-Context Learning

    – RLVR Is Not a Silver Bullet

WHERE DO THESE CRITIQUES LEAVE US?

HOW FAR CAN ENGINEERING, SIMULATION & SCAFFOLDING TAKE US?

FROM LIMITATIONS TO NEW DIRECTIONS

    – Bayesian Cognitive Models
      & Probabilistic Program Induction

    – Program synthesis & Neuro-Symbolic Reasoning

    – Active Inference & the Free Energy Principle

- What Does Computational Neuroscience Tell Us?
- Whole Brain Cognitive Architectures
- Agile Human-Like Memory Research
- Multimodal Data & World Models
  Meet Spatial & Embodied Intelligence
- Open-Endedness, Evolutionary
  & Creativity Research
- Transforming Transformers: New Architectures
  for Reasoning & Symbolic Integration
- Complexity Science: Less Is More
  & Brain-inspired Adaptive Systems

BENCHMARKS TO WATCH

SUMMARY FROM AN AGENT BUILDER'S PERSPECTIVE

Before you read this chapter, you may also want to re-read or skim Chapter 5 again, where we lay out a high-level *behavioral perspective* on the key challenges in building human-like AI agents. Now, let's get started, by looking at the thorny question of defining human intelligence.

The Challenge of Defining Human Intelligence

A crucial challenge is that there is no universally accepted definition of human intelligence, and therefore no accepted definition of Artificial General Intelligence or human-level AGI. This makes it difficult to measure progress in AI research. Some researchers focus on specific tasks, while others aim for a more holistic understanding of intelligence.[1]

---

[1]As a convenience, and to avoid repetition, I will treat ASI or Artificial Super Intelligence as simply an augmentation of essentially *all capabilities* by some meaningful factor (maybe 2x, maybe 10x, maybe 1000x) beyond the level of those capabilities when we have achieved human-level AGI.

One view of how to know when we have reached AGI is to avoid writing definitions altogether, and devote our energy to constructing benchmarks and continuously making them harder and more human-like. Perhaps at some point, when even our hardest benchmarks are solved by an AI system or agent, we will extinguish the last corners of doubt that we have reached AGI. In this view, the benchmark writers will also have to throw in the towel! We conclude this chapter with a look at some of the current challenging and important benchmarks to watch in this regard.

Other approaches, similar to what we took in Chapter 5, try to identify the broad cognitive categories that we see in humans (things like perception, memory, intrinsic motivation, goals and planning, reasoning, judgment, creativity, confronting novelty, data efficiency, etc.), and then consider AI's ability to exhibit these at human levels or beyond. This approach can dovetail with the benchmarks approach to the extent we *rigorously categorize* our benchmarks, and adopt a wide suite that gives coverage across cognitive categories, at various levels of granularity.

Still other definitions of AGI emphasize the ability to complete "all economically useful tasks" as well as the "median human." OpenAI publicly states in their charter that AGI will be achieved when we have "highly autonomous systems that outperform humans at most economically valuable work." OpenAI's definition must be taken with a grain of salt. They have contract obligations to Microsoft to share technology up to the point they reach an agreed definition of AGI. Beyond that point, they need not share. This gives OpenAI an economic incentive to reduce the requirements in their definition of AGI.

An important problem with these approaches is the emphasis on "economically useful" tasks, which seems a fairly arbitrary limitation. Much of what we see as human intelligence is not an economic task per se, but rather may be motivated by wide open goals like happiness, exploration and learning. An essential element, which OpenAI's definition at least acknowledges, is the need to see "highly autonomous" behavior from AIs. Something I would add, that they neglect, are intrinsic goals, and particularly *autonomy in goal formation*. In this broader view, AGI would require agents able to establish and pursue their own goals, and not just follow goals given by humans in prompts. I also place very strong emphasis on the ability to confront entirely novel situations not seen in training, and to do so with very limited data.

Still other definitions of human intelligence are more philosophical. They try to put their finger on certain elusive properties of human intelligence like consciousness (itself extremely hard to define). Alternatively, they may evoke subtle behaviors and capabilities that humans exhibit that we don't yet see in frontier LLMs and agents, like emotion, humor, taste, and judgment.

My goal is not to resolve the debate here, but simply to help you see the breadth of opinions and nuance. We should note, however, that the entire history of AI is famously one where every time computers complete a task that was previously believed to represent true intelligence, we change the definition. Early AI researchers famously believed that when computers beat humans in chess, that would mean true AI had been reached, but when that was achieved humans moved the goalposts. This pattern has repeated itself many times.

In 1988, roboticist and futurist Hans Moravec summarized this in a brilliant metaphorical passage in his paper, "When will computer hardware match the human brain?" He described AI as waters, slowly flooding a "landscape of human competence," moving from lowlands of easier tasks until it eventually should reach the highest peaks of human intelligence. Thankfully, Max Tegmark in 2017 took the liberty of converting Moravec's vision to an image, which I have reproduced roughly in Figure 29.1, with help from Claude 4.1. I am confident that even as AI improves, we will continue to tweak and expand our definition of human-level AGI for some time, meaning the peaks will rise even as the waters move in. In short, the benchmark writers have certainly not thrown in the towel yet!

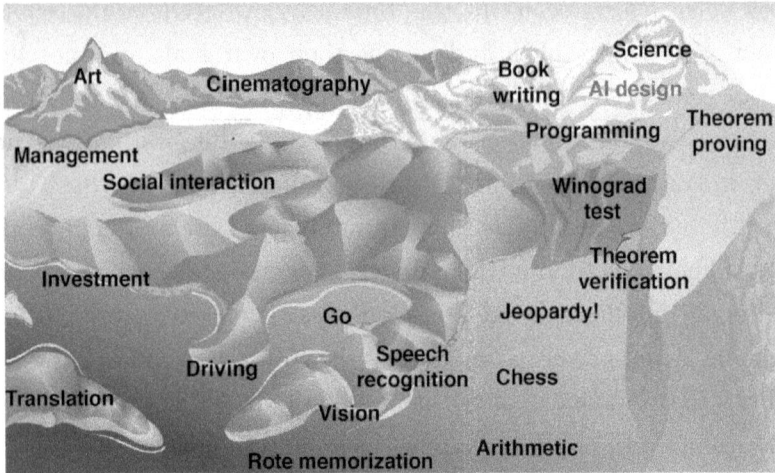

Figure 29.1: Claude 4.1's interpretation of Tegmark's rendition of Moravec's "landscape of human competence."

The Special Role of Novelty: Modern approaches to defining what still separates human and machine intelligence place a particular importance on adaptation to novelty. These approaches resonate with me. A strong example is Francois Chollet's notion of "fluid intelligence," which strikes me as a wonderful moniker for human intelligence. Chollet speaks of intelligence as being our "sensitivity to analogy," that is our ability to transfer subtle knowledge patterns to completely new situations, and to do so efficiently.[2] He has argued convincingly that intelligence should be seen as an "efficiency ratio" of how efficiently we spot connections between novel situations and our prior knowledge, and then leverage that similarity to build new solutions. This challenge is most associated with

---

[2]While I have not heard Chollet directly make this reference, the importance of analogy builds on foundational work on analogy-making AI by Melanie Mitchell in her dissertation, itself building on work by Douglas Hofstadter, which surfaces prominently in Chapter XIX of his tour de force *Gödel, Escher, Bach: an Eternal Golden Braid.*

the broad subfield of AI research known as "open-endedness."

Open-endedness, like the sciences of complex adaptive systems, can trace its roots to Norbert Wiener's landmark Cybernetics work, and John Von Neumann's work on the theory of automata in the 1940s. It also flourished in the 1960s and 1970s with John Holland's work on genetic and adaptive algorithms and with the work of Christopher Langton, John Conway and others on Artificial Life in the 1970s and 1980s. In recent years, open-endedness research has enjoyed a surge in popularity. We will examine this, and the closely related study of complex adaptive systems, when we look at new research directions later in this chapter.

For me, the ability to confront open-ended novelty efficiently and creatively is a crucial hallmark of human intelligence. Kenneth Stanley, one of the exciting researchers in the field, has written that open-endedness is likely "the last great challenge you've never heard of." Before we examine that challenge, however, we turn to a look at how we got to today's dominant paradigm in AI research.

✳ is All You Need: The Road to Today's Dominant Paradigm

Machine learning research is particularly fond of publishing papers with titles that play on the famous "Attention is All You Need" paper by Vaswani et al., which introduced the Transformer architecture in 2017. Each such new "✳ is All You Need" paper purports to reveal the one true remaining secret that will unlock boundless potential, and render previous approaches obsolete. It is appropriate that this trend started with the Transformer paper. Although the attention mechanism highlighted by Vaswani et al. significantly pre-dated the transformer itself, together they have been the basis of the most successful and widely adopted architectures in AI research over the last decade.[3]

Many of us in Silicon Valley shifted work into scaling models in the period after 2017.[4] More researchers began defending the idea that *next token prediction*, the primary goal of the Transformer, was in fact the only thing needed to get better and better performance. We just needed to keep increasing scale. To be fair, this approach turned out to be spectacularly successful. Paired with the tuning of transformers via Reinforcement Learning from Human Feedback (RLHF), this approach sparked the current AI revolution.

Following ChatGPT in November of 2022, the focus on further scaling of compute and data was relentless. Devotees of this "scale only" philosophy defended it like religious dogma. Transformers were still widely regarded by many in Silicon Valley as the only approach needed. The pursuit of pure scale, as the story was told, would lead to continuous, regular, step function improvements that would fairly quickly take us to AGI.

In time, doubts emerged. It began to appear that all available web data had been used up, and data started to look like the bottleneck. Focus then shifted to synthetic data. A mini breakthrough happened with DeepSeek. Following DeepSeek, there was widespread realization that training models using Reinforcement Learning with Verifiable Rewards (RLVR), often using synthetic data generated by specialized verifiers and simulators, could increase performance on critical tasks like math and coding. As we discussed in Chapters 15 and 16, gains from RL continue to evolve and bear fruit. Overall, this journey led us to the following definition of the "dominant paradigm" in AI today:

---

[3]The transformer, rather than the attention mechanism, was the novel contribution of the 2017 paper.

[4]I myself worked in the scalable machine learning and data platform team at Yahoo during this period. Our primary goal was making very large AI models possible to train and to use in production. To that end, Yahoo open-sourced a distributed training framework called TensorFlowOnSpark, as well as Vespa.ai, a large scale AI search platform.

Dominant Paradigm: The approach that rose to dominance in the year following the release of ChatGPT in late 2022, building on Transformer architectures introduced in 2017, but only consolidated as the field's orthodoxy once massive GPU clusters enabled scaling to unprecedented model sizes. Its core relies on next-token prediction at scale, paired with Reinforcement Learning from Human Feedback (RLHF), and Reinforcement Learning with Verifiable Rewards (RLVR), where verifiers and simulators generate synthetic data at large scale. The paradigm assumes that continued growth in compute, data, and model size under this recipe can deliver increasingly general and capable AI systems.

This paradigm has given us today's very powerful LLMs, which were unimaginable just a few years before. We now turn to some of the most important critiques of this dominant paradigm.

Critiques of the Dominant Paradigm

As we sit today, the prevailing paradigm is being challenged. Increasingly, researchers and industry players alike are observing that the recipe of scaling compute and data in training and inference, even augmented by reinforcement learning in various forms, is beginning to produce diminishing returns. The newest horizontal foundation models at the time of publishing this book are still improving, but incrementally. Moreover, the fundamental capabilities that still set humans apart are not emerging from the dominant recipe. We begin with a look at some of the hardest hitting research showing fundamental limits in the current paradigm.

Critiques come from a few distinct and very penetrating angles. One of the most mathematically rigorous examines the attention mechanism, which sits at the heart of transformers. This critique seeks to prove concrete limits on what attention alone can compute. The idea of attention is simple. Essentially, it allows transformers to "look in parallel" at long sequences of text and compute the degree to which each token "attends to" every other token. As noted, the 2017 Vaswani et al. paper set off an explosion of followers, and transformer models quickly became the most successful models for a wide variety of NLP tasks at the time. But research now shows that the current paradigm, based on transformers, attention and RL, is deficient in certain ways that may well impede its ability to take us to AGI. We will summarize and briefly explain four major critiques next.

Self-Attention as a Computational Primitive: Today's dominant transformer models rely internally on a mechanism known as self-attention. A series of research results put hard limits on the sorts of problems that constant-depth self-attention can solve. When researchers in the theory of computation say that a system cannot "solve a problem" they use some jargon that is worth learning when approaching research in this area. They say that a Turing Machine (an idealized model of computation) representing the system cannot "recognize" a particular formal "language" that represents the problem. In the case of attention-based transformers, Michael Hahn at Stanford University showed that transformers of fixed depth and width cannot solve two formal problems. These problems are called Parity and Dyck.

Roughly you can think of Parity as taking a Boolean problem (one that has a series of zeros or ones as input) and asking, "Does the current input have an odd or even number of 1's?" The Dyck problem (or more formally the Dyck language) was originally specified by Noam Chomsky and Marcel-Paul Schützenberger in 1963. It is the problem of matching and closing parentheses, imagining you confront a situation with many highly nested parentheses.[5] Transformers alone cannot solve these problems (or "recognize" these "languages" as a computation theorist would say) as the length of the problems grows. Yiding Hao and researchers at Yale University

---

[5]I appreciate that you may not obsess about these problems personally on a daily basis. But such seemingly esoteric formal problems are the bread and butter of testing the computational limits of different algorithms.

extended the result from Stanford, by proving transformers can recognize at most what are known as AC0 problems. These are the lowest level of complexity in a family of formal problems, built from AND and OR gates, known as "Alternating Circuits languages." The Dyck and Parity problems lie outside of AC0, and therefore Hao proved *why* attention-based transformers alone cannot solve them.

These deficiencies manifest themselves in some of the famous errors early ChatGPT models made counting the number of r's in the word "strawberry," or the more recent and more embarrassing struggles of GPT-5 thinking for several seconds and failing multiple times to get the number of b's in "blueberry" correct (see Figure 29.2). While these issues are often patched quite quickly, they illustrate the deficiencies today's transformer-based models face in solving classes of problems which are very basic for humans.

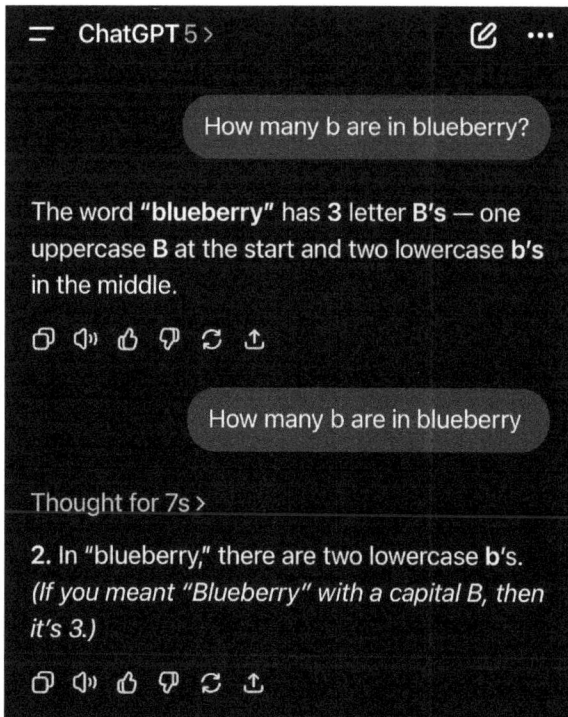

Figure 29.2: GPT-5 still struggles mightily to count the number of b's in "blueberry."

Additionally, these failures manifest themselves when models should know it is preferable to use tools, rather than try to "think through" a problem. Humans when faced with the word "blueberry" will quickly solve the number-of-bs problem mentally. If, however, you give a human a large block of code with hundreds of parentheses, and you ask if the opening parentheses match the closing ones (the Dyck problem), or if you give a human a book and ask if the number of words in it that equal the word "potato" is odd or even (the Parity problem), most sensible folks will use a computer. Even today's top LLMs do not turn to tools sensibly. These struggles of *knowing what strategy* to use to solve a problem also arise when LLMs need to combine separate reasoning steps together. We will look at this next.

Gaps in Compositional Reasoning: A defining feature of human reasoning is compositionality: we learn a small stock of operations and concepts and then recombine them, systematically and on the fly, to handle new situations. We do not need to see every possible arrangement of parts to understand a novel one. We reuse procedures and strategies adroitly. A growing line of recent work shows that today's large transformers do not reliably do this. They succeed when the test case resembles examples seen in training, but when a task demands recombining familiar pieces in a new structural arrangement, performance often collapses.

Nouha Dziri at the Allen Institute for AI, working with Yejin Choi's group at the University of Washington, carried out one of the clearest studies of how large language models failed at compositional reasoning. The paper was titled, "Faith and Fate: Limits of Transformers on Compositionality." The authors selected three specific tasks that could only be solved correctly by combining multiple intermediate steps: multi-digit multiplication, logic grid puzzles of the type often called Einstein puzzles, and a dynamic programming problem known as the maximum-weight independent set on a path.

The first task required the models to multiply numbers with several digits, such as 3-digit by 3-digit or 4-digit by 4-digit problems. Solving this type of problem demanded carrying out a sequence of additions and digit-by-digit multiplications in the correct order. The authors gradually increased the problem length by raising the number of digits in the numbers, testing whether the models could reuse the same basic procedure repeatedly as the numbers became larger. The results showed that the models performed moderately on smaller cases, but accuracy collapsed once the numbers grew to four digits or more. The longer the computation required, the more often small mistakes compounded, leading to wrong answers almost every time.

The second task used puzzles where several entities had to be assigned attributes based on a set of written clues. For example, each "house" in the puzzle had to be given exactly one nationality, one pet, one drink, and so forth, with the clues describing partial relationships between them. Solving such puzzles requires a sequence of logical deductions where each step restricts possible assignments until the full solution is identified. The authors increased the task length by adding more houses and more attributes, which expanded the number of steps needed to resolve all constraints. Models often succeeded on the smallest instances but failed sharply as the puzzles required deeper chains of deduction. The failures revealed that the models could not reliably follow constraints across longer reasoning sequences.

The third task was a standard dynamic programming problem. The input was a sequence of numbers arranged in a line, and the goal was to select a subset of the numbers that were not adjacent to one another while maximizing the total sum. The optimal solution required recursively comparing choices and building up subsolutions, a hallmark of dynamic programming. The authors increased the task length by giving longer sequences. As the sequence length grew, the models' performance degraded quickly. The models were not able to consistently apply the recurrence relation across many steps.

To evaluate systematically, the authors did not only look at whether the final answer was correct. They rewrote each task as a computation graph. In this representation, every intermediate step appeared as a node, and each node was connected to others according to how the solution was supposed to be built. This allowed the researchers to check whether the model was reproducing the correct intermediate subcomputations. The team also tested multiple model configurations. They ran base models directly on the tasks. They tried fine-tuned versions trained on many examples. They also used prompting methods such as chain of thought, which meant instructing the model to write out intermediate reasoning steps in text before giving the final answer. Another method was the use of scratchpads, where the model was trained to output explicit intermediate results in a structured format. They also explored reinforcement learning approaches where the model was trained with feedback to improve its reasoning traces.

Despite these efforts, the results showed a consistent pattern. The models appeared to treat the tasks as matching against known surface patterns or memorized fragments rather than carrying out full procedures. When the problem length increased, accuracy fell quickly no matter the training method. The conclusion of the paper was that large language models could not reliably generalize compositional reasoning procedures to longer or more complex tasks. Even with chain of thought, scratchpads, or reinforcement learning, the underlying limitation remained.

The results have been confirmed, and extended to heavily RL trained reasoning models, in more recent work by Apple researchers titled, "The Illusion of Thinking: Understanding the Strengths and Limitations of Reasoning Models via the Lens of Problem Complexity." Researchers found the same pattern of models appearing to approximate reasoning on small problems, but collapsing entirely when problem complexity crosses a threshold, independent of extensive or zero RLVR training. We turn next to another widely publicized ability of large language models known as in-context learning, and show that it too is not as general as often claimed.

Limits of In-Context Learning: In-context learning (ICL) refers to a model's ability to adapt its outputs based on examples or instructions provided within the same input sequence, without altering the model's parameters. A "zero-shot" ICL setting gives the model only an instruction or query, while "one-shot" includes a single example alongside the task description. "Few-shot" or "multi-shot" ICL extends this by including several examples, allowing the model to see the pattern or structure before producing an answer. ICL has become one of the most publicized abilities of large language models, and demonstrations on benchmark datasets have frequently been used to argue LLMs learn new skills from minimal data.

One of the most rigorous and up-to-date examinations of these claims was carried out by Xingxuan Zhang and colleagues in their 2025 paper "Understanding the Generalization of In-Context Learning in Transformers: An Empirical Study." This work tested whether ICL in advanced transformer models, including those optimized for reasoning, could truly serve as a general learning mechanism rather than a narrow form of pattern matching. The study evaluated ICL across three distinct forms of generalization.

First, the authors asked whether models could handle new examples drawn from the same family of problems as those seen in the prompt. For example, if the task was linear regression with noisy data, the model was prompted with some regression examples and then evaluated on fresh examples of the same type. Models performed strongly in this setting, especially when the examples in the prompt closely resembled the test cases.

Second, the authors increased the complexity within a given task. For instance, the model might see short sequences in the prompt but be asked to generalize to longer sequences of the same problem type. Accuracy dropped significantly here. The results showed that while models could imitate familiar examples, they struggled to extend the learned procedure to more demanding instances of the same task.

Third, the authors tested whether models could use ICL to solve entirely new tasks by analogy, such as learning a different function class or a different mapping rule that was not explicitly present in the training distribution. In this case, the models failed consistently, even when the new task shared structural similarities with those seen in training or prompting. The models did not construct a reusable internal representation of abstract task structure and instead relied on surface similarity.

The authors applied these tests to a diverse set of problems including function fitting, synthetic algorithmic reasoning, and natural language applications such as translation and API calling. They found that pretraining diversity and richer prompting strategies could improve performance somewhat, but the improvements were narrow and did not overcome the sharp failures in the second and third generalization settings.

This study made clear that ICL's apparent flexibility arose from statistical pattern recognition rather than from an open-ended capacity to acquire new concepts. The effectiveness of ICL depended on whether the test examples were close to patterns embedded in the model's pretraining data or prompt. When tasks demanded generalization beyond that envelope, performance collapsed.

Other studies support the same conclusions as those reached by Zhang and team. In-context learning is *not* a universal learning algorithm. Its limitations are systematic and fundamental. Transformer-based LLMs simply do not yet possess the ability to adapt and learn quickly and fluidly from small data in the way that humans do.

RLVR Is Not a Silver Bullet: Reinforcement learning from verifiable rewards (RLVR) has been marketed as a transformative addition to large model training, sometimes framed as a fundamental paradigm shift rather than an incremental optimization. In the public narrative, RLVR is described as pushing models into qualitatively new capabilities, bringing them closer to general intelligence. While there is solid evidence that RLVR can improve performance in certain kinds of tasks, and make it easier for a model to surface correct answers efficiently, recent work shows that these benefits are far from universal and in some cases, may come at a cost.

A clear example comes from work by researchers at Tsinghua University in 2025, which evaluates the impact of RLVR on problem-solving performance using the pass@k metric. Pass@k is a standard measure in problem-solving benchmarks: given k independent attempts to solve a problem, it records the probability that at least one of those k attempts included the correct answer. A higher k allows a model to try more times, while a low k tests whether the model can quickly get a correct answer.

The Tsinghua team fine-tuned a base model with RLVR and compared it to the same base model without RLVR across a variety of reasoning benchmarks. They found that RLVR-tuned models did indeed outperform their base counterparts at low k values, suggesting that RLVR improves the efficiency of producing correct answers when the model has only one or a few attempts. However, when k was increased to allow more retries, the base model often solved more problems than the RLVR-tuned model. In other words, RLVR appeared to sharpen

RLVR may be an important tool to create efficient, narrow skills in LLMs, but it does not lead to the kind of open-ended, flexible intelligence we see in humans. It may damage it in some cases.

the model's initial guesses, but at the expense of its broader exploratory ability to find solutions when more attempts are available.

The authors interpret this as evidence that RLVR training can narrow the model's search space in ways that make it more confident but also more rigid. Such *confidence sharpening* aligns with RLVR's optimization objective, which reinforces patterns that produce high-reward outputs during training. However, in domains where exploration of multiple strategies is valuable, this same narrowing can hinder performance. The result is a model that appears stronger in single-shot settings, but is actually less able to find non-obvious solutions when given more freedom to search.

This work highlights a more general point: RLVR is not a universal method for expanding a model's fundamental capabilities. It may be an important tool to create strong, narrow skills in LLMs, but it does not lead to the kind of open-ended, flexible intelligence we see in humans. In fact, it may damage it in some cases.

Where Do These Critiques Leave Us?

The preceding critiques are powerful. Along with others, they have persuaded many researchers that the dominant recipe of large transformers trained at scale, then optimized with rewards, will not deliver the missing ingredients we need for human-level general intelligence.

The industry has not stagnated, nor is it standing still. Organizations like Google, OpenAI, and Anthropic have the people, data, and compute to continue building stronger systems. They will tighten training pipelines, refine objectives, and fold in new components that raise practical utility. Agents will get better too, despite no sign of the "emergence of AGI" from scale alone that many predicted based on the original Kaplan OpenAI scaling-laws paper in 2020.

The next section looks squarely at these systems engineering efforts. We will examine compound systems that add orchestration layers on top of base models. These include mixture-of-experts (MoE) routing, tool and API selection, explicit verifiers, structured memory, and controller policies that attempt to manage multi-step work. Can such scaffolding substitute for true meta-recognition and adaptive reasoning? Likely, performance gaps *can* be narrowed, but by how much?

How Far Can Engineering, Simulation & Scaffolding Take Us?

Over the past two years, the major labs have invested heavily in compound systems that extend the capabilities of a single large model. The architectural trend is toward mixtures of experts with learned routing, search and retrieval, persistent memory stores, and tool-and-computer-use frameworks that orchestrate multi-step work. OpenAI has highlighted its unified agent with browser and desktop control. Anthropic has integrated tool schemas and persistent workspaces. These are fundamentally engineering approaches that support the model with components designed to improve utility by reaching outcomes more reliably. Google has made similar efforts with its "universal assistant" known as Project Astra, and its browser automation effort Project Mariner (both of which Google still calls "research prototypes" at the time this book goes to publication).

"Meta recognition" is the ability to classify a novel problem into the right *type*, to aid selection of an appropriate strategy to solve it. "Adaptive reasoning control" is the ability to govern how much computation to run, what algorithm or tool to choose, when to branch, when to verify, when to backtrack, when to replan, and when to stop. These concepts are *very similar* to Chollet, Mitchell, and Hofstadter's emphasis on the human ability to spot analogies we mentioned earlier.[6]

Recent research continues to show that these capabilities do not emerge natively in base LLMs. Subbarao Kambhampati and

---

[6]Perhaps my pointing this analogy out will convince you I'm human too?

colleagues demonstrate in work on planning that even extended chains of thought often produce steps without improving the quality of the plan itself. Benchmarks also show that performance often collapses when tasks shift from curated environments to live, noisy systems that require deciding which tools to use and when. Gains in meta recognition and adaptive reasoning due to scaffolding appear to plateau quickly.

Memory systems are an increasingly important part of the engineering response of major players. Humans rely on agile recall, retrieving just the relevant fragment from a past experience to guide current problem-solving. In contrast, current LLM-based agents suffer from "context rot": information from earlier steps in a long interaction is dropped, buried under irrelevant detail, or retrieved imperfectly. Compound systems now often add summarization pipelines to compact and compress context, improving some things, but often introducing new problems. We looked at these challenges in Chapter 21: compaction can discard key dependencies, and search over large, poorly structured stores can return irrelevant information that derails reasoning. Better structuring, filtering, and integration of retrieved memories into the slim, well-crafted context windows is still producing gains in specialized tasks, but is not yet showing open-ended generalization.

Mixture-of-Experts (MoE) architectures are another system-level approach that has seen growing adoption. MOEs increase system capacity by maintaining multiple specialized submodels (the "experts") and using a learned routing function to determine which experts should process which inputs. This selective activation can reduce compute cost, while allowing different experts to specialize in distinct parts of a problem. The router's decisions are typically based on local token distributions, not on a deeper recognition of the nuances of a novel problem. They do not implement the kind of strategic reasoning required for truly adaptive intelligence.

The type of controller we need would be like "executive decision-making" in humans. It would govern the choice and sequencing of modes and models based on a nuanced understanding of semantics, importance, goal relevance, and other factors. Building such an executive controller remains an open area of research, beyond the capability of today's compound systems.

Independent evaluations suggest a consistent pattern. Compound systems yield incremental improvements on benchmarks aligned with their scaffolding. They already produce commercially valuable agents, with solid narrow skills in constrained domains. But the same systems show persistent failures when faced with open-ended, messy environments. This is not entirely bad news for teams building highly vertical agents today. In the context of getting to AGI, however, systems engineering, memory augmentation, and better scaffolding are unlikely on their own to produce the kind of robust, open-ended intelligence of human-level AGI.

From Limitations to New Directions

Transformers may well end up playing an important role when we ultimately reach AGI, but the case against relying exclusively on the current dominant recipe is now evident to a growing number of serious researchers. Systems engineering matters, and will keep moving the curve, but it does not remove the need to explore new research directions.

The remainder of this chapter aims to provide what I hope will be an exciting tour of frontier research areas that attack these gaps from first principles, with novel and creative scientific thinking. The areas we will examine here are focused on the fundamental challenges that remain to be solved. As a reminder, here is a snippet from our earlier outline showing you what we will cover in the sections ahead:

NEW RESEARCH DIRECTIONS

- Bayesian Cognitive Models
  & Probabilistic Program Induction

- Program synthesis & Neuro-Symbolic Reasoning

- Active Inference & the Free Energy Principle

- What Does Computational Neuroscience Tell Us?

- Whole Brain Cognitive Architectures

- Agile Human-Like Memory Research

- Multimodal Data & World Models
  Meet Spatial & Embodied Intelligence

- Open-Endedness, Evolutionary
  & Creativity Research

- Transforming Transformers: New Architectures
  for Reasoning & Symbolic Integration

- Complexity Science: Less Is More
  & Brain-inspired Adaptive Systems

For each area, the goal is to separate promise from proof, and to give you an idea of where to go to learn more. The chapter ends with a discussion of key benchmarks to watch, followed by a summary aimed at those building AI agents today.

Bayesian Cognitive Models
& Probabilistic Program Induction

A central challenge in AI is learning new concepts quickly from very little data. Most large neural networks need vast numbers of examples to learn reliably, and they often fail when faced with situations that differ from their training data. In contrast, humans can learn a completely new category (such as a symbol in an unfamiliar alphabet) from just one example. Research in computational cognitive science has sought to explain this ability, and one influential explanation is the *Bayesian cognitive model.*

A Bayesian cognitive model treats learning as a process of updating beliefs about possible explanations for observed data. The "Bayesian" part refers to Bayes' Rule, a mathematical formula that combines prior knowledge (what you already believe is likely) with new evidence (what you observe) to produce updated beliefs. Formally, Bayes' Rule is often expressed as the probability of some hypothesis after you have received some evidence. This is known as the "posterior probability" and it is given as a formula of the prior probability of the hypothesis, and the likelihood of the evidence being what you would see *if* the hypothesis is true, divided by the total probability of the evidence. In practice, Bayesian machine learning (Bayesian modeling) often writes this as the probability of some model that explains the data, given that some data has been observed.

Classical notation (Hypothesis | Evidence)

$$P(H|E) = \frac{P(E|H)\,P(H)}{P(E)}$$

Bayesian modeling notation (Model | Data)

$$P(M|D) = \frac{P(D|M)\,P(M)}{P(D)}$$

Figure 29.3: Comparison of classical conditional probability notation with Bayesian modeling notation

Seeing the two formulations side by side in Figure 29.3 helps illustrate that these are completely equivalent. In the Bayesian modeler's language, the hypothesis becomes a "model," i.e. a structured, executable description of how the data might have been generated. This is where *probabilistic program induction* comes in. In this approach, each concept is represented as a small generative program. This set of instructions is a "model" that could produce examples of that concept (the "data"). The learning task is to infer the most likely program given the data. For example, a program for a handwritten letter might specify how to draw it using a sequence of pen strokes, with some randomness to capture variation between examples. The system searches over possible programs, balancing the prior probability of a program, (which favors simpler and more plausible ones), and the likelihood of the program generating the observed data (essentially the robustness of the program to the task at hand).

In 2015, Brenden Lake, Ruslan Salakhutdinov, and Josh Tenenbaum demonstrated this approach in their Bayesian Program Learning (BPL) model. Given just one image of a new handwritten character, BPL could infer a program that not only reproduced the character but could also generate new, stylistically consistent examples. The model reached human-level accuracy in one-shot classification on the Omniglot dataset and even fooled human judges in a "visual Turing test." It could also decompose characters into parts and recombine these parts to form new categories.

Beyond handwritten characters, Bayesian program induction has been applied to domains such as intuitive physics and understanding the actions of other agents. In physics learning, the system considers different "theories" of how objects move and interact (for example, whether they obey certain physical constraints), then uses Bayesian inference to decide which theory best explains the observed motion. In theory-of-mind models, the hypotheses encode possible goals and beliefs of an observed agent, and inference recovers these from limited behavioral data.

One strength of this approach is that it can operate at multiple levels of abstraction. A model can learn both specific concepts and higher-level principles that apply across concepts. This multi-level structure is what allows rapid learning in novel situations. The higher-level principles (corresponding to Bayesian priors) narrow down the possibilities for new concepts.

However, pure Bayesian program induction faces severe computational challenges. Searching through the vast space of possible programs is expensive, and scaling to complex data such as natural images or continuous audio is difficult. A promising direction is to combine these models with neural networks. The neural component can propose good candidate programs or set priors, while Bayesian inference refines them and provides principled uncertainty estimates. Probabilistic programming languages such as Gen and Pyro make it easier to build such hybrids.

In the context of current AI dominated by transformers, Bayesian cognitive models can address specific gaps. They offer a systematic way to recognize when a new type of reasoning or representation is needed (meta recognition), adapt reasoning strategies based on probabilistic evidence (adaptive reasoning), and handle novelty by constructing entirely new structured hypotheses instead of relying on surface pattern matching. Integrating them with transformer models could give systems the coverage and perceptual power of large-scale deep learning, combined with the structured reasoning and generalization ability that today's models still lack.

Program Synthesis & Neuro-Symbolic Reasoning

Another approach to bridging the gap between current AI and human-like reasoning focuses on *program synthesis*. Here, the goal is for an AI system to construct explicit, executable programs that solve a given problem. The specification for the program might come in the form of examples, logical constraints, natural language descriptions, or test cases. Once synthesized, the program can be run repeatedly, adapted to new inputs, and understood in terms of its exact steps.

Representing solutions as programs makes their structure explicit, which allows researchers to analyze them compositionally. Adding a loop to a program, for example, allows it to handle more repetitions without any retraining. This kind of systematic generalization is often absent in purely neural models, which tend to break down on problems outside their training data. You will likely also recognize this as similar to the tool-forming abilities we saw in the Voyager Minecraft agent, and which we discussed as a way agents can learn and add new skills over time in Chapter 20.

One prominent line of research comes from Kevin Ellis and colleagues, who developed the DreamCoder system which we reviewed in Chapter 10. DreamCoder works in a domain-specific language and alternates between two phases. In the wake phase, it searches for short programs that fit the current tasks. In the sleep phase, it compresses recurring fragments of these programs into new reusable library functions. Over time, this learned library makes it easier to solve new problems, because the building blocks are already in place. This process closely reflects how human programmers accumulate and reuse code.

Some recent approaches combine neural networks with symbolic program search, using the strengths of each together. In these systems, neural models act as guides through the vast program space by ranking or suggesting candidate steps that a symbolic process then evaluates. Examples include neural–symbolic theorem provers, where a neural network suggests the next proof step and a symbolic proof assistant checks its validity, and program synthesis systems that repeatedly draft, execute, and refine code until all test cases pass. In these systems, correctness is grounded by an external verifier, which prevents the drift and self-reinforcement problems that can occur when large language models generate reasoning steps without external feedback.

Program synthesis is not limited to traditional programming. In planning problems, such as robotics or games, symbolic planners can be thought of as synthesizing high-level programs that achieve a goal. If the planner has an accurate model of how actions affect the environment, it can produce sequences of actions that are interpretable, verifiable, and generalizable to new settings. Similar ideas apply in question answering, where the system might translate a natural language question into a formal query language like SQL, execute it, and return the result. The translation step is itself a form of program synthesis.

Paired with transformer models, program synthesis and neurosymbolic reasoning could partially remediate shortcomings in today's AI systems. In experiments, these approaches have helped handle novel tasks by composing known elements, though more work is needed to make these approaches truly adaptive to novelty.

Active Inference & the Free Energy Principle

In Chapter 18 where we discussed the infinite agentic meta loop, we crossed paths with the question of what drives organisms? Is it the environment or is it internal goals? This theme of what is *true agency* has been with us since the earliest chapters. Active inference is a fascinating theory born in neuroscience and biology that seeks to ground the question of what drives organisms at a very fundamental level. Active inference connects what an agent perceives and learns to how it acts. Developed primarily by Karl Friston and collaborators, Active Inference is built on the *Free Energy Principle*, a mathematical framework that describes how systems maintain themselves in a changing environment.

The free energy principle begins with the observation that an agent, whether a cell, an animal, or a machine, must keep its sensory states within ranges compatible with survival. A single-celled organism that drifts into water that is too hot may die within seconds. A human whose core temperature rises only a few degrees above normal risks organ failure. Robots face the same constraint in physical terms, since a machine that overheats in direct sunlight or drains its battery below safe levels will soon shut down. This separation of the agent from its environment is described by the idea of a *Markov blanket*, which defines the probabilistic boundary between the agent and the external world that can vary widely. Active inference treats survival as the ongoing task of keeping states inside that boundary, either by changing beliefs to better anticipate inputs or by acting to avoid conditions that would push them out of range.

Friston formalized active inference as the process of an agent minimizing a quantity called "variational free energy," which approximates the reduction of *surprise*.[7] Can you spot the similarities with Bayesian inference? The agent has a generative world model that predicts its sensory data given hidden states of the world, and it updates beliefs about those hidden states to minimize prediction error.

Active inference extends this process to action. Instead of only adjusting beliefs to match incoming data, the agent can also act on the world to make the data match its predictions. For example, if the model predicts that a certain view should be visible and it is not, the agent might move its sensors to bring that view into sight. Active inference postulates a unified loop of perception, inference, and action, where the agent continuously selects actions that minimize expected free energy. The "expected" part means the agent evaluates possible futures and chooses actions that will reduce uncertainty, achieve preferred outcomes, or both.[8]

The framework integrates exploration and exploitation within the same formalism. Agents act to reduce surprise, either by updating their internal models to better match the world or by intervening in the world so that it matches their predictions. In machine

---

[7]In information theory, surprise is a measure of how unlikely or unexpected an event is. For an agent, you can think of this as the gap between predicted and actual sensory inputs.

[8]Do you notice the strong similarity between active inference and the difference engine we discussed in Chapter 18?

learning terms, active inference offers a single mathematical objective that ties together model learning and policy learning, rather than treating them as separate processes as in much of reinforcement learning.

For AGI research, active inference supports meta recognition by embedding the decision of whether to gather more information directly into the meta loop. It supports adaptive reasoning by adjusting the balance between exploration and goal pursuit in response to uncertainty. And it handles novelty by treating surprising observations not as failures but as opportunities to refine the internal model. If combined with transformer-based reasoning, and the architectures we discussed in Part IV, active inference could support agents that plan and act in an infinite meta loop, guided by world models for both prediction and action.

What Does Computational Neuroscience Tell Us? (Language, Space, Physics, Social Cognition)

Computational neuroscience leverages computers to model the algorithms the brain uses, and how those algorithms are implemented in neural circuits. Computational principles learned about the brain may in turn guide AI model architecture and evaluation. Computational neuroscience has a rich history and studies models ranging from individual neurons up to whole-brain networks as shown in Figure 29.4.

Insights Into Language: Human language processing relies on specialized neural systems that work differently from networks supporting general problem-solving. One of the key discoveries in cognitive neuroscience is that there is a "language network" in the brain located in regions such as Broca's and Wernicke's areas. These regions respond selectively to linguistic input, such as sentences. This network operates largely independently of the "multiple-demand network," which spans frontal and parietal re-

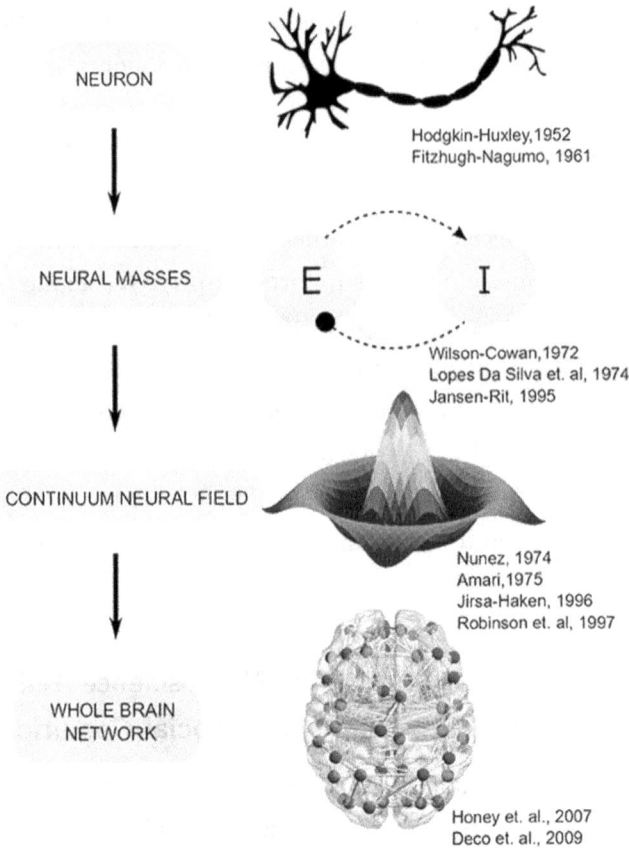

Figure 29.4: Computational neuroscience builds models from individual neurons up to whole brain networks.

gions and activates during tasks that require effortful reasoning, logic, or complex planning. MIT researchers led by Evelina Fedorenko used fMRI experiments to show these two systems respond differently. The language network responds to grammatical, meaningful sentences but not to sequences of unrelated words or nonwords, whereas the multiple-demand network reacts when a task requires deliberate effortful reasoning,[9] even when linguistic material is present. This suggests that the brain does not repurpose

---

[9] What Kahneman termed System 2 thinking.

general-purpose circuits for parsing language, but instead devotes a specialized substrate to it.

The findings suggest that the brain depends on a specialized network for language. That network is sensitive to structure and expectation, distinct from general reasoning circuits, and appears to use hierarchical representations to support prediction. For AI, the implication is that next token prediction may capture some aspects of human language processing, but lacks the structured, hierarchical approach that the brain appears to use. Architectures that embed explicit hierarchical structure, maintain working memory states akin to surprisal tracking, or separate linguistic processing from general reasoning systems may yield models that generalize more robustly and in a more human-like way.

Insights Into Spatial Reasoning: The spatial domain is also rich with insights. In the brain, mammals build an internal, flexible representation of space that supports navigation, planning, and memory. Our understanding of this began with the discovery of distinct neurons that signal location and movement. Place cells, first described by John O'Keefe, activate when an animal enters a specific area, effectively marking "you are here." Surrounding them, grid cells, identified by Edvard and May-Britt Moser, form a regular, hexagonal lattice across the environment: as the animal moves, these cells fire at periodic intervals acting like a neural coordinate system.

Further studies revealed other spatially tuned neurons, such as head-direction cells signaling orientation, and boundary-vector or object-vector cells that fire relative to landmarks or walls. These form a structured, map-like code for space. Computational models show how these neural representations support planning. The successor representation (SR) is one such model that relies heavily on the formalisms of matrix operations in linear algebra. SR encodes each location in terms of expected future visits under a given behavior policy. Remarkably, grid-cell activity patterns can emerge from analysis of the eigenvectors of a state transition matrix, suggesting grid cells act like a compact basis for forecasting future states in a spatial model.

Outside of strictly spatial tasks, SR principles can also explain generalization. A preprint by Yu and colleagues (2021) also argues that grid-like codes can serve as efficient basis functions for predicting relationships, even in abstract, non-spatial domains! If these models can be verified experimentally, it would strongly imply that the same neural logic governing navigation in the brain could support learning to navigate more abstract spaces, and might be part of how humans confront novelty more broadly. If you recall our discussion of the difference engine in Chapter 18, you will see a strong similarity here as well. Something *akin to* the predictive state transition matrix of SR (but able to handle non-spatial goals and states) would be needed to support the kind of predictive goal, world-state, action alignment we discussed in that chapter.

Insights Into Intuitive Physics: Infants, even before they can speak, develop a basic understanding of how objects behave. They expect solid things not to pass through one another, they notice when objects disappear or change, and they understand that unsupported objects should fall. Psychologists such as Elizabeth Spelke have demonstrated this through violation-of-expectation experiments: when babies are shown scenes that defy these physical principles, such as an object vanishing into thin air, they look longer, and show surprise. This suggests that humans are born with intuitive models of physics.

Researchers like Peter Battaglia and Josh Tenenbaum have turned this into a computational framework. They model intuitive physics as a generative inference engine: systems simulate scenes using objects, forces, and rules of collision, then compare predictions to observed outcomes. Crucially, these models represent scenes in an object-centric way, breaking down the world into individual entities with properties rather than ingesting raw pixels. This structure makes their predictions more stable and interpretable, particularly when dealing with unseen configurations. For improved AI, this implies that models with object-based structure and explicit physical simulation are more likely to generalize to new environments. This is essential for planning, flexible interaction, and robustness.

Insights Into Social Cognition: Social cognition refers to the brain's ability to represent and reason about the mental states of others. Neuroscience has shown that this capacity depends on a distributed network, with two regions playing consistently central roles. The temporo-parietal junction (TPJ) is strongly engaged when people evaluate another person's beliefs, especially when those beliefs differ from reality. This was demonstrated in work by Rebecca Saxe and Nancy Kanwisher, where images from fMRI scans revealed TPJ activation when participants judged a character's false belief compared to a matched control task involving outdated photographs. The medial prefrontal cortex (mPFC), by contrast, is more active when people consider the traits, preferences, or long-term dispositions of others. A study by Jason Mitchell, C. Neil Macrae, and Mahzarin Banaji found that mPFC activity shifted depending on whether participants judged people similar to themselves or very different, suggesting a role in self–other comparison and perspective taking.

Beyond these two hubs, other brain structures such as the superior temporal sulcus and the posterior cingulate cortex contribute to interpreting gaze, body language, and context-specific social cues. Lesion studies reinforce these findings: damage to the TPJ or mPFC often impairs the ability to track others' beliefs or to adapt behavior in social contexts.[10]

For AI systems that need to work with humans or other agents, these insights suggest new designs. Specifically embedding models that can represent other actors' goals and beliefs can support for

---

[10]These studies on social cognition make me think back to Forrest Gump, and how he innocently interprets other people in his world.

better planning, coordination, negotiation, and adaptation. This could enable agents that act with a more human-like level of social awareness.

Summary of Insights: These insights point to concrete ingredients that current large models lack. Language understanding benefits from structured prediction with control over memory and composition. Navigation requires an explicit map-like state and predictive coding of transitions. Physical reasoning works better with object representations and learned forward models. Social interaction calls for inference over latent beliefs and goals. Harnessing these insights in AI systems is the subject of many of the other research areas we are examining in this chapter.[11]

Whole Brain Cognitive Architectures

Cognitive architectures are attempts to specify how the major capacities of intelligence fit together. They emerged from cognitive science as "whole brain" models that sought to capture perception, memory, reasoning, planning, and action within a unified framework. Classic systems such as ACT-R and Soar, developed from the late 1970s onward, treated these capacities as explicit submodules and experimented with methods for their interaction. The current interest in cognitive architectures revives this systems perspective for the age of neural networks. Instead of only building ever-larger monolithic models, the question becomes how to divide functions across modules, how to learn their interfaces, and how to assemble them into agents. This perspective is very similar to the overall multi-loop, multi-model architectural vision we adopted in Part IV for building AI agents.

A persistent difficulty for classical cognitive architectures has been representation of information. Passing data from module to

---

[11]There are a couple additional insights about memory from modern neuroscience, which I have put in that section just a bit later in this chapter.

module often required inflexible hand-designed messages. Modern approaches attempt to overcome this by learning distributed representations in shared latent spaces. This makes it possible to gain parallelism and modularity and yet avoid fixed symbolic interfaces. The challenge of how best to represent and transfer information across subsystems remains central to the field. Increasingly, AGI research is returning to cognitive architectures as a way to organize and integrate the many capabilities that human-like agents must exhibit.

Yann LeCun, a Turing Award recipient and former chief AI scientist at Meta, has argued that LLMs alone will not yield human-level intelligence. In his view, token prediction will not produce agents that can perceive the world, form predictive internal models, pursue goals, or plan multi-step actions. In his 2022 paper, "A Path Towards Autonomous Machine Intelligence," he proposes a systems-level architecture for agents rather than a single model.

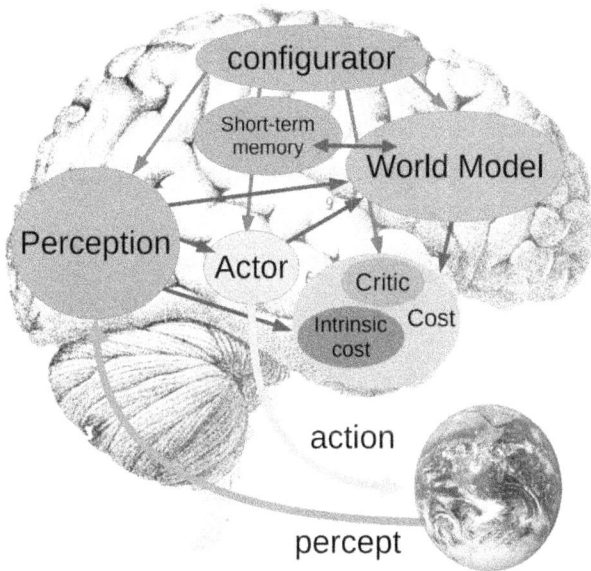

Figure 29.5: LeCun's systems-level architecture for autonomous intelligence involves multiple interacting subsystems.

Figure 29.5 summarizes LeCun's proposed architecture. The configurator provides executive control. Given a task, it modulates the parameters and attention of other modules so that each operates in a goal-directed mode. Perception turns raw sensory streams into a structured current state that can be queried at multiple levels of abstraction. For any task only a fraction of the sensory stream is relevant, so the configurator primes perception to extract the right subset.

The world model is the core predictive engine. It fills in aspects of the current state that perception did not observe, and forecasts multiple futures under hypothetical action sequences. The model operates in an abstract representation space so that it can reason without reconstructing pixels or tokens. LeCun emphasizes multi-timescale prediction and uncertainty, so that different tasks induce different prediction granularities.

The cost module has an intrinsic part and a trainable critic. The intrinsic component encodes hard requirements and drives such as safety, resource sufficiency, and curiosity. The critic learns to predict future intrinsic costs from states, including states imagined by the world model. Because both pieces are differentiable, gradients can back-propagate from the cost module to the world model, perception module, and the actor.

Short-term memory stores recent states, predicted states, and their associated costs. The world model queries and updates this memory while completing spatial information and while rolling predictions forward in time. The critic trains by retrieving past state–cost pairs. LeCun points to key-value memory designs as a useful template, with a role analogous to the vertebrate hippocampus but implemented as a task-configurable neural module.

In LeCun's architecture, the actor module has both a fast policy and a slower optimizer. The fast policy maps state estimates to actions for immediate control. The optimizer proposes multi-step action plans to the world model, receives predicted futures and their costs, and then uses gradients of those costs with respect to the proposed actions to refine the sequence.

Within this broader system, the Joint Embedding Predictive Architecture (JEPA), supplies a concrete learning principle for the world model. A JEPA learns by predicting representations of missing or future parts of its input from representations of the observed context. The prediction happens in latent space rather than in the raw input space. This allows the model to discard nuisance detail and focus on causal structure at the right level of abstraction for downstream control.

Two features really distinguish LeCun's architecture from the classic cognitive architectures. First, the insistence on differentiable interfaces across all modules, so that optimization signals can propagate through the entire system, avoiding the inflexible hand-designed messages of old. Second, the configurator, which sets targets, and allocates attention, acts as an executive controller across modules.

An older but instructive cognitive architecture to compare to LeCun's is the LIDA architecture. LIDA, short for Learning Intelligent Decision Agent, was developed by Stan Franklin and colleagues as a computational implementation of Global Workspace Theory, a prominent theory of consciousness. LIDA centers cognition on a fast cycle that repeats perception, attention, global broadcast, and action selection. Perceptual associative memory constructs structured descriptions from sensory input. Transient episodic memory holds recent events. Contents compete for attention via what are called "codelets." Winning coalitions of codelets gain entry to the global workspace and are broadcast, giving the signals they carry greater influence. Procedural memory and an action selection mechanism then choose a behavior. We will see codelets again when we discuss complexity science and adaptive systems later in this chapter.[12]

LIDA is not a neural end-to-end learner. It is a hybrid architecture that mixes symbolic and connectionist components, and treats the global workspace as a control hub. The explicit separation of memory types, and the broadcast of codelets, remain a novel and flexible way to coordinate subsystems. These ideas map well to architectures like LeCun's. One can view LeCun's configurator as a learned, differentiable successor to LIDA's attention and broadcast control, with the critic deciding which contents are worth pursuing.

Today's transformer-based language models provide valuable components for recognition, knowledge retrieval, and sequence prediction, but they do not produce true agency (as we saw in Chapter 4). Whole-brain cognitive architectures attempt to model agents that have goals, drives, perception, predictive world models, memory across multiple timescales, and the capacity to face novelty. They provide concrete testing grounds for how these capacities interact. Many of these ideas were incorporated into the multi-loop, multi-model architecture for agents we discussed in the engineering chapters. I encourage readers to return frequently to this area for more implementation inspiration.

Agile Human-Like Memory Research

Human memory is not a single mechanism but a layered system that balances rapid learning with long-term stability. In the mid-1990s, James McClelland, Bruce McNaughton, and Randall O'Reilly introduced the influential "Complementary Learning Systems" theory, which remains a touchstone in cognitive science. They argued that the hippocampus specializes in encoding specific episodes quickly, while the neocortex accumulates gradual, structured knowledge over time. Interaction between these sys-

---

[12]Thanks again to Melanie Mitchell and Douglas Hofstadter for giving us the delightfully evocative term "codelets."

tems allows new experiences to be consolidated, reorganized, and integrated into broader knowledge, often through replay during periods of rest or sleep. This model highlights why human memory can adapt to novelty while still protecting older knowledge.

Modern language models face similar tensions but lack such architecture. Longer input contexts make it possible to carry large amounts of text around, but, as we discussed in Chapter 21, studies show that models underuse information in the middle of the context window, and are highly sensitive to where facts appear. Retrieval Augmented Generation (RAG), which we also discussed, emerged as a practical workaround, inserting relevant information into the model's context at query time. While these approaches do aid recall, they fall well short of human-like memory. They store and retrieve, but they do not distill and reshape knowledge in an adaptive or natural way.

Several research programs are now attempting to move beyond this stage by drawing more directly on cognitive science. One direction has been episodic segmentation. Models such as EM-LLM identify event boundaries in a stream of text using measures of surprise, then store and retrieve experiences in units that resemble human episodes. Another line of work has turned to hierarchical architectures. Projects like MemGPT and MemoryOS treat an LLM as if it were running an operating system, with layers of short-term, mid-term, and long-term memory that can be paged in and out of context. Paging creates an adaptive mechanism for reading, writing, and forgetting, and mirrors the idea that the brain has distinct but interacting stores that balance flexibility with endurance. The MemoryBank framework adds forgetting curves and reinforcement schedules that resemble those studied in psychology, allowing memory traces to fade or strengthen based on recency and importance. These designs shift from simple retrieval toward adaptive policies for storage, decay, and recall.

Foundational theories of associative memory also continue to shape modern designs. Pentti Kanerva's work on sparse distributed memory, developed in the 1980s, remains influential. By storing information in high-dimensional space and retrieving it by similarity rather than exact match, it anticipates the associative nature of human recall. Another stream of theory comes from Jeff Hawkins and colleagues at Numenta, who proposed hierarchical temporal memory as a model of cortical processing. Both frameworks suggest that robust memory requires distributed, flexible representations rather than static indexing.

As noted earlier in the section on neuroscience, I held back insights specific to memory until now, as they fit a bit better here. For much of the twentieth century, memory was assumed to reside in the strengthening and weakening of synapses in the brain, a view rooted in Donald Hebb's famous maxim that "neurons that fire together wire together." Synaptic plasticity remains the dominant model, and it underpins theories such as the complementary learning systems framework, where cortical columns slowly encode stable patterns that complement the rapid storage of episodes in the hippocampus.

More recent work by Leo Kozachkov, Jean-Jacques Slotine, and Dmitry Krotov at MIT suggests that memory is not confined to synapses. Astrocytes, a class of glial cells[13] once thought to play only a supporting role, appear to participate directly in memory storage through dense networks of signaling and metabolic regulation. These findings are still under debate, but they point to memory as a more distributed and resilient process than previously assumed. This highlights how much richer biological memory is than the stores engineered into today's AI systems. It supports the idea that we will likely need to build agents with much richer forms of memory that are capable of persistence, forgetting, abstraction

---

[13]Glial cells are non-neuronal cells in the brain that provide structural support, regulate the chemical environment, and interact with neurons in ways that influence signaling and plasticity.

and detail.

Agile memory matters for the gaps identified earlier. Meta recognition (sensitivity to analogies) clearly depends on recalling the right prior memory as a cue for the present situational analysis. Adaptive reasoning depends on maintaining intermediate results and revising them as new evidence arrives. Confronting novelty depends on analogical retrieval of partial matches and on integrating them into reasoning without rigid symbolic schemas. For this reason, advancing beyond retrieval pipelines toward human-like memory systems is central to progress toward human fluid intelligence.

Multimodal Data & World Models
Meet Spatial & Embodied Intelligence

As we laid out in Chapter 18, a world model is an agent's complete model and knowledge of the world and how it works. Critically, because a lot of popular use gets this wrong, this must include *not only* how the physical environment works but also the motivations, behaviors, and potential reactions of other actors. Humans are believed to rely on such models. Kenneth Craik, a Scottish psychologist and philosopher, argued in 1943 that the brain carries "small-scale models" of external reality that it can use to test possible actions before taking them. His book *The Nature of Explanation* is often credited with introducing the idea of internal world models in cognitive science, decades before the term was adopted in AI research. More recent work in neuroscience, such as Karl Friston's free energy framework, discussed earlier in this chapter, describes perception and action as processes of prediction within a generative model of the world. These perspectives suggest that strong multimodal world models are not just a tool for AI systems but a central feature of human intelligence, and likely a requirement for human-level AGI.

In AI agents, the purpose of a world model is prediction. If the agent moves, or if something in the world around it changes, the model should give a reasonable guess about what will happen next. In practice, this might involve predicting the next video frame, estimating how objects or agents will move or act, and then using those predictions to choose its own actions. This should be pretty familiar from our architectural discussions.

Recent approaches try to build rich world models from multiple kinds of data rather than text alone. Video provides motion and dynamics, audio gives cues about materials and events, language adds abstraction and goals, and embodied interaction supplies feedback from acting in the world. When these sensory channels are fused, the agent develops a world model it can use to decide what to do next to reach its goals.

Large multimodal datasets have been central to this shift. Egocentric corpora such as Ego4D capture daily activities from a first person viewpoint and expose supervision signals that matter for action, including hand–object contact, occlusion, and near field geometry. Research teams at Meta and Google have trained models that align video segments with text and audio and then predict masked or future segments, which forces the latent representation to encode physical regularities and event structure. Work on joint embedding for many modalities aims to learn a shared "latent representation space" where different signals that refer to the same thing end up *near* one another.[14] A picture of a dog, the word "dog," the sound of barking, and even a motion trace of a dog running can all map to nearby points in such a space. This makes it easier to transfer knowledge between modalities, such as retrieving an image from a sound cue. The broader hope is that such alignments will help agents connect language with events and objects in the physical world.

---

[14]Mathematically, the embedding spaces of LLMs are high-dimensional vector spaces. The concept of "nearness" in embedding spaces is subtle and still hotly debated in AI research.

Embodied data plays a special role in robotics because it connects perception to real consequences. Groups led by Andy Zeng and Sergey Levine at Google and Berkeley have gathered thousands of hours of robot experience data, with tasks such as picking up objects or moving through rooms, and used this data to train large models called Robotics Transformers. These models take in camera images and language instructions and learn to output actions for the robot to perform. Because the training covers many different objects and situations, the models are pushed to learn general patterns about how objects can be grasped or moved. As a result, they can handle new objects or new room layouts better than older, more narrowly trained models.

Because real world data is costly, simulation remains essential. DeepMind's XLand and related open-ended platforms generate families of tasks with changing goals, rules, and opponents. In the Minecraft ecosystem, projects such as Voyager used a large language model to write and revise its own tool library while exploring, and then store skills in a persistent code base.

Simulation has long been central to robotics because it provides cheap and controllable data, but the fidelity gap has always been controversial. Futurist and roboticist Hans Moravec in the 1980s warned that small mismatches in sensors and contact dynamics can derail transfer, a concern later echoed in Ken Goldberg's phrase "Sim2Null." For years this meant that results in simulation rarely carried over to real robots. More recently, advances in physics engines, domain randomization, and photorealistic rendering have begun to close this gap. Systems trained in engines such as MuJoCo, Isaac Gym, or Habitat can transfer grasping, locomotion, and navigation skills with less need for fine-tuning than before. The debate continues, but the trajectory suggests simulation is becoming not just a pretraining tool but a generator of synthetic data distributions that complement scarce real-world interaction.

How objects are represented in space is a crucial foundational question. Agents that can build maps or scene graphs tend to perform better at navigation and manipulation because they have a structured place to store and retrieve spatial information. In robotics, this often involves combining modern learning methods with classical SLAM (Simultaneous Localization and Mapping). Such systems let a robot estimate where it is while at the same time building a map of its surroundings.

Object-centric models, influenced by the work of Peter Battaglia, Josh Tenenbaum, and others, factor a scene into discrete entities and learn forward dynamics for each, enabling predictions that generalize to new layouts and contact patterns. Neural scene graph methods extend this by learning both geometry and semantic relations, supporting relational queries like "what is inside which container" or "which object is blocking the target." In vision, latent predictive encoders such as Generative Query Networks and the family of neural radiance field models (NeRFs) learn internal 3D structure by predicting unseen views, which supports occlusion reasoning, mental rotation, and geometry-aware planning. These advances matter for adaptive agents because they give the agent a manipulable internal world model, not just a reactive mapping from pixels to actions.

Important challenges remain. Scaling up senses like touch and proprioception is difficult. Touch refers to detecting external contact, such as pressure or texture, while proprioception tracks the robot's own body state, like joint angles and motion. Moving skills from simulation into the physical world is still unreliable, because small mismatches in noise, friction, or contact dynamics often cause policies that worked in simulation to fail on real hardware. Another challenge is data quality. Large multimodal datasets often have weak alignment, such as subtitles that do not match a video or audio that drifts out of sync. Evaluation methods also need to move beyond average benchmark scores and test whether agents stay reliable when conditions change.

Open-Endedness, Evolutionary
& Creativity Research

Biological evolution, human culture, and even personal creativity all unfold without a fixed end state, producing novelty after novelty, building on what came before, and sometimes stumbling onto radical new forms. A growing community of AI researchers has argued that if we want machines to be as inventive and adaptive as nature, our algorithms must also be designed not to converge on a single so-called "optimal" solution, but to keep exploring, practically indefinitely. Kenneth Stanley and Joel Lehman have been among the most pioneering advocates of this view. Their work challenges the traditional "objective-first" mindset in AI, showing that by chasing a single performance metric we often miss the crucial stepping stones that lead to real breakthroughs.

Their 2008 introduction of novelty search was a turning point. Instead of rewarding agents for moving toward a predefined goal, the algorithm rewards them for doing something different from anything seen before. In a maze-navigation experiment, this meant giving points for exploring new locations or movement patterns rather than for getting closer to the exit. Counterintuitively, this open-ended approach often solved the maze faster than a direct objective-based search, because it avoided being trapped in deceptive local optima. Stanley and a graduate student Jimmy Secretan applied a similar philosophy to collaborative human–AI creativity with Picbreeder, an online platform where users evolved images starting from random blobs through successive generations of variation and selection.

No one explicitly told the Picbreeder system to make faces or butterflies, yet those emerged through the cumulative effect of thousands of novelty-driven choices. Picbreeder revealed a key property of open-ended systems: meaningful features can emerge as byproducts of unrelated explorations. This happened, for example, when an "alien eyes" pattern in one image unpredictably morphed into

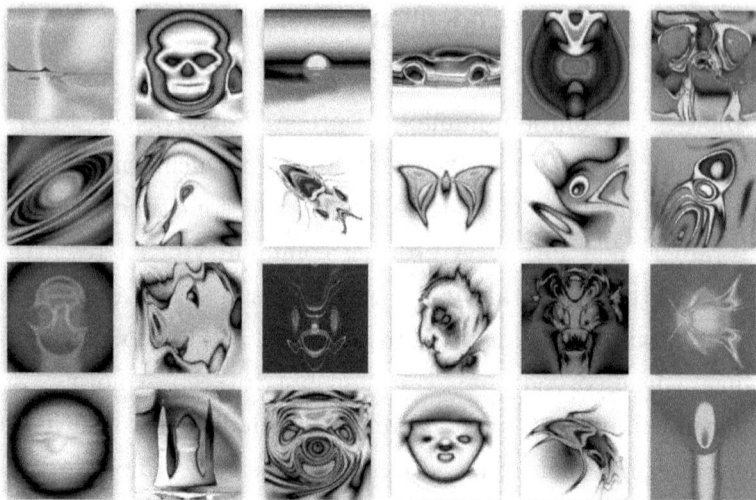

Figure 29.6: Guided by human selection, Picbreeder produced startlingly recognizable images like faces and butterflies when people bred images *without* seeking an objective. Image used under permission of the University of Central Florida.

the tires of a sleek, futuristic car several generations later.

This emphasis on continual exploration is also a response to what Stanley, Lehman, and collaborators like Akarsh Kumar and Jeff Clune have called "representational optimism" in deep learning. This is the generally unsupported belief that the internal representations of neural networks must be improving if the network outputs performs better on tasks. Their 2025 paper, "Questioning Representational Optimism in Deep Learning: The Fractured Entangled Representation (FER) Hypothesis" argues that representations generated by backpropagation of errors tend to be tangled, noisy, and poorly suited for recombination, whereas open-ended systems continually generate representations that are cleaner, more composable and more interpretable.

Large-scale experiments have tested open-endedness approaches in ambitious ways. Uber AI's 2020 paper Enhanced Paired Open-Ended Trailblazer (Enhanced POET) built on and went beyond the original 2019 POET paper. In Enhanced POET, as agents mastered one terrain, the system mutated and introduced new environments, while maintaining a population of diverse environment–agent pairs so that different agents specialized and excelled across different niches. DeepMind's 2021 XLand project took the concept further, procedurally generating 3D games and letting agents learn entirely through nearly endless play. After 200 billion training steps across 700,000 unique games, some agents displayed high-level skills (e.g. cooperation and active exploration) that let them adapt to games they had never seen before. These systems illustrated the promise of open-endedness: not memorizing fixed solutions, but developing general strategies for novelty itself. They also underscored the challenges, from the immense compute demands to the risk of "trivial novelty" (agents doing meaningless but new things, like spinning in place). To keep progress meaningful, researchers often blend novelty rewards with measures of quality. This family of methods is known as Quality-Diversity (QD) algorithms. MAP-Elites, for example, maps from a higher-dimensional search space to a lower-dimensional behavioral space and tries to fill that map with diverse, high-performing solutions.

In parallel, evolutionary algorithms have re-emerged as a powerful tool for fostering novelty and creative problem-solving. Where gradient descent incrementally adjusts a single model's parameters, evolutionary methods maintain populations of solutions, iteratively selecting and mutating them. This population-based search can excel in discrete or non-differentiable spaces, domains where gradients are unavailable or misleading. Stanley's 2002 paper with Risto Miikkulainen, "NeuroEvolution of Augmenting Topologies NEAT," demonstrated evolving both neural network weights and architectures. Starting from minimal structures, NEAT progressively added complexity, yielding architectures well-adapted to their tasks.

Evolutionary strategies (ES) have also been applied to large-scale policy learning. OpenAI's 2017 work by Tim Salimans and colleagues showed that a simple ES could match reinforcement learning performance on complex control tasks while being trivially parallelizable and more robust to sparse rewards. But the link between evolution and creativity becomes strongest when combined with open-endedness. Novelty Search with Local Competition, for instance, balances novelty against local performance, producing a diverse set of moderately high-performing solutions rather than a single winner. This approach has evolved modular robot controllers, gaits, and strategies that objective-first optimization never discovered.

Classic work by Karl Sims (1994) and by Hod Lipson and Jordan Pollack (2000) on evolving virtual creatures showcased evolution's capacity for structural creativity: given only physics and a fitness measure for movement, evolution produced bizarre yet functional morphologies, walking, swimming, or hopping in ways no human designer anticipated. Evolution has also delivered unexpected engineering innovations in the real world, like the unusual but highly effective antenna designs evolved for NASA spacecraft, which exploited electromagnetic principles in ways that surprised even seasoned engineers.

Open-endedness and evolutionary algorithms thus share a deep conceptual kinship. Both reject the notion that intelligence emerges from following a single path or objective. Instead, they explore entire landscapes, preserving diversity so that dead ends on one path become possible directions toward another. Additionally, these approaches are closely linked to complexity science and the study of adaptive systems, which we will examine later in this chapter, but next we turn to research focused on reshaping today's dominant transformers themselves.

Transforming Transformers: New Architectures for Reasoning & Symbolic Integration

Much of the work on advancing beyond today's transformers comes from direct modifications to the architecture itself. The aim is not to discard transformers, but to extend them with features that allow more systematic reasoning, more reliable use of memory, and closer integration with symbolic methods and external tools. These changes are motivated by specific weaknesses of current models: their fixed depth of computation, their tendency to blur structure, and their difficulty with tasks that demand exactness or multi-step planning.

Search and Recombination: One line of research focuses on using population-based methods to generate new models. Instead of refining a single transformer by gradient descent, multiple pretrained models are treated as a set of building blocks. Search methods then explore ways of merging or recombining their weights, producing new networks without the full cost of pretraining. The goal here is efficiency and reuse: rather than scale each model from scratch, researchers look for novel compositions hidden in existing networks.

An example comes from David Ha and colleagues at Google Brain, who applied evolutionary strategies to the problem of model merging. Recipes for how to combine weights were encoded and mutated, and strong variants were selected in a loop. They showed that competitive models could be assembled from populations without exhaustive retraining, making concrete the idea that diversity in pretrained networks can be a resource to exploit.

Variable Depth and Recurrence: A fixed stack of transformer layers gives every input the same number of processing steps, which limits the ability to tackle problems that demand deeper or more iterative reasoning. New designs address this by allowing computation to run for a variable number of steps. Some separate a slow "planner" path from a fast "executor" path, enabling hierarchical control over how long to think about a problem. Others tie weights across layers and add a halting mechanism, so that the model itself decides when enough processing has been done.

The Universal Transformer, developed by Mostafa Dehghani and colleagues at Google Brain, is a strong example of adding recurrence. Instead of fixing the number of layers in advance, it ties weights across layers and adds a halting mechanism so that the model itself decides how many steps to apply to each token. Some inputs are processed quickly, others are iterated on for longer, and the computation depth becomes adaptive rather than rigid. This approach directly addresses the depth problem in transformers, showing that variable-step processing can improve generalization on algorithmic and reasoning tasks where fixed stacks fall short.

Higher-Order Representation: Another direction aims to address a deeper limitation of transformers: they blur semantic relations and roles together in flat embeddings. A standard transformer reduces meaning to undifferentiated vectors, which makes it difficult to support abstract reasoning, analogy, or planning, all of which are crucial to AGI and rely on keeping track of higher-order structures. Alternatives try to enrich internal representations so that distinctions are preserved. The larger goal is to give transformers representations that support the forms of reasoning human intelligence depends on.

This line of work includes the Large Concept Models from Meta AI, which operate not on tokens but on units such as sentences or discourse segments, and then predict directly in that higher-order space. By operating on units that already carry larger-chunks of meaning, these models extend the effective context and make discourse relations easier to represent. Earlier explorations of this idea came from work on structured embeddings, such as Maximilian Nickel and Douwe Kiela's knowledge graph embeddings at Facebook AI Research (FAIR), and Paul Smolensky's tensor-product representations at Johns Hopkins, which showed how roles and fillers could be combined into vectors. Neural theorem proving projects at DeepMind took those principles further, demonstrating that simple logical rules such as transitivity and set inclusion can be learned and applied compositionally once the underlying representations carry structure.

Memory and Recurrence: Transformers are constrained by the length of their attention window. Information outside that window must be re-encoded repeatedly, which makes it difficult to carry knowledge across long horizons. To address this, researchers have introduced mechanisms for persistence. Some designs attach explicit external memories with learned read–write operations, allowing information to be stored and retrieved as needed. Others replace attention altogether with architectures that maintain a recurrent state evolving over time. Both strategies aim to give models the capacity to retain and use information over extended sequences.

State space models are the clearest example here. The S4 family, led by Albert Gu and colleagues at Stanford, and its successor Mamba, are built on ideas from control theory and signal processing. They maintain a compact recurrent state that can stretch over thousands of steps with linear complexity, in contrast to the quadratic cost of attention. This has made them attractive for speech recognition, reinforcement learning, and long-document modeling, domains where the persistence problem is most acute.

Graph-Aware Hybrids: Another family of architectures couples transformers with graph-based reasoning. In these systems, the transformer extracts entities and relations from text, constructs a graph, and then uses a graph neural network to propagate constraints before producing an answer. The transformer supplies broad linguistic coverage, while the graph component enforces relational structure, motivated by the fact that many domains benefit from explicit multi-hop reasoning across structured knowledge.

A representative example is work from Ruochen Yasunaga and collaborators at Stanford, who built biomedical concept graphs from language model outputs and then used graph networks to refine answers. Their results showed clear gains on medical QA benchmarks where reasoning over multi-step causal chains was essential. The same hybrid pattern now appears in domains from program verification to scientific question answering.

What can we conclude? These designs do not solve general intelligence, and each brings its own costs in training stability and system complexity. They do, however, address longstanding shortcomings of transformers alone, and offer alternatives that may be closer to implementation ready than some of the other research frontiers we have discussed.

Complexity Science: Less Is More & Brain-Inspired Adaptive Systems

Complexity science treats intelligence as an emergent property of many interacting parts. The Santa Fe Institute (SFI) has been central to this view for four decades, shaping the study of complex adaptive systems in biology, economics, and computation. John Holland, who later served for many years as an SFI professor and external professor, set the tone with *Adaptation in Natural and Artificial Systems* in 1975, which introduced genetic algorithms and a general theory of adaptive schemata. His book predates SFI's founding but became a touchstone for its research culture and for the Institute's ongoing work on adaptation and emergence. Kenneth Stanley's later advocacy for open-ended novelty, developed with Joel Lehman and popularized in *Why Greatness Cannot Be Planned*, was written while Stanley was on sabbatical at SFI, and it sits naturally in this lineage that links evolution, open-ended creativity, and complex adaptive architectures for intelligence.

It may be obvious, but it's worth saying, the human brain is not a "single forward pass through a stack of transformer layers." It is a highly parallel network of specialized, recurrent, and plastic subsystems. These subsystems operate at different time scales, and communicate continuously through billions of parallel spike trains. This has motivated designs that try to harness rich internal parallel dynamics, rather than rely entirely on gradient descent through a static set of layers. One such design space (which does not fully capture brain dynamics, but offers an alternative to transformers) is known as "reservoir computing," a specific variant of which is called a "liquid state machine."

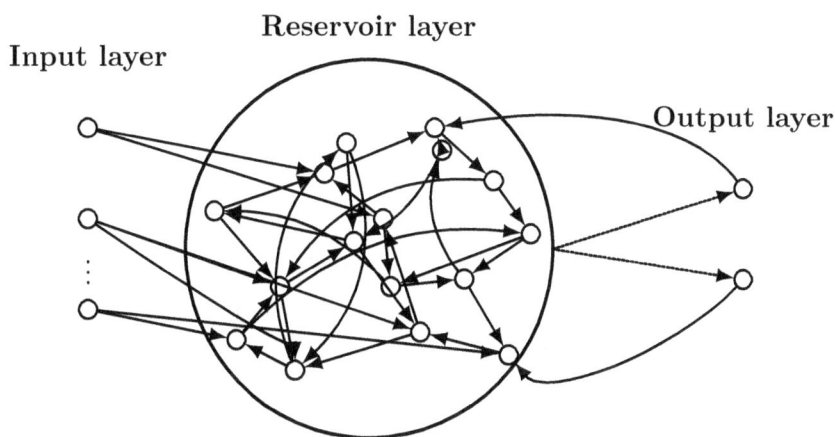

Figure 29.7: Schematic of a reservoir computing system showing the input, reservoir, and output layers. The reservoir layer forms a large recurrent network with random internal connections that transform the input signals into a high-dimensional dynamical state, from which the outputs are linearly read out.

In these systems, a recurrent (looping) network is built, with connections chosen at random and then kept fixed. Unlike a transformer, which processes information in a single direction through pretrained layers, such a network continually feeds activity back into itself so that past inputs influence future states. The "reservoir" is this shifting pool of activity. A simple linear readout learns to map those states to outputs. A liquid state machine is a reservoir that uses spiking neurons and continuous time, so that inputs leave ripples of activity that fade gradually, much like ripples in water. Researchers have found that when reservoirs operate near the boundary between stability and chaos, sometimes called the critical regime, they may capture temporal structure well, preserve memory, and adapt quickly with minimal weight changes.

A different line of work focuses on intelligence as the interaction of many small, semi-independent processes. We discussed this in some detail in Chapter 18. Recall that in the 1980s, Marvin Minsky argued in *Society of Mind* that human cognition emerges from a society of "agents," each one simple, but collectively powerful. Recent machine learning work has rediscovered this principle in technical form. Graph-based and message-passing networks distribute reasoning across many nodes, and multi-agent control divides tasks into populations of interacting subagents. The key is not tidy modules but small parts that can specialize, compete, and cooperate in parallel. Minsky's insight, that agency can arise from the interplay of many loosely coupled processes, remains a guide for today's researchers to think about the emergence of human-like thought.

Complex adaptive systems also continuously change themselves. Development and plasticity matter as much as instantaneous computation. Work inspired by neurodevelopment evolves or grows architectures during learning, adding units and connections when needed and pruning when they become unnecessary. This covers ideas from Holland's genetics of search to modern neural architecture search and topology evolution. It also motivates local learning rules and neuromodulation so that parts of a large system can adapt without catastrophic interference elsewhere. The goal is a network that keeps learning, rather than a static model that must be retrained wholesale when the task changes. SFI researchers like Melanie Mitchell have long emphasized the role of feedback loops in such systems. That emphasis has filtered into cognitive architectures that combine top–down influence and recurrent refinement across levels of representation.

Large-scale brain models illustrate what becomes possible when many specialized parts are wired with realistic dynamics and control. Chris Eliasmith's "Spaun" model, built at the University of Waterloo, was one of the first large-scale simulations of the brain. It instantiated about 2.5 million spiking neurons across visual, motor, memory, and decision circuits and performed a battery of tasks using the same underlying network. Spaun did not solve human cognition, but it demonstrated that a coordinated assembly of specialized subsystems can flexibly switch tasks, maintain working memory, and integrate perception with action in one unified model. That lesson aligns with the complexity view as well as with Minsky's "society" vision.

Less Is More: In 2025, David Krakauer, the current President of SFI, published a delightful paper with his brother, John Krakauer, of the Johns Hopkins School of Medicine and with Melanie Mitchell titled "Large Language Models and Emergence: A Complex Systems Perspective." The paper provides a neat summary of how the LLM scaling philosophy of "more is more" contrasts with the view of intelligence as a measure of efficiency in adaptation to novel situations. They go on to argue that simply observing unexpected or surprising behavior from an LLM is not sufficient grounds to claim that LLMs have emergent intelligence. They separate the idea of emergent capabilities from emergent intelligence, arguing that task performance might be enough to justify the former, but that the latter requires more efficient coarse-grained representations to be developed within the transformer network. It is interesting to read this research in light of Kumar, Clune, Lehman and Stanley's work on the FER hypothesis, particularly the results that show evolutionary approaches may yield cleaner, more composable representations.

In many ways, the open-endedness work discussed earlier is very complementary to the work in complexity science. Mechanisms like Stanley and Lehman's novelty search take complex systems through a sequence of adaptations, avoiding premature convergence and discovering stepping stones that objective-driven training might miss. These processes can produce repertoires of skills, morphologies, and composition-friendly representations that can be recombined when a task changes, resembling the adaptive designs found in biological systems.[15] Complexity science increasingly provides the principles, and a growing set of computational results shows that when many simple parts interact and rewire under the right constraints, they can acquire new capacities. This is compatible with famed American psychologist Herbert Woodrow's 1921 definition of intelligence as "the capacity to acquire capacity."

Benchmarks to Watch

This chapter has surveyed many research directions, each aimed at closing part of the gap between today's transformer-based models and human-level AGI. To see whether these ideas are turning into real progress, it helps to track a handful of demanding benchmarks that test agents in situations much closer to the messy, unpredictable challenges of the real world. The tests differ in structure and intent, but all aim to measure how well a model adapts to new and unfamiliar challenges. The benchmarks below were chosen because they capture distinct, hard-to-fake abilities and are already being used to evaluate the most advanced agents.

---

[15]Kumar, Clune, Lehman and Stanley call these representations UFRs, for Unified Factored Representations, emphasizing that modular designs may generalize and adapt more efficiently.

Table 29.1: Selected AI benchmarks for measuring progress toward general intelligence

Benchmark	*Description*
ARC / ARC-AGI-2 / ARC-3 (preview)	The Abstraction and Reasoning Corpus probes pattern discovery and analogical reasoning in grid puzzles. ARC-AGI-2 adds interactive tasks to test on-the-fly adaptation, and ARC-3 has further formats planned for the ARC family.
Humanity's Last Exam (HLE)	A multimodal, multi-domain exam with thousands of expert-authored questions spanning math, science, and the humanities. It prioritizes reasoning across unfamiliar contexts rather than narrow recall.
GAIA	The General AI Assistant benchmark contains 466 complex, real-world-like tasks involving multiple steps and tool use. It evaluates whether an assistant can plan, browse, execute code, and coordinate tools to complete end-to-end tasks.
Terminal-Bench	A real terminal environment for evaluating AI agents on complex, end-to-end CLI tasks. Tasks span code compilation, ML training, server setup, and debugging, run in containerized sandboxes with verification scripts and an evaluation harness for execution-based scoring.

Benchmark	Description
Big-Bench Hard (BBH)	A curated subset of BIG-Bench that remains difficult for large models, emphasizing logical deduction, novel analogies, and compositional generalization. Many tasks reward systems that integrate structured intermediates or tools.
MATH and Coding Competitions	MATH targets olympiad-style problems that require multi-step derivations. Coding challenges such as Codeforces probe algorithm design and error-handling under novel constraints. Both emphasize precise reasoning under distribution shift.
The Agent Company (CMU)	An extensible benchmark for agents that behave like digital coworkers: browsing the web, writing code, running programs, and communicating with teammates. It measures consequential task completion, collaboration, and end-to-end robustness in realistic workflows.
OSWorld	A real computer environment for multimodal agents across operating systems. Tasks involve operating arbitrary applications with execution-based evaluation and interactive learning, testing long-horizon UI control and tool competence.
Mind2Web / RealWebAssist	Mind2Web covers instruction-following on real websites across many domains to test generalization to unseen sites. RealWebAssist emphasizes long-horizon, evolving user goals with GUI grounding and ambiguity resolution during live web interactions.

Benchmark	Description
MCPToolBench	MCPToolBench provides a large-scale AI agent tool calling benchmark focused specifically on 231 real-world tasks involving tools enabled via the Model Context Protocol.

These benchmarks give a concrete view of where the frontier lies. They differ in modality, required skills, and the extent to which they allow tool use or interaction. Watching them over time reveals not only raw accuracy gains but also shifts in how systems solve problems, whether through larger monolithic models, or increasingly, through modular, agent-like designs.

Summary from An Agent Builder's Perspective

Hats off for making it this far! We've covered a lot in this chapter. I began with a sharp set of critiques of the dominant transformers-plus-RL paradigm, followed by how the large AI players are adding scaffolding, routers, memory stores, specialized submodels, and other system-level concepts to expand what builders can achieve. From there, the discussion moved through a wide span of research aimed at closing the gap between current AI systems and the capabilities needed for general intelligence.

The following table summarizes the ground we have covered. We outline the gap areas and highlight the engineering patches and research levers that could help close them. In the next chapter, we go down the dangerous path of trying to predict how all this unfolds over the course of the next decade.

Table 29.2: Agent AGI gaps. Possible near-term engineering and deeper research responses by problem area.

Engineering Patch	Research Lever

Advanced reasoning and algorithmic computation

Engineering Patch	Research Lever
• Chain-of-thought with verifiers	• Program synthesis and neuro-symbolic methods
• Code execution and sandboxes	• Differentiable interpreters and verifiers
• Self-consistency and tree search	• GNN graph reasoning
• CAS and exact math tools	• Looping, HRM, Universal Transformers

Meta-recognition and strategy selection

Engineering Patch	Research Lever
• Heuristic routers and task classifiers	• Active inference and expected free energy
• Prompt policies and tool-choice	• Bayesian model selection and hypothesis testing
• Controller heuristics for depth and verification	• Cognitive architectures with planners
	• JEPA state as input to control

Confronting novelty and open-ended generalization

Engineering Patch	Research Lever
• Data augmentation	• Novelty search and quality-diversity
• Procedural task generators	• POET or XLand self-play
• Web and tool orchestration for exploration	• Evolutionary design
• Experience and skill libraries	• Intrinsic motivation in RL

Engineering Patch	*Research Lever*

Agile memory and long-horizon context

- RAG with vector databases
- Episodic logs and summaries
- Long-context caches and compression
- kNN-LM overlays

- Complementary learning
- Event segmentation indexing
- Hierarchical episodic and semantic memory
- Learned write and read policies

Grounded world models and spatial reasoning

- Video-text-audio pretraining
- SLAM with semantic mapping
- Scene graphs and object trackers
- Knowledge-graph retrieval

- JEPA world models
- Object-centric dynamics
- GQN and NeRF latent 3D structure
- Successor representations

Planning and long-horizon control

- Planners (MPC, A*)
- Hierarchical workflows and subgoals
- Tool-call schedulers and goal checkers

- Model-based RL
- Active inference control
- Hierarchical RL and options
- HRM with recurrent control

Data efficiency and learning from little data

- Synthetic data and distillation
- Retrieval of exemplars
- Curated instruction tuning

- Bayesian program induction
- Hierarchical Bayesian priors
- Amortized inference proposals

Engineering Patch	Research Lever
Tool use and software UI use	
• Tool registries and API schemas • Browser and desktop control frameworks • Tested skill libraries	• Program synthesis • Planners and verifiers • Graph-based reasoning over UIs

Chapter 30

Perilous Predictions

Takeaways: The next decade will see an incomplete but substantial transition away from traditional software products designed to be used by humans toward AI agents capable of functioning more like humans. In this chapter, we outline the potential major phases in this transition, providing a rough guide, not a statement of certainty.

ANY ATTEMPT TO PREDICT the years ahead is risky. Nonetheless, the path ahead is becoming more and more clear. Here I will lay out my thoughts on roughly the next decade of evolution from our current software product world to a world heavily populated by AI agents, where humans spend less and less time interacting directly with traditional software tools.

The Present Reality
Agentification of Existing Software

The present is still dominated by traditional software vendors, many of whom are very large and have strong, entrenched positions and powerful distribution advantages in the markets they serve. I include in this picture not just major enterprise software vendors like Salesforce, Adobe, Microsoft and IBM, but also the large-scale consumer platforms like Facebook, Netflix, Google, Airbnb, DoorDash, Uber and numerous other consumer-facing technology companies. All of these companies are already aggressively adopting AI, and many of them are well along the way to adding co-pilots, generative AI, and agentic assistance to their existing products.

Stated simply, incumbent players will do very well as AI will drive price increases, stickiness, and product upgrades. Disruptors trying to reach large markets will face stiff competition.

2025-2027
The Emergence of Agentic Micro-SaaS

2025 looks to be the year of early generalist agents, deep-research agents, and the early middle maturity phase for agentic software engineering. These foundational agents are already spawning a new opportunity that I call "agentic micro-SaaS." The agentic micro-SaaS opportunity is being driven by a number of factors and is leading to a new opportunity space with features very different from traditional SaaS businesses.

The cost of software creation and domain knowledge research has dropped dramatically, making the creation of high-quality software with agentic features feasible for industries and niches where software adoption today is low. These are typically smaller markets or specialized sub-segments where the high cost of software creation previously made addressing them infeasible. Large players will be occupied "agentifying" their existing software, as well as creating platforms and ecosystems for new software, where they can be the channel for more specialized and lower market size tools.[1] Sales velocity into niche markets will likely separate winners from losers, as the cost of reasonable quality software falls, and as the differences between software products narrow.

I do *not* anticipate there will be many billion-dollar opportunities in this space, but there will be many companies with tens of millions in revenue. More interesting in some ways, there will be a huge long-tail of very simple software products in this space that

---

[1]This is already happening with things like "Apps in ChatGPT" from OpenAI, which is attempting to make ChatGPT a channel and platform for software and commerce from other apps.

may generate low revenues from a large company or venture capital perspective, but perfectly acceptable low millions or hundreds of thousands in annual revenue that can sustain smaller businesses. A big part of this business may also be agency-driven as well, consisting of one-of-one software created for medium-sized businesses as a service.

2028-2030
More Agent - Less Software

While full-blown agents are already on the scene in future-leaning areas like software development, social media, and crypto, they will likely be held off a bit by agentic micro-SaaS and not start to become mainstream until 2028. The next phase, which I put as 2028 to 2030, will essentially see a rapid transition from "Software as a Service to Service as Software." It must be noted that many forward-thinking technologists and venture capitalists already see this coming, and the concept is by no means new. In 2024, Microsoft CEO Satya Nadella declared SaaS would be almost entirely replaced by agents. For founders, this is important. Funding is already available for new entrants who are prepared to potentially start with Micro-SaaS, but transition to full-blown agents over time and as their businesses grow.

In this period, agents will become more and more specialized, and focus more and more on delivering full business outcomes for customers. The idea of buying a piece of software that you have to learn to use, and that may or may not help your business will be replaced by the idea that you hire many specialized AI agents, who work with your systems and your remaining employees to deliver value. Already in 2025, we see pioneering companies like Sierra experimenting with outcome-based pricing and only charging customers when AI agents fully solve a business problem. This trend toward "hiring and firing" software agents based on whether they can "do the job" will only grow.

Although our focus throughout this book has been more on software, and less on robotics, it is important to note that robots and agents will increasingly go hand in hand. Specialized as well as humanoid robots are improving rapidly, and costs are declining such that this period will also see significant growth in the overall deployed robot population. Specialized agents will need to fully understand the physical production and control processes as they enter more and more industries such as agriculture, manufacturing, food production, and health care where physical processes are as important as information processes.

As we stressed in Chapter 6, an agent's mind need not be confined to a single robot body, and agents can, in a sense, be everywhere at once. They can show up for humans in multiple forms of embodiment. Stated more plainly, an agent mind will be able to use multiple robot bodies, depending on the task at hand.

Many small agentic micro-SaaS companies will not survive this era. As platforms shift to include robots, and customers begin to demand agents that operate seamlessly across many platforms, smaller software companies will struggle to keep pace. People in general will tire of directly using software, just as many of us have already tired of downloading new mobile apps.

2031-2035
Full-Blown Agents & the Spread of Robotics

The world is still built for humans, and in many situations, we will want it to be even more tailored to us. This strongly suggests that robots that are designed *like us* will be the form factor that is best able to operate in our world and serve our needs. Increasingly, as software AI agent products seek to serve more and more of our needs, they will need physical embodiment.

The high costs of humanoid robot construction, maintenance,

and delivery, as well as the fact that many customers will need lease, rental and other financing options, means humanoid robotics will be a very capital-intensive business. Over time, it will likely be dominated by a handful of large global companies. As a result, AI agent companies that are software-only, will have to determine which robot platforms will control their path to market. Today, developers are wholly dependent on Apple and Google to put their mobile apps onto consumer devices. In the future, AI agent product companies will increasingly have to deal with robotics companies as platform gatekeepers, as well as other platforms (such as smart cars) that directly reach the consumer.

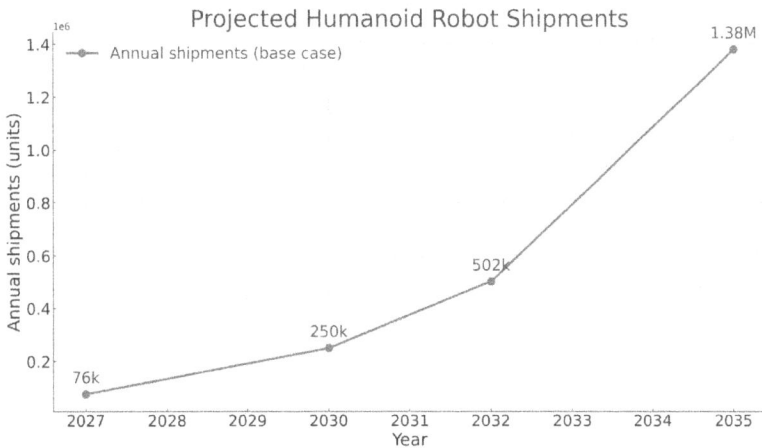

Figure 30.1: Goldman Sachs humanoid robots base case projection is conservative compared to other forecasts.

Foundational tech giants, particularly those that offer hardware or robotics platforms, will simultaneously be competing and cooperating with future agent provider companies. Each of them will likely offer some version of an "agent / app store" to reach the customer. Much like today, the foundational model, app store, or large social platform providers will be able to wipe out markets for smaller players quickly with changes to their own offerings. Survival as a new entrant agent company will depend upon strong vertical specialization and integration, and an adroit choice of the platforms and partners that provide the best path to market.

In specialized industries, robotics, software, and the required domain knowledge to operate them will create multiple opportunities for sustainable agent businesses. Competition will be fierce. Mega tech giants will enter many new industries like financial services, and of course media. Companies like Amazon already compete in groceries through Whole Foods and have come to dominate retail. Mega tech companies will continue to vertically integrate to stay ahead of rivals. Just as today we see Google, Amazon and Microsoft investing in nuclear energy to make sure they have access to the electricity that AI may require, they will likely enter new areas to vertically integrate further and drive efficiencies.

Conclusions

Beyond 2035, these dynamics will no doubt continue. There will be sectors of the economy that due to their need for highly specialized manual labor, or due to already low costs of production, where AI will be under-adopted, even in a decade. I have chosen not to discuss the social, employment, and societal forces that will develop in parallel. They will be equally significant, but could easily occupy another full book.

Factors that could strongly affect the pace of these changes include AI regulation (or lack thereof), as well as if any foundational AI companies begin to exhibit clear evidence of "recursive self-improvement," where their AI can improve itself largely without the aid of humans. There is also a possibility that public backlash against AI, caused by rising electricity costs, huge job losses, or examples of AI causing high-profile human harm, could slow the timelines.

Chapter 31

Product Manager as Behavioral Psychologist

> *Takeaways*: The skills required for product managers will change quickly as AI agents become a major path to market for new software businesses. Increasingly, they will need skills more like those of behavioral psychologists, as the product surface becomes the agent's behavior and disposition, rather than the UI or UX of a traditional software product. This requires new skills in understanding and shaping goals, personality, and behavior.

A RECENT POSTING from OpenAI titled "Product Manager, Model Behavior" highlights a shift: leading AI companies now expect product managers to blend psychology, philosophy, and human-computer interaction alongside traditional product chops. Soon enough, product managers will no longer merely be shipping features. They will be shaping the dispositions of an intelligent colleague who must be competent, prudent, reliable, and engaging.

Why Behavior Is the New Product Surface

When a product *is* an autonomous agent, the real touchpoint is the agent's personality and demeanor. A bug is no longer a misplaced button or a broken UI flow, but rather a habit or quirk your agent acquires that irritates their human supervisor, or simply makes your agent "that guy" that nobody wants to work with. The Stanford "Generative Agents" study, which we looked at in Chapter 9, demonstrated how even simple LLM-based characters develop emergent routines, social ties, and collective folklore once they are given memory, reflection, and planning. Those emergent behaviors are the *surface* your customers touch. To shape them will increasingly require the toolkit of a behavioral psychologist: hypothesis-driven observation, longitudinal studies, and interventions designed to shift underlying cognitive priors.

I have found that instrumenting an agent can feel a bit like running a laboratory experiment. Product managers have to think about holistic measurement objectives. They will work with engineers to set up controlled, repeatable environments with careful logging to capture results. The team needs tooling to vary prompts possibly at multiple levels, then measure changes in personality, judgments, or cooperation rates. Recent work in an emerging area known as "activation engineering" shows you can move an LLM toward strong human-interpretable personality traits without retraining. Meanwhile, researchers from the Shanghai Institute of AI for Education and the University of Minnesota collaborated to use standard Big-Five psychometrics to show GPT-4 can sustain coherent, test-retest-stable personalities. This kind of research shows how the process of building effective AI agents increasingly overlaps with clinical assessment. Learning tools from psychology can help when you need to know if your agent's self-concept is "drifting" or "dissociating."

As we have examined in detail in Chapter 9, while user feedback still matters, a more global perspective and greater reliability will come from multi-agent simulations that let you rehearse large-scale social and professional interactions before your agent enters the workforce. Certain position papers on LLM social simulation report that synthetic populations already predict ~90% of treatment-effect variance across dozens of preregistered experiments.[1] Traditional UX testing operates at a much lower scale, and is not currently aimed at social interaction in environments with multiple humans

---

[1] These numbers strike me as high, but research in this area is very active.

collaborating, as it has traditionally focused more on the use of a software tool by one person. Running regular scaled multi-agent simulation scenarios can help you spot emergent misalignment as well as opportunities for additional value your agent can bring.

Goals & Personality Are the Real Moat

Hiring trends reflect the shift. Chinese LLM startup DeepSeek, for example, is recruiting PMs who can "translate behavioral insights into intelligent products," a request that would have sounded odd not long ago. Forums such as Mind the Product now pair backlog grooming advice with essays on cognitive bias. If you are a product manager, your edge will come from diagnosing and reshaping adaptive behaviors, not pushing UI features.

Beyond specialized domain skills, what will differentiate your agent is how intentionally you craft its enduring goals, including its deep curiosity for your domain, and the persona through which those goals manifest. This will require new hats for product managers, but learning to operate from these new perspectives will help you create agents that earn loyalty through predictable helpful behavior no matter how sophisticated their cognitive architectures become.

Chapter 32

Finding Your Personal Path

> *Takeaways*: We all face challenges navigating the economic and social changes that are on the horizon with AI agents. Your human experience, judgment, and relationships remain deeply important, and you can play an active role in shaping the future you want. Outcomes are not inevitable, so please double down on your humanity and find ways to contribute that resonate deeply for you.

CONGRATULATIONS ON APPROACHING the end of the book. I hope that the preceding chapters have captured some of the excitement, uncertainty, and pace of change of the period of time we are in. My intention in writing this book has been to help you rapidly see the bigger picture of what is happening to software product development, so that you can be prepared to be part of it in a way that is right for you. And while this book is specifically about product development, it is also part of a much larger discussion about the unfolding impact of AI on society, education, the economy, and our way of life.

As MIT cosmologist turned AI researcher Max Tegmark put it in his thought-provoking 2017 book *Life 3.0: Being Human in the Age of Artificial Intelligence*, this discussion around AI is the "most important conversation of our time." I share Tegmark's viewpoint that what the future holds as it relates to AI is still vitally dependent on what each of us does now to participate in the debates around AI that will shape that future. If this book helps you participate more deeply in that conversation, I will be very satisfied.

I have found that the amount of change people have already experienced from AI varies a good bit by the type of industry, job function, and organizational culture they are part of. Consistently though, over the past several years, I've seen the teams I advise failing to fully grapple with the pace of change that is underway. In his acclaimed 2006 book, *The Singularity is Near*, Ray Kurzweil argues that humans are wired by evolution to understand linear rates of change, not exponential ones like we experience today. This is a core reason that facing the type of change we see now is so difficult for most of us.

So, how do you make the preceding chapters most valuable to you personally? I'd like to offer some thoughts and principles from my own journey that I hope can be helpful.

First, I would encourage you to accept that your journey will be unique, and only you control it. I meet many people who are perpetually waiting to start, waiting for someone to give them a perfect step-by-step roadmap. They hold back from taking action, awaiting certainty. While my goal has been to bring together as much of this subject as I could, there is no one book that can summarize it all, nor deal with the myriad fractal realities of each person's goals and situation. So embrace your unique situation and create a personal learning and experimentation journey driven by your curiosity, taste, and sense of what matters to you. You won't be far off the mark.

Second, I would let you know that your experience and your human judgment are still *highly* valuable. Whether you are looking to break into something new, just getting started in your career, or a seasoned expert in a domain, your unique perspectives can bring deep value to teams creating new products in this AI agent future. Despite what can appear daunting, I'm still inspired by how open humans are to helping other humans, across cultures and countries.[1] Sharing your perspectives builds culture, which in turn builds enduring products and organizations and movements.

Lastly, in an age of AI, I will give an "old school" perspective. I would strongly encourage you to think as much about your relationships, and how you position yourself, as you do about your skills and knowledge. Learning and skill building alone will not be enough to set you apart. Going forward, all of us will be competing with AIs that have much of the same knowledge, and probably better and more diverse skills than we do in many dimensions. They will have read a thousand times as much as we have, and they will make fewer mistakes than we do. They also won't need to sleep, or to take care of a sick child or an elderly parent. But even then, your story, your judgments, and your connections to other humans will be yours alone. They will be the source of real insights, and can be a big part of what sets you apart.

Open-ended exploration, combined with creatively connecting the dots, is one area where I personally believe humans still hold a considerable, possibly eternal, lead over AIs. Join us. We need more brave explorers.

M.P.
Taos Research Corporation
taosresearch.ai
Tampa, Florida
December 2025

Homo liber de nulla re minus quam de morte cogitat et ejus sapientia non mortis sed vitæ meditatio est. (Spinoza, Ethica, PROPOSITIO LXVII)

---

[1]Despite what headlines would have you believe.

References

Chapter 1: Software as Colleague & Teammate

Chapter 1 ideas including the Jennifer business story are those of the book author, but inspired by the countless brilliant books of Isaac Asimov among others.

Chapter 2: The Evolution of Software Products

Condon, Dan 2002. *Software Product Management: Managing Software Development from Idea to Product to Marketing to Sales.* Boston, Mass: Aspatore. ISBN: 978-1-58762-202-1.

History of the Software Industry 2005. *History of the Software Industry: The Challenge.* https://www.researchgate.net/publication /239856310_History_of_the_software_industry_the_challenge.

Manifesto for Agile Software Development 2001. https://agilemanifesto.org/.

Moore, Geoffrey A. 1991. *Crossing the Chasm: Marketing and Selling Technology Products to Mainstream Customers.* New York: HarperCollins. ISBN: 978-0-88730-519-1.

Orozco, Sondra 2024. *The Real History of Product Management.* https://blog.academyofpm.com/p/product-management-history.

Chapter 3: Where We Are Today

Maslej, Nestor 2025. "Stanford Artificial Intelligence Index Report 2025". In: *Artificial Intelligence* 2025.

The State of AI: Global Survey | McKinsey 2025.

Chapter 4: What is True Agency?

Campbell, John W. 1942. *Astounding Science Fiction: March, (1942).*

Formosa, Paul, Inês Hipólito, and Thomas Montefiore Apr. 2025. *Artificial Intelligence (AI) and the Relationship between Agency, Autonomy, and Moral Patiency.* DOI: 10.48550/arXiv.2504.08853. arXiv: 2504.08853 [cs].

Isaac, Asimov 1950. *I, Robot.* Gnome Press.

Schlosser, Markus 2019. "Agency Stanford Philosophy". In: *The Stanford Encyclopedia of Philosophy*. Ed. by Edward N. Zalta. Winter 2019. Metaphysics Research Lab, Stanford University.

Tallam, Krti Feb. 2025. *Alignment, Agency and Autonomy in Frontier AI: A Systems Engineering Perspective*. DOI: `10.48550/arXiv.2503.05748`. arXiv: `2503.05748` [cs].

Chapter 5: Adapt, Specialize, Survive, Flourish

AI-powered Threat Hunting.

akaBot May 2025. *Supply Chain Resilience: AI Agents Mitigating Disruptions and Optimizing Logistics.*

Beeonline June 2024. *The Key Role of AI, Automation, and Robotics in Port Efficiency.*

Bhardwaj, Chirag May 2025. *10 Use Cases and Real Examples of How AI Is Used in the Restaurant Industry.*

Critical Raw Materials Act.

DJI Enterprise. *Precision Agriculture with Drone Technology.*

Hosny, Ahmed et al. Aug. 2018. "Artificial Intelligence in Radiology". In: *Nature Reviews Cancer* 18.8 Aug. 2018, pp. 500–510.

Jiang, Yinjie et al. Aug. 2022. "Artificial Intelligence for Retrosynthesis Prediction". In: *Engineering (Beijing, China)* Aug. 2022.

Ocana, Alberto et al. Mar. 2025. "Integrating Artificial Intelligence in Drug Discovery and Early Drug Development: A Transformative Approach". In: 13.1 Mar. 2025, p. 45.

Park, Joon Sung et al. Aug. 2022. "Social Simulacra: Creating Populated Prototypes for Social Computing Systems". In: Aug. 2022. arXiv: `2208.04024` [cs.HC].

PYMNTS May 2025. *Marketplaces' Third-Party Sellers to Face Full Impact of Tariffs in Second Half.*

Smarter Streets: How California Is Using AI and IoT to Reinvent Traffic.

Treasury Releases Proposed Guidance to Continue U.s. Manufacturing Boom in Batteries and Clean Vehicles, Strengthen Energy Security.

World Water Day: The Water Impacts of Lithium Extraction Mar. 2023.

Chapter 6: Agents Can Be Everywhere at Once

AI Agent Marketplace: Add AI Agents to Your Assistant in Minutes. https://marketplace.moveworks.com/.

Google Agentspace. https://cloud.google.com/products/agentspace.

Chapter 7: Feedback: The New Beautiful UI

Magazine, U. X. Apr. 2025. *Secrets of Agentic UX: Emerging Design Patterns for Human Interaction with AI Agents.*

Shao, Yijia et al. June 2025. *Future of Work with AI Agents: Auditing Automation and Augmentation Potential across the U.S. Workforce.* DOI: 10.48550/arXiv.2506.06576. arXiv: 2506.06576 [cs].

Zhu, Aaron June 2025. *Designing Trustworthy AI Agents: 30+ UX Principles That Turn "Wow" into Daily Habit.*

Chapter 8: New Challenges for Designers

D'Anastasio, Cecilia June 2023. "Meet Neuro-sama, the AI Twitch Streamer Who Plays Minecraft, Sings Karaoke, Loves Art". In: *Bloomberg.com* June 2023.

Soul Machines to Unveil Digital Marilyn Monroe at SXSW 2024 2024. https://www.licenseglobal.com/new-media-social/soul-machines-to-unveil-digital-marilyn-monroe-at-sxsw-2024.

Chapter 9: The Insight Factory: Simulate Your Domain

CAMEL-AI Finding the Scaling Laws of Agents. https://www.camel-ai.org/?utm_source=chatgpt.com.

Pan, Xuchen et al. July 2024. *Very Large-Scale Multi-Agent Simulation in AgentScope.* DOI: 10.48550/arXiv.2407.17789. arXiv: 2407.17789 [cs].

Park, Joon Sung, Joseph C O'Brien, et al. Apr. 2023. "Generative Agents: Interactive Simulacra of Human Behavior". In: Apr. 2023. arXiv: 2304.03442 [cs.HC].

Park, Joon Sung, Lindsay Popowski, et al. Aug. 2022. "Social Simulacra: Creating Populated Prototypes for Social Computing Systems". In: Aug. 2022. arXiv: 2208.04024 [cs.HC].

Park, Joon Sung, Carolyn Q Zou, et al. Nov. 2024. "Generative Agent Simulations of 1,000 People". In: Nov. 2024. arXiv: 2411.10109 [cs.AI].

ter Hoeven, Ewout et al. Mar. 2025. *Mesa 3: Agent-based Modeling with Python in 2025.* DOI: 10.21105/joss.07668.

Xu, Frank F. et al. May 2025. *TheAgentCompany: Benchmarking LLM Agents on Consequential Real World Tasks.* DOI: 10.48550/arXiv.2412.14161. arXiv: 2412.14161 [cs].

Chapter 10: Dream, Distill, Differentiate: Your Agent's Data Moat

"Dreaming with ARC" Nov. 2020. In: Nov. 2020.

Ellis, Kevin, Catherine Wong, et al. June 2021. "DreamCoder: Bootstrapping Inductive Program Synthesis with Wake-Sleep Library Learning". In: *Proceedings of the 42nd ACM SIGPLAN International Conference on Programming Language Design and Implementation.* Virtual Canada and New York, NY, USA: ACM.

Ellis, Kevin, Lionel Wong, et al. July 2023. "DreamCoder: Growing Generalizable, Interpretable Knowledge with Wake-Sleep Bayesian Program Learning". In: *Philos. Trans. A Math. Phys. Eng. Sci.* 381.2251 July 2023, p. 20220050.

Feng, Tongtong et al. Feb. 2025. *EvoAgent: Agent Autonomous Evolution with Continual World Model for Long-Horizon Tasks.* DOI: 10.48550/arXiv.2502.05907. arXiv: 2502.05907 [cs].

File Sept. 2018. *File:Polysomnography Model.Jpg - Wikimedia Commons.* https://commons.wikimedia.org/wiki/File:Polysomnography_model.jpg.

"How Gen AI Can Improve Enterprise Data Management" Aug. 2025. In: *ResearchGate* Aug. 2025. DOI: 10.55041/IJSREM46621.

Hudachek, Lauren and Erin J. Wamsley Dec. 2023. "A Meta-Analysis of the Relation between Dream Content and Memory Consolidation". In: *Sleep* 46.12 Dec. 2023, zsad111. ISSN: 1550-9109. DOI: 10.1093/sleep/zsad111.

Kandogan, Eser et al. Apr. 2025. *Orchestrating Agents and Data for Enterprise: A Blueprint Architecture for Compound AI.* DOI: 10.48550/arXiv.2504.08148. arXiv: 2504.08148 [cs].

Lehman, Joel and Kenneth O. Stanley 2011. "Novelty Search and the Problem with Objectives". In: *Genetic Programming Theory and Practice IX.* Ed. by Rick Riolo, Ekaterina Vladislavleva, and Jason H. Moore. New York, NY: Springer, pp. 37–56. ISBN: 978-1-4614-1770-5. DOI: 10.1007/978-1-4614-1770-5_3.

Pan, Chaofan et al. June 2025. *A Survey of Continual Reinforcement Learning.* DOI: 10.48550/arXiv.2506.21872. arXiv: 2506.21872 [cs].

Rasch, Björn and Jan Born Apr. 2013. "About Sleep's Role in Memory". In: *Physiological Reviews* 93.2 Apr. 2013, pp. 681–766. ISSN: 1522-1210. DOI: 10.1152/physrev.00032.2012.

Seizing the Agentic AI Advantage | McKinsey 2025. https://www.mckinsey.com/capabilities/quantumblack/our-insights/seizing-the-agentic-ai-advantage?utm_source=chatgpt.com.

Siclari, F. et al. June 2017. "The Neural Correlates of Dreaming". In: *Nature neuroscience* 20.6 June 2017, pp. 872–878. ISSN: 1097-6256. DOI: 10.1038/nn.4545.

Stanley, Kenneth O., Joel Lehman, and Lisa Soros Dec. 2017. *Open-Endedness: The Last Grand Challenge You've Never Heard Of.* https://www.oreilly.com/radar/open-endedness-the-last-grand-challenge-youve-never-heard-of/.

Wang, Rui et al. 2020. "Enhanced POET: Open-ended Reinforcement Learning through Unbounded Invention of Learning Challenges and Their Solutions". In: 2020.

Wong, Catherine et al. June 2021. "Leveraging Language to Learn Program Abstractions and Search Heuristics". In: June 2021. arXiv: 2106.11053 [cs.LG].

Chapter 11: A Skeptic's Point of View

Marcus, Gary Feb. 2023. *Happy Groundhog Day, The AI Edition.* Substack Newsletter.

Shojaee, Parshin et al. 2025. "The Illusion of Thinking: Understanding the Strengths and Limitations of Reasoning Models via the Lens of Problem Complexity". In: 2025.

Xu, Frank F. et al. May 2025. *TheAgentCompany: Benchmarking LLM Agents on Consequential Real World Tasks.* DOI: 10.48550/arXiv.2412.14161. arXiv: 2412.14161 [cs].

Yue, Yang et al. May 2025. *Does Reinforcement Learning Really Incentivize Reasoning Capacity in LLMs Beyond the Base Model?* DOI: 10.48550/arXiv.2504.13837. arXiv: 2504.13837 [cs].

Chapter 12: The Role of Reinforcement Learning

Faldor, Maxence et al. Oct. 2024. *Synergizing Quality-Diversity with Descriptor-Conditioned Reinforcement Learning.* DOI: 10.48550/arXiv.2401.08632. arXiv: 2401.08632 [cs].

Su, Yi et al. Apr. 2025. *Crossing the Reward Bridge: Expanding RL with Verifiable Rewards Across Diverse Domains.* DOI: 10.48550/arXiv.2503.23829. arXiv: 2503.23829 [cs].

Chapter 13: Tool Use Explosion

Abhyankar, Reyna, Qi Qi, and Yiying Zhang June 2025. *OSWorld-Human: Benchmarking the Efficiency of Computer-Use Agents.* DOI: 10.48550/arXiv.2506.16042. arXiv: 2506.16042 [cs].

Bhan, Lekha Priyadarshini May 2025. *Model context protocol (MCP) — the backbone of tool-using AI agents.*

Knight, Will May 2025. "Jack Dorsey's Block Made an AI Agent to Boost Its Own Productivity". In: *Wired* May 2025.

Liu, Xiao et al. Aug. 2023. "AgentBench: Evaluating LLMs as Agents". In: Aug. 2023. arXiv: 2308.03688 [cs.AI].

Mialon, Grégoire et al. Nov. 2023. *GAIA: A Benchmark for General AI Assistants.* DOI: 10.48550/arXiv.2311.12983. arXiv: 2311.12983 [cs].

Renschni 2025. *In-Depth Investigation Manus AI Agent, Focusing on Its Architecture, Tool Orchestration, and Autonomous Capabilities.* https://gist.github.com/renschni/4fbc70b31bad8dd57f3370239dccd58f.

Schick, Timo et al. Feb. 2023. "Toolformer: Language Models Can Teach Themselves to Use Tools". In: Feb. 2023. arXiv: 2302.04761 [cs.CL].

Wang, Guanzhi et al. May 2023. "Voyager: An Open-Ended Embodied Agent with Large Language Models". In: May 2023. arXiv: 2305.16291 [cs.AI].

Wang, Xingyao et al. Feb. 2024. "Executable Code Actions Elicit Better LLM Agents". In: Feb. 2024. arXiv: 2402.01030 [cs.CL].

Yao, Shunyu et al. Oct. 2022. "ReAct: Synergizing Reasoning and Acting in Language Models". In: Oct. 2022. arXiv: 2210.03629 [cs.CL].

Chapter 14: Simulating Agency & Hierarchical Goals

Formosa, Paul, Inês Hipólito, and Thomas Montefiore Apr. 2025. *Artificial Intelligence (AI) and the Relationship between Agency, Autonomy, and Moral Patiency*. DOI: 10.48550/arXiv.2504.08853. arXiv: 2504.08853 [cs].

Minsky, Marvin 1988. *The Society of Mind*. New York: Simon & Schuster. ISBN: 978-0-671-65713-0.

Newell, Allen, J. C. Shaw, and Herbert A. Simon 1958. "Elements of a Theory of Human Problem Solving". In: *Psychological Review* 65.3 1958, pp. 151–166. ISSN: 1939-1471. DOI: 10.1037/h0048495.

Newell, Allen, J.C. Shaw, and Herbert Simon 1958. *Report On a General Problem-Solving Program*.

Tallam, Krti Feb. 2025. *Alignment, Agency and Autonomy in Frontier AI: A Systems Engineering Perspective*. DOI: 10.48550/arXiv.2503.05748. arXiv: 2503.05748 [cs].

Chapter 15: Higher Order Cognition: Creativity, Taste, Humor & Judgment

Chayka, Kyle June 2025. "A.I. Is Homogenizing Our Thoughts". In: *The New Yorker* June 2025. ISSN: 0028-792X.

Chollet, François Nov. 2019. *On the Measure of Intelligence*. DOI: 10.48550/arXiv.1911.01547. arXiv: 1911.01547 [cs].

Kahneman, Daniel 2013. *Thinking, Fast and Slow*. First paperback edition. New York: Farrar, Straus and Giroux. ISBN: 978-0-374-53355-7.

Kim, Sean and Lydia B. Chilton Feb. 2025. *AI Humor Generation: Cognitive, Social and Creative Skills for Effective Humor*. DOI: 10.48550/arXiv.2502.07981. arXiv: 2502.07981 [cs].

Koivisto, Mika and Simone Grassini Sept. 2023. "Best Humans Still Outperform Artificial Intelligence in a Creative Divergent Thinking Task". In: *Scientific Reports* 13.1 Sept. 2023, p. 13601. ISSN: 2045-2322. DOI: 10.1038/s41598-023-40858-3.

LeCun, Yann 2022. "A Path Towards Autonomous Machine Intelligence Version 0.9.2, 2022-06-27". In: 2022.

Mirowski, Piotr et al. June 2024. "A Robot Walks into a Bar: Can Language Models Serve as Creativity SupportTools for Comedy? An Evaluation of LLMs' Humour Alignment with Comedians". In: *The 2024 ACM Conference on Fairness Accountability and Transparency*. Rio de Janeiro Brazil: ACM, pp. 1622–1636. ISBN: 979-8-4007-0450-5. DOI: 10.1145/3630106.3658993.

Yampolskiy, Roman 2025. *Towards Solving Humor: Why the Funniest AI Joke Will Not Be Funny*.

Chapter 16: Coding Agents: A Bellwether

Barr, Alistair 2025. *'Inference Whales' Are Eating into AI Coding Startups' Business Model.* https://www.businessinsider.com/inference-whales-threaten-ai-coding-startups-business-model-2025-8.

Gallagher, Dan Aug. 2025. *Software's Death by AI Has Been Greatly Exaggerated.* https://www.wsj.com/finance/softwares-death-by-ai-has-been-greatly-exaggerated-b639c0cd.

Letters from Andrew Ng | The Batch July 2025. https://www.deeplearning.ai/the-batch/tag/letters/.

Medina, Manny July 2025. *A New Framework for AI Agent Pricing.* https://www.growthunhinged.com/p/ai-agent-pricing-framework.

Roychoudhury, Abhik Aug. 2025. *Agentic AI for Software: Thoughts from Software Engineering Community.* DOI: 10.48550/arXiv.2508.17343. arXiv: 2508.17343 [cs].

Sapkota, Ranjan, Konstantinos I. Roumeliotis, and Manoj Karkee May 2025. *Vibe Coding vs. Agentic Coding: Fundamentals and Practical Implications of Agentic AI.* DOI: 10.48550/arXiv.2505.19443. arXiv: 2505.19443 [cs].

Thammineni, Prasad Apr. 2025. *Pricing Strategies Among Agentic Startups — A Competitive Analysis.*

Wang, Huanting et al. Aug. 2025. *AI Agentic Programming: A Survey of Techniques, Challenges, and Opportunities.* DOI: 10.48550/arXiv.2508.11126. arXiv: 2508.11126 [cs].

Wang, Yanlin et al. Sept. 2024. *Agents in Software Engineering: Survey, Landscape, and Vision.* DOI: 10.48550/arXiv.2409.09030. arXiv: 2409.09030 [cs].

Chapter 17: The Wild West of Social & Crypto Agents

Blorm-Network/ZerePy Aug. 2025. Blorm.

Dan Boneh and David Mazières (CS) to Co-Lead a New Lab | Stanford Electrical Engineering 2025. https://ee.stanford.edu/dan-boneh-and-david-mazieres-cs-co-lead-new-lab.

DeFAI 2025. *DeFAI: DeFi x AI.* https://crypto.com/en/research/defai-jan-2025.

ElizaOS/Eliza Sept. 2025. ElizaOS.

Lucas, George 1977. *Star Wars: Episode IV – A New Hope.*

Pippinlovesyou/Pippin Aug. 2025. pippinlovesyou.

Rig - Build Powerful LLM Applications in Rust 2025. https://rig.rs/.

Virtuals Protocol | Society of AI Agents 2025. https://app.virtuals.io.

Chapter 18: The Infinite Agentic Loop

Chen, Junjie et al. Apr. 2025. *Enhancing LLM-Based Agents via Global Planning and Hierarchical Execution.* DOI: 10.48550/arXiv.2504.16563. arXiv: 2504.16563 [cs].

Erdogan, Lutfi Eren et al. Apr. 2025. *Plan-and-Act: Improving Planning of Agents for Long-Horizon Tasks.* DOI: `10.48550/arXiv.2503.09572`. arXiv: `2503.09572 [cs]`.

Feng, Tongtong et al. Feb. 2025. *EvoAgent: Agent Autonomous Evolution with Continual World Model for Long-Horizon Tasks.* DOI: `10.48550/arXiv.2502.05907`. arXiv: `2502.05907 [cs]`.

Hafner, Danijar et al. Apr. 2025. "Mastering Diverse Control Tasks through World Models". In: *Nature* 640.8059 Apr. 2025, pp. 647–653. ISSN: 1476-4687. DOI: `10.1038/s41586-025-08744-2`.

Minsky, Marvin 2007. *The Emotion Machine: Commonsense Thinking, Artificial Intelligence, and the Future of the Human Mind.* New York: Simon & Schuster. ISBN: 978-0-7432-7664-1.

New Tools for Building Agents. https://openai.com/index/new-tools-for-building-agents/.

Song, Yunpeng et al. Oct. 2024. "VisionTasker: Mobile Task Automation Using Vision Based UI Understanding and LLM Task Planning". In: *Proceedings of the 37th Annual ACM Symposium on User Interface Software and Technology*, pp. 1–17. DOI: `10.1145/3654777.3676386`. arXiv: `2312.11190 [cs]`.

swyx Apr. 2025. *2024 in Agents [LS Live! @ NeurIPS 2024].* https://www.latent.space/p/2024-agents.

Wang, Guanzhi et al. May 2023. "Voyager: An Open-Ended Embodied Agent with Large Language Models". In: May 2023. arXiv: `2305.16291 [cs.AI]`.

Chapter 19: Agent Situational Awareness: Harness Hallucinations

Atmakuru, Anirudh et al. Oct. 2024. "CS4: Measuring the Creativity of Large Language Models Automatically by Controlling the Number of Story-Writing Constraints". In: Oct. 2024. arXiv: `2410.04197 [cs.CL]`.

Béchard, Patrice and Orlando Marquez Ayala Apr. 2024. "Reducing Hallucination in Structured Outputs via Retrieval-Augmented Generation". In: Apr. 2024. arXiv: `2404.08189 [cs.LG]`.

Dhuliawala, Shehzaad et al. Sept. 2023. "Chain-of-Verification Reduces Hallucination in Large Language Models". In: Sept. 2023. arXiv: `2309.11495 [cs.CL]`.

Jiang, Xuhui et al. Feb. 2024. "A Survey on Large Language Model Hallucination via a Creativity Perspective". In: Feb. 2024. arXiv: `2402.06647 [cs.AI]`.

Ko, Joonho, Jinheon Baek, and Sung Ju Hwang Jan. 2025. "Real-Time Verification and Refinement of Language Model Text Generation". In: Jan. 2025. arXiv: `2501.07824 [cs.CL]`.

Lin, Sheng-Chieh et al. May 2024. "FLAME: Factuality-aware Alignment for Large Language Models". In: May 2024. arXiv: `2405.01525 [cs.CL]`.

Manakul, Potsawee, Adian Liusie, and Mark J F Gales Mar. 2023. "SelfCheckGPT: Zero-resource Black-Box Hallucination Detection for Generative Large Language Models". In: Mar. 2023. arXiv: 2303.08896 [cs.CL].

Viereck, George Sylvester Oct. 1929. "What Life Means to Einstein". In: *The Saturday Evening Post* Oct. 1929.

Wei, Jerry et al. Mar. 2024. "Long-Form Factuality in Large Language Models". In: Mar. 2024. arXiv: 2403.18802 [cs.CL].

Chapter 20: Tools, Tuning, Reasoning & Protocols

RULER: Easy Mode for RL Rewards | OpenPipe 2025. https://openpipe.ai/blog/ruler.

Abhyankar, Reyna, Qi Qi, and Yiying Zhang June 2025. *OSWorld-Human: Benchmarking the Efficiency of Computer-Use Agents*. DOI: 10.48550/arXiv.2506.16042. arXiv: 2506.16042 [cs].

Agentic Commerce Protocol 2025. https://www.agenticcommerce.dev/.

Bhan, Lekha Priyadarshini May 2025. *Model context protocol (MCP) — the backbone of tool-using AI agents*.

MegaETH | The First Real-Time Blockchain 2025. https://www.megaeth.com.

Mialon, Grégoire et al. Nov. 2023. *GAIA: A Benchmark for General AI Assistants*. DOI: 10.48550/arXiv.2311.12983. arXiv: 2311.12983 [cs].

Renschni 2025. *In-Depth Investigation Manus AI Agent, Focusing on Its Architecture, Tool Orchestration, and Autonomous Capabilities*. https://gist.github.com/renschni/4fbc70b31bad8dd57f3370239dccd58f.

Schick, Timo et al. Feb. 2023. "Toolformer: Language Models Can Teach Themselves to Use Tools". In: Feb. 2023. arXiv: 2302.04761 [cs.CL].

Wang, Xingyao et al. Feb. 2024. "Executable Code Actions Elicit Better LLM Agents". In: Feb. 2024. arXiv: 2402.01030 [cs.CL].

Chapter 21: Context Engineering, Memory & Knowledge

Agrawal, Lakshya A. et al. July 2025. *GEPA: Reflective Prompt Evolution Can Outperform Reinforcement Learning*. DOI: 10.48550/arXiv.2507.19457. arXiv: 2507.19457 [cs].

Asai, Akari et al. Oct. 2023. *Self-RAG: Learning to Retrieve, Generate, and Critique through Self-Reflection*. DOI: 10.48550/arXiv.2310.11511. arXiv: 2310.11511 [cs].

Béchard, Patrice and Orlando Marquez Ayala Apr. 2024. "Reducing Hallucination in Structured Outputs via Retrieval-Augmented Generation". In: Apr. 2024. arXiv: 2404.08189 [cs.LG].

Code Execution with MCP 2025. *Code Execution with MCP: Building More Efficient AI Agents*. https://www.anthropic.com/engineering/code-execution-with-mcp.

Edge, Darren et al. Feb. 2025. *From Local to Global: A Graph RAG Approach to Query-Focused Summarization.* DOI: 10.48550/arXiv.2404.16130. arXiv: 2404.16130 [cs].

Fan, Shiqing et al. Aug. 2025. *MCPToolBench++: A Large Scale AI Agent Model Context Protocol MCP Tool Use Benchmark.* DOI: 10.48550/arXiv.2508.07575. arXiv: 2508.07575 [cs].

Hierarchical Temporal Memory (HTM) Whitepaper 2011.

Hinton, Geoffrey E. and James A. Anderson 1981. *Parallel Models of Associative Memory.* Hillsdale, NJ: Lawrence Erlbaum Associates Inc,US. ISBN: 978-0-89859-105-7.

Kanerva, Pentti 1988. *Sparse Distributed Memory.* Cambridge, MA, USA: MIT Press. ISBN: 978-0-262-51469-9.

Meyerson, Elliot et al. Nov. 2025. *Solving a Million-Step LLM Task with Zero Errors.* DOI: 10.48550/arXiv.2511.09030. arXiv: 2511.09030 [cs].

Niu, Cheng et al. May 2024. *RAGTruth: A Hallucination Corpus for Developing Trustworthy Retrieval-Augmented Language Models.* DOI: 10.48550/arXiv.2401.00396. arXiv: 2401.00396 [cs].

Packer, Charles et al. Feb. 2024. *MemGPT: Towards LLMs as Operating Systems.* DOI: 10.48550/arXiv.2310.08560. arXiv: 2310.08560 [cs].

Yan, Shi-Qi et al. Oct. 2024. *Corrective Retrieval Augmented Generation.* DOI: 10.48550/arXiv.2401.15884. arXiv: 2401.15884 [cs].

Zhang, Qizheng et al. Oct. 2025. *Agentic Context Engineering: Evolving Contexts for Self-Improving Language Models.* DOI: 10.48550/arXiv.2510.04618. arXiv: 2510.04618 [cs].

Chapter 22: Beyond Vibes:
Rigorous AI Software Development

Karpathy, Andrej Feb. 2025. *There's a New Kind of Coding I Call "Vibe Coding"* ... Tweet.

Roychoudhury, Abhik Aug. 2025. *Agentic AI for Software: Thoughts from Software Engineering Community.* DOI: 10.48550/arXiv.2508.17343. arXiv: 2508.17343 [cs].

Sapkota, Ranjan, Konstantinos I. Roumeliotis, and Manoj Karkee May 2025. *Vibe Coding vs. Agentic Coding: Fundamentals and Practical Implications of Agentic AI.* DOI: 10.48550/arXiv.2505.19443. arXiv: 2505.19443 [cs].

Wang, Huanting et al. Aug. 2025. *AI Agentic Programming: A Survey of Techniques, Challenges, and Opportunities.* DOI: 10.48550/arXiv.2508.11126. arXiv: 2508.11126 [cs].

Chapter 23: Open Source Agentic Frameworks

Celi, Mariama, Serafim De Oliveira, and Davide DI Ruscio. "A Comparative Analysis of LLM-Based Multi-Agent Frameworks". In.

Derouiche, Hana, Zaki Brahmi, and Haithem Mazeni Aug. 2025. *Agentic AI Frameworks: Architectures, Protocols, and Design Challenges*. DOI: 10.48550/arXiv.2508.10146. arXiv: 2508.10146 [cs].

Surveying the LLM Application Framework Landscape 2024.

Yu, Chaojia et al. May 2025. "A Survey on Agent Workflow – Status and Future". In: *2025 8th International Conference on Artificial Intelligence and Big Data (ICAIBD)*, pp. 770–781. DOI: 10.1109/ICAIBD64986.2025.11082076. arXiv: 2508.01186 [cs].

Chapter 24: The Future of Scrum, Kanban, Agile, etc.

Alliata, Zorina, Tanvi Singhal, and Andreea-Madalina Bozagiu 2025. "The AI Scrum Master: Using Large Language Models (LLMs) to Automate Agile Project Management Tasks". In: *Lecture Notes in Business Information Processing*. Lecture Notes in Business Information Processing. Cham: Springer Nature Switzerland, pp. 110–122.

Cabrero-Daniel, Beatriz et al. Apr. 2024. *Exploring Human-AI Collaboration in Agile: Customised LLM Meeting Assistants*. DOI: 10.48550/arXiv.2404.14871. arXiv: 2404.14871 [cs].

Chinta, Swetha Oct. 2021. "The Impact of Ai-Powered Automation on Agile Project Management: Transforming Traditional Practices". In: 8 Oct. 2021, pp. 2025–2036. DOI: 10.2139/ssrn.5034076.

Khan, Salman and Mendus Daviglus Feb. 2025. *AI-driven Automation in Agile Development: Multi-agent Llms for Software Engineering*. DOI: 10.13140/RG.2.2.20682.89281.

Manifesto for Agile Software Development 2001. https://agilemanifesto.org/.

Spinach | The 8 Top AI Use Cases for Scrum Masters. https://www.spinach.ai/content/ai-use-cases-for-scrum-masters.

Chapter 25: Transparency from the Ground Up

Boisvert, Leo et al. Apr. 2025. *DoomArena: A Framework for Testing AI Agents Against Evolving Security Threats*. DOI: 10.48550/arXiv.2504.14064. arXiv: 2504.14064 [cs].

Buterin, Vitalik 2024. *The Promise and Challenges of Crypto AI Applications*. https://vitalik.eth.limo/general/2024/01/30/cryptoai.html?utm_source=chatgpt.com.

Clifton, Casey, Richard Blythman, and Kartika Tulusan Nov. 2022. *Is Decentralized AI Safer?* DOI: 10.48550/arXiv.2211.05828. arXiv: 2211.05828 [cs].

Editor, OwaspgenAIProject. *OWASP Top 10 for LLM Applications 2025*.

Li Ξ Liøη July 2025. *Deterministic Vs Probabilistic Systems: The Frontier Between Blockchain And Artificial Intelligence*.

Mitre/Advmlthreatmatrix Aug. 2025. The MITRE Corporation.

Qureshi, Haseeb Mar. 2024. *Don't Trust, Verify: An Overview of Decentralized Inference.*

Srinivasan, Balaji June 2024. *AI Makes Everything Fake Crypto Makes It Real Again AI Generates Crypto Authenticates.* Tweet.

Tabassi, Elham Jan. 2023. *Artificial Intelligence Risk Management Framework (AI RMF 1.0).* Tech. rep. NIST AI 100-1. Gaithersburg, MD: National Institute of Standards and Technology (U.S.), NIST AI 100–1. DOI: 10.6028/NIST.AI.100-1.

Chapter 26: Simulation for Security & Robustness

Fujitsu Develops World's First Multi-AI Agent Security Technology to Protect against Vulnerabilities and New Threats 2024. https://www.fujitsu.com/global/about/resources/news/press-releases/2024/1212-01.html.

OpenAI et al. Mar. 2024. *GPT-4 Technical Report.* DOI: 10.48550/arXiv.2303.08774. arXiv: 2303.08774 [cs].

Zou, Andy et al. Dec. 2023. *Universal and Transferable Adversarial Attacks on Aligned Language Models.* DOI: 10.48550/arXiv.2307.15043. arXiv: 2307.15043 [cs].

Chapter 27: Controlling Agent Autonomy

(25) When AI Agents Act on Your Behalf: The New Identity and Access Management (IAM) Challenge | LinkedIn. https://www.linkedin.com/pulse/when-ai-agents-act-your-behalf-new-identity-access-iam-polavarapu-xvtcc/.

10 LLM Observability Tools to Know in 2025.

Handling AI Agent Permissions 2025. https://stytch.com/blog/handling-ai-agent-permissions/.

Meinke, Alexander et al. Jan. 2025. *Frontier Models Are Capable of In-context Scheming.* DOI: 10.48550/arXiv.2412.04984. arXiv: 2412.04984 [cs].

Navigating DeepSeek R1, Security Concerns, and Guardrails | Solo.Io 2025. https://www.solo.io/blog/navigating-deepseek-r1-security-concerns-and-guardrails.

Orseau, Laurent and Stuart Armstrong 2016. "Safely Interruptible Agents". In: Unknown 2016.

Yeddula, Sanjana July 2025. *LLM Observability for AI Agents and Applications.* https://arize.com/blog/llm-observability-for-ai-agents-and-applications/.

Chapter 28: Agent Identity, Agent Liability

An Autonomy-Based Classification 2024. https://www.interface-eu.org/publications/ai-agent-classification.

Gabison, Garry A. and R. Patrick Xian 2025. "Inherent and Emergent Liability Issues in LLM-based Agentic Systems: A Principal-Agent Perspective". In: *Proceedings of the 1st Workshop for Research on Agent Language Models (REALM 2025)*, pp. 109–130. DOI: 10.18653/v1/2025.realm-1.9. arXiv: 2504.03255 [cs].

Herbosch, Maarten 2025. "LIABILITY FOR AI AGENTS". In: 2025.

Kumayama, Ken, Pramode Chiruvolu, and Daniel Weiss 2025. *AI Agents: Greater Capabilities and Enhanced Risks | Reuters*. https://www.reuters.com/legal/legalindustry/ai-agents-greater-capabilities-enhanced-risks-2025-04-22/.

O'Keefe, Cullen et al. May 2025. *Law-Following AI: Designing AI Agents to Obey Human Laws*.

The Law of AI Is the Law of Risky Agents Without Intentions | The University of Chicago Law Review 2024. https://lawreview.uchicago.edu/online-archive/law-ai-law-risky-agents-without-intentions.

Chapter 29: AGI Research Frontiers

Akiba, Takuya et al. Jan. 2025. "Evolutionary Optimization of Model Merging Recipes". In: *Nature Machine Intelligence* 7.2 Jan. 2025, pp. 195–204. ISSN: 2522-5839. DOI: 10.1038/s42256-024-00975-8. arXiv: 2403.13187 [cs].

Asai, Akari et al. Oct. 2023. *Self-RAG: Learning to Retrieve, Generate, and Critique through Self-Reflection*. DOI: 10.48550/arXiv.2310.11511. arXiv: 2310.11511 [cs].

Assran, Mahmoud et al. Apr. 2023. *Self-Supervised Learning from Images with a Joint-Embedding Predictive Architecture*. DOI: 10.48550/arXiv.2301.08243. arXiv: 2301.08243 [cs].

Baars, Bernard J. 1988. *A Cognitive Theory of Consciousness*. https://philpapers.org/rec/BAAACT.

Baker, Chris L., Rebecca Saxe, and Joshua B. Tenenbaum Dec. 2009. "Action Understanding as Inverse Planning". In: *Cognition*. Reinforcement Learning and Higher Cognition 113.3 Dec. 2009, pp. 329–349. ISSN: 0010-0277. DOI: 10.1016/j.cognition.2009.07.005.

Barrault, Loïc et al. Dec. 2024. *Large Concept Models: Language Modeling in a Sentence Representation Space*. DOI: 10.48550/arXiv.2412.08821. arXiv: 2412.08821 [cs].

Battaglia, Peter W., Jessica B. Hamrick, and Joshua B. Tenenbaum Nov. 2013. "Simulation as an Engine of Physical Scene Understanding". In: *Proceedings of the National Academy of Sciences* 110.45 Nov. 2013, pp. 18327–18332. DOI: 10.1073/pnas.1306572110.

Brohan, Anthony et al. Aug. 2023. *RT-1: Robotics Transformer for Real-World Control at Scale*. DOI: 10.48550/arXiv.2212.06817. arXiv: 2212.06817 [cs].

Cai, Weilin et al. 2025. "A Survey on Mixture of Experts in Large Language Models". In: *IEEE Transactions on Knowledge and Data Engineering* 2025, pp. 1–20. ISSN: 1041-4347, 1558-2191, 2326-3865. DOI: 10.1109/TKDE.2025.3554028. arXiv: 2407.06204 [cs].

Chollet, François Nov. 2019. *On the Measure of Intelligence*. DOI: 10.48550/arXiv.1911.01547. arXiv: 1911.01547 [cs].

Chomsky, N. and M. P. Schützenberger Jan. 1963. "The Algebraic Theory of Context-Free Languages*". In: *Studies in Logic and the Foundations of Mathematics*. Ed. by P. Braffort and D. Hirschberg. Vol. 35. Computer Programming and Formal Systems. Elsevier, pp. 118–161. DOI: 10.1016/S0049-237X(08)72023-8.

Craik, K. J. W. 1943. *The Nature of Explanation*. Cambridge: Cambridge University Press. ISBN: 978-0-521-04755-5.

Dehghani, Mostafa et al. Mar. 2019. *Universal Transformers*. DOI: 10.48550/arXiv.1807.03819. arXiv: 1807.03819 [cs].

Diachek, Evgeniia et al. June 2020. "The Domain-General Multiple Demand (MD) Network Does Not Support Core Aspects of Language Comprehension: A Large-Scale fMRI Investigation". In: *Journal of Neuroscience* 40.23 June 2020, pp. 4536–4550. ISSN: 0270-6474, 1529-2401. DOI: 10.1523/JNEUROSCI.2036-19.2020.

Driess, Danny et al. Mar. 2023. *PaLM-E: An Embodied Multimodal Language Model*. DOI: 10.48550/arXiv.2303.03378. arXiv: 2303.03378 [cs].

Dziri, Nouha et al. Oct. 2023. *Faith and Fate: Limits of Transformers on Compositionality*. DOI: 10.48550/arXiv.2305.18654. arXiv: 2305.18654 [cs].

Edge, Darren et al. Feb. 2025. *From Local to Global: A Graph RAG Approach to Query-Focused Summarization*. DOI: 10.48550/arXiv.2404.16130. arXiv: 2404.16130 [cs].

Eliasmith, Chris et al. Nov. 2012. "A Large-Scale Model of the Functioning Brain". In: *Science* 338.6111 Nov. 2012, pp. 1202–1205. DOI: 10.1126/science.1225266.

Ellis, Kevin, Catherine Wong, et al. June 2021. "DreamCoder: Bootstrapping Inductive Program Synthesis with Wake-Sleep Library Learning". In: *Proceedings of the 42nd ACM SIGPLAN International Conference on Programming Language Design and Implementation*. Virtual Canada and New York, NY, USA: ACM.

Ellis, Kevin, Lionel Wong, et al. July 2023. "DreamCoder: Growing Generalizable, Interpretable Knowledge with Wake-Sleep Bayesian Program Learning". In: *Philos. Trans. A Math. Phys. Eng. Sci.* 381.2251 July 2023, p. 20220050.

Faldor, Maxence et al. Oct. 2024. *Synergizing Quality-Diversity with Descriptor-Conditioned Reinforcement Learning*. DOI: 10.48550/arXiv.2401.08632. arXiv: 2401.08632 [cs].

Fan, Shiqing et al. Aug. 2025. *MCPToolBench++: A Large Scale AI Agent Model Context Protocol MCP Tool Use Benchmark*. DOI: 10.48550/arXiv.2508.07575. arXiv: 2508.07575 [cs].

Fountas, Zafeirios et al. Oct. 2024. *Human-like Episodic Memory for Infinite Context LLMs*. DOI: 10.48550/arXiv.2407.09450. arXiv: 2407.09450 [cs].

Franklin, Stan 2006. *The LIDA Architecture: Adding New Modes of Learning to an Intelligent, Autonomous, Software Agent*.

Friston, Karl, James Kilner, and Lee Harrison July 2006. "A Free Energy Principle for the Brain". In: *Journal of Physiology-Paris* 100.1-3 July 2006, pp. 70–87. ISSN: 09284257. DOI: 10.1016/j.jphysparis.2006.10.001.

Gauthier, Daniel J. et al. Sept. 2021. "Next Generation Reservoir Computing". In: *Nature Communications* 12.1 Sept. 2021, p. 5564. ISSN: 2041-1723. DOI: 10.1038/s41467-021-25801-2.

Girdhar, Rohit et al. May 2023. *ImageBind: One Embedding Space To Bind Them All*. DOI: 10.48550/arXiv.2305.05665. arXiv: 2305.05665 [cs].

Grauman, Kristen et al. Mar. 2022. *Ego4D: Around the World in 3,000 Hours of Egocentric Video*. DOI: 10.48550/arXiv.2110.07058. arXiv: 2110.07058 [cs].

Griffiths, Thomas L., Nick Chater, and Joshua B. Tenenbaum, eds. 2024. *Bayesian Models of Cognition: Reverse Engineering the Mind*. Cambridge, Massachusetts: The MIT Press. ISBN: 978-0-262-04941-2.

Gu, Albert and Tri Dao May 2024. *Mamba: Linear-Time Sequence Modeling with Selective State Spaces*. DOI: 10.48550/arXiv.2312.00752. arXiv: 2312.00752 [cs].

Hahn, Michael Jan. 2020. "Theoretical Limitations of Self-Attention in Neural Sequence Models". In: *Transactions of the Association for Computational Linguistics* 8 Jan. 2020, pp. 156–171. ISSN: 2307-387X. DOI: 10.1162/tacl_a_00306.

Hao, Yiding, Dana Angluin, and Robert Frank July 2022. "Formal Language Recognition by Hard Attention Transformers: Perspectives from Circuit Complexity". In: *Transactions of the Association for Computational Linguistics* 10 July 2022, pp. 800–810. ISSN: 2307-387X. DOI: 10.1162/tacl_a_00490.

Hebb, D.O. 1949. *The Organization of Behavior: A Neuropsychological Theory*. John Wiley & Sons.

Hendrycks, Dan et al. Nov. 2021. *Measuring Mathematical Problem Solving With the MATH Dataset*. DOI: 10.48550/arXiv.2103.03874. arXiv: 2103.03874 [cs].

Hierarchical Temporal Memory (HTM) Whitepaper 2011.

Hinton, Geoffrey E. and James A. Anderson 1981. *Parallel Models of Associative Memory*. Hillsdale, NJ: Lawrence Erlbaum Associates Inc,US. ISBN: 978-0-89859-105-7.

Höfer, Sebastian et al. Dec. 2020. *Perspectives on Sim2Real Transfer for Robotics: A Summary of the R:SS 2020 Workshop*. DOI: 10.48550/arXiv.2012.03806. arXiv: 2012.03806 [cs].

Hofstadter, Douglas R. 1979. *Godel, Escher, Bach: An Eternal Golden Braid*. New York: Basic Books. ISBN: 978-0-465-02685-2.

Holland, John H. 1992. *Adaptation in Natural and Artificial Systems: An Introductory Analysis with Applications to Biology, Control, and Artificial Intelligence.* Cambridge, Mass.: Bradford Books. ISBN: 978-0-262-58111-0.

Hong, Kelly, Anton Troynikov, and Jeff Huber 2025. *Context Rot: How Increasing Input Tokens Impacts LLM Performance.* https://research.trychroma.com/context-rot.

Jaderberg, Max et al. "Open-Ended Learning Leads to Generally Capable Agents". In.

Kalyan, Ashwin et al. Sept. 2018. *Neural-Guided Deductive Search for Real-Time Program Synthesis from Examples.* DOI: 10.48550/arXiv.1804.01186. arXiv: 1804.01186 [cs].

Kambhampati, Subbarao et al. June 2024. "Position: LLMs Can't Plan, But Can Help Planning in LLM-Modulo Frameworks". In: *Forty-First International Conference on Machine Learning.*

Kanerva, Pentti 1988. *Sparse Distributed Memory.* Cambridge, MA, USA: MIT Press. ISBN: 978-0-262-51469-9.

Kang, Jiazheng et al. May 2025. *Memory OS of AI Agent.* DOI: 10.48550/arXiv.2506.06326. arXiv: 2506.06326 [cs].

Kaplan, Jared et al. Jan. 2020. *Scaling Laws for Neural Language Models.* DOI: 10.48550/arXiv.2001.08361. arXiv: 2001.08361 [cs].

Kotseruba, Iuliia and John K. Tsotsos Jan. 2018. *A Review of 40 Years of Cognitive Architecture Research: Core Cognitive Abilities and Practical Applications.* DOI: 10.48550/arXiv.1610.08602. arXiv: 1610.08602 [cs].

Kozachkov, Leo, Jean-Jacques Slotine, and Dmitry Krotov July 2024. *Neuron-Astrocyte Associative Memory.* DOI: 10.48550/arXiv.2311.08135. arXiv: 2311.08135 [q-bio].

Krakauer, David C., John W. Krakauer, and Melanie Mitchell June 2025. *Large Language Models and Emergence: A Complex Systems Perspective.* DOI: 10.48550/arXiv.2506.11135. arXiv: 2506.11135 [cs].

Kumar, Akarsh et al. May 2025. *Questioning Representational Optimism in Deep Learning: The Fractured Entangled Representation Hypothesis.* DOI: 10.48550/arXiv.2505.11581. arXiv: 2505.11581 [cs].

Kumon, Ryoma, Daiki Matsuoka, and Hitomi Yanaka 2024. "Evaluating Structural Generalization in Neural Machine Translation". In: *Findings of the Association for Computational Linguistics ACL 2024*, pp. 13220–13239. DOI: 10.18653/v1/2024.findings-acl.783. arXiv: 2406.13363 [cs].

Lake, Brenden M., Ruslan Salakhutdinov, and Joshua B. Tenenbaum Dec. 2015. "Human-Level Concept Learning through Probabilistic Program Induction". In: *Science* 350.6266 Dec. 2015, pp. 1332–1338. ISSN: 0036-8075, 1095-9203. DOI: 10.1126/science.aab3050.

LeCun, Yann 2022. "A Path Towards Autonomous Machine Intelligence Version 0.9.2, 2022-06-27". In: 2022.

Lehman, Joel 2007. "Evolution through the Search for Novelty". In: 2007.

Lehman, Joel and Kenneth O. Stanley 2011. "Novelty Search and the Problem with Objectives". In: *Genetic Programming Theory and Practice IX*. Ed. by Rick Riolo, Ekaterina Vladislavleva, and Jason H. Moore. New York, NY: Springer, pp. 37–56. ISBN: 978-1-4614-1770-5. DOI: 10.1007/978-1-4614-1770-5_3.

Liu, Nelson F. et al. Nov. 2023. *Lost in the Middle: How Language Models Use Long Contexts*. DOI: 10.48550/arXiv.2307.03172. arXiv: 2307.03172 [cs].

Livi, Lorenzo, Filippo Maria Bianchi, and Cesare Alippi 2016. "Determination of the Edge of Criticality in Echo State Networks through Fisher Information Maximization". In: *IEEE Transactions on Neural Networks and Learning Systems* 29.3 2016, pp. 706–717. ISSN: 2162-237X, 2162-2388. DOI: 10.1109/TNNLS.2016.2644268. arXiv: 1603.03685 [physics].

McClelland, James L., Bruce L. McNaughton, and Randall C. O'Reilly 1995. "Why There Are Complementary Learning Systems in the Hippocampus and Neocortex: Insights from the Successes and Failures of Connectionist Models of Learning and Memory". In: *Psychological Review* 102.3 1995, pp. 419–457. ISSN: 1939-1471. DOI: 10.1037/0033-295X.102.3.419.

Mialon, Grégoire et al. Nov. 2023. *GAIA: A Benchmark for General AI Assistants*. DOI: 10.48550/arXiv.2311.12983. arXiv: 2311.12983 [cs].

Millhouse, Tyler, Melanie Moses, and Melanie Mitchell Oct. 2021. *Frontiers in Evolutionary Computation: A Workshop Report*. DOI: 10.48550/arXiv.2110.10320. arXiv: 2110.10320 [cs].

Minsky, Marvin 1988. *The Society of Mind*. New York: Simon & Schuster. ISBN: 978-0-671-65713-0.

Mitchell, Jason P., C. Neil Macrae, and Mahzarin R. Banaji May 2006. "Dissociable Medial Prefrontal Contributions to Judgments of Similar and Dissimilar Others". In: *Neuron* 50.4 May 2006, pp. 655–663. ISSN: 0896-6273. DOI: 10.1016/j.neuron.2006.03.040.

Mitchell, Melanie 1990. "Copycat: A Computer Model of High-Level Perception and Conceptual Slippage in Analogy Making." In: 1990.

— 2011. *Complexity: A Guided Tour*. New York, NY: Oxford University Press ISBN: 978-0-19-979810-0.

Morales, Guillermo B. and Miguel A. Muñoz July 2021. "Optimal Input Representation in Neural Systems at the Edge of Chaos". In: *Biology* 10.8 July 2021, p. 702. ISSN: 2079-7737. DOI: 10.3390/biology10080702.

Moravec, Hans 1980. "Obstacle Avoidance and Navigatio n in the Real World by a Seeing Robot Rover". In: 1980.

Moravec, Hans 1988. *Mind Children: The Future of Robot and Human Intelligence.* Cambridge, Mass.: Harvard Univ Pr. ISBN: 978-0-674-57616-2.

— 1988. "When Will Computer Hardware Match the Human Brain?" In: *Journal of Evolution and Technology* 1 1988.

Nickel, Maximilian and Douwe Kiela May 2017. *Poincaré Embeddings for Learning Hierarchical Representations.* DOI: 10.48550/arXiv.1705.08039. arXiv: 1705.08039 [cs].

Niu, Cheng et al. May 2024. *RAGTruth: A Hallucination Corpus for Developing Trustworthy Retrieval-Augmented Language Models.* DOI: 10.48550/arXiv.2401.00396. arXiv: 2401.00396 [cs].

OpenAI Charter. https://openai.com/charter/.

Packer, Charles et al. Feb. 2024. *MemGPT: Towards LLMs as Operating Systems.* DOI: 10.48550/arXiv.2310.08560. arXiv: 2310.08560 [cs].

Parr, Thomas, Giovanni Pezzulo, and Karl J. Friston 2025. *Active Inference: The Free Energy Principle in Mind, Brain, and Behavior.* S.l.: The MIT Press. ISBN: 978-0-262-55399-5.

Pathak, Anagh, Dipanjan Roy, and Arpan Banerjee May 2022. "Whole-Brain Network Models: From Physics to Bedside". In: *Frontiers in Computational Neuroscience* 16 May 2022. ISSN: 1662-5188. DOI: 10.3389/fncom.2022.866517.

Phan, Long et al. Apr. 2025. *Humanity's Last Exam.* DOI: 10.48550/arXiv.2501.14249. arXiv: 2501.14249 [cs].

Pierrot, Thomas et al. Apr. 2021. *Learning Compositional Neural Programs with Recursive Tree Search and Planning.* DOI: 10.48550/arXiv.1905.12941. arXiv: 1905.12941 [cs].

Polu, Stanislas and Ilya Sutskever Sept. 2020. *Generative Language Modeling for Automated Theorem Proving.* DOI: 10.48550/arXiv.2009.03393. arXiv: 2009.03393 [cs].

"Probabilistic Programming" June 2025. In: *Wikipedia* June 2025.

Pyro Deep Universal Probabilistic Programming 2025. https://pyro.ai/.

Salimans, Tim et al. Sept. 2017. *Evolution Strategies as a Scalable Alternative to Reinforcement Learning.* DOI: 10.48550/arXiv.1703.03864. arXiv: 1703.03864 [stat].

Saxe, R and N Kanwisher Aug. 2003. "People Thinking about Thinking People: The Role of the Temporo-Parietal Junction in "Theory of Mind"". In: *NeuroImage* 19.4 Aug. 2003, pp. 1835–1842. ISSN: 1053-8119. DOI: 10.1016/S1053-8119(03)00230-1.

Shojaee, Parshin et al. 2025. "The Illusion of Thinking: Understanding the Strengths and Limitations of Reasoning Models via the Lens of Problem Complexity". In: 2025.

Smolensky, Paul 1990. "Tensor Product Variable Binding and the Representation of Symbolic Structures in Connectionist Systems". In: 1990.

Snell, Charlie et al. Aug. 2024. *Scaling LLM Test-Time Compute Optimally Can Be More Effective than Scaling Model Parameters.* DOI: 10.48550/arXiv.2408.03314. arXiv: 2408.03314 [cs].

Spelke, Elizabeth S. 2000. "Core Knowledge". In: *American Psychologist* 55.11 2000, pp. 1233–1243. ISSN: 1935-990X. DOI: 10.1037/0003-066X.55.11.1233.

Stachenfeld, Kimberly L, Matthew M Botvinick, and Samuel J Gershman Nov. 2017. "The Hippocampus as a Predictive Map". In: *Nature Neuroscience* 20.11 Nov. 2017, pp. 1643–1653. ISSN: 1097-6256, 1546-1726. DOI: 10.1038/nn.4650.

Stanley, Kenneth O. 2007. *Compositional Pattern Producing Networks: A Novel Abstraction of Development.*

Stanley, Kenneth O., Joel Lehman, and Lisa Soros Dec. 2017. *Open-Endedness: The Last Grand Challenge You've Never Heard Of.* https://www.oreilly.com/radar/open-endedness-the-last-grand-challenge-youve-never-heard-of/.

Stanley, Kenneth O. and Risto Miikkulainen June 2002. "Evolving Neural Networks through Augmenting Topologies". In: *Evolutionary Computation* 10.2 June 2002, pp. 99–127. ISSN: 1063-6560, 1530-9304. DOI: 10.1162/106365602320169811.

Stanley, Kenneth O. O. and Joel Lehman 2015. *Why Greatness Cannot Be Planned: The Myth of the Objective.* Cham Heidelberg New York Dordrecht London: Springer. ISBN: 978-3-319-15523-4.

Strobl, Lena et al. May 2024. "What Formal Languages Can Transformers Express? A Survey". In: *Transactions of the Association for Computational Linguistics* 12 May 2024, pp. 543–561. ISSN: 2307-387X. DOI: 10.1162/tacl_a_00663.

Sumers, Theodore R. et al. Mar. 2024. *Cognitive Architectures for Language Agents.* DOI: 10.48550/arXiv.2309.02427. arXiv: 2309.02427 [cs].

Suzgun, Mirac et al. Oct. 2022. *Challenging BIG-Bench Tasks and Whether Chain-of-Thought Can Solve Them.* DOI: 10.48550/arXiv.2210.09261. arXiv: 2210.09261 [cs].

Tegmark, Max 2018. *Life 3.0: Being Human in the Age of Artificial Intelligence.* First Vintage books edition. New York: Vintage Books, A Division of Penguin Random House LLC. ISBN: 978-1-101-97031-7.

Tenenbaum, Joshua B. et al. Mar. 2011. "How to Grow a Mind: Statistics, Structure, and Abstraction". In: *Science* 331.6022 Mar. 2011, pp. 1279–1285. DOI: 10.1126/science.1192788.

Valmeekam, Karthik et al. Nov. 2023. "On the Planning Abilities of Large Language Models - A Critical Investigation". In: *Thirty-Seventh Conference on Neural Information Processing Systems.*

VanRullen, Rufin and Ryota Kanai Sept. 2021. "Deep Learning and the Global Workspace Theory". In: *Trends in Neurosciences* 44.9 Sept. 2021, pp. 692–704. ISSN: 0166-2236. DOI: 10.1016/j.tins.2021.04.005.

Vaswani, Ashish et al. Aug. 2023. *Attention Is All You Need*. DOI: 10.48550/arXiv.1706.03762. arXiv: 1706.03762 [cs].

Vespa.Ai 2025. https://vespa.ai/.

von Neumann, J. 1951. "The General and Logical Theory of Automata". In: *Cerebral Mechanisms in Behaviour*. Ed. by L. A. Jeffress. Wiley.

Von Neumann, John 1966. *Theory Of Self Reproducing Automata*. University of Illinois Press. ISBN: 978-0-252-72733-7.

Wang, Guan et al. Aug. 2025. *Hierarchical Reasoning Model*. DOI: 10.48550/arXiv.2506.21734. arXiv: 2506.21734 [cs].

Wang, Guanzhi et al. May 2023. "Voyager: An Open-Ended Embodied Agent with Large Language Models". In: May 2023. arXiv: 2305.16291 [cs.AI].

Wang, Rui, Joel Lehman, Jeff Clune, et al. Feb. 2019. *Paired Open-Ended Trailblazer (POET): Endlessly Generating Increasingly Complex and Diverse Learning Environments and Their Solutions*. DOI: 10.48550/arXiv.1901.01753. arXiv: 1901.01753 [cs].

Wang, Rui, Joel Lehman, Aditya Rawal, et al. 2020. "Enhanced POET: Open-ended Reinforcement Learning through Unbounded Invention of Learning Challenges and Their Solutions". In: 2020.

Watters, Nicholas et al. 2017. "Visual Interaction Networks: Learning a Physics Simulator from Video". In: *Advances in Neural Information Processing Systems*. Vol. 30. Curran Associates, Inc.

Wiener, Norbert 1948. *Cybernetics or Control and Communication in the Animal and the Machine*. The Technology Press//Wiley. ISBN: 978-1-114-35934-5.

Woodrow, Herbert Apr. 1921. "Intelligence and Its Measurement: A Symposium—XI." In: *Journal of Educational Psychology* 12 Apr. 1921, pp. 207–210. DOI: 10.1037/h0067806.

Wu, Yaxiong et al. Apr. 2025. *From Human Memory to AI Memory: A Survey on Memory Mechanisms in the Era of LLMs*. DOI: 10.48550/arXiv.2504.15965. arXiv: 2504.15965 [cs].

Xie, Tianbao et al. May 2024. *OSWorld: Benchmarking Multimodal Agents for Open-Ended Tasks in Real Computer Environments*. DOI: 10.48550/arXiv.2404.07972. arXiv: 2404.07972 [cs].

Xu, Frank F. et al. May 2025. *TheAgentCompany: Benchmarking LLM Agents on Consequential Real World Tasks*. DOI: 10.48550/arXiv.2412.14161. arXiv: 2412.14161 [cs].

Yahoo/TensorFlowOnSpark 2017. Yahoo.

Yan, Shi-Qi et al. Oct. 2024. *Corrective Retrieval Augmented Generation*. DOI: 10.48550/arXiv.2401.15884. arXiv: 2401.15884 [cs].

Yasunaga, Michihiro et al. Dec. 2022. *QA-GNN: Reasoning with Language Models and Knowledge Graphs for Question Answering*. DOI: 10.48550/arXiv.2104.06378. arXiv: 2104.06378 [cs].

Ying, Lance et al. July 2025. *Assessing Adaptive World Models in Machines with Novel Games*. DOI: 10.48550/arXiv.2507.12821. arXiv: 2507.12821 [cs].

Yu, Linda Q. et al. June 2021. *Do Grid Codes Afford Generalization and Flexible Decision-Making?* DOI: 10.48550/arXiv.2106.16219. arXiv: 2106.16219 [q-bio].

Yue, Yang et al. May 2025. *Does Reinforcement Learning Really Incentivize Reasoning Capacity in LLMs Beyond the Base Model?* DOI: 10.48550/arXiv.2504.13837. arXiv: 2504.13837 [cs].

Zhang, Xingxuan et al. Mar. 2025. *Understanding the Generalization of In-Context Learning in Transformers: An Empirical Study*. DOI: 10.48550/arXiv.2503.15579. arXiv: 2503.15579 [cs].

Zhong, Wanjun et al. May 2023. *MemoryBank: Enhancing Large Language Models with Long-Term Memory*. DOI: 10.48550/arXiv.2305.10250. arXiv: 2305.10250 [cs].

Zhou, Hattie et al. Oct. 2023. *What Algorithms Can Transformers Learn? A Study in Length Generalization*. DOI: 10.48550/arXiv.2310.16028. arXiv: 2310.16028 [cs].

Chapter 30: Perilous Predictions

Bg2 Pod Dec. 2024. *Satya Nadella | BG2 w/ Bill Gurley & Brad Gerstner*.

Hanbury, Peter, Arjun Dutt, and Emanuele Veratti Apr. 2025. *Humanoid Robots at Work: What Executives Need to Know*. https://www.bain.com/insights/humanoid-robots-at-work-what-executives-need-to-know/.

Outcome-Based Pricing for AI Agents Dec. 2024. https://sierra.ai/blog/outcome-based-pricing-for-ai-agents.

The Global Market for Humanoid Robots Could Reach $38 Billion by 2035 2024. https://www.goldmansachs.com/insights/articles/the-global-market-for-robots-could-reach-38-billion-by-2035.

Tong, Yuchuang, Haotian Liu, and Zhengtao Zhang 2024. "Advancements in Humanoid Robots: A Comprehensive Review and Future Prospects". In: *IEEE/CAA Journal of Automatica Sinica* 11.2 2024, pp. 301–328. ISSN: 2329-9266. DOI: 10.1109/JAS.2023.124140.

Chapter 31: Product Manager as Behavioral Psychologist

Allbert, Rumi A., James K. Wiles, and Vlad Grankovsky Jan. 2025. *Identifying and Manipulating Personality Traits in LLMs Through Activation Engineering*. DOI: 10.48550/arXiv.2412.10427. arXiv: 2412.10427 [cs].

Cognitive Bias - Product Management Content - Mind the Product 2025.

Jiang, Hang et al. Apr. 2024. *PersonaLLM: Investigating the Ability of Large Language Models to Express Personality Traits*. DOI: 10.48550/arXiv.2305.02547. arXiv: 2305.02547 [cs].

Park, Joon Sung et al. Nov. 2024. "Generative Agent Simulations of 1,000 People". In: Nov. 2024. arXiv: 2411.10109 [cs.AI].

Turner, Alexander Matt et al. Oct. 2024. *Steering Language Models With Activation Engineering*. DOI: 10.48550/arXiv.2308.10248. arXiv: 2308.10248 [cs].

Wang, Yilei et al. Jan. 2025. "Evaluating the Ability of Large Language Models to Emulate Personality". In: *Scientific Reports* 15.1 Jan. 2025, p. 519. ISSN: 2045-2322. DOI: 10.1038/s41598-024-84109-5.

Chapter 32: Finding Your Personal Path

Kurzweil, Ray 2006. *The Singularity Is near: When Humans Transcend Biology*. New York: Penguin Books. ISBN: 978-0-14-303788-0.

Spinoza, Benedict. *The Ethics of Spinoza (Bilingual Latin - English): Ethica Ordine Geometrico Demonstrata*. Trans. by Robert Elwes.

Tegmark, Max 2018. *Life 3.0: Being Human in the Age of Artificial Intelligence*. First Vintage books edition. New York: Vintage Books, A Division of Penguin Random House LLC. ISBN: 978-1-101-97031-7.

Production Methods

This book was produced using LaTeX, specifically the XeLaTeX typesetting engine. Visual Studio Code with the LaTeX Workshop extension was used for editing and compilation. The main text font is Latin Modern. Helvetica Neue is used on the cover and title page. Gil Sans is used for subsection headings and chapter titles.

Except as otherwise noted, diagrams and technical illustrations throughout this book were created using TikZ, a LaTeX graphics library. AI tools assisted in the generation of the TikZ code. Unless otherwise noted, images and illustrations in this book were generated using artificial intelligence image generation tools.

AI was used extensively in the research process for this book, largely in lieu of traditional search tools to find papers or other works on a topic. All outputs generated by AI research tools were checked carefully against source papers and books for accuracy. AI was also used to help create much of the code that powers the book's build system, including scripts for automating compilation, managing dependencies, and generating various editions of the book.

AI was *not* used in the actual writing of this book's content. AI tools and other scripts were employed for mechanical tasks such as checking for typographical errors, identifying misplaced punctuation, flagging potential grammatical issues, and layout and other LaTeX issues.

Index

A

A2A, *see* agent to agent protocol
AC0, 321
ACP, *see* agentic commerce
    protocol
activation engineering, 380
active inference, 161, 312, 332,
    337–339
agent to agent protocol, 194, 203,
    216, 217
AgentBench, 123
agentic loop, 268
agentic micro-SaaS, 374–376
agentic workflows, 27, 29
AgentScope, 84
Agentspace, 216
Agile, 277
Agile Manifesto, 277
Aixbt, 144, 145, 150
AlphaGo, 114
Architectural Decision Records
    (ADRs), 257
Arize, 300, 301
attention mechanism, 319
authorization, 300, 301, 303
AutoGen, 122
AutoGPT, 29

B

backlog grooming, 381
Bayesian AI, 99
BMAD, *see* business, manager,
    architect, developer
business, manager, architect,
    developer, 255

C

call deflection, 27
Camel AI, 84
Chain-of-Verification, 191
Claude, 79
Claude 3.5 Sonnet, 120
Claude Code, 109, 139
co-pilot, 28, 30, 66
CodeAct, 123
computer-use agent, 116
context bloat, 195, 235
context collapse, 247
context rot, 235
context window, 174, 235, 349
Cursor, 256

D

data distillation, 94
DeepSeek, 112–114, 318
DefAI, 150
Devin, 141
difference engines, 125
direct preference optimization, 207
Discord, 64, 75, 84, 146
DoomArena, 296
DPO, *see* direct preference
    optimization
DreamCoder, 99
Dyck language, 320

E

Eliza Labs, 145
ElizaOS, 145–147
end goal, 126
end-of-sequence token, 162
Ethereum, 145, 147
Ethereum's Base, 143

F

FAIR, 360
fMRI, *see* functional magnetic
    resonance imaging
Forrest Gump, 7
free energy principle, 312, 332, 337
functional magnetic resonance
    imaging, 340, 343

G

Gemini, 79
GitHub SpecKit, 255
goals, 109
group relative policy optimization,
    208, 210
GRPO, *see* group relative policy
    optimization
guardrail, 290

H

hallucination, 110, 123
Haystack, 29
HITL, *see* human in the loop
human in the loop, 30, 304

I

ICL, *see* in-context learning
in-context learning, 325, 326
inference-time, 132
Instagram, 8
instrumental goal, 128
instrumenting, 380

J

JEPA, *see* joint embedding
    predictive architecture

Jira, 280
joint embedding predictive
    architecture, 347
JSON web token, 300
JWT, *see* JSON web token

K

Kanban, 279
kill switch, 301
Kimi K2 Thinking, 213
Kozuchi, 296

L

LangChain, 29
Langfuse, 300
LangGraph, 122
LangSmith, 300
Language for Abstraction and
    Program Search, 103
LAPS, *see* Language for
    Abstraction and
    Program Search
large reasoning model, *see also*
    thinking model, 212
law-following AI, 306
learning intelligent decision agent,
    347
least privilege, 300
Lee Sedol, 114
LIDA, *see* learning intelligent
    decision agent
liquid state machine, 363
LlamaIndex, 29
LLM-as-a-judge, 184, 210, 233
LoRA, *see* low-rank adaptation
Lost in the Middle, 235
low-rank adaptation, 207
LRM, *see* large reasoning model

M

Manus, 120
MAP-Elites, 357
Markov blanket, 338

MCP, *see* model context protocol

MCTS, *see* Monte Carlo tree
     search

memory, 108

memory vaccination, 296

Mesa, 84

metaverse, 148

Microsoft Teams, 64

Minecraft, 123

mixture of experts, 328, 330

model context protocol, 66, 118,
     121, 122, 194, 195, 235

MoE, *see* mixture of experts

Monte Carlo tree search, 213

Moonshot AI, 213

N

next token prediction, 162, 318

novelty search, 355

O

o1 model, 113

Open Worldwide Application
     Security Project, 258

open-endedness, 117, 317, 356–358

OpenLLMetry, 301

OpenSpec, 254

OpenTelemetry, 300

overconfidence, 110

OWASP, *see* Open Worldwide
     Application Security
     Project

P

Paired Open-Ended Trailblazer,
     356

Pareto front, 247

Parity, 320

Perplexity, 10

persona, 80, 381

Phoenix, 301

Picbreeder, 355

planning, 108, 380

principal-agent, 306

product liability, 304

Prompt-injection, 295

Q

Quality-Diversity, 357

R

RAG, *see* retrieval augmented
     generation

ReAct, 122

Reasoning Models, 212

recursive self-improvement, *see*
     Self-Improvement,
     Recursive

reinforcement learning, 111–117,
     207–211

reinforcement learning from
     human feedback, 178,
     318, 319

reinforcement learning with
     verifiable rewards, 112,
     115, 116, 208, 210, 318,
     319, 327, 328

relative universal LLM-elicited
     rewards, 210

reservoir computing, 363

retrieval augmented generation,
     27, 28, 30, 349

reward hacking, 115, 211

RL, *see* reinforcement learning

RLHF, *see* reinforcement learning
     from human feedback

RLVR, *see* reinforcement learning
     with verifiable rewards

robotic process automation, 29

RPA, *see* robotic process
     automation

RULER, *see* relative universal
     LLM-elicited rewards

S

SaaS, *see* software as a service
Santa Fe Institute, 362, 364, 365
scaffolding, 109
Scrum, 277, 279
Scrum Masters, 280
self-attention, 320
Self-Improvement, Recursive, 378
self-prompting, 99, 129
SelfCheckGPT, 190
Service as Software, 375
SFI, *see* Santa Fe Institute
SFT, *see* supervised fine-tuning
shrink-wrapped software, 17
simulation, 128, 297, 380
situational awareness, 165, 166,
        177–193, 289
skills, 236
Slack, 64, 75
software as a service, 18, 19, 91
software engineering agents, 45,
        137, 250
spec-driven development, 140, 252,
        253
SpecKit, 255
subagent, 237
supervised fine-tuning, 207, 208
SWE agents, *see* software
        engineering agents

system 1, 132, 177

T

Telegram, 64, 75, 84, 144, 146
temperature, 162
test-driven development, 256
theory of mind, 130, 164
thinking model, *see also* large
        reasoning model, 113,
        194, 213
tool bloat, 195, 235
tool forming, 204
Toolformer, 122
traceability, 306
Trulens, 300

V

vector database, 28
vibe coding, 251, 252
Virtuals, 143–145, 147
Vision Language Model, 207
Voyager, 123

W

Windsurf, 141
world model, 164

X

XLand, 357